Principles and Practice of

CRIMINALISTICS

The Profession of
Forensic Science

A Volume in the
Protocols in Forensic Science Series

Principles and Practice of
CRIMINALISTICS
The Profession of
Forensic Science

Keith Inman, M.Crim.

Senior Criminalist, California Department of Justice

Norah Rudin, Ph.D.

Forensic Science Consultant

CRC Press
Boca Raton   London   New York   Washington, D.C.

Library of Congress Cataloging-in-Publication Data

Inman, Keith.
   Principles and practices of criminalistics : the profession of forensic science / Keith
Inman, Norah Rudin.
      p.   cm. -- (Protocols in forensic science)
   Includes bibliographical references and index.
   ISBN 0-8493-8127-4 (alk. paper)
   1. Forensic sciences.   I. Rudin, Norah.   II. Title.   III. Series.

HV8073.I443 2000
363.25--dc21   00-034316

Thinking is Allowed. This is one of the major themes of the book. Critical thinking is the first skill to be invoked at the beginning of a case, and continues through every phase of an analysis and interpretation. Too often, our thinking is constricted by what we believe is true, by what we expect to be true, or by commands from the god of productivity. The competent analyst will not sacrifice thoughtfulness at any stage of his work.

Series Introduction

Principles and Practice of Criminalistics: The Profession of Forensic Science, is the flagship book of the *Protocols in Forensic Science* series. It provides the intellectual basis for the work of the forensic scientist. In *Principles*, we review the evolution of criminalistics, discuss the foundational concepts, and explore general professional issues unique to forensic science. In each subsequent volume of the *Protocols* series, an expert in a specific forensic discipline will provide an enumeration and comprehensive discussion of hands-on protocols in that particular area or will address a specific professional issue. The *Protocols* series is written by the working professional for the working professional.

Preface

Why do we need another book about criminalistics? Many books have been written on this subject over the last century, and several are currently in print (Kirk, 1953, 1974; Saferstein, 1981, 1988, 1993, 1998; DeForest, 1983; Fisher, 2000). The majority of writings addressing subjects relating to science and crime have been aimed at the police investigator or the lay public. This is perhaps not surprising. The investigator or detective plays the unquestionably critical role of identifying and collecting evidence from the crime scene. These actions profoundly influence any subsequent analysis and interpretation, so it is imperative that those duties are performed with knowledge and expertise. Although investigators are usually not trained scientists, they must understand enough about the analytical procedures to avoid confounding them by their actions at the scene. Thus many books have been written with this goal in mind.

The lay public, including crime and mystery writers, has always had a morbid obsession with criminals, crime, and its detection. Many of the fascinating tales recounting both the commission of crimes and their solution have been recorded in various volumes directed toward the interested layperson. As technology has advanced and more-sophisticated methods have been applied to the analysis of physical evidence, the interested public wants to know not only about the criminal and the crime, but also about the various analytical techniques and what they can contribute to the solution of the crime (Ragle, 1995; Houde, 1999).

This book is not aimed at the investigator, attorney, crime or mystery writer, career switcher, or beginning student. Although all of these groups may find the information presented here both useful and interesting, they may have to employ other resources to fill in gaps in scientific or forensic knowledge. Rather, this volume is by and for forensic scientists; it is directed toward the practicing or soon to be practicing criminalist. It is not introductory in nature and assumes a strong background and familiarity with the physical and forensic sciences.

Strangely, few volumes have been written for the forensic science professional, and the majority of those tend to be simply compilations of laboratory methods and techniques (Kirk, 1953, 1974; Saferstein, 1981, 1988, 1993; DeForest et al., 1983). While detailed and standardized procedures are obviously indispensable to quality laboratory work, without the proper cognitive framework the laboratory results may be worse than useless. Therefore, we do not present here yet another overview of forensic science or introduction to laboratory techniques. Rather, we concentrate on topics that are discussed in lunchrooms, around watercoolers, and on electronic mail lists by practicing forensic scientists.

We outline here a logical framework for a forensic investigation, an approach rather than a compendium of methods, a way of thinking rather than a set of instructions. We most definitely emphasize the role of physical evidence in providing information about criminal actions. However, as we will stress throughout the book, physical evidence does not exist in a vacuum and, to maximize its value, it must be considered in the total context of the circumstances of the case. The technician who only pushes buttons and twiddles dials, even on the most-sophisticated instrument, remains just that — a technician. The criminalist must synthesize and interpret laboratory results in the greater context of the crime, or risk misinterpreting them. Thinking is allowed — consider this a framework on which to hang your thoughts.

THINKING IS ALLOWED

We unabashedly build on the ideas of previous icons such as Edmund Locard and Paul Kirk, both pioneers in thinking about the particular conundrums created by the application of scientific techniques to forensic situations. We also incorporate the ideas from leading thinkers on today's forensic landscape — Dave Stoney, Ian Evett, John Buckleton, and John Thornton, to name a few. We reexamine the ideas of these men and others in light of both technical and intellectual advances. Although others working in the field of criminalistics are unquestionably more qualified to organize, summarize, and comment on the current state of forensic thinking, no one has done so. Therefore, we have decided to fill the vacuum.

The reputation of forensic science has been significantly tarnished in recent years. A number of unethical, unprofessional, and immoral acts have clearly been perpetrated and we condemn them. However, because of the public impact of forensic investigations and analyses, they often become fodder for journalists, the most well intentioned of whom has little or no scientific expertise and likely no forensic background. We cannot allow the media or political bodies to police our profession, especially in the forum of public opinion. We must enforce standards from within the profession; if we are unwilling to monitor analyst integrity on our own, it will be done for (and to) us. Therefore, some of the subjects that will be addressed at various points in these writings are standards for professional work, and professional, ethical, and moral obligations of both the primary analyst and outside reviewers.

Some of the ideas we present here challenge conventional wisdom and will certainly provoke discussion, if not argument, among the forensic community. In one sense we present what we perceive to be the "state of the debate." We look forward to a continuation of this healthy debate and hope this book may provide a point of discussion of some of the important dilemmas facing the practicing criminalist.

To paraphrase a 1970s icon, "You can't consider yourself a member of the congregation [read that profession] until you offend everybody" — Daniel Berrigan, Chaplain at Yale, 1995.

References

DeForest, P., Lee, H., and Gaensslen, R., *Forensic Science: An Introduction to Criminalistics*, McGraw-Hill, New York, 1983.

Fisher, B. J., *Techniques of Crime Scene Investigation*, 6th ed., CRC Press, Boca Raton, FL, 2000.

Houde, J. *Crime Lab: A Guide for Nonscientists*, Calico Press, Ventura, CA, 1999.

Kirk, P. L., *Crime Investigation*, Interscience, John Wiley & Sons, New York, 1953.

Kirk, P. L., *Crime Investigation*, 2nd ed., Krieger Publishing Co. (by arrangement with John Wiley & Sons), Malabar, FL, 1974.

Ragle, L., *Crime Scene*, Avon Books, New York, 1995.

Saferstein, R., *Forensic Science Handbook*, Vol. 1, Prentice-Hall, Englewood Cliffs, NJ, 1981.

Saferstein, R., *Forensic Science Handbook*, Vol. 2, Prentice-Hall, Englewood Cliffs, NJ, 1988.

Saferstein, R., *Forensic Science Handbook*, Vol. 3, Prentice-Hall, Englewood Cliffs, NJ, 1993.

Saferstein, R., *Criminalistics: An Introduction to Forensic Science*, 6th ed., Prentice-Hall, Englewood Cliffs, NJ, 1998.

The Authors

Keith Inman holds a B.S. and M. Crim., both from the University of California at Berkeley. He is a fellow of the American Board of Criminalistics. In his professional career he has been employed as a criminalist by the Orange County Sheriff's Department, the Los Angeles County Sheriff's Department, the Los Angeles County Chief Medical Examiner-Coroner, and the Oakland Police Department. He was in private practice for 6 years at Forensic Science Services of California, Inc., a private crime laboratory that undertook both prosecution and defense work. Mr. Inman is currently employed as a senior criminalist by the California Department of Justice DNA Laboratory. He has coauthored *An Introduction to Forensic DNA Analysis*, a book that has become the preeminent reference for both attorneys and crime laboratories. He has taught in the Criminal Justice Administration Department at California State University, Hayward, and currently teaches a variety of general forensic science and forensic DNA courses for the University of California at Berkeley Extension and online.

Norah Rudin holds a B.A. from Pomona College and a Ph.D. from Brandeis University. She is a diplomate of the American Board of Criminalistics. After completing a postdoctoral fellowship at Lawrence Berkeley Laboratory, she worked for 3 years as a full-time consultant for the California Department of Justice DNA Laboratory and has also served as consulting technical leader for the DNA programs at the Idaho Department of Law Enforcement DNA Laboratory, the San Francisco Crime Laboratory, and the San Diego County Sheriff's Department. Dr. Rudin divides her time among consulting, writing, and teaching about forensic DNA and forensic science as well as more general topics in biology. Dr. Rudin has co-authored *An Introduction to DNA Forensic Analysis*, a book that has become the preeminent reference for both attorneys and crime laboratories. She is also the author of the *Dictionary of Modern Biology*, Barron's Educational, 1997. Dr. Rudin teaches a variety of general forensic and forensic DNA courses for the University of California at Berkeley Extension and online. She is active as a consultant and expert witness in forensic DNA for both prosecution and defense.

Please visit the *Forensic Education and Consulting* Web page at ***www.forensicdna.com.***

Acknowledgments

The seed for this book was planted during the first class we taught at the University of California at Berkeley Extension when a student asked us how the principle of *transfer* applied to physical match evidence. Our search for an answer to her question led us to propose the new principle of *divisible matter*, and subsequently to reexamine the prevailing ideas and conventional wisdom in forensic science. The constant challenges and critical thinking from our students comprised the major driving force behind the writing of this book.

We are eternally grateful to Harvey Kane who rescued the proposal for this book from apparent oblivion and insisted that it was a worthwhile project. He remains our "Godfather." Becky McEldowney, who inherited the responsibility of editor for two demanding and high-maintenance authors, helped bring the book to fruition. Her patience with our missed deadlines and at times odd requests is appreciated. Likewise, Andrea Demby, our project editor, maintained both a sense of perspective and a sense of humor while expertly guiding us through the details of the publishing process. We also would like to acknowledge the folks, many of whom we have never even met, who labor behind the scenes in the CRC production department.

A number of individuals provided material or assistance with specific items. E.J. Wagner and Peter Martin contributed to the Birmingham Six sidebar; John Houde provided us with one of the original Locard quotes, and Sharon Kruzic assisted us with the translation; Elliot Beckleman gave us permission to reproduce the results chart from one of his cases; Jeff Silvia and Roger Moore provided us with case transcripts; Ron Linhart and Mark Stolorow reviewed the Fred Zain sidebar; Duayne Dillon provided assistance in checking various historical details; John Buckleton gave us permission to use his "absence of evidence" example previously posted to a mailing list. Carl Selavka, Greg Matheson, Hiram Evans, Jay Henry, Peter Striupaitis, Frank Hicks, and Joe Polski assisted us in obtaining permission for the logos used to illustrate Chapter 12.

Finally, we are especially grateful to Peter Barnett, Ann Bradley, and Ray Davis who provided both encouragement and a number of suggestions which significantly improved the manuscript. Any remaining errors are our responsibility alone.

Dedication

To my father, Walter Inman, and my father-in-law, Robert Petersen, who, in their own ways, taught me that what we see depends on how we look.

KPI

To my co-author and continuing partner in crime, Keith Inman, who insisted that I was a criminalist long before I became convinced of it. Fortunately, he always lets me have his opinion when I don't have one.

NR

Table of Contents

Section I
Background and History of Forensic Science

Figure 1.1 Physical evidence. Any bit of physical matter can become evidence, including a puff of smoke, a Mack truck, or a dab of peanut butter. Certain items are frequently encountered in violent crimes; some are represented in this collage.

Introduction

1

Contents

I have no data yet. It is a capital mistake to theorize before one has data. Insensibly one begins to twist facts to suit theories, instead of theories to suit facts.

Arthur Conan Doyle
—*A Scandal in Bohemia*

A. Scope and Definitions

Any profession, discipline, craft, or art may potentially be invited into the judicial arena. As criminal activity and creativity grows, and our society

becomes more litigious, it is not unusual for the court to call upon experts
in the most esoteric of pursuits to provide testimony. While acknowledging
the diversity of expertise that may impinge on legal matters, we will direct
our commentary according to our own area of expertise, the application of
the physical sciences to the solution of crime. Even so, there remains a
discussion of semantics, intent, and, to no small extent, integration of all the
various disciplines that may be called upon in any investigation. Many of the
ideas that we present here most certainly apply to areas beyond strict science,
if for no other reason than the science must integrate with the greater effort
of an investigation. But to begin, we will tackle the classic struggle to define
our territory. Even if you do not agree with the following definitions, at least
you will be able to read the rest of this book without ambiguity.

1. What is Forensic Science; Who Is a Forensic Scientist?

Put three forensic scientists in a room together and ask for an opinion on
any subject — you will receive at least six opinions. If you ask these same
folk — "What is forensic science?" and "Who is a forensic scientist?" — the
number of opinions will increase exponentially. Why should the combination
of two simple words produce such heated debate?

First of all, the noun *forensics* strictly refers to the art of debate. Although
the common origin of the adjective and the noun are obvious (the Latin root
is *forum*, and the court is a place of debate), we distinguish between them in
modern usage. We suggest that the common use of forensics to refer to *forensic
science* unnecessarily obscures an already imprecise term. Our natural tendency to reduce any word to its most simplistic form does not legitimize its use.

The adjective *forensic* simply designates a connection with, or use in,
public discussion and debate or, more specifically, a court of law (*Webster's*,
1996). The use of forensic as an adjective is becoming appropriately common
for practically any activity than might be invited into a courtroom: forensic
art, forensic accounting, forensic knot analysis, and so on. But do these
activities fall into the purview of forensic *science*? Although forensic anthro-
pology, forensic chemistry, forensic medicine, and forensic psychiatry receive
nominal definitions in the 1996 edition of *Webster's*, *forensic science* is notable
for its absence.

It appears that the *science* part of *forensic science* is what instigates so
much consternation. Why should this be? Perhaps a partial answer may be
found in modern society's perception of science. Science is believed by the
average person to offer hard facts, definite conclusions, and uncompromised
objectivity. Therefore, any discipline called a science gains a certain legitimacy
and credibility in society's (the judge's? the jury's?) view. Conversely, other

professions (some of which are, interestingly, called the "soft sciences" by academicians) perceive themselves to lose credibility and worth if they are somehow excluded from designation as a science. This unfortunate view only detracts from the unique and useful contributions that experts in many diverse fields may offer a case investigation.

2. The Science in Forensic Science

Science is an oft-misused term, frequently employed to lend credibility to an idea or statement as if the aura of science automatically confers trustworthiness. (It's scientific, it must be true.) Just as often, it is used to discredit a concept, as if ideas outside the realm of science have no merit. (It's not scientific, we can't trust it.) The reality lies in understanding that science is a process not a truth. Laboratory scientists engaged in research or development in the natural sciences will recognize the following assertions.

a. What Is Science?

Science is the method of study we use in our attempts to understand and describe the physical universe. We do this by identifying repeating patterns, either spatial or temporal, and using the pattern data to try to establish general rules. This is called inductive reasoning — extrapolating from the specific to the general. If we think we have established a general principle, we attempt to test that principle by predicting what will happen in a specific situation. This is an example of deductive reasoning. The scientist obtains qualitative data by observation and quantitative data by measurement, all in the attempt to understand and categorize the universe. Although the quantitative description of data increasingly dominates our view of science, in no small part due to advances in measuring instruments, it is important to understand that both qualitative and quantitative descriptions of data are useful tools — it all depends on the question (Houck, 1999).

Classical science is defined by the notion of hypothesis testing. In very simple terms, the scientist proposes a hypothesis, performs experiments to test the hypothesis, and obtains results that either tend to confirm or invalidate the hypothesis. To classify an endeavor as science, one must be able not only to state a hypothesis, but to imagine a way to test the hypothesis (Popper, 1962). The **scientific method** provides a framework for hypothesis testing. In reality, we can never prove that an idea, concept, or theory is true — we can only fail to prove that it is false. In the absence of information that a theory is untrue or incorrect, we accept it as correct until new information is obtained that demonstrates otherwise. Both in science and forensic science, we frequently have an idea in mind — this bullet came from that gun. This is called the **null hypothesis*** (Fisher, 1949). While we cannot scientifically prove our hypothesis, we can try very hard to disprove it. If we perform discriminating and adequate testing, and repeatedly fail to disprove the null hypothesis, we may become convinced that our original hypothesis is true — that the bullet did pass through the gun. If the testing does, in fact, disprove the null hypothesis, we must accept the alternate hypothesis (Neyman and Pearson, 1928) — that the bullet was not fired from the gun. Although this idea is a basic tool of the working criminalist, it is rarely recognized or articulated. Another way of examining hypotheses is in a Bayesian framework where competing hypotheses are compared and their relative likelihood calculated (Evett, 1983; Taroni et al., 1998). As we will see, both logical frameworks find a use in forensic science, and one may be more useful than another at various stages in the process.

An experimental result has no standing until it is disseminated to the relevant scientific community for review. This is usually accomplished by presentation at a scientific meeting or publication in a peer-reviewed journal. Publication of the methods used in obtaining the data provides a chance for other colleagues to repeat and reproduce the experimental result. Thus, science is a product of the community, not individuals. It is much too easy to be led astray without the foil of other scientists to refute one's ideas. In basic research, an experimental result is not accepted until it can be reproduced by an independent worker (Maddock, 1989). This concept is followed in forensic science when specific techniques are developed or adapted for forensic use. Laboratories will, for instance, carry out collaborative studies to confirm that a new method yields equivalent results in different hands.

In actual casework, however, duplication of testing is not always possible for a variety of reasons, not the least of which may be an inherent limitation in sample size. Thus, in forensic casework, the confirmation of work product frequently takes the form of independent review, either by another analyst in the laboratory or by an expert assisting opposing counsel. It is essential that the work be reviewed both to catch and correct any clerical errors and to establish that the conclusions are supported by the data. It is the obligation of the forensic scientist to interpret the data objectively and to form and state a conclusion regarding the results.

b. Science Is Dynamic

Another common misconception about science is that it embraces immutable truths. In fact, nothing could be further from reality. At any point in time,

---

* Much confusion and misunderstanding exists around the idea of the null hypothesis. The most useful working definition is that the null hypothesis must be falsifiable (Stark, 2000). When the null hypothesis is disproved by experimentation, we must accept one or more alternative hypotheses.

science provides us with our best estimate of how the universe works. But soon enough, an idea or discovery comes along either to refine or to refute what we once "knew to be true." This is simply the nature of scientific discovery; our understanding changes with new information. This revelation can be somewhat disconcerting to the layperson who perceives that science can provide hard and fast, black and white, irrefutable answers to questions about the physical realm. All science can provide is the best answer based on all the information available at that point in time. This concept becomes excruciatingly clear in forensic science when newer, more discriminating techniques are able to distinguish between two items that were previously indistinguishable using older techniques. One of the best examples of this concept at work is that of convictions that have been overturned with the advent of DNA testing. Barring the exceptional case in which an accidental or malicious error has been committed, the previous work would not be considered wrong; it is simply that two individuals with, for example, blood type "O" will likely show different DNA profiles.

c.   *Science Is Durable*

In spite of some well-known historical exceptions (the world is flat, the Earth is the center of the solar system), most ideas in science tend to change rather slowly and in small increments. The newer idea is usually a small variation on the old one and tends to add rather than discard information. Our current understanding is simply a refinement of the previous concept; one can follow the evolution of the idea along a logical path. This idea is demonstrated in forensic science by exactly the same example we used above to demonstrate that science is dynamic. The methods that were originally used to include each of these people in a class of individuals who could have perpetrated a crime did not produce "wrong" results; repeated today (again barring cases of intentional misrepresentation), they would provide exactly the same answers. Rather, increasingly discriminating methods of detection enable us to add knowledge to the previous results, allowing us to refine rather than refute the answer. The two individuals with blood type "O" would still be indistinguishable using that test; only with a more discriminating DNA test are they differentiated. The critical distinction between these two kinds of tests resides in the limitations inherent in each one. Qualified by the appropriate limitations, each conclusion remains valid.

d.   *Forensic Science Is an Applied Science*

The realm of science can be divided into pure science, or research, and applied science. Basic research seeks to understand the physical world for its own sake; in applied science we seek to use the physical principles discovered to obtain a desired goal. Like medicine or engineering, the forensic analysis of physical evidence is an applied science, resting firmly on a foundation of the basic scientific principles of physics, chemistry, and biology. As such, every experiment and every case must follow the scientific method of hypothesis testing described above. It is worth clarifying that forensic casework is not strictly experimental in nature. By definition, the conditions under which a scientific experiment is performed are controlled, and variables are intentionally changed one at a time; in casework, reality dictates that the sample is completely uncontrolled until its recognition and recovery by a responsible party. Aspects of the sample are tested using procedures that have been experimentally validated on known samples, but the results obtained from a forensic sample are those of an examination or analysis, not an experiment. It is worth emphasizing that this process is inherently inductive. The analyst is gathering facts about a piece of evidence that will later be combined with other facts and assumptions to form a theory of what happened in the case.

3.   Science Lessons from History

E. O. Wilson, in his most recent work, *Concilience* (Wilson, 1998), reminds us that science has not always been so narrowly defined. During the 18th-century Enlightenment, the first scientific philosophers began to explore the borders of knowledge. Francis Bacon, the father of the philosophy of science, defined science more broadly as a method of investigation available to any branch of learning including psychology, the social sciences, and even the humanities (Bacon, 1620). He was a proponent of *induction*, which may be described as amassing large amounts of data, then attempting to discern patterns (Bacon, 1620). This was in counterpoint to *deductive reasoning*, the main method of scientific inquiry in classical and medieval times, and reclaimed later by the reductionists over the next several centuries of Western scientific development. In simplistic terms, deductive reasoning may be defined as proceeding from the general to the specific — suggesting a theory and performing experiments to see if the results are predicted by the theory. It is important to realize that inductive reasoning (proceeding from the specific to the general), whether performed consciously or not, is necessary, *a priori*, to generate the theory.

A case investigation, including the laboratory analysis of physical evidence, practically defines inductive reasoning if it is performed correctly. Interestingly, a common pitfall is to slip into deductive reasoning, latching onto a convenient theory that may or may not follow from the data collected. Temptation then leads us to try to fit the facts to the theory, however poor the fit. Bacon also emphasized the importance of a minimum of preconceptions, as did Descarte* (1637), who insisted on systematic doubt as the first

* *Cogito, ergo sum* — I think therefore I am.

principle of learning. Clearly, an open mind is prerequisite to a search for the truth in the solution of crime.

Wilson's definition of science harks back to those 18th-century scientific philosophers to encompass a wider range of possibilities. He suggests that science is "the organized systematic enterprise that gathers knowledge about the world and condenses the knowledge into testable laws and principles." His corollaries share many common points with the elements of science outlined above, but emphasize slightly different aspects of the scientific process:

> The diagnostic features of science that distinguish it from pseudoscience are first, repeatability: The same phenomenon is sought again, preferably by independent investigation, and the interpretation given to it is confirmed or discarded by means of novel analysis and experimentation. Second, economy: Scientists attempt to abstract the information into the form that is both simplest and aesthetically most pleasing — the combination called elegance — while yielding the largest amount of information with the least amount of effort. Third, mensuration: If something can be properly measured, using universally accepted scales, generalizations about it are rendered unambiguous. Fourth, heuristics: The best science stimulates further discovery, often in unpredictable new directions; and the new knowledge provides an additional test of the original principles that led to its discovery. Fifth and finally, consilience: the explanations of different phenomena most likely to survive are those that can be connected and proved consistent with one another. (Wilson, 1998)

Sidestepping, for our limited purpose, the larger debate in the scientific community over Wilson's sociobiological meaning of *consilience* (Naess, 1998), we can certainly apply the concept to the interpretation of facts and analyses in a case investigation. In fact, it is the goal of a criminal inquiry to provide a reconstruction consistent with all known facts and stated assumptions. Additionally, the concept that the simplest explanation is often the best is not lost in attempting crime reconstruction.*,**

Perhaps, in the end, a more flexible notion of the definition of science will provide a stronger framework upon which to hang our notion of forensic science. Although we will be concentrating on the natural sciences, certainly the ideas we will present may be adopted by any branch of learning willing to systematize its knowledge and use it to generate fundamental, testable laws and principles.

* In the 14th century, the British monk and philosopher, William of Occam, argued that the best explanation of a given phenomenon is generally the simplest, the one with the fewest assumptions. This principle, called *Occam's razor*, was the downfall of the Ptolemaic model of the solar system in the Middle Ages (Horgan, 1996).
** On the other hand, we have all had the experience that truth is stranger than fiction, particularly in the context of a criminal case.

4. Forensic Science and Criminalistics

So far, we have explained to you our understanding of the forensic part and the science part of the term forensic science. But where does this leave us? Better men and women than we have tackled this same semantic problem. The term *criminalistics*, derived from the German *Kriminalistic*, was coined in the late 1800s, probably by Hans Gross, in an attempt to describe better the emerging discipline of "police science." *Criminalistics* has the unfortunate property of being even longer and harder to pronounce than forensic science. This may lead to its common confusion with *criminology*, the application of psychology and sociology to crime, criminals, and the judicial system. Perhaps because of its seemingly unwieldy and slightly esoteric nature, the term *criminalistics* has been left to the crime laboratories. In the United States the job of the crime laboratory (public or private) is to examine physical evidence that arises as a result of a criminal event; private laboratories extend their services into the venue of civil law.* The person who analyzes evidence in a crime laboratory may be properly referred to as an analyst, a forensic scientist, or a criminalist.

This practical definition of criminalistics has taken on a life of its own, expanding to encompass a more general philosophy and cognitive framework. It is this forensic way of thinking that will comprise the central theme of this book. Although we discuss many specific examples and practical applications, they find a common root in the cognitive framework we will describe. We do not take credit for inventing this approach; it has clearly evolved with the discipline. However, little attempt has been made in the literature to define the paradigm of criminalistics in an organized fashion. By nature, criminalists tend to be fiercely independent thinkers, sometimes to a fault. This has slowed a convergence of ideas in the field. While the autonomy of the individual criminalist must be preserved, it is also essential to formulate a common platform from which to explore each investigation.

The dictionary definitions of *criminalist* and *criminalistics* (*Webster's*, 1996) contribute little to our understanding and are, in fact, discordant with each other, reflecting the general confusion in this area. Webster's suggests the following:

> *criminalist* (n.) 1. an expert in criminalistics. 2. one who studies or practices criminology; criminologist. 3. an expert in criminal law.

> *criminalistics* (n.) 1. The scientific study and evaluation of physical evidence in the commission of crimes. 2. the science dealing with the detection of crime and the apprehension of criminals.

* In Europe, where the term criminalistics originated, the laboratory's work may be less restricted.

An expert in criminal law is not a criminalist at all, but a criminal lawyer (pun optional) and, as we have discussed previously, criminology is the study of the psychological and social aspects of criminal behavior. Although, "the science dealing with the detection of crime" is accurate, the "apprehension of criminals" falls strictly outside the purview of the scientist. The first definition of criminalistics, "The scientific study and evaluation of physical evidence in the commission of crimes," is new to this edition of Webster's and is, in fact, an accurate if skeletal description.

Van Heerden, in his 1982 book *Criminalistics*, takes a somewhat novel approach to relating forensic science and criminalistics. He suggests that a forensic expert is an expert in only one discipline (e.g., chemistry or medicine) and that one can perform a limited examination of physical evidence for forensic purposes without being a criminalist. While we strongly disagree that anyone without at least an appreciation of the larger criminalistic scope should ever lay hands on a piece of evidence, Van Heerden's description of criminalistics as the more general discipline required to integrate a variety of physical analyses provides a useful starting point. He joins with Ceccaldi (1974) in recognizing that "Because of its multidisciplinary, composite and coordinating nature, criminalistics is not regarded as a separate* discipline..."; it relies on the fundamental sciences for its methods and techniques and depends on progress in those sciences for advancement. Van Heerden quotes Ceccaldi as saying that criminalistics is "a technique in thinking; an art in the collection of facts; in other words as a systematized scientific approach to the solution of crime problems on the basis of scientifically acquired facts." He further quotes Jones and Gabard (1959) to say, "In this sense criminalistics is equated with *scientific crime detection*: in other words the application of science and scientific equipment to the analysis, comparison and identification of objects and phenomena associated with legal problems," and Williams (1967) "in an effort to reveal the full truth of criminal activities."

The California Association of Criminalists (CAC) defines criminalistics as

> That professional occupation concerned with the scientific analysis and examination of physical evidence, its interpretation, and its presentation in court. It involves the application of principles, techniques and methods of the physical sciences and has as its primary objective a determination of physical facts which may be significant in legal cases.

The American Academy of Forensic Sciences (AAFS) defines criminalistics in a slightly different way as

---

* We understand separate, in this context, to mean autonomous.

The analysis, comparison, identification, and interpretation of physical evidence. The main role of the criminalist is to objectively apply the techniques of the physical and natural sciences to examine physical evidence, thereby prove the existence of a crime or make connections.

A concrete definition of the profession that we call criminalistics remains both elusive and morphotic. In large measure, this derives from our acknowledged role as the flea on the hair of the dog on the leash of the judicial system. As the needs and expectations of the criminal justice system change, our contribution shifts accordingly. Perhaps a circumscribed definition is neither appropriate nor useful.

5. Physical Evidence: From Art to Science

Any endeavor, when performed at its pinnacle, is an art. The genius inherent in a musical prodigy is not fundamentally different from the genius required to solve a recalcitrant mathematical proof (Hofstadter, 1979). Both require a leap beyond pedestrian rationality and the courage and faith to take that leap. Scientific breakthroughs stand on a bedrock of many small, insignificant advances; but the final solution is often rooted in an intuition that is not fully understandable based simply on previous data.* We do not mean to imply that a forensic analysis is an act of genius, only that the boundaries between art and science are perhaps less distinct than is commonly understood. The nature of forensic science lends itself to an artistic and intuitive approach. Facts are often in short supply, analytical results are rarely textbook, and human nature prompts us to fill in the gaps. The very recognition of this proclivity, however, and the institution of rigorous review procedures, serves as an effective counter to our natural tendencies.

At the same time that we strive to maintain scientific objectivity, however, we must realize that the comparison between evidence and reference, regardless of whether the items of interest are two fingerprints or two spectra, is not free of human subjectivity. Nor should it be. Two items derived from the same source are nevertheless two unique items, having experienced different paths through time and space. The question before the forensic scientist is not, as the uninitiated might assume, are these two items the same, but rather, can we exclude the possibility that they originate from the same source? Even the most-sophisticated instrumentation cannot overcome imperfections in the samples themselves; analysts must rely on their education, training, and experience to determine whether small differences observed between evidence and reference samples qualify as *significant* or *explainable*. It is worth

---

* In an interview with John Horgan for *The End of Science*, Karl Popper insisted that a scientific theory is an invention, an act of creation as profoundly mysterious as anything in the arts (Horgan, 1996).

emphasizing that training in any of the forensic disciplines includes (or at least should include) examining many patterns, some of which are known to come from the same source and some of which come from different sources (Murdock and Biasotti, 1997). It is the process of testing the limits — gaining experience with the variation that occurs in samples from the same source and knowledge of the similarity that samples from different sources might exhibit — that generates an appropriately skeptical and cautious, yet confident, examiner.

Because this process of comparison, and the expertise to accomplish it, is acquired through a lifetime of trial and error, it is not always a conscious process. Part of the effort in systematizing a body of knowledge is to explicate the guidelines for the interpretation of a particular type of analysis. This not only encourages consistency by compelling the analyst to consciously define the comparison process, but also allows other colleagues working in the field to understand the guidelines by which an analyst has arrived at a conclusion. The explication, organization, and dissemination of a common set of ground rules provide a universal starting point for critical review by both peers and independent reviewers. However, no matter how clear and well reasoned the guidelines, and no matter how conscientiously applied, two competent scientists may still ultimately disagree about the interpretation of a result. This is simply the nature of science. One could program a computer with all the interpretation guidelines in the world, but a human being still must designate and input the guidelines. Two computers, programmed with different interpretational guidelines, may also assert different conclusions.

One effort in this direction has been standardization. Is standardization the answer? To some extent, yes. Standardization allows scientists to begin the discussion on common ground, understand each other's data, and share results. However, to constrict an analyst to a particular detail in some analytical procedure, or to a set of immutable interpretational rules, risks misanalyzing or misinterpreting any particular piece of evidence, the special nature of which might have been unforeseen at the time the guidelines were established. And if anything is true about forensic evidence, it cannot be predicted. Thinking is allowed.

It is crucial to recognize that, even among physical evidence, some categories may not fit a traditional or commonly understood definition of science, particularly with regard to quantitation of the data (Houck, 1999). To some extent, this is due to the historical acceptance of these types of analyses in court without having demanded a demonstration of rigorous scientific underpinning, including an articulation of interpretational guidelines and a statistical frequency estimate. In particular, we refer to those examinations that require no laboratory analysis, but "only" a visual comparison. Such examinations include physical match comparison, microscopic comparison of hairs and fibers, and print and impression evidence. Rarely will an analyst be asked about the fingerprint database on which a conclusion of common source has been based (Cole, 1998; 1999), or the number or proportion of microscopic striae that must concord between an evidence and test bullet for the analyst to conclude that they were fired from the same gun. Some argue that inherent differences in the nature of each type of evidence preclude a universal statistical or interpretational model for all physical evidence (Houck, 1999).

An evolving standard for the legal admissibility of scientific evidence has prompted a review and closer scrutiny of all methods, some of which have been accepted without question for the last century (Cole, 1998; 1999). While DNA analysts (recent FBI pronouncements notwithstanding) are expected to provide an estimated frequency of a genetic profile in the relevant population, the print or firearms analyst simply renders an opinion that the association between evidence and reference is unique. It has been suggested that comparison evidence might fall within the purview of an acquired skill or expert opinion. Therefore, examiners should be able to express opinions of identity without having to provide numeric estimates or systematic scientific justification (Ashbaugh, 1996; Murdock and Biasotti, 1997). Recent court decisions (*Daubert*, 1993; *Kumho*, 1999) that comment directly on the admissibility and definition of scientific evidence, and to what standard it should be held, have provoked this discussion anew among the forensic community.

Certainly, defining the elements of a valid shoe print or glass fracture comparison presents a greater challenge than defining the elements of similarity necessary for a DNA or solid dose drug analysis. This follows directly from the nature of the evidence. Shoe wear and breaking glass generate highly random and complex patterns that may actually require greater expertise, or at least more experience, to interpret than the much simpler and more constrained patterns found in a spectrum or autoradiograph. Certainly, some criminalists debate whether any useful purpose would be served by demanding a more scientific treatment of disciplines that have traditionally relied on the experience and expertise of each individual examiner (Ashbaugh, 1996; Murdock and Biasotti, 1997). In a 1997 editorial, John Thornton, one of the leading forensic minds of our day, wrote, "To master statistical models to explain much of our evidence may be a slow, reluctant march through enemy territory, but we must begin to plan for that campaign" (Thornton, 1997). We agree that, at least for physical evidence, providing a statistical justification for the analyst's opinion should be a goal. This may take different forms for different evidence; it may be limited for certain types of evidence until further work is done, and remain limited for some kinds of evidence due to its nature. However, in our opinion, it is an objective that we should be actively pursuing. The discussion within the forensic community remains heated and current.

B.   Forensic Science and the Law

Although the definition of forensic science may be debated, the relationship of forensic science to the law is clear. Without the judicial system, the criminalist has no function. The job of the analyst is to provide scientific information to the legal community and, in doing so, to translate the story the evidence has to tell. The scientific analysis is only performed at the behest of someone seeking to introduce the evidence into a court of law. This could be an investigator or the prosecuting attorney. It could also be the defendant through a defense attorney. The evidence comes to the forensic analyst because someone has deemed it relevant to the reconstruction of an event in time, an event that is associated with a suspected crime.

The frequently opposing aims of science and law must be acknowledged before they can be surmounted. While the scientist is trained to be objective to the point of skepticism, and to present alternative explanations equally, the U.S. legal system is constructed around a system of advocacy. The prosecution is expected to strongly argue the case that she at least believes to be the truth, and the defense attorney is required to strongly advocate for his client and may elect to emphasize the interpretation that best supports his position. These contradictory goals frequently make for an uneasy alliance between science and law, with both representatives battling to maintain their own professional ethics. Each case presents these challenges anew.

1.   What Is the Question?

If you don't ask the right question, you won't get the right answer, no matter how brilliant your analysis. Although that aphorism could describe most situations in life, its consequence becomes excruciatingly clear when applied to a case investigation. Asking the right question will be a continuing theme throughout this book.

a.   Translating the Legal Question into the Scientific Question

Before the criminalist ever picks up a magnifying glass, pipette, or chemical reagent, he must have an idea of where he is headed; he must define a question that science can answer. That question is determined by the circumstances of each individual case and calls into play the experience, education, and knowledge of the analyst. It is critical to understand that this question depends directly on the legal question framed by the investigator or attorney. In a criminal action, these all derive from the legal definition of the crime itself and in some cases from the circumstances surrounding the crime. For the legal action to proceed, the law must establish that a crime has, in fact, been committed by defining the *corpus delicti* (literally, "body of the crime"). All of the elements that legally define any particular crime must be present to proceed. In this setting, the only germane questions are the legal questions. The role of the forensic scientist is to translate the relevant legal question into a scientific question. If this cannot be done, then forensic science has no role to play.

One way the criminalist can assist law enforcement and legal professionals is by helping them to translate a legal question correctly (Did O. J. Simpson kill Ron Goldman and Nicole Brown Simpson?) into a question that science can answer (What genetic types are found in the bloodstains from the scene?). The answer to the scientific question will then assist in answering the legal question. Conversely, one of the most effective counters to the presentation of physical evidence is to show that the wrong question was asked. For instance, finding the suspect's blood on the suspect's shoes is irrelevant to whether he attacked the victim. Similarly, the finding of an unusual collection of fibers on the murder weapon becomes meaningless if both the suspect and the victim were wearing uniforms composed of the rare fiber set. Analysis of physical evidence in a crime laboratory is best suited to answering *who*, *what*, *where*, and *how*; it is less adept at answering *when* and can almost never answer *why*. Because the design or selection of appropriate tests depends completely on the initial hypothesis, it must be carefully framed at the beginning of the investigation rather than on the witness stand.

It is crucial to note that the moment the question is translated into science, the component of guilt or innocence is lost. Forensic science seeks to establish connections (or lack thereof) between evidence and its source, and secondarily, between items that may be associated by the evidence. Said in another way, we consider the probability of the evidence in light of competing hypotheses, often the prosecution's allegation and the defense proposition. Guilt or innocence may only be considered by the legal system and decided by a judge or jury.

The focus of an analysis and its interpretation are dictated by the circumstances of the case and the question(s) facing the criminal justice system. This is the reason the most common and useful answer to any general criminalistics question is, "it depends." The analysis of a sexual assault case serves as a good example of this point. Sexual assault, and rape in particular, is distinguished from other crimes in that it is not necessarily evident by mere observation that a crime has occurred. We know that if we come home, the window has been forced open, and our stereo is missing, that a burglary has taken place. This is generally obvious to any other observer as well. It is rarely possible to look at a woman or man and determine that she or he has been raped. The crime of rape can be summarized as the act of sexual intercourse accomplished through fear or force. Science can assist in substantiating one of the elements (that of sexual intercourse) by determining that sperm are present. This, of course, says nothing about the fear or force part. The meaning of the scientific finding may change dramatically depending on the circumstances of the case.

The use of science in the arena of civil law has grown as pioneering and developing societies have achieved the economic stability necessary to support elective activities. Civil litigation almost always concerns money; to argue about it, one must have both the time and means to do so. Many of the common areas of civil litigation, such as medical malpractice, money fraud, and engineering, are outside the scope of this volume. Of the areas of inquiry shared by criminal and civil investigations, the legal standards obviously differ, leading to, among other things, different questions, but the scientific analyses remain the same.

b. Physical Evidence and Circumstantial Evidence

Before we proceed further, it is worth reviewing the concepts of **circumstantial evidence** and **physical evidence**. Most physical evidence is circumstantial evidence — that is, its involvement in the scenario requires some further inference or assumption. Exceptions to this generality include substances that by their very presence are illegal, such as illicit drugs. Circumstantial evidence need not be physical, although most of it is. The term circumstantial evidence carries with it the connotation of untrustworthiness, while eyewitness evidence tends to be considered conclusive. Nothing could be farther from the truth. In fact, numerous studies have shown eyewitness evidence to be remarkably unreliable (Loftus, 1996).

Consider the following scenario. You are camping in a cabin deep in the woods in Alaska. It is the depth of winter and the snow pack is many feet. You hear a sound in the middle of the night and go to the window to see what it is. The moon is new, and it is practically pitch dark. You see a quickly moving shadow that seems to blend in with the snow. Is it a polar bear? Is it a potential burglar dressed in white? You really can't be sure. In the morning you venture outside to behold — very clear snowshoe tracks. There is no question in your mind that the previous night's visitor was a human, not a bear. You then also notice that the lock to your toolshed is hanging open, and a reconnaissance of the interior reveals that some of your tools are missing. Which evidence was more convincing — your midnight glimpse (eyewitness evidence) or the prints in the snow (circumstantial evidence) combined with the burglary? More important, which evidence will be more convincing to the local police — your description of a dark blur or casts of the tracks in the snow. Even if you had had a really good look at the burglar, it's still your word against his; the physical evidence of the tracks is inarguable. (The issue of the significance of a match to the suspect's snowshoes is another issue). So much for the assertion that "the evidence is only circumstantial."

C.   Summary

In writing this book, we found that our subject area logically divided itself into three sections. In Section 1, Background and History of Forensic Science, we introduce you to definitions and concepts to that we will refer throughout the book. We also spend some time looking backward to see how the evolution of forensic science can help us understand the issues we face today. In Section 2, The Principles of Forensic Science, we introduce you to a unifying paradigm for thinking about forensic science. Included in this paradigm is a new principle, **divisible matter**, that we propose is necessary to invoke the well-known principle of *transfer*, attributed to the great forensic scientist Edmund Locard (Locard, 1920). We also discuss at length the forensic principles of *identification, classification, individualization, association*, and *reconstruction*. In Section 3, The Practice of Forensic Science, we address some of the pragmatic issues facing the criminalist today. We start with recognizing an item as evidence, progress through analysis and interpretation guidelines, and finish with a discussion of ethics and accountability. We hope we have at least intrigued you to read further.

References

Ashbaugh, D. R., *Quantitative–Qualitative Friction Ridge Analysis: An Introduction to Basic and Advanced Ridgeology*, CRC Press, Boca Raton, FL, 2000.

Bacon, F., *The Great Instauration*. Originally published 1620, The Great Instauration and the New Atlantis, Weinberger, J., Ed. AMH Publishing Co., Arlington Heights, IL, 1980.

Ceccaldi, P. F., From crime to evidence, *Int. Police J.*, 1974.

Cole, S., Witnessing identification: latent fingerprinting evidence and expert knowledge, *Soc. Stud. Sci.*, 28(5–6), 687, 1998.

Cole, S., What counts for identity? The historical origins of the methodology of latent fingerprint identification, *Sci. Context*, 12(1), 139, 1999.

Daubert v. Merrill Dow Pharmaceuticals, 509 U. S., 1993.

Decartes, R. *Discourse on Method*, 1637.

Doyle, A. C., The Adventures of Sherlock Holmes: A Scandal in Bohemia, *The Strand Magazine*, 1891.

Evett, I., What is the probability that this blood came from that person? A meaningful question? *J. Forensic. Sci. Soc.*, 23, 35, 1983.

Fisher, R. A., *The Design of Experiments*, Oliver and Boyd, London, 1949.

Hofstadter, D. R., *Gödel, Escher, Bach: An Eternal Golden Braid*, Basic Books, New York, 1979.

Horgan, J., *The End of Science*, Addison-Wesley, New York, 1996.

Houck, M., Statistics and Trace Evidence: The Tyranny of Numbers, *Forensic Science Communications*, Federal Bureau of Investigation, Virginia 1(3), 1999, available at *http://www.fbi.gov/programs/lab/fsc/current/houck.htm*.

Jones, L. V. and Gabard, C., *Scientific Investigation and Physical Evidence; Handbook for Investigators*, Charles C Thomas, Springfield, MA, 1959.

Kumho Tire Co., Ltd., et al. v. Carmichael. 97-1709 U.S., 1999.

Locard, E., *L'enquete Criminelle et Les Methodes Scientifique*, Ernest Flammarion, Paris, 1920.

Loftus, E. F., *Eyewitness Testimony*, Harvard University Press, Cambridge, MA, 1996.

Maddock, J., No evidence for cold fusion neutrons, *Nature*, 340, 1989.

Murdock, J. E. and Biasotti, A. A., The scientific basis of firearms and toolmark identification, in Firearms and Toolmark Identification, in *Modern Scientific Evidence*, Faigman, D. L., et al., Eds., West Law, San Francisco, 1997.

Naess, A., Book review, *New Scientist*, August, 1998.

Neyman, J. and Pearson, E. S. On the use and interpretation of certain test criteria for purposes of statistical inference, Part I and II, *Biometrika*, 20, 174–240, 263–294, 1928.

Popper, K. R., *Conjectures and Refutations: The Growth of Scientific Knowledge*, Basic Books, New York, 1962.

Stark, P. B., SticiGui© Glossary of Statistical Terms, 2000, available at *http://www.stat.berkeley.edu/~stark/SticiGui/Text/gloss.htm#n*.

Taroni, F., Champod, C., and Margot, P., Forerunners of Bayesianism in early forensic science, *Jurimetrics J.*, 38, 183–200, 1998.

Thornton, J., The DNA statistical paradigm vs. everything else, correspondence, *J. Forensic Sci.*, 42(4), 758, 1997.

Van Heerden, T. J., Criminalistics, University of South Africa, Muakleneuk, Pretoria, 1982.

Webster's Encyclopedic Unabridged Dictionary of the English Language, Gramercy Books, New York, 1996.

Williams, E. W., *Modern Law Enforcement and Police Science.* Charles C. Thomas, Springfield, MA, 1967.

Wilson, E.O., *Consilience: The Unity of Knowledge*, Knopf, New York, 1998.

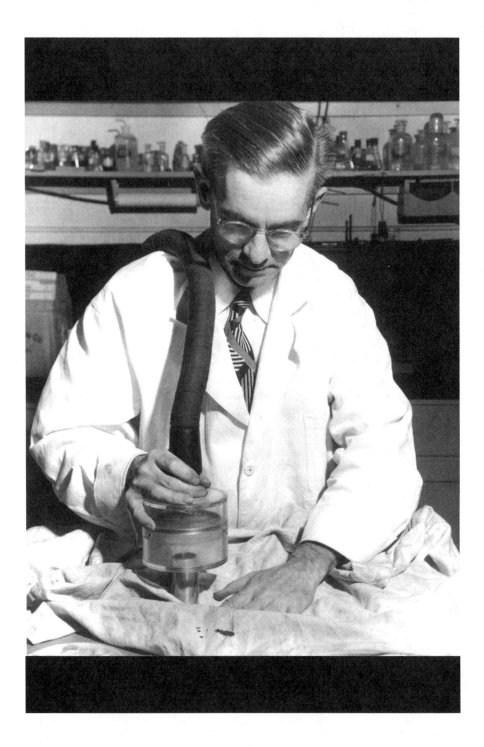

The Evolution of Forensic Science

2

Contents

Figure 2.1 Dr. Paul Kirk. Dr. Paul Kirk both searches for and collects evidence with one of his inventions. Dr. Kirk pioneered many technical and conceptual advances in criminalistics. He proposed that individualizing the evidence that we find is the defining principle of the criminalistics effort. (Courtesy of Bancroft Library, University of California, Berkeley.)

It was a dark and stormy night; the rain fell in torrents — except at occasional intervals, when it was checked by a violent gust of wind which swept up the streets (for it is in London that our scene lies), rattling along the housetops, and fiercely agitating the scanty flame of the lamps that struggled against the darkness.

Edward George Earl Bulwer-Lytton
—*Paul Clifford*, 1830

As with any endeavor, it is useful to study the lessons of the past so that one can at least make new mistakes rather than recycle the old ones. For reasons that remain unclear to the authors, those involved, either integrally or peripherally, in the practice of forensic science seem to insist on repeating the same mistakes over and over again. In this chapter we identify the roots of forensic science, trace some of the history, and highlight the evolution of concepts as well as practice. We hope that a brief reflection on the past will prove useful in guiding the future course of forensic science. Please refer to Appendix A for a Timeline of Forensic Science.

A. The Literary Beginnings

From its inception, forensic science has evoked an air of mystery and intrigue. It is probably both the least understood and most misunderstood of all scientific disciplines. Because speculation immediately expands to fill an informational void, rumor and gossip have become the stuff upon which the lay public judges the forensic profession. Certainly, forensic practitioners have historically contributed to the perception that the reconstruction of a criminal event from limited evidence can only be achieved by a few talented individuals with a special aptitude for such work. Even those whose methods were scientifically defensible could not resist encouraging the bit of celebrity and notoriety that seems to follow those known for solving difficult crimes. The accordance of these attributes, combined with the understandable inability of legal professionals to separate true experts from charlatans, has unfortunately also encouraged a proliferation of self-appointed experts whose motives are based solely in greed and infamy.

However, even the most scientifically inclined and professionally oriented forensic practitioners have historically overestimated their ability to draw grand conclusions from limited data. This may follow, at least in part, from the literary beginnings of criminal investigation. In these stories, fictional detectives were able to recreate an entire detailed sequence of events from a few small clues. An example is found in one of Voltaire's lesser-known works, *Zadig*, written in 1747. The chapter entitled "The Dog and the Horse" takes place in ancient Babylon (Voltaire, 1748).

Zadig was walking through the woods when he encountered the Queen's eunuch and the King's huntsman. They inquired anxiously whether he had seen the Queen's dog and the King's horse. Shaking his head, Zadig asked if they were referring to a bitch, slightly lame with long ears who had recently had puppies, and a horse with small hoofs, about five feet tall and with a tail three and a half feet long. Although he vehemently denied it, the eunuch and the huntsman were in no doubt that Zadig had stolen both the King's horse and the Queen's dog, else how could he have known such details? He was arrested, found guilty, and sentenced to flogging and banishment to Siberia.

However, the sentence had scarcely been passed when the missing animals reappeared. The sentence was reduced to a heavy fine to punish Zadig for declaring that he had not seen what he had seen and he was allowed to plead his case as follows:

"... I noticed the tracks of an animal in the sandy soil, which I readily took to be those of a little dog. Some long but delicate furrows, traced in the sand wherever it was raised between the prints of the paws, showed me that it was a bitch with hanging dugs, which must therefore have had puppies a few days before. Other tracks of a different kind, which always appeared to have brushed the sand at either side of the forefeet, showed me that its ears were very long; and as I noticed that the sand was always more deeply impressed by one paw than by the other three, I concluded that our august Queen's little bitch was a trifle lame, if I may dare to say so.

"As for the horse which belongs to the King of Kings, you must know that as I was walking along the paths of this wood, I noticed some horseshoe prints all at equal distances.... In a straight stretch of path only seven feet wide, the dust had been lightly brushed from the trees on both sides at a distance of three and a half feet from the centre of the path. 'This horse.' Said I, 'has a tail three and a half feet long, which must have swept off the dust on both sides as it waved.' The trees formed an arcade five feet high. When I noticed that some of the leaves were newly fallen, I deduced that the horse must have touched them, and that he was therefore five feet high also. As for the bit it must be made of twenty-three carat gold, because the horse had rubbed the bosses against a stone which I knew to be touchstone, and which I therefore tested And finally I judged from the marks which the horseshoes had left on a different kind of stone that it was shod with silver of eleven deniers proof."

The king's court was so greatly impressed by Zadig's deductive powers that he was promptly vindicated and his gold returned.

In scientific endeavors, advances are commonly foretold in fiction before becoming reality. Forensic science is no exception and the influence of detective literature on the development of modern forensic science cannot be underestimated. Edmund Locard, to whom the concept of transfer is attributed, gives direct credit to Arthur Conan Doyle, innovator of the fictional detective Sherlock Holmes, as the true instigator of modern forensic science. In "The Analysis of Dust Traces," a three part series published in 1930 in *The American Journal of Police Science*, Locard wrote:

> I hold that a police expert, or an examining magistrate, would not find it a waste of his time to read Doyle's novels. For, in *The Adventures of Sherlock Holmes*, the detective is repeatedly asked to diagnose the origin of a speck of mud, which is nothing but moist dust. The presence of a spot on a shoe or pair of trousers immediately made known to Holmes the particular quarter of London from which his visitor had come, or the road he had traveled in the suburbs. A spot of clay and chalk originated in Horsham; a peculiar reddish bit of mud could be found nowhere but at the entrance to the post office in Wigmore Street. Nevertheless, one is not to be persuaded that even with the genius of a Sherlock Holmes there would not be the risk of numerous failures in identification of such spots by merely viewing them at a distance. But even such an inspection may develop something significant and one might profitably re-read from this point of view the stories entitled: *A Study in Scarlet, The Five Orange Pips*, and *The Sign of Four*. Elsewhere Holmes insists upon the interest and fascination to be found in collecting tobacco ashes, on which he says he has "written a little monograph concerning one hundred and forty varieties." (*The Boscombe Valley Mystery*) On the latter point one should again read *The Sign of the Four* and also *The Resident Patient* (Locard, 1930).

It is worth pointing out several other references by Conan Doyle, a physician by training, to the importance of physical evidence. In "A Study in Scarlet," Sherlock Holmes devises a specific test for blood which ostensibly improved on the guaiacum test in use at the time. He also points out several attributes of a useful forensic test for blood.

> "I've found it! I've found it," he shouted to my companion, running toward us with a test-tube in his hand. "I have found a re-agent which is precipitated by haemoglobin, and by nothing else." ... "Why, man, it is the most practical medico-legal discovery for years. Don't you see that it gives us an infallible

test for blood stains?" … "Beautiful! Beautiful! The old guaiacum test was very clumsy and uncertain. So is the microscopic examination for blood corpuscles.* The latter is valueless if the stains are a few hours old. Now, this appears to act as well whether the blood is old or new. (Doyle, 1887)

In "The Adventure of the Cardboard Box," he brings to our attention individualizing attributes of the human ear (Figure 2.2). We also see an example here of literary license in deducing kinship from ear traits.

"As a medical man, you are aware, Watson, that there is no part of the body which varies so much as the human ear. Each ear is as a rule quite distinctive and differs from all other ones. In last year's *Anthropological Journal* you will find two short monographs from my pen upon the subject. I had therefore examined the ears in the box with the eyes of an expert and had carefully noted the anatomical peculiarities. Imagine my surprise, then, when on looking at Miss Cushing I perceived that her ear corresponded exactly with the female ear which I had just inspected." … "Of course I at once saw the enormous importance of the observation. It was evident that the victim was a blood relation and probably a very close one." (Doyle, 1893)

It is not unusual, even today, for a young person to choose a career in forensic science because of an early fascination with the Sherlock Holmes stories. In fact, the smoking pipe and deerstalker's cap have become immediately recognizable symbols of crime detection to an entire generation of aspiring criminalists. Unfortunately, the somewhat pompous and omniscient attitude that draws us to Sherlock Holmes as a literary character becomes a liability when transferred to reality. Humbleness and modesty are generally better companions to a seeker of the truth.

Although less commonly recognized in the forensic community, Edgar Allen Poe is credited in literary circles as creator of the detective genre. In an odd twist, Doyle acknowledges Poe's C. Auguste Dupin as the inspiration for the Sherlock Holmes character ("Study in Scarlet"), and, in typical Holmesian fashion, immediately derides him as an inferior template.

"It is simple enough as you explain it," I said, smiling. "You remind me of Edgar Allan Poe's Dupin. I had no idea that such individuals did exist outside of stories." … Sherlock Holmes rose and lit his pipe. "No doubt you think that you are complimenting me in comparing me to Dupin," he observed. "Now, in my opinion, Dupin was a very inferior fellow. That trick of his of breaking in on his friends' thoughts with an apropos remark after a quarter of an hour's silence is really very showy and superficial. He had

---

* No doubt a reference to Orfila's work in the early 1800s.

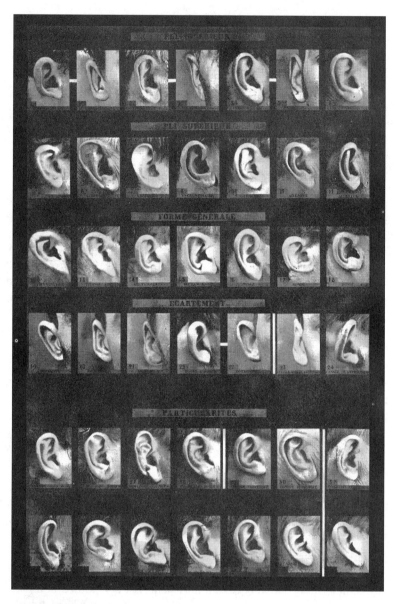

Figure 2.2 Locard's ears. Human ears develop into a wide variety of forms. Edmund Locard collected photographs of ears from numerous people to demonstrate that each one is unique.

some analytical genius no doubt; but he was by no means such a phenomenon as Poe appeared to imagine."

Doyle, through the Holmes character, continues his derision of Holmes' literary predecessors.

"Have you read Gaboriau's works?" I asked. "Does Lecoq come up to your idea of a detective?" ... Sherlock Holmes sniffed sardonically. "Lecoq was a miserable bungler." He said in an angry voice; "he had only one thing to recommend him, and that was his energy. That book made me positively ill. I could have done it in twenty-four hours. Lecoq took six months or so. It might be made a textbook for detectives to teach them what to avoid."

In fact, in Poe's stories, written before the word detective existed, we find several foretellings of forensic concepts that Doyle embellishes for his own stories. It is unlikely to be incidental that Poe establishes Dupin in France, the birthplace of Alphones Bertillon, Edmund Locard, and others comprising a veritable forensic dynasty. He also gives due derision to Eugène François Vidocq, a reformed Parisian criminal, who in 1810 established the first investigative unit ever.

The results attained by them are not unfrequently surprising, but for the most part, are brought about by simple diligence and activity. When these qualities are unavailing, their schemes fail. Vidocq, for example, was a good guesser, and the persevering man. But, without educated thought, he erred continually by the very intensity of his investigations. He impaired his vision by holding the object too close. He might see, perhaps, one or two points with unusual clearness, but in so doing he, necessarily, lost sight of the matter as a whole. (Poe, 1841)

In Poe's *The Murders in the Rue Morgue*, we find possibly the first reference to asking the right question, "It should not be so much asked 'what has occurred,' as 'what has occurred that has never occurred before.'" We also find the forerunner to the famous Holmesian quote "When you have eliminated the impossible, whatever remains, however improbably, must be the truth" in Dupin's "because here it was, I knew, that all apparent impossibilities must be proved to be not such in reality." Perhaps the most prescient concept introduced by Poe was the application of statistics to the interpretation of forensic results.

Coincidences, in general, are great stumbling-blocks in the way of that class of thinkers who have been educated to know nothing of the theory of probabilities — that theory to which the most glorious objects of human research are indebted for the most glorious of illustration. (Poe, 1841)

And one can't help but notice the element of the pipe, complete with drifting smoke, introduced in "The Purloined Letter" (Poe, 1845).

Although not known primarily for detective stories per se, Mark Twain (a.k.a. Samuel Clemens) immediately capitalized on one of the most important developments in police science, individualization using fingerprints. In

The Tragedy of Pudd'nhead Wilson, written in 1894, a lawyer with a hobby of collecting fingerprints exonerated twin brothers by showing that bloody prints on a knife were not theirs. From his descriptions, it is quite clear that Twain had carefully studied the theories and capabilities of fingerprints. At least one source indicates that, in 1892, while the details of the plot were still evolving, Twain acquired a copy of *Finger Prints*, by Francis Galton, and decided to feature fingerprints in the story (Railton, 1998). His proficient use of them in this story certainly predates their wide use and general acceptance by several years at least.

> The fad without a name was one which dealt with people's finger marks. He carried in his coat pocket a shallow box with grooves in it, and in the grooves strips of glass five inches long and three inches wide. Along the lower edge of each strip was pasted a slip of white paper. He asked people to pass their hands through their hair (thus collecting upon them a thin coating of the natural oil) and then making a thumb-mark on a glass strip, following it with the mark of the ball of each finger in succession.... Sometimes he copied on paper the involved and delicate pattern left by the ball of the finger, and then vastly enlarged it with a pantograph so that he could examine its web of curving lines with ease and convenience.
>
> ...Every human being carries with him from his cradle to his grave certain physical marks which do not change their character, and by which he can always be identified — and that without shade of doubt or question. These marks are his signature, his physiological autograph, so to speak, and this autograph can not be counterfeited, nor can he disguise it or hide it away, nor can it become illegible by the wear and mutations of time. This signature is not his face — age can change that beyond recognition; it is not his hair, for that can fall out; it is not his height, for duplicates of that exist; it is not his form, for duplicates of that exist also, whereas this signature is each man's very own — there is no duplicate of it among the swarming populations of the globe! One twin's patterns are never the same as his fellow twin's patterns ... there was never a twin born in to this world that did not carry from birth to death a sure identifier in this mysterious and marvelous natal autograph.

Interestingly, unlike the other two authors mentioned, Twain reserves his literary license for the story, sticking strictly to the limitations of the technique in his use of fingerprints. Clemens also used fingerprints to further the plot in *Life on the Mississippi*, in which a thumbprint is used to identify a murderer (Thorwald, 1964).

As we will see in subsequent sections, even the most revered of our forensic forefathers succumbed to an occasional indulgence in overinterpretation. Under the current microscope of ever-increasing scrutiny, the current trend is to step back from leaps of intuition. In some cases, this has led to an overreaction in the opposite direction, with technical specialists retreating to a corner of the laboratory to provide an isolated analysis of a lone piece of evidence. We suggest that a balance between these two extremes might be achieved by interpreting the evidence with appropriate limitations and in the context of the case.

B.   Evolution of the Practice

As with many applied sciences, the practice of the craft of forensic science evolved undeterred by any restrictions such as fundamental principles or universal concepts. In deference to the order of evolution, we will describe the progress of the profession as it proceeded throughout the last couple of centuries, then, in the next section, identify the points at which certain fundamental principles were first discerned.

1.   Physical Evidence

a.   Biological Evidence — Who?

Because friction ridge patterns on fingers are immediately obvious to simple visual examination, they were the first physical aspect of personal identity to be perceived. The complex patterns inherent in fingerprints were noticed even by primitive man, as evidenced by their incorporation in prehistoric paintings and rock carvings (Ashbaugh, 1996). The use of fingerprints for identification by both the Babylonians and later the Chinese seems clear from the archaeological relics of clay tablets and other legal documents bearing the prints of interested parties (Morland, 1950). Although several scientists, among them Marcello Malpighi in the 17th century and John Purkinji, in the early 19th century, remarked on the nature of fingerprints, it was not until the late 19th century that their usefulness in establishing individual identity and solving crimes was fully realized (Morland, 1950; Thorwald, 1964; Moore, 1999).

The acceptance of fingerprints, however, was preceded by a foray into what is now known as **anthropometry**. Although it seems innately obvious that we all recognize individuals by their unique aspects and proportions, Alphonse Bertillon developed this practice into a science of sorts (Thorwald, 1964). Based on the work of Adolphe Quetelet, a Belgian statistician best known for his statistical innovations in the social sciences, Bertillon developed a system of body measurements that, if performed with exquisite care, were claimed to be unique to each individual. Although initially met with great skepticism, he was finally allowed to put his innovation into practice for the French police force. In 1883, he was given 3 months to prove its worth. Bertillon's successful identification of a recidivist criminal convinced the administration to let him expand the system and compile a database of personal measurements of current prison inmates. Anthropometry, or Bertillonage, was hailed as the latest, greatest crime-solving tool, and quickly spread throughout the world as an accepted and much-used technique.

Meanwhile, the credit for recognition of fingerprints as a crime detection tool was being contested by Henry Faulds, a Scottish physician working in Japan, and by Sir William Hershel, a British officer working for the Indian Civil Service. Hershel had been using fingerprints since the mid-1800s, both as a substitute for written signatures for illiterates and to verify document signatures. It was not lost on him that the indigenous Indian population considered a transfer of body material as a binding contract. However, it fell to Faulds to specifically recognize the possibility that fingerprints at the scene of a crime could identify the offender. Ironically, in one of the first recorded uses of fingerprints to solve a crime, Faulds eliminated an innocent suspect before implicating the perpetrator in a Tokyo burglary (Thorwald, 1964). Much to Hershel's dismay, Faulds published the first paper detailing the nature and uses of fingerprints in the journal *Nature* in 1880. In the end, it was left to Sir Francis Galton, first cousin to Charles Darwin, to consolidate the information and publish the first paper dealing with the statistics and significance of fingerprints (Galton, 1888). Galton also published the first comprehensive book on the nature of fingerprints and their use in solving crime (Galton, 1892). Interestingly, in this book, *Finger Prints*, he gives Hershel, rather than Faulds, credit for the initial publication in Nature (Cole, 1999).

As with all physical evidence, the strength of a fingerprint association could not be determined without an estimation of its frequency in the population. Although Galton predicted the first theoretical probability of discrimination based on mathematical models, the development of working fingerprint classification systems was pioneered by Juan Vucetich, an Argentinean police researcher, and Sir Edward Henry, another Briton working as an Inspector General in India. Vucetich's system became entrenched in Latin America, while the system Henry invented on his shirt cuff during a train ride to Calcutta (Thorwald, 1964) continues to be used in Europe and North America. A standardized classification system enabled the collection and storage of large volumes of fingerprint data that could be organized into searchable databases and shared between institutions. Although a number of workers, from Galton forward, have attempted to introduce mathematical models that would allow for the estimation of the rarity of a fingerprint, none of these has been adopted for use by the field (Stoney and Thornton, 1986a).

As with many scientific advances, the use of fingerprints was not immediately accepted as a replacement for anthropometry. It took the death of

Bertillon, who had come to be a revered although disgruntled figure in police science, to finally allow the changeover. However, one specific incident finally convinced the skeptics that fingerprinting was the more appropriate and useful technique. In 1903, a new inmate by the name of Will West was brought to Leavenworth State Prison in Kansas. Leavenworth was one of the first correctional institutions in the United States to add fingerprint data to the anthropometric measurement database of its inmates. A particularly observant prison guard noticed that another Will West was already in residence at the prison and, surprisingly, had the same anthropometric measurements as the new arrival. As an experiment, fingerprints of the two men were compared and found unquestionably to differ. That the two men were later suspected to be estranged identical twins (German, 1999) only strengthened the obvious advantages of fingerprint identification over anthropometry. Ironically, Bertillon, during his later years, was the first to solve a crime on the continent using fingerprints, which he had begun to collect along with other anthropometric data (Thorwald, 1964).

Prints of other body areas containing friction ridges, such as the soles of the feet and palms of the hands, have also found forensic application, as have prints of various body orifices. Since the acceptance of fingerprints into general use, major advances have come mainly in two areas. Numerous methods have been developed to visualize latent prints, such as cyanoacrylate fuming and laser detection, making it possible to collect a print from practically any surface. On the other hand, the development of computerized databases has made it possible to store an enormous amount of fingerprint data in a form that is readily searched.*

It is worth pointing out that both fingerprinting and anthropometry, questions of validity aside, share the characteristic of being directly related to a person. They attempt to answer the *who* question in a case investigation. Of the constellation of tests used in forensic science, the only other tests that share that ability depend on the transfer and subsequent analysis of biological material, such as blood, semen, saliva, or hair. With the exception of microscopic hair comparison (perhaps better classified as a fiber examination), these examinations all require laboratory testing, explaining their later development.

At first, forensic testing of biological evidence was limited to determining the *what* question. In the mid-1800s, Ludwig Teichmann, in Kracow, Poland, developed the first microscopic crystal test for hemoglobin, indicating the presence of blood. In 1912, Masao Takayama developed a similar microscopic test for hemoglobin based on another crystal formation. Both tests are still used today, and remain exquisitely sensitive and specific. In 1863, the German

---

* It should be noted that the all the computer does is retrieve prints with similar patterns for a human being to compare.

scientist, Schönbein developed the first presumptive test for blood. It was based on the ability of heme to oxidize hydrogen peroxide, making it foam. Around the same time, the Dutch scientist Van Deen developed another presumptive blood test using a West Indian shrub called guaiac. Both tests, however, depended on the oxidizing property of heme, and thus had the limitation of sometimes producing false positives with substances other than blood. This was also true of the luminol test, originated by Walter Specht in 1937, and remains a caveat with all presumptive blood tests used even today. The next major advance in serology occurred at the turn of the century when Paul Uhlenhuth, a German professor, developed the antigen–antibody precipitin test for species. Now it was possible to at least tell *which*, if not *who*. The technique was not refined for forensic use until the 1960s, when Maurice Müller, a Swiss chemist, adapted the Ouchterlony antigen–antibody diffusion test for species testing (Thorwald, 1964; 1966; Gaensslen, 1983).

The first whisperings of a blood test that could indicate *who* were heard in 1900, when Karl Landsteiner first discovered human blood groups. This advance was so significant to medicine (it enabled the determination of donor–recipient compatibility for blood transfusions) that it earned him the Nobel prize in 1930. As a relatively minor sidelight, ABO testing enabled, for the first time, some differentiation between which human beings could have left biological evidence at a scene. Landsteiner, along with various collaborators, pioneered much of the basic research that would lead to serological typing systems. In 1915, Leon Lattes, professor at the Institute of Forensic Medicine in Turin, Italy, developed the first antibody-based test for ABO blood groups, thus greatly expanding their utility. Max Richter adapted Landsteiner's technique to type dried stains, one of the first instances of specifically developing and validating a technique for use in forensic situations. In 1923, Vittorio Siracusa, working under Lattes, developed the absorption–elution test for ABO typing of blood stains. In 1930, Franz Holzer extended ABO typing further with a refinement of the absorbtion–inhibition method that was subsequently adopted by crime laboratories. Weiner and colleagues contributed another major advance in 1958, when they introduced the use of H-lectin to positively determine blood type O (no naturally occurring human antibodies to blood type O exist, as they do against the A and B blood types) (Thornwald, 1966; Gaensslen, 1983).

Of course, biological material other than blood is also frequently shed or deposited in connection with a crime. In 1839, H. Bayard published the first reliable procedures for the microscopic detection of sperm (Figure 2.3). The acid phosphatase test, a widely used method for the presumptive detection of seminal fluid, was developed by Frank Lundquist in 1945. Along with Meüller's suggestion in 1928 of using salivary amylase as an indicator for saliva, this completed the constellation of presumptive tests for the most

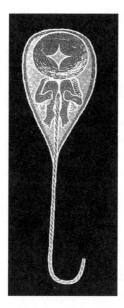

Figure 2.3 Homunculus. In the early days of microscopy, analysts believed that they could discern a little man in the spermatozoa that would later grow and emerge from the uterus as a human being. Later advances in the manufacture of microscope lenses, and in our knowledge of biology, would suggest a slightly more complex mechanism for the propagation of life.

common body fluids that might be found at a crime scene. Additional tests for seminal fluid, including seminal protein p30 (prostate specific antigen; PSA), have been developed more recently (Gaensslen, 1983).

Throughout the first half of the 20th century, a number of additional antigenic markers were developed and adapted for forensic use. With each additional marker, it was possible to exclude an ever-greater segment of the population as possible donors of a biological sample. As blood-typing systems were being developed, it was also realized that the same antigenic markers were present on other cell types such as buccal cells in saliva and sperm cells in semen. In most cases they were also detectable as free antigens in body fluids and secretions. These discoveries greatly expanded the usefulness of biological typing systems to the forensic community. In the 1950s and 1960s, advances in immunology and biochemistry led to the development of two more classes of serological markers. Testing systems were developed for several isoantibodies and also for a number of isoenzyme systems. It was not until the beginning of the next decade, however, that the now vast body of work on serological typing systems was consolidated. This was accomplished under the direction of Brian Culliford of the Metropolitan Police Laboratory in London. His book, *The Examination and Typing of Bloodstains in the Crime Laboratory*, published in 1971, is considered responsible for disseminating reliable protocols for the typing of polymorphic protein and enzyme markers to the United States and worldwide.

Although the ability to type biological material had been available for much of the 20th century, a dermatoglyphic fingerprint was still considered the ultimate in human identification. That all changed abruptly in the mid-1980s when Sir Alec Jeffreys initiated the greatest advance since Landsteiner with his discovery of "multilocus" restriction fragment length polymorphism (RFLP) testing (Jeffreys et al., 1985). During its adoption for use by the FBI and others, the testing was modified to test one locus at a time, and eventually more than a dozen markers became available for standard forensic testing. Around the same time, another invention revolutionized not only forensic DNA typing, but the very face of molecular biology. In 1983, Kerry Mullis conceived the idea of the polymerase chain reaction (PCR) while driving on a lonely highway to his backwoods cabin (Saiki et al., 1985; Mullis et al., 1986). The idea was introduced at Cetus corporation, where he was employed, and subsequently developed by the human genetics group there led by Henry Erlich. Because PCR can selectively amplify any desired region of the genome, it was an obvious choice for minute, degraded forensic samples. All of the genetic systems developed for forensic DNA typing since then depend on PCR as an initial step.

Although the potential to individualize using DNA has always been apparent, it was not fully realized with the earlier systems, in particular the first PCR-based markers. Ironically, Jeffreys' original multilocus "DNA fingerprint" probably was individualizing. Today, most scientists would agree that a 6 to 9 locus RFLP profile effectively supports an opinion of a one-to-one correspondence between a stain and a donor. Nevertheless, the capability was immediately apparent and the obvious possibilities sparked a scrutiny and challenge to which a forensic technique has never before been subjected. Once Pandora's box was opened, the scrutiny turned toward other disciplines of forensic science, provoking, for the first time in history, a mobilization of the profession as a whole. While formal standards and quality assurance measures such as analyst certification, laboratory accreditation, and educational standards had long been promulgated by small groups within the profession, the greater forensic science community was now impelled to embrace such measures formally. DNA laboratories have begun to implement the newest genetic system, short tandem repeats (STRs), along with a universal move toward automation, allowing more than a dozen DNA markers to be analyzed in just a couple of runs. A moment of clarity occurs when we realize that, more than a century later, DNA typing is close to being accepted as individualizing evidence of *who?* with the confidence that has almost automatically been accorded to fingerprints for almost a century.

b. Nonbiological Evidence — What, How, Where?

i. Documents.   Because documents, like fingerprints, are easily visible, their recognition as possible evidence and their analysis began relatively early in history. Before chemical analysis of inks and paper was well developed, it was still possible to compare handwriting patterns. The first known treatise on systematic document examination, written by Frenchman François Demelle, dates back to 1609, and a second was written by another Frenchman, Jacques Raveneau in 1665. C. Ainsworth Mitchell, in Great Britain, worked extensively on questioned document identification. He not only focused on handwriting comparison, but engaged in a comprehensive study of the chemistry of inks, a different aspect entirely. American Albert Osborn is generally considered the foremost document examiner of his time. In 1910, he published *Questioned Documents*, a book which remained the standard for many years (Dillon, 1977).

ii. Physical match.   Similarly, an often-ignored, but highly useful category of evidence is physical matching. Probably the first recorded case in which physical matching led to a suspect was that of John Toms in England in 1784. The torn edge of a piece of newspaper used for wadding in his pistol matched a remaining piece in his pocket (Kind and Overman, 1972). Because of the random nature of its generation, physical matching is often very strong evidence. However, because the analysis of physical match evidence requires no fancy instrumentation or chemical reactions, and the interpretation is based on common sense, cases in which it plays a significant role do not tend to make the history annals. Physical matching does relate specifically, however, to the new concept of *divisible matter* which we will discuss briefly in the next section and in depth in Chapter 4.

iii. Trace.   One of the most important historical figures in forensic science, Edmund Locard, popularized perhaps the most nebulous category of physical evidence, trace evidence. Locard was a pupil of Alexander Lacassagne in forensic medicine at the University of Lyons, France, and eventually succeeded him to that position. In Lyons, Locard also established the first police laboratory in 1910. The concept of transfer, with which history credits Locard, and with which Locard credits Alexandre Lacassagne, Arthur Conan Doyle, and Hans Gross, was a turning point in the conceptualization of forensic science; we discuss it at length later in this chapter. Locard wrote profusely and produced many volumes dedicated to the tortured description of various *dusts*, *mud*, and *grime* that might indicate a person's whereabouts or occupation. However, the very nature of trace evidence — that it is everywhere — also undermines its potential significance; it is notoriously difficult to determine the strength of trace evidence. Although several investigators have attempted to estimate the frequency of particular fiber or particle in the environment,* only rarely are the results from a particular case considered in a quantitative manner (Houck, 1999). A major advance in trace analysis was something as simple as the invention of the tape lift by Swiss criminalist, Max Frei-Sulzer (Thorwald, 1966). A tape lift preserves the spatial orientation of the particles and fibers to the item as well as to each other, adding a useful second dimension to the interpretation. Because, by definition, the analysis of trace depends on optical magnification, its development coincides with refinements in microscopy. Without question, the polarizing microscope, invented in 1828 by William Nichol (Solbello, 1999), has been the most influential tool in the study of trace evidence.

iv.   Firearms.   The subject of firearms is always highly inflammatory (pun optional), no matter what the aspect, and the forensic analysis of guns and their related accoutrements fulfills that tradition with vigor. It must be emphasized, however, that bullet markings are no more than a subset of toolmarks, yet another category of comparison evidence. Luke May, one of the first American criminalists, pioneered the organized study of toolmarks, in particular striation analysis (May, 1930; 1936). Because bullets generally kill more directly than tools, the art of bullet comparison took center stage directly following World War I. Because the origin of toolmarks is random in nature, toolmarks, including bullet comparison, have the potential to be individualizing evidence. Several workers, in particular Biasotti (1959), have performed seminal studies aimed at provided a statistical basis for the interpretation of toolmark evidence. However, the firearms community has yet to embrace a truly quantitative basis to support a conclusion of individuality; most examiners continue to rely on personal experience and judgment (Murdock and Biasotti, 1997; Nichols, 1997). In 1835, Henry Goddard, one of Scotland Yard's original Bow Street Runners, linked a bullet to its mold on the basis of an easily visible flaw that coincided in both (Thorwald, 1964). In 1889, after rifling had been developed, Lacassagne individualized a bullet to a gun on the basis of the number of lands and grooves (Thorwald, 1964). We can only hope that the right man was convicted. In 1913, Victor Balthazard, professor of forensic medicine at the Sorbonne, published the first article discussing breach block, firing pin, extractor, and ejector markings on

---

* Although some studies have been performed, they have been relatively limited in geography and scope. However, we also recognized the scope of the problem and give credit to these investigators for attempting a complex, arduous, and generally thankless task. (Pounds and Smalldon, 1975; Home and Dudley, 1980; Kidd and Robertson, 1982; Robertson et al., 1982; Robertson and Lloyd, 1984; Deadman, 1984a,b; Cordiner et al., 1985; Parybyk and Lokan, 1986; Allard and Wiggins, 1987; Coxon et al., 1992; Palmer and Chinherende, 1996; Grieve and Biermann, 1997; Roux and Margot, 1997; Houck and Siegal, 1999).

cartidge cases for the purpose of determining from which weapon they were fired (Thorwald, 1964). This was the beginning of the realization that, like all comparison evidence, the minutiae contained within the gross markings of firearms evidence provide the individualizing potential.

The nature of firearms evidence seems to have attracted one the earliest concentrations of self-professed experts. In its earliest incarnation, bullet comparison required little more than a passing knowledge of firearms, a magnifying glass, and the ability to provide an opinion, whether based in fact or not. "Dr." Albert Hamilton was the most grandiose of the new class of "professional experts," advertising himself as an expert in practically every aspect of criminalistics including firearms. In 1917, he testified at the trial of Charles Stielow that "the bullets that killed the defendant's employer could have been fired by no other weapon." Charles Waite had languished as an employee at the New York State Prosecutor's office until he was selected to act as an assistant to a governor-appointed commission formed to reexamine the firearms evidence from the Stielow case. Fortunately, before Stielow sat in the electric chair, the evidence was, at Charles Waite's urging, reexamined by Max Posner of Bauch and Lomb. Posner discovered and documented a manufacturing flaw in the barrel that produced the bullets in question, but not in the murder weapon, excluding any association between the two. Thus, a charlatan inadvertently paved the road for the development of legitimate bullet comparison, a cause that was to be ably championed by Charles Waite (Thorwald, 1964).

It was not until after World War I that Charles Waite in New York first set out to catalogue manufacturing data about weapons. The Stielow trial, in which he worked directly with Posner, was his introduction to forensic firearm examination. The realization that even modern mass-production methods left individualizing marks on weapon barrels and moving parts led to his use of microscopic techniques to compare bullet markings. His work eventually attracted Calvin Goddard (no relation to Henry), who led the group's effort to perfect the comparison microscope, enabling bullets to be compared side by side in the same visual field (Thorwald, 1964).

The trial of Sacco and Vanzetti in the mid-1920s in Bridgewater, Massachusetts, engendered the equivalent of a full-employment act for all firearms experts of the day, both legitimate and charlatan. In the final analysis, Calvin Goddard's opinion that "bullet III" was fired from Sacco's gun led to the convictions of both defendants and to their deaths in the electric chair. In 1961, Goddard's analyses were duplicated by the forensic firearms community, and his conclusions decisively upheld. Goddard's work on the Saint Valentine's day massacre in Chicago in 1929 led to the establishment of one of the first criminalistics laboratories in the United States on the campus of Northwestern University, Evanston, Illinois. As with several other forms of evidence, the most recent developments have been centered around developing a computer database that can be accessed by federal, state, and local crime laboratories around the country. NIBIN, the FBIs answer to firearms evidence (guns, bullets, and cartridge cases), is particularly useful in attempting to link serial shooting investigations.

The other aspect of firearms investigations, detection of gunshot residue (GSR) on the hands of a shooter, had a pretty sorry beginning. The original method used to test for the presence of nitrates on a suspect's hands consisted of exposing a paraffin cast to diphenylamine and sulfuric acid. The production of a blue color was supposedly indicative of recent exposure to gunpowder residue. Unfortunately, the test was so nonspecific, reacting to most oxidizing agents, including common substances such as those contained in cigarettes and playing cards, that it was quickly abandoned (Hatcher et al., 1957). Subsequently, elemental tests for the lead, barium, and antimony found in primer residue were adopted for this use. Atomic absorption (AA) and neutron activation analysis (NAA) were both explored for possible use in detecting primer residue, and both were abandoned because of interpretational problems. Most recently, scanning electron microscopy using energy dispersive X-ray analysis (SEM-EDX) has been employed in the elemental analysis of GSR. Although scientists agree that this procedure reliably detects primer residue by a combination of visual detection of stereotypical spheres and X-ray analysis for the characteristic elements, the probative value of any type of GSR test is still a topic of heated debate within the forensic community. An example of misuse of the paraffin test to convict six Irishmen in the bombing of Birmingham pub in 1974 (the Birmingham Six) is illustrated in Sidebar 1.

v. Drugs.   The analysis of solid dose drugs, and even more pertinent, the toxicological analysis of drugs in the body, more or less paralleled advances in medical knowledge. Because foreign chemicals in the body are often present at extremely dilute concentrations, they present a more difficult detection and identification problem than do solid dose drugs. Additionally, organics, especially those derived from plants, are notoriously difficult to separate chemically from human tissues and may be immediately metabolized into by-products. Mathiew Orfila, a Spaniard who became a physician and professor of forensic chemistry at the University of Paris, is generally recognized as the father of modern toxicology. In 1813, he published *Traité des Poisons Tires des Regnes Mineral, Vegetal et Animal, ou Toxicologie Général*, the first handbook detailing the effects of poisonous chemicals in the body. But James Marsh, an English chemist, was the first to develop a robust test for arsenic in the body and present it in a jury trial in 1836. It was not until 1851 that Jean Servais Stas, a chemistry professor from Brussels, Belgium was able to identify vegetable

Sidebar 1

The Birmingham Six — A Miscarriage of Justice

On November 21, 1974, at 8:15 in the evening, a bomb exploded at the Rotunda pub in Birmingham, England. Seconds afterward, another bomb exploded at the Tavern. A third bomb, planted at the tax office, failed to explode. The two live bombs resulted in 21 deaths and 162 injured persons. Minutes before, the *Birmingham Post and Mail* newspaper had taken a call from a man with an Irish accent tipping it off to the placement of bombs in all three locations.

That same evening, five Irishmen traveling from England to a funeral in Belfast were stopped as they attempted to board a ferry to cross the channel. The five had spent the evening on a train from London to Heysham. During their journey, they had played cards and smoked cigarettes. Shortly after midnight, all five had been apprehended and taken to the police station.

Sometime in the early hours of the morning, Dr. Frank Skuse, a forensic scientist with the Home Office, showed up at the jail. He swabbed each suspect's hands with ether and performed a Greiss test, ostensibly to check for the presence of explosives on the men's hands. The Greiss reagent turns pink in the presence of nitro-containing compounds, including nitrates, a common ingredient in explosives. However, it is extremely nonspecific and reacts with many different nitro-containing compounds. According to Dr. Skuse's records, two of the men showed no reaction at all on either hand; two others showed positive reactions on one hand. The fifth man's hands gave a negative result for the Greiss test, but apparently showed a faint positive for a water-based test to detect the presence of ammonium ions. Although a control test on Skuse's own hands showed a similar reaction, he would later testify that the man could have handled explosives. Dr. Skuse was later to maintain that if a suspect showed a positive reaction to the Greiss test, he would be "99 percent certain" that the suspect had been in contact with nitroglycerine, a common explosive used to make bombs.

According to the men's accounts they were brutalized by the police throughout the night and into the next day. One of them reported being coerced into implicating a sixth suspect, leading to his detention as well. Four of the six eventually signed statements amounting to confessions to the Birmingham bombings.

Mr. Justice Bridge presided over the criminal trial that took place at Lancaster Crown Court during June of 1975. Dr. Skuse testified for the prosecution. He presented his original results from the presumptive Greiss tests performed at the jail, and also the results of confirmatory tests performed on the same material at the laboratory. Skuse apparently performed either thin layer chromatography (TLC) or gas chromatography–mass spectrometry (GC-MS), or both, on the remainder of each sample that had given a positive Greiss reaction. According to Skuse, only one sample, from one man's hand, was confirmed to contain nitroglycerine by one of the more-discriminating tests, and even that interpretation was challenged by Dr. Hugh Black from Leeds University, an independent expert working for the defense. Nevertheless, the jury, apparently at the urging of the judge, convicted all six men, and recommended life sentences.

The verdict was appealed, at least partly on the grounds that Judge Bridge had overstepped his judicial function by conveying his views so forcefully to the jury that the opinion of Dr. Black, the defense witness, was worthless and should be ignored. The appeal was heard on March 30, 1976, and although the justices lamented that Justice Bridge "unhappily went somewhat far," they rejected the notion that the conviction was influenced by the forensic results at all and dismissed the appeal.

In 1978, Mr. John Yallop, a former Home Office forensic scientist who first introduced the technique of testing hand swabs for explosives residue, wrote to the solicitors acting on behalf of the six men, now known, somewhat infamously, as the Birmingham Six. Yallop mentioned that he had conducted tests on himself after, for instance, smoking a cigarette, and obtained the same positive results that Dr. Skuse insisted were definitive evidence of nitroglycerine.

In 1985, working at the behest of the Granada Television "World in Action" program, Professor Brian Caddy set up a team to determine the reliability of the Griess test. The team tested many different samples, including cigarettes, playing cards, and nitrocellulose-containing wood varnish, all of which gave positive reactions to the Griess reagent. Shortly after the airing of this program, Dr. Skuse unexpectedly took an early retirement from the Home Office forensic laboratory. Almost simultaneously, the Home Office itself commissioned a detailed study of the Griess test.

In 1985, Chris Mullin published *Error in Judgment*, a book about the Birmingham Six. In large part because of this book, the men were granted a new appeal which was heard in November, 1987. Although the court now allowed that "as a result of fresh evidence there is now a grave doubt as to the nature of the method used for testing by Dr. Skuse at Morecambe, ..." they continued to disregard the forensic evidence as central to the convictions. They remained convinced by the eyewitness and testimonial evidence presented, and dismissed the appeal.

Ultimately, the case would be referred back to the British Court of Appeals three times before the chief prosecutor publicly admitted that the forensic evidence was worthless and that the confessions had been beaten out of the suspects. In March 1991, the Court of Appeal quashed the convictions and the six men were released after serving more than 16 years in prison. The Griess test was liberally used throughout the 1970s and early 1980s to provide evidence against a number of Irish Nationals who were convicted of various bombings in England. Many of these convictions have now been overturned, including those of the Guildford four and the Maguire seven.

Reference: Based on Mullin, C., *Error of Judgment: The Truth about the Birmingham Bombings,* Chatto & Windus Ltd., London, 1986.

poisons in body tissue successfully. However, like ignitable fluid analysis in a fire-cause investigation, a toxicological analysis only addresses the *what* and maybe *how* questions in a case investigation. The most exquisitely performed drug analysis cannot relate directly to *who*. Interestingly, it is one of the subset of forensic analyses for which answering the *what* question is an end in itself, for example, the identification of illegal drugs.

Advances in instrumentation over the last half of the 20th century have enabled the detection of chemicals with exquisite sensitivity and specificity. In particular, Fourier transform infrared (FTIR) spectroscopy and the coupling of a mass spectrometer to a gas chromatograph (GC-MS) have virtually transformed the fields of drug analysis, toxicology, arson, and explosives. Immunological tests using antibodies developed against specific drugs have also revolutionized toxicological testing. However, probably no invention has had more impact on the everyday lives of normal citizens than R. F. Borkenstein's development, in 1954, of the Breathalyzer for field-sobriety testing (Saferstein, 1998).

2. From Generalist to Specialist (and Back Again)

The comparative advantages of a specialist vs. a generalist remain one of the more-enduring sources of contention in practically any craft or discipline. In the scientific arena, the pendulum has swung across and back again. The earliest Greek scientists were, by default, generalists simply because not enough knowledge existed to create the need or even the opportunity for specialization. As science progressed, then exploded throughout the Enlightenment, and into the 20th century, specialization became inevitable. To understand string theory requires so much dedicated time and energy that one is left with little time to devote to quantum mechanics, much less its relation to cosmic evolution. However, of late, the value of interdisciplinary relationships has received increased attention. It has become clear that no one discipline can continue to exist, much less flourish, in isolation; the borders between disciplines have become gathering places for the convergence of knowledge. This trend is exemplified in E. O. Wilson's book *Consilience* (1998), where he advocates a common framework and interdependency of all knowledge.

Forensic science has also taken a journey from generalist to specialist, and back again. A few of the very first criminalists were generalists. Although he was not, by training, a scientist, Hans Gross was most definitely the first declared generalist. In 1891, the Austrian magistrate and professor of criminal law published *Criminal Investigation*, the first comprehensive description of the uses of physical evidence in solving crime. This tradition was continued by the distinguished line of French forensic scientists. Bertillon quite naturally expanded the taking of physical measurements to the gathering of fingerprints and the photographing of both convicts and crime scenes. He even began to dabble in impression evidence and document examination. Because he had become internationally renowned as an expert "police" scientist, questions about all kinds of physical evidence were directed his way and he responded. Mathiew Orfila, primarily known for his work on toxicology, also made significant contributions to the identification of blood and seminal stains, both macroscopically and microscopically (Gaensslen, 1983). Although Lacassagne, Balthazard, Orfila, and Locard each specialized in a particular area, they all handled diverse types of evidence simply by virtue of the forensic nature of their work. In fact, in the beginning of the 20th century, it was not uncommon to find "Institutes of Forensic Medicine," on the continent in particular, where both pathology and physical evidence analysis resided.

However, as criminalistics entered its adolescence, it became more common for scientists already educated in specific disciplines to apply their particular expertise to the emerging discipline of forensic science. Illustrative examples include Leon Lattes (blood typing), Calvin Goddard (firearms), and Albert Osborn (documents). Although these men and many others contributed immeasurably to the specific methods and techniques used in the various branches of criminalistics, the trend toward specialization also created a vacuum in precisely the aspect of forensic science that distinguishes it from other basic or applied sciences. Paul Kirk was the first modern criminalist to espouse a return to generalist thinking. It is perhaps significant that Kirk also championed the term *criminalist* to describe the new breed of expert that would be trained in the University of California at Berkeley program. Although the designation was probably first contrived by Hans Gross, Kirk is often credited (or variously blamed) for its current use. Kirk's thesis was based on his conviction that the criminalist is an expert in what he considered to be the defining aspect of criminalistics, individualization (Kirk, 1953).

In Kirk's first edition of *Crime Investigation*, published in 1953, he writes several paragraphs addressing this issue:

> Furthermore, a very artificial idea is current regarding the nature of crim-inalistic specialization, viz., that it must follow either (1) the type of crime, e.g., homicide, murder, or arson; or (2) the type of evidence, e.g., docu-ments, firearms, etc. ... It is clear that the methods of investigating both the various kinds of crime, and the various types of evidence, center actually on methods of establishing identity or non-identity, and, as such involve the application of common techniques to many types of crime and a large variety of evidence.
>
> Neither is it necessary that he be an expert in the manufacture of paper in order to determine whether two pieces of paper are identical. To hold otherwise is a self-evident delusion, and not more sensible than to say that a man must be an expert automobile mechanic in order to qualify as a driver, or that he must know the lumbering industry before he can become a carpenter.
>
> These difficulties of qualification arise from overlooking the fact that the expert witness in criminalistics is first and foremost an expert in iden-tification and comparison. He understands the methods of testing identities and is qualified to state whether two objects are identical or not, and whether they had or had not a common origin. He moreover is qualified to evaluate the significance of his identity.

Although graduates of the U.C. Berkeley program, many of whom found influential positions in public laboratories, continued to disseminate the generalist dogma, the idea was never fully embraced outside of the U.S. West Coast. As the techniques for analyzing different types of physical evidence became more sophisticated and case load increased, those who believed in and were trained as generalists have become members of a diminishing minority. This has been due both to the hiring and training practices of laboratories worldwide and to the persistent lack of a focused academic program in forensic science. Due mostly to competitive funding decisions, rather than lack of student interest, the Berkeley program was deconstructed in 1995, abdicating the only U.S. program that had offered a doctoral-level degree in forensic science.* Although a few high-quality criminalistics programs remain in North America, they offer only the possibility of master's-level work. A doctoral program in forensic science is available at Strathclyde University in Glasgow, Scotland, but the absence of such programs from North American academia is both remarkable and unfortunate. We will discuss education in forensic science further in Chapter 12.

Because of continual pressure to increase case clearance, analysts are more often than not hired and trained in a specific technique, such as DNA or drug analysis; often no training in, or appreciation of, other forensic disciplines is required or even provided. In the United States, the forensic community has responded to this growing insulation in the context of board certification. Before an analyst may test in a specialty, she must first pass a rigorous exam covering topics taken from all of criminalistics. However, support for this program is not universal and participation is currently voluntary. In addition, as access to true apprenticeship training has decreased, the lack of academic support for forensic science has become glaring. In particular, a scientific framework for forensic thinking has not been well articulated. We present such a framework in this book. It is our hope that this contribution will assist journeymen criminalists to, at the very least, understand their specialty within the greater context of a case investigation.

C.   Evolution of Concept

Although a few core concepts have been articulated by thoughtful individuals, the field of criminalistics has operated for most of its tenure without a comprehensive paradigm. The maturation of the discipline, and a full measure of respect from the scientific community, requires the development of a unifying framework specific to the practice of forensic science. The following section traces the evolution of integral but fragmented concepts such as transfer and individualization. In the next chapter, we present a unified paradigm that incorporates those concepts as well as others.

1.   Transfer

To become evidence, material must first be transferred to or from an item relevant to the crime. This concept has been historically understood in terms of trace evidence such as particles and fibers. Implicit in the understanding of the concept has been the assumption that the transfer is inadvertent and

---

* Although a number of American universities offer the opportunity to perform doctoral research in forensic science or criminalistics under the umbrella of a criminal justice or chemistry program, at this writing, none has a full-fledged doctoral program in forensic science.

unheeded. Edmund Locard is universally credited with articulating the concept of "exchange" or **transfer** as "every contact leaves a trace." Because most of Locard's writings were in French, tracing the origin of this aphorism has been somewhat circuitous. The most likely candidate appears to be a passage from *L'enquete criminelle et les methodes scientifique*, published by Locard in 1920. The original passage in French is reproduced below with an English translation following. We've left the grammatical alternatives provided by the translator.*

> *Nul ne peut agir avec l'intensité que suppose l'action criminelle sans laisser des marques multiples de son passage, tantot le malfaiteur a laissi sur les lieux des marques de son activité, tanto par une action inverse, il a emporti sur son corps ou sur ses vetements les indices de son sejour ou de son geste.*
>
> No one can act [commit a crime] with the force [intensity] that the criminal act requires without leaving behind numerous signs [marks] of it: either the wrong-doer [felon; malefactor, offender] has left signs at the scene of the crime, or, on the other hand, has taken away with him — on his person [body] or clothes — indications of where he has been or what he has done.

Locard was the first to undertake an extensive study of "dusts," "mud," and "grime." His mentor at the University of Lyons, Alexandre Lacassagne, was among the first to propose the study of dust on clothing or body parts as an indicator of occupation and whereabouts (Thorwald 1966). Locard had also been exposed to the writings of Hans Gross and French translations of the Sherlock Holmes stories. He gives due credit to both these sources as inspiring his dust investigations (Locard, 1928). Just about the time that Doyle, tired of writing and fresh out of ideas, sent Holmes plunging into Reichenbach gorge to die what later turned out to be a quite virtual death, Gross had just finished *Criminal Investigation*. Although it is unclear if either he or Doyle were influenced by the other, they were unique in their time in suggesting that microscopic evidence — what we now call trace evidence — could provide valuable clues to the solution of crime.

In early 1910, when Locard had just established his Lyon laboratory and begun his enormous effort to catalog dusts, "scientific criminology" was occupied with the shift from anthropometry to fingerprints. Although Locard's thoughts on dust were initially ignored by police officials, his successful solution of several crimes finally caught their attention and produced funding and support (Thorwald, 1966). By 1920, Locard had completed his encyclopedic work of cataloging and classifying the microscopic and microchemical characteristics of various dust particles (Thorwald, 1966). Whether or not he ever uttered the exact phrase that we now quote as representing

---

* Translations courtesy of Sharon Kruzic.

the principle of transfer, he is certainly to be credited with inspiring and disseminating it.

Other than an occasional quoting of the "exchange principle," there does not appear to be evidence of any great intellectual progress in this area until Paul Kirk revived its consideration in the 1950s. Kirk was among the first to consider the strength and significance of trace evidence. He performed studies on the occurrence and transfer of fibers in urban environments (Kirk, 1953). Although the concept of transfer is universally accepted today as key to the understanding of forensic evidence, very little has been done since Kirk to explore its consequences, establish its limitations, or specifically relate it to various types of evidence. There has been no consensus regarding how the strength of an association established by transfer evidence should be determined, nor how its significance might be understood in the context of a case. With the increasing expectation that experts provide a rigorous scientific basis to support their opinions, it will be interesting to see how the trace evidence community meets this challenge. Certainly an excellent start has been made with the guidelines put forth in 1999 by the Scientific Working Group in Material Analysis and Testing (SWGMAT). We will discuss the concept of transfer in depth in Chapter 4, including some aspects of transfer that are not usually considered, such as "macro-transfer."

2. Individualization

a. Biological Evidence

The concept of individualization is clearly central to the consideration of physical evidence. Even before it was formally articulated, it seems impossible that the early civilizations who used fingerprints and other biometric measurements did not presume their uniqueness to an individual. Adolphe Quetelet, the Belgian statistician who provided the foundation for Bertillon's work, may have been the first to express formally the inherent assumption that no two human bodies are exactly alike (Thorwald, 1964; Block, 1979). Bertillon, of course, created the first systematized knowledge base for personal identification. He even attempted to provide a statistical foundation for his conclusions. Bertillon suggested that if 14 proscribed measurements were taken, the chances of any two individuals having exactly the same measurements were 268,435,456 to 1 (Thorwald, 1964).* This was based on Quetelet's (unproven) assumption that each measurement would decrease the frequency of the total profile by 1/4. Whether or not a mathematical basis existed for this calculation, it was certainly one of the first allusions (illusions?) to the potential multiplicative value of added traits. Never mind that

---

* Thorwald (pg. 10), reports this number as 286,435,456 to 1. We can hope the transposition of digits occurred in Thorwald's transcription of the data rather than in the original source.

Bertillon apparently failed to account for any possible dependence of anthropometric traits on each other.

As soon as fingerprints replaced anthropometry, they became the standard of individuality against which every other kind of physical evidence was measured. Even today, when someone wants to tout the power of some particular test, the description of DNA fingerprint, drug fingerprint, or retinal fingerprint is invoked. Interestingly, there is no agreed-upon standard for individualization by fingerprint comparison (Cole, 1998; 1999). Although a number of mathematical models have been proposed, starting with Galton, none has proved fully adequate to describe the process, significance, and limitations of fingerprint comparison (Stoney and Thornton, 1986a). One of the models, proposed by Balthazard in 1911, may have provided the historical basis for what was to become widely accepted rules regarding fingerprint individuality* (Stoney and Thornton, 1986a), and in 1918 Edmond Locard wrote that if 12 points (Galton's details) were the same between two fingerprints, it would suffice as a positive identification. This may be where the often quoted 12 points originated (Moore, 1999). Other theories have also been proffered (Kingston and Kirk, 1965). One of those is detailed in Sidebar 2.

To this day, no comprehensive statistical study has ever been undertaken to determine the frequency of occurrence of different ridge characteristics and their relative locations (Saferstein, 1998; Cole, 1998; 1999). In 1973, frustrated by the imposition of artificial thresholds, the North American fingerprint community, under the auspices of the International Association for Identification (IAI), adopted a resolution rejecting an arbitrary number of corresponding points as the basis to accept or reject an individualization.

> The International Association for Identification assembled in its 58th annual conference in Jackson, Wyoming, this first day of August, 1973, based upon a three-year study by its Standardization Committee, Hereby states that no valid basis exists at this time for requiring that a pre-determined minimum of friction ridge characteristics must be present in two impressions in order to establish positive identification. The foregoing reference to friction ridge characteristics applies equally to fingerprints, palmprints, toeprints and soleprints of the human body.

---

* Using a world population of 15 billion human fingers, Balthazard determined that 17 corresponding minutiae would be needed to conclude a unique association between a print and a finger. (Under his model, 17 corresponding minutiae would be found with a frequency of only about 1 in 17 billion.) Balthazard considered a lesser number of corresponding minutiae (for example 11 or 12) to be sufficient for an unequivocal identification if one could be certain that the fingerprint donor was restricted to a particular geographical area (Stoney and Thornton, 1986a).

In 1995, the International Fingerprint community endorsed this standard in the *Ne'urim Declaration* (Israel National Police, 1995; Cole, 1999).

In other words, the decision to "make" a print has been left entirely up to the experience and intuition of the examiner.*

In the first edition of *Crime Investigation* (1953), Kirk, in an attempt to explain the probabilistic nature of fingerprint evidence, gives an example of how individual fingerprint traits may be multiplied to produce a composite frequency.

> Assume that, on the average, one person in every twenty is found to have a whorl on the left thumb. Assume further that one in every ten is found to have a whorl on the right index finger. Then the probability that an individual picked at random will have both whorls is 1/20 times 1/10, or 1/200. To generalize, the probability of any combination of characteristics being found in a given person is the product of the probabilities of each of the individual characteristics. With the ordinary methods of classifying fingerprints, the probability of any but the one person in question having a particular fingerprint classification is so minute as to be negligible. For this reason only, fingerprints may be accepted as definite identification.

The problem, which Kirk sidesteps along with everyone else, is the lack of scientific basis for the actual frequencies of the individual traits; Kirk gives no foundation for his 1/20 or 1/10 assumption** and fails to even address the issue of independence. Perhaps it is telling that, although his premise remains the same in the second edition, edited by John Thornton, the specific example has disappeared.

In 1986, Stoney and Thornton (1986b) published an article in which they reviewed fingerprint individuality models proposed throughout history and defined a list of features that they resolved should be incorporated in a comprehensive and utilitarian model. They conclude with the caution that the value of any fingerprint for identification is inversely proportional to the chance of false association and that this chance depends on the number of comparisons that are attempted. These ideas have yet to be developed and put to practical use.

One consequence of the growing emphasis on individualization has been the tendency to overinterpret evidence that does not necessarily hold individualizing potential. The history of microscopic hair comparison exemplifies

* It should be noted that the IAI resolution is not binding and many agencies continue to adhere to a minimum number of corresponding points to conclude identity. For instance, Great Britain continues to hold tenaciously to a standard of 16 points.
** Some basis for these estimates may be found in historical fingerprint models such as that of Gupta (Stoney and Thornton, 1986a), but Kirk provides no reference.

Sidebar 2

Alphonse Bertillon — The Case of the Missing Minutiae

Many students of criminalistics have heard of a case in which fingerprints were doctored in such a way as to produce an apparently false match. Although Bertillon studied fingerprints in great detail and was, in fact, the first on the Continent to solve a crime using them, he insisted until his death that fingerprints alone could not identify an individual with absolute certainty. The following passage, taken verbatim from Henry Rhodes biography of Bertillon, may well be the source of this story. It is not a case, per se, simply an instance of Bertillon apparently attempting to point out what he believed to be a limitation to fingerprint comparison.

> In 1912, two years before his death, he [Bertillon] published an article in the *Archives of Lacassagne* that purported to show that the points of resemblance upon two fingerprints of different origin might in certain circumstances show an apparent correspondence. The article was illustrated with the excellent photographs he knew so well how to take. They were ingeniously reproduced to indicate how, if certain portions of the pattern were not shown, what remained might suggest correspondences which would produce an appearance of identity in different fingerprints. This thesis was purely academic. It did not explain how the artificial conditions he created to produce these fragmentary designs could have occurred in practice. Advocates of the fingerprint system, which was now well established, also declared that his "points of resemblance" were not points of resemblance at all, since they showed only the same general form.

In 1993, Champod, Lennard, and Margot reproduced Bertillon's photographs (see figure) along with several passages translated from the French. From these passages, it is clear that, no matter how crude or unrealistic his mock-ups of apparently matching prints, he possessed a fundamental understanding of the nature of dermal ridge print evidence, and an appreciation of the limitations. In particular, he points out the value of inspecting the prints for dissimilarities as well as similarities, and the fact that even one unexplainable dissimilarity must lead to an exclusion, no matter how many other corresponding points.

> At the same time, one must note the total absence of dissimilarities in the clearly visible parts of the prints.

And in an interesting foreshadowing of issues that many a DNA analyst would do well to heed,

> The only way to completely eliminate this hypothesis, in the case where the accused has a brother who may also be a suspect, is to record the brother's fingerprints and check that his prints do not show all the particularities found in the evidential marks.

He, in fact, does explain his fabrication of the falsely matching prints and expresses his realization that they would be virtually impossible to reproduce in a true case.

> It can be seen that by appropriate cut-outs, it would be possible, through the consultation of numerous documents, to obtain fairly extensive fingerprint zones that show a certain number of common particularities without any notable dissimilarities. However, it is evidently unlikely that portions of fingerprints left at random by a criminal would precisely reproduce such artificially chose zones.

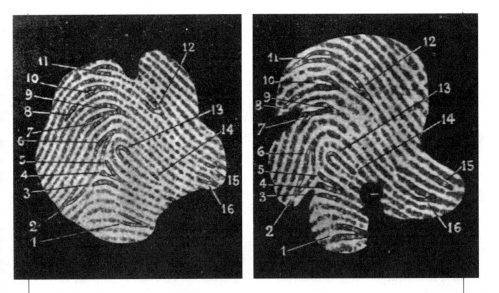

Bertillon fingerprint. The photograph Bertillon produced to illustrate his "points." (Courtesy of Professor Pierre Margot, Institut de Police Scientifique et de Criminologie de l'Université de Lausanne, Switzerland.)

He also admits that they would likely not stand up to a meticulous comparison.

It is also necessary to add that these patterns, which appear so similar after a preliminary observation would not stand up to a meticulous comparison.

We are left to ponder his fascinating conclusion that echoes the lament of many a defendant whose DNA profile is indistinguishable from the evidence.

The two examples of deceiving similarities that have just been presented show that the assertion of identity relies less on the number of common particularities than on the undoubted absence of dissimilarities. It is therefore, in the end, an *induction based on a negative result* [emphasis added].

In the end, he rescues fingerprinting from the oblivion where he apparently intended to send it by giving the nod to personal expertise.

However, from a point of view purely philosophical, such conclusions are generally unconvincing. Their value is uniquely derived from the accepted and already proven competence of the expert. It is totally personal, whereas a non-identify may be shown without discussion by the finding of obvious dissimilarities that may be verified by anyone.

We refer the interested reader to the full article by Champod, Lennard, and Margot listed in the references below.

References

Champod, C., Lennar, C., and Margot, P., Alphonse Bertillon and Dactyloscopy, *J. Forensic Ident.*, 43(6), 604–617, 1993.

Rhodes, H. T. F., *Alphonse Bertillon, Father of Scientific Detection*, George G. Harrap, London, 1956.

this concern. As early as 1879, Dr. Rudolph Virchow, a German pathologist, realized the limitations of hair evidence. In comparing hairs, he accounted for the reality that visible traits vary between different hairs of an individual, even along the same hair, and that hairs from different people can look similar. His understanding is evident in a portion of his testimony, "The appearance of the hair is such that it is not inconsistent with having come from the accused" (Thorwald, 1966). Unfortunately, not all hair analysts since that time have followed his example. In the now infamous Canadian case of Guy Paul Morin (*Commission on Proceedings Involving Guy Paul Morin*, 1998) Morin was arrested almost solely on the basis of a single hair of dubious quality found adhering to the necklace of the murder victim. This case is a poster child for the necessity of the criminalist conveying, and the investigators and attorneys understanding, the limitations of the evidence.

In the last paragraph of the chapter on hair in the first edition of *Crime Investigation* (1953), Kirk writes of his hopes for the individualizing potential of hair, in the process employing the inevitable fingerprint comparison:

> That hair is actually characteristic of the individual is very probable since, if it were not, it would be the exception to the general rule of biological individuality. It therefore merits the most careful and extensive investigation aimed at fulfilling the tremendous possibilities that it presents in this direction.... Simple and rapid methods capable of producing decisive results in this field may be possible, but not without much more extensive and thorough research investigation.... It seems safe to predict that such efforts might well be rewarded ultimately with one of the most valuable sets of techniques for establishing personal identification, using evidence that cannot readily be kept from the possession of law enforcement agents, as fingerprints are at present.

Earlier in the chapter Kirk intimates that the individualizing potential of hair might lie in its transient chemical makeup rather than its inherent biological properties.

> The *minor constituents* of hair have received only limited attention and it is possible that these may lead to considerable advance from the standpoint of criminal investigation.... The intake of arsenic, lead, silica, and other minor constituents which are regularly detected in hair is certainly variable and to some extent a function of the occupation, diet, and medication of the individual. Thus these constituents might be expected to vary accordingly and to be useful in determining the source of a hair, provided that sensitive enough methods for the analysis can be developed and applied without destruction of a prohibitively large amount of available evidence.

In the second edition of *Crime Investigation* (1974), buried in a section about using neutron activation analysis to detect trace elements in hair, is the acknowledgment that:

> It may be mentioned, however, that the analysis of a single hair has not been found adequate for personal identification to date, both because of the difficulty of making a complete analysis of a single hair, and because of the fact that variations may be considerable from hair to hair of the same person.

Interestingly, his final paragraph in the 1974 edition, which rests on assumptions that hair evidence will necessarily exhibit "biological individuality," remains virtually the same.

In 1953, the same year Watson and Crick elucidated the structure of DNA, Kirk predicted, "The criminalist of the future may well be able to identify him directly through the hair he dropped, the blood he shed, or the semen he deposited." About 30 years later, Alec Jeffreys of the United Kingdom in fact presented the first "DNA fingerprint." Jeffreys makes no apology for his very deliberate descriptor of this technique. To set the record straight, it is worth pointing out that Jeffreys' first efforts, using a technique known as multilocus RFLP, may well have been individualizing. In this technique, a single DNA probe is used to investigate numerous locations (*loci*) in the genome simultaneously. Complex patterns, containing substantial amounts of information, are produced and initial calculations (Jeffreys et al., 1985) suggested that the pattern produced by a single probe might well be unique to an individual.

However, technical considerations and interpretation concerns led to the eventual adoption of a single-locus system, in which only one location at a time is analyzed. With each locus-specific result, a segment of the population is eliminated but, in and of itself, the result is not individualizing. This was even more true of the loci initially used for PCR-based techniques, because each locus generally exhibited less variability. For both kinds of systems, much of the power depends on the same concept that Bertillon employed, multiplication of individual trait frequencies to reduce sequentially the portion of the population exhibiting the combined traits. The difference is that population data for genetic traits have been amassed in great amounts allowing a truly quantitative assessment of the rarity of a composite profile. In fact, genetic-based analyses (serology and DNA) are the only forensic tests for which hard data exist from which to estimate the frequency in the population of an evidence sample exhibiting a particular. This same concept could certainly be employed in dermatoglyphic fingerprint analysis, but the underlying population data (available in a raw form in the national finger-print database, AFIS) has not been systematically organized and analyzed.

No doubt exists that DNA analysis provides the potential to individual-ize.* This was not true when the first few single-locus RFLP probes came online, however this conclusion can no longer be escaped. When 9 RFLP probes or 13 PCR-amplified STR loci produce population frequencies as low as 1 in quadrillions (that's 15 zeros), the odds of the evidence coming from another person are so small that a reasonable person is convinced of indi-viduality. Interestingly, many in the forensic community continue to hold up fingerprints and toolmarks, including bullet comparison, as the standard for determining individuality. But without the hard frequency data now begin-ning to be expected because of the work performed for DNA, these claims are starting to be reexamined.

b. Nonbiological Evidence

Because physical match evidence seems so self-evident, the basis for assuming an individualization of two pieces of an object to each other are not often discussed. Nevertheless, the random nature of the generation of physical match evidence predicts its individualizing potential. As we will discuss in the next chapter, the understanding of how matter divides is so fundamental that it deserves a place as a tenet of forensic science. The apparent obviousness of physical matching seems to have precluded much mention of notable cases involving its use in historical reviews. One of the few examples tells of John Toms of Lancaster, England, who was convicted of murder based on physical match evidence (Kind and Overman, 1972). The piece of newsprint that he had used as wadding in the murder pistol was judged exactly complementary to the piece remaining in his pocket. Even with physical matching, we are not without the inescapable fingerprint comparison. In 1949, O'Hara and Osterburg (1949) wrote of a glass fracture: "The elements in this case which correspond to the characteristics of a fingerprint are the points of the curves when they are regarded as being plotted in some system of coordinates."

Like fingerprints, toolmarks, including their most prominent manifesta-tion as bullet markings, have always been accepted as inherently individual-izing evidence. With the exception of Balthazard's first attempts to systematize firearms evidence with respect to marks conferred on a cartridge case by the moving parts of a gun (Thorwald, 1964), the emphasis seems to

---

* Individualizing potential should not be confused with certain individualization. Whether or not a piece of evidence may be individualized using DNA depends on many factors, including the state of the sample (quality and quantity), which loci are analyzed, how many loci are analyzed, and the population frequencies of the alleles involved. And, as with any forensic analysis, the veracity of the results rests on the reliability of the analysis and thoughtful interpretation of the data.

have been directed toward perfecting the mechanics of detection and visualization. From the first documented experience of Henry Goddard in 1835, through the first attempts at photomicrography by Jesrich in 1898, to Waite and Goddard's adaptation of the comparison microscope for bullet analysis in about 1920 (Thorwald, 1964), no one worried much about the basis for a conclusion of individuality. Like fingerprints, the markings left on a bullet by both the barrel and the various moving parts of the weapon are complex and irregular. Consequently, individualizing potential is assumed, and a rich oral history is likely to exist around its justification. However, like fingerprint examiners, the opinions of toolmark and firearm examiners have been accepted almost without challenge regarding the individualization of an impression to a tool or a bullet to a gun. A landmark exception to this trend is presented in a paper published in *The American Police Journal* in 1930 by Luke May, in which he presents his methods for toolmark comparison and some case examples. In *Wash. v. Clark* he individualized a knife to a cut in a fir tree. May presents the following calculation to substantiate his conclusion:

> Considering only the major marks on this cut, it can be mathematically determined that no other blade in the world would make a cut like this. Invoking the law of probabilities, using the algebraic formula for determining combinations and permutations, with only one-third of the marks here shown as factors, there would be only "one" chance of there being another blade exactly like this if everyone of the hundred million people in the United States had six hundred and fifty quadrillion knives each. Using all of the marks, and the factors of depth, width, shape, etc., it would be carried to infinity.

Unfortunately, he gives us no clue as to any statistical studies on which his numbers might be based, nor does he provide the details of the mathematical determination or his algebraic formula for determining combinations and permutations. He also fails to inform us regarding his assumptions about independence. One is left to wonder just how his rather oddly expressed frequency of the [population of the U.S.] × [six hundred and fifty quadrillion knives] has been determined.

It is not as if no work has been performed since May's time to address these questions. The study mentioned previously by Biasotti (1959) and numerous other analyses of consecutively manufactured gun barrels and other tools (reviewed in Murdock and Biasotti, 1997; Nichols, 1997) are commendable efforts. Although isolated pockets of work continue (Tulleners and Giusta, 1998), the greater toolmark and firearms community has shown relatively little interest in exploiting and continuing this work to provide a more quantitative presentation of their data.

Interestingly, Kirk, in the second edition of *Crime Investigation* (1974), mentions that increased mass-production methods were generating tools that were initially indistinguishable by the impressions they made. He hastens to add that this situation is quickly "remedied" by use of the tool; nevertheless, it is one of the few admissions of a limitation to toolmark analysis. And like fingerprint examiners, firearms and toolmark examiners may soon be called upon to substantiate their opinions based on experience with scientific studies and provide statistics supported by databases.

c.   Uniqueness vs. Common Source

One point about which the current coterie of practitioners in the forensic field seem to agree is that individualization in the forensic context refers to the assignment of items to a common source or origin rather than the determination of the uniqueness of any one object. For this reason the process of individualization always requires a comparison between at least two items.

According to Saferstein (1998):

> A comparison analysis subjects a suspect specimen and a control specimen to the same tests and examinations for the ultimate purpose of determining whether or not they have a common origin.

Similarly, DeForest, Lee, and Gaensslen (1983) write:

> It [individualization] may also refer to the demonstration that a questioned piece of physical evidence and a similar known sample have a common origin. The nature of these individual characteristics varies from one type of evidence to another, but forensic scientists try to take advantage of them in efforts to individualize a piece of physical evidence by some type of comparison process.

We will continue a discussion of these concepts in depth in Section 2, The Principles of Forensic Science.

3.   Identification

The use of the word *identification* in the context of forensic science has been and continues to be a major source of confusion. The first quandary results from the common lay usage of the word identification as a descriptor of a unique item. In particular the standard usage in the context of "human identity" or "human identification" confers the impression of uniqueness because we have an innate understanding that each human being is unique. The second source of ambiguity comes from within forensic science. The word *identification* has often been restricted to describing the appearance or composition of an item and using those characteristics to place it in a class or category with other items; sometimes this is a step on the way to individualization and sometimes it is an end in itself. In any case, the field has not agreed on a consistent usage of the term *identification* and the ambiguity is conveyed in a passage from the first edition of Kirk's *Crime Investigation*:

> The determination of identity is of importance to the criminalist in two ways: (1) in establishing between two objects an identity of origin; and (2) in determining the nature of a specimen of evidence. The first category is ordinarily the more significant because on it rests the final determination of the value of the evidence. It is, for example, more valuable to say that two bullets, one of known origin, were fired from the same gun, than to say that the bullets are the same type of ammunition. It is more valuable to be able to say that two hairs have come from the same head, than say that both hairs are human in origin.

Contrary to widespread conventional wisdom, individualization may not be the necessary or even expected goal in every forensic analysis. An example is the analysis of solid dose drugs. If controlled substances are identified, it may well not matter from which laboratory or field they came; mere possession fulfills the element of illegality. According to Saferstein (1998):

> Identification has as its purpose the determination of the physical or chemical identity of a substance with as near absolute certainty as existing analytical techniques will permit.

Interestingly, Kirk also points out that when simply identifying the nature of a substance, rather than suggesting an individualization, statistical estimates may not be relevant because the answer is a qualitative yes or no, rather than a quantitative estimation of the frequency of occurrence. However, he also emphasizes, particularly with respect to presumptive chemical testing, the necessity to state clearly other substances that might give the same result.

> Probability is a factor in virtually every phase of the study of evidence. The most important exceptions are matters of straight chemistry, physics, or other exact science when applied directly to testing for a constituent or property on a single choice basis.... This type of problem in which a positive or negative but definite answer is provided by the test is not one requiring statistical treatment.... Even in chemical testing, however, there are instances in which a test established only a probability of identity. For example, many of the commonly used tests for alkaloidal poisons are not specific. That is, the same color may be given when the reagent is added to different alkaloids.

In the next several chapters, we will discuss a modification to the forensic paradigm in which we suggest that identifying the nature of a piece of evidence as an end in itself should be distinguished from the classification that takes place as an intermediate to possible individualization.

One of the most cogent commentaries on individualization and statistics was written by David Stoney (1991) in response the then new application of DNA profiling. Stoney draws distinctions between our acceptance of dermatoglyphic fingerprints as inherently individualizing and our seeming need to prove uniqueness for DNA profiling.

> Secondly, we must look realistically at the individualization process. Are we really trying to prove uniqueness? I would offer to you that it is a ridiculous notion. The contrast with fingerprint comparisons is important. We hold fingerprint specificity and individuality up as our ideal, yet this is achieved only through a subjective process. In fingerprint work, *we become subjectively convinced of identity; we do not prove it* [emphasis ours].

If we were to pick one concept that the criminalist must appreciate, this would be it.

4.   Association

Association may be the most misunderstood concept in the forensic arena. Although it is intimately associated with the concept of transfer, and entirely dependent on the processes of classification and individualization, few records exist of any academic discussion of association per se or its relationship to other forensic concepts. Kirk (1953) skirts the edges of this discussion when he suggests that inanimate objects can serve as intermediary evidence in the course of linking a person with a crime.

> The central problem of the criminal investigator is the establishment of personal identity. Usually this is the identity of the criminal, sometimes the identity of the victim. Supplementary to the establishment of personal identity is the establishment of the identity of physical objects, which in turn contributes to the desired personal identification. The identification of a murder weapon may lead to its possessor at the time of the crime. Identification of handwriting leads to the writer and so forth.

Osterburg (1968) describes associative evidence merely as "linking a person to a crime scene." Likewise in DeForest, Lee, and Gaensslen's *Forensic Science: An Introduction to Criminalistics* (1983), only a couple of sentences are devoted to this essential notion.

> Depending on the degree of individuality exhibited by the samples, various conclusions can be drawn about the association between people and the physical evidence in the case.... These kinds of considerations need to be kept in mind when evaluating the value of *associative* physical evidence comparisons.

Even here, we are not sure whether association is a synonym for individualization or a completely different concept. As we will see in the next chapter, association may best fit into the forensic paradigm as the culmination of classification or individualization. In fact, it best describes the basis for a conclusion of contact between two objects.

Probably the most recent thinking on the matter comes from Evett et al. (1998). These workers propose a "hierarchy of propositions" within which to consider levels of association in casework. The levels they suggest are (1) *source* (e.g., the glass fragments came from window X; (2) *activity* (Mr. A is the man who smashed window X); (3) *offense* (e.g., Mr. A committed the burglary). They emphasize that at each level, the scientist must also consider the alternative hypothesis, i.e., the glass fragments came from some other broken glass item; Mr. A did not smash the window; another person committed the burglary. In Section 2 of this book, we will see that Evett's hierarchy simply provides different terms for concepts with which we are already familiar. *Source* is analogous to *classification/individualization*; *activity* we understand as *association*, and *offense* directly correlates to *reconstruction*.

5.   Reconstruction

Reconstruction entices us to indulge our every temptation to create a videotape replay of the crime event. As we'll see in the next chapter, reconstruction is more properly viewed as an ordering of events in relative space and time, using physical evidence plus any other available information. However, historically, some criminalists' overinflated belief in their powers of reconstruction have led to skewed expectations by both the public and judicial system regarding the information that can be provided by physical evidence associated with a crime. Perhaps because of pressure to "solve" a particularly horrendous crime, even the most well-intentioned and educated criminalists have succumbed to overinterpreting the results of a physical analysis.

Fiction writers gave the science of detection a jump start, in the process quite unintentionally paving the way for far-reaching and often unreasonable expectations. Unfortunately, news reporters and journalists, in their incessant quest for sensationalism, have continued to inflate the capabilities of physical evidence analysis carelessly, completing a vicious circle in which the public expects miracles and some scientists feel compelled to comply. In 1958,

Eugene Block, formerly a San Francisco police reporter, published a book entitled *The Wizard of Berkeley*, hardly an unassuming title. The short leader on the book jacket promises, "The extraordinary exploits of American's pioneer scientific criminologist, the world-famous Edward Oscar Heinrich." The first anecdote tells of a well-known case involving a Southern-Pacific railroad murder on the California–Oregon border. In keeping with the book title, Heinrich was apparently able to discern that a pair of dirty overalls found at the scene

> …were worn by a left-handed lumberjack accustomed to working around fir trees. He is a white man between 21 and 25 years of age, not over five feet ten inches tall and he weighs about 165 pounds. He has medium light brown hair, a fair complexion, light brown eye-brows, small hands and feet, and he is rather fastidious in his personal habits. Apparently he has lived and worked in the Pacific Northwest. Look for such a man. You will be hearing more from me shortly.

We almost expect Heinrich to tell us what the man had for breakfast the morning of the crime. (A detailed description of the case may be found in Sidebar 3.

These leaps of faith seem to have reached their heyday in the 1950s in the infamous breeding ground of modern criminalistics, Berkeley, California. In the first edition of *Crime Investigation*, Kirk reports his deductions from an examination of a glove left at the scene of a burglary.

a. The culprit was a laborer associated with building construction
b. His main occupation was pushing a wheelbarrow
c. He lived outside the town proper, on a small farm or garden plot
d. He was a southern European
e. He raised chickens, and kept a cow or horse

He reports that after apprehension of the suspect, all of the inferences were confirmed except that the individual in question drove a tractor rather than pushed a wheelbarrow. This, he rationalizes, was a reasonable misinterpretation because his observation of greater wear on the inside surfaces of the fourth and fifth fingers of the glove, as compared with the other three fingers, could have been caused either "by thrusting forward on wheelbarrow handles, but it also could be — and was — caused by pulling on sloping tractor levers."

Our intent in calling attention to these common examples of how criminalistics was practiced in the earlier part of the century is not to demean these two very capable scientists, without whom the profession would not be what it is today, but to emphasize how the pressures of the media and the public might encourage overinterpretation of physical evidence, and to point out the shift in the thinking of the field that has occurred since that time.

Sidebar 3

Edward O. Heinrich — Murder
on the Southern Pacific Express

On October 11, 1923, just outside the small town of Siskiyou, Oregon, in the mountains of the same name, the Portland–San Francisco Express Train No. 13 approached Tunnel 13, not far from the California border. Unbeknownst to the crew and passengers, two bandits hopped the mail car as it slowly approached the north entrance to the tunnel, and a third waited on a hillside just outside the south exit with his trigger finger on a bomb detonator. The train stopped unexpectedly just as the engine and the first few cars emerged from the south side of the tunnel; the mail car was halfway out, and the passenger and baggage cars remained in the tunnel. The bomb, planted in the mail car and presumably meant only to breach its integrity, exploded and, much to the horror of the robbers, not to mention the crew and passengers, ignited a fire. The mail clerk burned to death at his post, while the engineer, fireman, and brakeman were shot to death on a nearby hillside. The bandits were forced to abandon their loot, presumably the securities and sums of money carried in the mail car, and disappeared into the surrounding hills. The conductor, who had been riding in a rear car, and therefore escaping detection by the robbers, emerged and immediately called the authorities from an emergency telephone located at the south end of the tunnel.

Soon deputy sheriffs and other officers from nearby towns converged on the scene. On the slope just outside the southern end of the tunnel, they found the remains of a detonator with two batteries attached and with wires running to the train tracks. Close to the detonator, they found a revolver, a pair of greasy blue-denim overalls, and a pair of gunnysack shoes soaked in creosote, presumably to keep tracking dogs from detecting the scent. A knapsack, a suit of underwear, a pair of socks, a canteen, and a water bag were collected from a cabin close to the site. A local tramp reported seeing two men jump aboard the mail car as the train approached the northern end of the tunnel.

Posses and canine searches led nowhere. It was suggested that the batteries from the detonator might have come from a local shop. A group of men converged on the shop and, convinced that the grime on the lone mechanic's hands and face resembled that on the overalls found at the scene, forced him to try them on. Convinced of a perfect fit, the men hauled the mechanic, over his protests of innocence, off to the local jail. However, the police failed to connect him to the crime in any other way.

The blue overalls were sent to Edward O. Heinrich in Berkeley, along with a description of the garage mechanic. After carefully examining the overalls, he issued the following report:

> You are holding the wrong man.... The overalls you sent me were worn by a left-handed lumberjack accustomed to working around fir trees. He is a white man between 21 and 25 years of age, not over five feet ten inches tall and he weighs about 165 pounds. He has medium light brown hair, a fair complexion, light brown eye-brows, small hands and feet, and he is rather fastidious in his personal habits. Apparently he has lived and worked in the Pacific Northwest. Look for such a man. You will be hearing more from me shortly.

The garage mechanic was release on the strength of Heinrich's report.

How did Heinrich reach such astounding inferences? He concluded that, instead of oil and grease, the apparent grime was tree pitch, more specifically, fir pitch. From the right-hand pocket, he extracted a variety of grains, particles, and chips. From a microscopic examination, he determined that the particulate matter comprised bits of Douglas fir needles, fir chips, and fingernail clippings. He also recovered a strand of hair caught in a button. From the pocket contents, he surmised that the wearer was a lumberjack who worked around fir trees; the color, cross-sectional shape, and width of the hair apparently allowed him to determine that it came from the head of a Caucasian between the ages of 21 and 25.

Heinrich was convinced that the man was left-handed. This conclusion was based on the finding of wood chips in the right pocket, where he said they would land while a left-handed person chopped a tree (his right side would be facing the tree, and the wood chips would fly in), the wear on the left side pockets, and his observation that the overall had been buttoned exclusively from the left side. The neatness of the fingernail trimmings convinced him of the fastidious nature of the man. The height, he calculated by measuring the overalls between the shoulder buckles and the bottoms of the trouser legs. Heinrich maintained that the fact that the left buckle was ¾ inch higher than the right was further proof of left-handedness. The creases on the bottom of each leg told him that they had been tucked into shoe tops, "just as a lumberjack does."

The most concrete finding, extricated from a deep narrow pencil pocket in the bib, was a registered mail receipt for $50 sent by Roy D'Autrement from Eugene, Oregon to his brother in Lakewood, New Mexico. This piece of information led police to Paul D'Autrement, father of three sons, Roy and Ray (who were twins), and Hugh. The elder D'Autrement recounted that his sons had vanished the day before the train was held up. His description of Roy appeared to coincide with Heinrich's description, and he was a left-handed lumberjack.

A number of personal items were collected from the D'Autrement house. Heinrich matched a hair from a towel used by Roy to the one from the overall button. From the items in the cabin, he determined that the knapsack contained fir needle fragments and was mended with the same coarse black thread that had been used to mend the overalls — it was "identical." From measurements of the underwear and socks, he calculated the stature and physique of the wearer, and, deciding that the person was larger than the owner of the overalls, concluded that such a person exactly matched the description of Ray given by his father.

From the Colt automatic revolver, from which the external serial number had been partially obliterated, he found a second, internal serial number. The gun was traced to a store in Seattle and had been sold to, and signed for, by a William Elliott. Elliott's signature was sent to Heinrich, who established that it was — "identical" — to that of Roy D'Autrement. According to the gun dealer, the gun buyer fitted the description of Roy. Finally, a canteen and water bag were reported to have been sold from an army surplus store in Eugene to three men who had come in together. According to Block, "Obviously, these were the three brothers, and they must have used the cabin as their rendezvous before the robbery."

Three years later, in March, 1927, Hugh D'Autrement was arrested after a former military colleague recognized his photograph on a wanted poster. A month later, an elderly gentleman, recognized the twins' photographs from an article in the Sunday paper. They were picked up from the Ohio steel mill where they had been working under false names. Hugh was tried first, and convicted, inspiring the twins to confess, as finally did Hugh himself. They were all sentenced to life imprisonment in the Oregon State Penitentiary at Salem.

It is difficult to know from a historical account what part the forensic evidence actually played in the investigation and conviction of the D'Autrement brothers. Most forensic scientists working today would agree that Heinrich's conclusions, the significance he accorded them, and the confidence with which they were proffered, far exceeded the data on which they were based. However, no one can disagree that Heinrich was instrumental in popularizing forensic science, and educating law enforcement and the public about the potential contributions of physical evidence to the solution of crime.

Source: Based on Block, E. B., *The Wizard of Berkeley*, Coward-McCann, New York, 1958.

Few working criminalists today would support the extrapolation of such specific details about a person's life and habits from the examination of physical evidence, let alone a single glove or pair of overalls. Such inferences were probably overstatements even for the time, but with the increasingly mobile and eclectic nature of our society, they become irresponsible at best, misleading at worst. Most forensic scientists practicing in the current climate shy away from grand sweeping Holmesian deductions, instead limiting themselves to commenting on whether evidence and reference samples could have a common origin, and inferences about whether two items were ever in contact.

Both DeForest and Saferstein emphasize the role of physical evidence in reconstruction as either corroborating or confuting eyewitness reports, or providing information in the absence of any eyewitness evidence. DeForest, Lee, and Gaensslen (1983) suggest that:

> Reconstruction refers to the process of putting the "pieces" of a case or situation together with the objective of reaching an understanding of a sequence of past events based on the record of physical evidence that has resulted from the events. Reconstructions are often desirable in criminal cases in which eyewitness evidence is absent or unreliable. Identification and individualization of physical evidence can play important roles in providing data for reconstructions in some cases.

According to Saferstein (1998):

> The physical evidence left behind at a crime scene plays a crucial role in reconstructing the events that took place surrounding the crime. Although the evidence alone does not describe everything that happened, it can support or contradict accounts given by witnesses and/or suspects. Information obtained from physical evidence can also generate leads and confirm the reconstruction of a crime to a jury. The collection and documentation of physical evidence is the foundation of a reconstruction. **Reconstruction supports a likely sequence of events by the observation and evaluation of physical evidence, as well as statements made by witnesses and those involved with the incident** [emphasis in the original].

Clearly, the more experienced we become in the use of physical evidence to provide information about crimes, the greater caution we take in interpreting results and making inferences about actual events. For the most part, modern-day criminalists understand that grand feats of detection are best left in the literary venue. However, perhaps some have even retreated too far into their havens of specialty within the laboratory. Few criminalists today consider it within their purview to suggest a reconstruction, and for those with only specialty training, they are correct. Associating objects and events in space and time tends to be left to the old-timers or, more commonly, the detective or attorney. In our opinion, the well-rounded and properly trained criminalist is still the best-qualified person to perform a reconstruction.

Even in the midst of discerning detailed event sequences from a single blood spatter patter, Kirk tempers his enthusiasm with the understanding that:

> A single piece of evidence is rarely sufficient in itself to establish proof of guilt or innocence.

D.   The State of the Practice

1.   Continuing Themes

Throughout the short history of forensic science, some common themes have
developed, mostly in the form of controversies and complaints. In the closing
section of this chapter, we enumerate the most pervasive of these and comment briefly on the current state of the profession with regard to some of
these concerns.

a.   Recognition and Collection of Evidence

Perhaps the most bitter and persistent complaint throughout the history of
criminalistics has been the lack of adequate training in crime scene procedures. In fact, most of the "police science" or "crime detection" books*
specifically address, at least in part, the audience of nonscientifically oriented
police officers and detectives who are virtually always the first to arrive at a
scene. More often than not, a law enforcement officer or evidence collection
technician with minimal scientific training is the person tasked with the all-
important charge of recognizing and collecting evidence. Less and less often
will a criminalist from the laboratory be called to the crime scene, and the
decision to do so is usually that of those already there. The individual making
decisions about what evidence to collect and the person given the responsibility to collect it vary widely between jurisdictions, so it is difficult to gen-
eralize. Although numerous well-credentialed authors have stressed the
importance of allowing the criminalist access to the scene,** budget constraints and resource management often preclude even the possibility. For
instance, even in those jurisdictions where a homicide might justify the
services of a criminalist, dusting for prints at the site of a burglary might not.

O'Hara and Osterburg, then members of the New York City Police
Department, in *Introduction to Criminalistics*, published in 1949, are particularly critical of this situation. They speak of the "inability of civil service to
attract competent personnel" and, in the face of the already present separation of the criminalist from the crime scene, emphasize the "importance of
field work for the working criminalist," describing the analysis as "a routine
affair which may be entrusted to an ordinary technician." They also point
out the paucity of texts written "to make a detective out of the scientist,"
noting, even then, the trend toward training specialized officers to collect
evidence for the criminalist waiting in the laboratory.

---

* A great number of these books have been written throughout history. They include Gross,
1891; Else and Garrow, 1934; May, 1936; Grant, 1941; Svensson and Wendel, 1955; Nickolls,
1956; Cuthbert, 1958; Jones and Gabard, 1959; Williams, 1967; Kind and Overman, 1972;
Fisher, 1992.
** *Ibid.*

In Kirk's 1953 *Crime Investigation*, he points out that "The investigator ... must understand (a) what physical evidence is; (b) how to collect and preserve it; (c) how to obtain from it the information it carries; and (d) how to interpret the information so obtained." He espouses the presence of the criminalist at the scene stating "categorically that more laboratory failures are due to inadequate collection of the existing evidence than are caused by the failure of the laboratory to examine it properly." Svensson (Svensson and Wendel, 1955) a Swedish author, in *Crime Detection*, provides one of the first specific descriptions of proper crime scene procedure. He emphasizes the duty of the responding officer in preserving the scene and stresses the care with which evidence should be handled.

L. C. Nickolls, then director of the Metropolitan Police Laboratory, New Scotland Yard, in *The Scientific Investigation of Crime*, published in 1956, provides some of the most compelling justification for calling the analyst to the scene. He describes the functions of the *scientist* as:

- To examine the general circumstances of the crime and form an opinion from the scientific angle of the nature of the events preceding the police investigation.
- To examine the scene of the crime for any unusual articles or fragments of material which have meaning to him in his special capacity as an expert but for some reason might not be suspected as being of value to the lay mind.
- To suggest from the examination of the scene what possibilities of future scientific action exist and, therefore, what kind of samples the police can expect to find of scientific value.
- Most important — to see for himself what the exact circumstances of the crime have been so that at the subsequent examination of the various scientific exhibits and also, if necessary, at the trial, the expert will know these circumstances. He will thus not be making examinations or giving evidence when has no first-hand knowledge of the reason why he is making the examination or of what value or purpose is his subsequent evidence.

In 1959, Leland Jones, one-time commander of the Scientific Investigation Division of the Los Angeles Police Department (LAPD), and Gabard wrote *Scientific Investigation and Physical Evidence; A Handbook for Investigators*. In a surreal prescient comment (re: the Simpson case) he ironically suggests that the most valuable physical evidence may be worthless if inefficiently handled. He divides the handling of physical evidence into four phases:

1. Gathering all potential evidence at scene or elsewhere.
2. Marking it correctly.
3. Keeping the chain of continuity straight.
4. Preventing contamination.

For reasons that continue to elude us (which means they must be administrative or fiscal), the system continues to try to force square pegs into round holes, placing the onus of all-important evidence collection on those least trained to recognize it, and sequestering the criminalist in the laboratory with the expensive equipment.

b.   Is Criminalistics an Autonomous Scientific Discipline?

Criminalistics is sometimes regarded, especially by those outside of the profession, as a bastard child, essentially a parasitic branch of knowledge completely dependent on the academic sciences for its continued existence (O'Hara and Osterburg, 1949). In his 1963 monograph, *The Ontogeny of Criminalistics* Kirk already had the foresight to address the question of whether criminalistics is an autonomous branch of learning. In addition to recognizing the basic attributes that categorize any particular endeavor as scientific, Kirk inquires whether criminalistics qualifies as an independent body of knowledge.

> *Is criminalistics a science?* According to most definitions, a science consists of an orderly and consistent body of knowledge, based on fundamental principles that can be clearly stated. Such a body of knowledge allows prediction as well as interpretation. Recognized sciences are characterized by research effort that produces constantly increasing theoretical and technical knowledge. Does criminalistics qualify? It is based on apparently simple but not clearly enunciated principles of individualization and individuality. In this sense it does not encroach on other sciences, but is a separate and unique area. It is unfortunate that the great body of knowledge which exists in this field is largely uncoordinated and has not yet been codified in clear and simple terms. The body of knowledge is constantly being increased by a moderate research effort, largely technical rather than theoretical. It seems fair to state that criminalistics may now be considered a science in its own right, but that it lacks at this time the full development that will allow general recognition. Even in its present state, it allows prediction as well as interpretation. It should be developed so as to achieve full recognition as a separate scientific discipline.

The situation, unfortunately, hasn't changed much since Kirk described it 40 years ago. Technical innovations, especially in instrumentation, have far outdistanced any attempts to establish a theoretical framework for criminalistics as an autonomous discipline. The dearth of, and recent alarming decrease in, academic programs in forensic science only serves to underscore the dangers of analysis without a framework for thoughtful interpretation. As Kirk so succinctly states, "a thoroughly competent investigator without much equipment is far better off than an incompetent investigator with unlimited equipment."* With this volume, we hope to contribute to the ongoing effort to provide a rational framework within which the results of forensic comparisons and analyses may be thoughtfully interpreted.

c.   Is Criminalistics a Profession?

In *The Ontogeny of Criminalistics* (1963), Kirk lists three criteria that a profession must meet: (1) extensive training at a high educational level, (2) a generally recognized and accepted code of behavior or ethics, and (3) establishment of competence. The parameters that Kirk promulgates seem both reasonable and comprehensive. Did criminalistics in 1963 satisfy the requirements of a profession? Has the situation changed over the last 40 years? Kirk cites the slow but finite expansion of academic programs in forensic science to meet his first standard; currently this situation seems to be in flux. He mentions the ethical code adopted by the California Association of Criminalists (CAC) to meet his second standard, but clearly acknowledges a lack of formal adherence in the field as a whole, relying mostly on his generous assumption that, "As a rule, even those practitioners not bound by any official code of ethics tend to be objective, fair and just in their relations to the people and the law." His rationalization that, "The exceptions are not more glaring than those in many of the established professions," is at best equivocal. The field has progressed in this area in that at least two national forensic organizations, the American Association of Forensic Sciences (AAFS) and the American Board of Criminalistics (ABC) each have codes of ethics, as have other regional associations (see Appendices B, C, D). However, membership in these organizations, hence adherence to any code, is still voluntary. Kirk concedes the absence of any objective assessment of competence, such as certification, to meet his third criterion. Quite recently, only in the 1990s, the ABC was formed and began to administer both general and specialty certification exams. However, like adherence to an ethical code, participation in certification procedures is still voluntary. Kirk concludes, "Despite the limitations still apparent in this relatively new field, the practice of criminalistics is clearly meeting the requirements of a professional discipline." Although he may have been indulging in a bit of wishful thinking with his assessment of the state of the practice in his day, Kirk clearly set the standard and paved the way for ongoing progress in this area. We will discuss specific aspects of ethics and accountability in greater detail in the last chapter of this book.

Thorwald provides a pertinent historical comment that may explain, though not excuse, some of the lack of focus and cohesion that seems to have

---

* A concertmaster can make a cigar box sound like a Stradivarius; a beginning student can make a Stradivarius sound like a cigar box. — Doug Emerson, San Gorgonio High School, California, band director, 1970.

characterized the forensic profession in recent times. The second world war, even more than the first, redirected a technological explosion toward military efforts. Personnel and resources were pulled from academic pursuits to assist their country of citizenship in the war effort. While civilian science would ultimately benefit from advances instigated by wartime progress, the immediate effect on the newly emerging forensic field was a dissipation of focus leading to a disorganization of the profession from which we are still recovering. Although methods and procedures continued to be disseminated, the accompanying training in analytical details and interpretation guidelines was less than uniform, and the importance of quality assurance was often lost in the haste to get laboratories up and running. The urbanization instigated by the baby boom population explosion, along with the more effective firearms spawned by the war, created a predictable environment for the growth of violent crime, as did the increase in recreational drug use. The need for physical evidence analysis was increasing both in quantity and variety.

As forensic science has matured, the need for high standards, professional cohesion, and an intellectual framework has slowly come to be acknowledged. A systematic literature, one of the earmarks of an autonomous discipline has emerged. Current technological advances are directed more toward automation, efficiency, and increasing sensitivity, than toward discovering novel or revolutionary methods. While the battle between the obligatory pragmatism of an applied science and the essential cerebral discourse of an academic discipline remains in the balance, we can be assured that it is only the continuing conflict that will lead to progress.

E.   Summary

In this chapter, we have taken you from the literary beginnings of crime detection, through the development of the practice of criminalistics, and into some of the preliminary concepts and principles that have evolved, although somewhat belatedly, along with the practice. We've described the evolution of biological evidence as a tool in crime detection. Although fingerprints are not traditionally grouped with blood and tissue typing, conceptually, they are completely analogous; both kinds of evidence contain the potential to be individualized directly to a person. The development of nonbiological evidence has also been reviewed. By definition, nonbiological evidence may link a person to a crime only indirectly. Therefore, inherent differences arise in interpreting and presenting the results from the comparison or analysis of nonbiological and biological evidence. We will continue to explore this counterpoint throughout the book. However, in the broader sense, certain unifying concepts and principles apply to all physical evidence. We will also introduce additional layers that interact to impact the forensic work product, including the inherent nature of the evidence and the decisions introduced by the analyst and the forensic community. In the next chapter, we introduce a unifying paradigm for forensic science.

References

Allard, J. E. and Wiggins, K. G., The evidential value of fabric car seats and car seat covers, *J. Forensic Sci. Soc.*, 27(2), 93–101, 1987.

Ashbaugh, D. R., *Quantitative-Qualitative Friction Ridge Analysis: An Introduction to Basic and Advanced Ridgeology*, CRC Press, Boca Raton, FL, 2000.

Biasotti, A., A statistical study of the individual characteristics of fired bullets, *J. Forensic Sci.*, 4(1), 133–140, 1959.

Block, E. B., *The Wizard of Berkeley*, Coward-McCann, New York, 1958.

Block, E. B., *Science vs. Crime: The Evolution of the Police Lab*, Cragmont Publications, San Francisco, 1979.

Cole, S., Witnessing identification: latent fingerprinting evidence and expert knowledge, *Soc. Stud. Sci.*, 28(5–6), 687, 1998.

Cole, S., What counts for identity? The historical origins of the methodology of latent fingerprint identification, *Sci. Context*, 12(1), 139, 1999.

Commission on Proceedings Involving Guy Paul Morin, The Honourable Fred Kaufman, C.M., Q.C., Queen's Printer for Ontario, 1998, and available at *http://www.attorneygeneral.jus.gov.on.ca/reports.htm*

Cordiner, S. J., Stringer, P., and Wilson, P. D., Fiber diameter and the transfer of wool fiber, *J. Forensic Sci. Soc.*, 25(6), 425–426, 1985.

Coxon, A., Grieve, M., and Dunlop, J., A method of assessing the fibre shedding potential of fabrics, *J. Forensic Sci. Soc.*, 32(2), 151–158, 1992.

Culliford, B. J., *The Examination and Typing of Bloodstains in the Crime Laboratory*. U.S. Government Printing Office, Washington, D.C., 1971.

Cuthbert, C. R. M., *Science and the Detection of Crime*, Hutchinson, London, 1958.

Deadman, H., Fiber evidence and the Wayne Williams trial, Part I, *FBI Law Enforcement Bull.*, 53(3), 12–20, 1984a.

Deadman, H., Fiber evidence and the Wayne Williams trial, Part II, *FBI Law Enforcement Bull.*, 53(5), 10–19, 1984b.

DeForest, P., Lee, H., and Gaensslen, R., *Forensic Science: An Introduction to Criminalistics*, McGraw Hill, New York, 1983.

Dillon, D., A History of Criminalistics in the United States 1850–1950, Doctor of Criminology thesis, University of California, Berkeley, 1977.

Doyle, A. C., A Study in Scarlet, *Beeton's Christmas Annual*, 1887.

Doyle, A. C., The Adventure of the Cardboard Box, *The Strand Magazine*, 1893.

Else, W. M. and Garrow, J. M., *The Detection of Crime,* published at the office of *The Police Journal,* London, U.K., 1934.

Evett I. W. et al., A hierarchy of propositions: deciding which level to address in casework, *Sci. Justice,* 38(4), 231–239, 1998a.

Evett I. W. et al., A model for case assessment and interpretation, *Sci. Justice,* 38(3), 151–156, 1998.

Faulds, H., On the skin furrows of the hand, *Nature,* 22, 605, 1880.

Fisher, B. J., *Techniques of Crime Scene Investigation,* 5th ed., CRC Press, Boca Raton, FL, 1992.

Gaensslen, R. E., *Sourcebook in Forensic Serology,* U.S. Government Printing Office, Washington, D.C., 1983.

Gaensslen, R. E., Ed., *Sourcebook in Forensic Serology, Unit IX: Translations of Selected Contributions to the Original Literature of Medicolegal Examination of Blood and Body Fluids,* National Institute of Justice, Wasington, D.C., 1983.

Galton, F., *Finger Prints,* Macmillan, London, 1892.

Galton, F., Personal Identification and Description II, *Nature,* 38, 201–202, 1888.

German, E., The History of Fingerprints, 1999, available at *http://www.onin.com/fp/fphistory.html.*

Grant, J., *Science for the Prosecution,* Chapman & Hall, London, 1941.

Grieve, M. C. and Biermann, T. W., The population of coloured textile fibres on outdoor surfaces, *Sci. Justice J. Forensic Sci. Soc.,* 37(4), 231–239, 1997.

Gross, H., *Criminal Investigation,* 1891.

Hatcher, J. S., Jury, F. J., and Weller, J., *Firearms Investigation, Identification, and Evidence,* Samworth, T. G., Ed., The Stackpole Co., Harrisburg, PA, 1957.

Home, J.M. and Dudley, R. J., A summary of data obtained from a collection of fibres from casework materials, *J. Forensic Sci. Soc.,* 20, 253–261, 1980.

Houck, M., Statistics and Trace Evidence: The Tyranny of Numbers, Forensic Science Communications, Federal Bureau of Investigation, Virginia 1(3), 1999, available at *http://www.fbi.gov/programs/lab/fsc/current/houck.htm.*

Houck, M. and Siegal, J., A large scale fiber transfer study, paper presented at the American Academy of Forensic Sciences, Orlando, FL, February, 1999.

Israel National Police, International Symposium on Fingerprint Detection and Identification, *J. Forensic Identification,* 45, 578–84, 1995.

Jeffreys, A. J., Wilson, V., and Thein, S. L., Individual-specific "fingerprints" of human DNA, *Nature,* 316(4), 76, 1985.

Jones, L. V. and Gabard C., *Scientific Investigation and Physical Evidence; Handbook for Investigators,* Charles C Thomas, Springfield, MA, 1959.

Kidd, C. B. M. and Robertson, J., The transfer of textile fibers during simulated contacts, *J. Forensic Sci. Soc.,* 22(3), 301–308, 1982.

Kind, S. and Overman, M., *Science against Crime*, Aldus Book Limited, published by Doubleday, New York, 1972.

Kingston, C. R. and Kirk, P. L., Historical development and evaluation of the "12 point rule" in fingerprint identification, *Int. Criminal Police Rev.*, 186, 62–69, 1965.

Kirk, P. L., The ontogeny of criminalistics, *J. Criminal Law, Criminol. Police Sci.*, 54, 235–238, 1963.

Kirk, P. L., *Crime Investigation*, Interscience, John Wiley & Sons, New York, 1953.

Kirk, P. L., *Crime Investigation*, 2nd ed., Thornton, J., Ed., Krieger (by arrangement with John Wiley & Sons), Malabar, FL, 1974.

Locard, E., Dust and its analysis, *Police J.*, 1, 177, 1928.

Locard, E., *L'enquete criminelle et les methodes scientifique*, Ernest Flammarion, Paris, 1920.

Locard, E., The analysis of dust traces, Part I–III, *Am. J. Police Sci.*, 1, 276, 401, 496, 1930.

May, L. S., The identification of knives, tools and instruments, a positive science, *Am. Police J.*, 1, 246, 1930.

May, L. S., *Crime's Nemesis*, Macmillan, New York, 1936.

Moore, G., Brief History of Fingerprint Identification, 1999, available at *http://onin. com/fp/fphistory.html*.

Morland, N., *An Outline of Scientific Criminology*, Philosophical Library, New York, 1950.

Mullis, K. B. et al., Specific enzymatic amplification of DNA in vitro: the polymerase chain reaction, *Cold Spring Harbor Symp. Quant. Biol.*, 51, 263–273, 1986.

Murdock, J. E. and Biasotti, A. A., The scientific basis of firearms and Toolmark Identification, in Firearms and Toolmark Identification, in *Modern Scientific Evidence*, Faigman, D. L., et al., Eds., West Law, San Francisco, 1997.

Nichols, R. G., Firearm and toolmark identification criteria: a review of the literature, *J. Forensic Sci.*, 42(3), 466–474, 1997.

Nickolls, L. C., *The Scientific Investigation of Crime*, Butterworth, London, 1956.

O'Hara, C. E. and Osterburg, J. W., *An Introduction to Criminalistics; The Application of the Physical Sciences to the Detection of Crime*, Macmillan, New York, 1949.

Osterburg, J. W., *The Crime Laboratory; Case Studies of Scientific Criminal Investigation*, Indiana University Press, Bloomington, 1968.

Palmer, R. and Chinherende, V., A target fiber study using cinema and car seats as recipient items, *J. Forensic Sci.*, 41, 802–803, 1996.

Parybyk, A. E. and Lokan, R. J., A study of the numerical distribution of fibers transferred from blended fabrics, *J. Forensic Sci. Soc.*, 26(1), 61–68, 1986.

Poe, E. A., The murders in the rue morgue, *Graham's Mag.*, 1841.

Poe, E. A., The Purloined Letter, *The Gift*, 1845.

Pounds, C. A. and Smalldon, K. W., The transfer of fibers between clothing materials during simulated contacts and their persistence during wear: part I: fiber transference, *HOCRE Report*, Home Office Central Research Establishment, Aldermaston, 1975a.

Pounds, C. A. and Smalldon, K. W., The transfer of fibers between clothing materials during simulated contacts and their persistence during wear: part II: fiber persistence, *HOCRE Report*, Home Office Central Research Establishment, Aldermaston, 1975b.

Pounds, C. A. and Smalldon, K. W., The transfer of fibers between clothing materials during simulated contacts and their persistence during wear: part III: a preliminary investigation of the mechanisms involved, *HOCRE Report*, Home Office Central Research Establishment, Aldermaston, 1975c.

Railton, S., University of Virginia, Mark Twain in His Times, Pudd'nhead Wilson sources, 1998, available at *http://etext.lib.virginia.edu/railton/wilson/pwsrcs.html.*

Robertson, J. and Lloyd, A. K., Observations on redistribution of textile fibers, *J. Forensic Sci. Soc.*, 24(1), 3–7, 1984.

Robertson, J., Kidd, C. B. M., and Parkinson, H. M. P., The persistence of textile fibers transferred during simulated contacts, *J. Forensic Sci. Soc.*, 22(4), 353–360, 1982.

Roux, C. and Margot, P., An attempt to assess the relevance of textile fibres recovered from car seats, *Sci. Justice J. Forensic Sci. Soc.*, 37(4), 225–230, 1997.

Saferstein, R., *Criminalistics: An Introduction to Forensic Science*, 6th ed., Prentice-Hall, Englewood Cliffs, NJ, 1998.

Saiki, R. K. et al., Enzymatic amplification of beta-globin genomic sequences and restriction site analysis for diagnosis of sickle cell anemia, *Science*, 230, 1350, 1985.

Solbello, L., Application of PLM in the Industrial Minerals Laboratory, paper presented at *Inter/Micro 99*, Chicago, IL, July 1999.

Stoney, D. A. and Thornton, J. I., A critical analysis of quantitative fingerprint individuality models, *J. Forensic Sci.*, 31(4), 1187–1216, 1986a.

Stoney, D. A. and Thornton, J. I., A method for the description of minutia pairs in epidermal ridge patterns, *J. Forensic Sci.*, 31(4), 1217–1234, 1986b.

Stoney, D. A. and Thornton, J. I., A systematic study of epidermal ridge minutiae, *J. Forensic Sci.*, 32(5), 1182–1203, 1987.

Stoney, D. A., What made us ever think we could individualize using statistics? *J. Forensic Sci. Soc.*, 3(2), 197–199, 1991.

Svensson, A. and Wendel, O., *Crime Detection*, Elsevier, New York, 1955.

Thorwald, J. T., *Crime and Science*, Harcourt, Brace & World, New York, 1966, Translation, Richard and Clara Winston.

Thorwald, J. T., *The Century of the Detective*, Harcourt, Brace & World, New York, 1964, Translation, Richard and Clara Winston, 1965.

Tulleners, F. A. J. and Giusto, M., Striae reproducibility on sectional cuts of one Thompson Contender barrel, *AFTE J.*, 30(1), 62–81, 1998.

Twain, M. [Samuel Clemens], The tragedy of Pudd'nhead Wilson, *Century Magazine*, 1894.

Voltaire, F., *Zadig*, 1748.

Williams, E. W., *Modern Law Enforcement and Police Science*, Charles C Thomas, Springfield, MA, 1967.

Wilson, E. O., *Consilience: The Unity of Knowledge*, Knopf, New York, 1998.

Section 2
The Principles of
Forensic Science

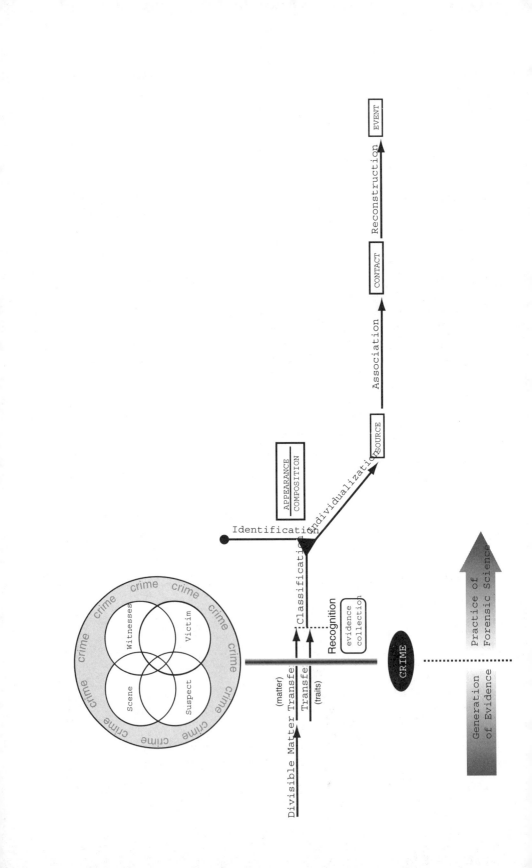

Overview — A Unifying Paradigm of Forensic Science

3

> The study of paradigms ... is what mainly prepares the student for membership in the particular scientific community with which he will later practice. Because he there joins men who learned the bases of their field from the same concrete models, the subsequent practice will seldom evoke overt disagreement over fundamentals. Men whose research is based on shared paradigms are committed to the same rules and standards for scientific practice. That commitment and the apparent consensus it produces are prerequisites for normal science, i.e., for the genesis and continuation of a particular research tradition.
>
> **—Thomas Kuhn**
> *The Structure of Scientific Revolutions, 3rd edition, 1996*

Figure 3.1 The paradigm. Individuals practicing a profession need a common map to guide them through their work. While never fully articulated in an organized fashion, over the years a map of the discipline of criminalistics has emerged. Numerous workers have contributed to the conceptual framework presented in this book. The paradigm includes the principles of evidence formation (the origin of evidence) and the processes of analysis that describe the profession of criminalistics.

A.   Introduction

In 1963, Paul Kirk published a short monograph entitled *The Ontogeny of Criminalistics*. In it he states:

> With all of the progress that has been made in this field, and on a wide front, careful examination shows that for the most part, progress has been technical rather than fundamental, practical rather than theoretical, transient rather than permanent. Many persons can identify the particular weapon that fired a bullet, but few if any can state a single fundamental principle of identification of firearms. Document examiners constantly identify handwriting, but a class of beginners studying under these same persons would find it difficult indeed to distinguish the basic principles used. In short, there exists in the field of criminalistics a serious deficiency in basic theory and principles, as contrasted with the large assortment of effective technical procedures.

Remarkably, although Kirk goes on to suggest that "criminalistics is the science of individualization," he fails to offer us the comprehensive set of fundamental principles whose absence he deplores.

Over the last several decades, a theoretical framework of sorts has, in fact, evolved. These fundamental precepts provide a philosophical and rational framework for the application of scientific knowledge to the forensic arena. They are concepts that guide a forensic analysis in a logical progression, starting with understanding the origin of evidence, and culminating in a statement of the significance of the analytical result. Unfortunately, these concepts have evolved in a fragmented manner and, in fact, no published record of a comprehensive organized paradigm exists. Traditionally, forensic science practitioners have come to understand the major paradigm of their work to comprise five basic concepts:

1. **Transfer** (*Locard exchange principle*) — The exchange of material between two objects (Locard, 1928; 1930)
2. **Identification** — Defining the physicochemical nature of the evidence (Saferstein, 1998)
3. **Classification/Individualization** — Attempting to determine the source of the evidence (Kirk, 1963; DeForest, 1983)
4. **Association** — Linking a person with a crime scene (Osterburg, 1968)
5. **Reconstruction** — Understanding the sequence of past events (DeForest et al., 1983)

We will propose an as yet unarticulated fundamental principle necessary to the understanding of forensic evidence, which we call *divisible matter*. This precedes *transfer* in the generation of physical evidence, and brings to six the number of principles that we feel are necessary to understand and practice the science of criminalistics. For purposes of this section, we will incorporate all six into the paradigm, leaving it to the reader to return after finishing the section on divisible matter for a better understanding of the interdependence of these six principles.

In attempting to relate them to each other, we conclude that only two, divisible matter and transfer, define scientific principles that relate to the generation of evidence; the other concepts, *identification*, *association* through *class* and *individualizing* characteristics, and *reconstruction*, are integral to the *practice* of forensic science, and are *processes* we use in our attempt to answer the various investigative questions, "who? what? where? why? when? and how?"

Figure 3.1 is a pictorial representation of the paradigm as we understand it. All of the ideas we have discussed are arranged around a physical and temporal focus, the *crime*. The interactive elements of a scene, a victim, a suspect, and witnesses are not novel. However, they are usually depicted as a triangle with the victim, suspect, and witnesses as apices surrounding the physical scene. We prefer to think of these elements as overlapping domains. Regardless, the crime defines the border between the generation of evidence and the recognition and subsequent analysis and interpretation of evidence.

B.   The Principles

Only two of the concepts we have discussed thus far emerge from the fundamental nature of matter, divisible matter and transfer. These principles exist independently of any human intervention, or even recognition; therefore we accord them a different status than the processes that begin with the recognition of evidence by human beings. However, although all matter is constantly dividing and transferring, it does not become evidence until division and transfer occur in conjunction with a criminal event. Note that for some types of evidence the contact necessary for transfer may be the force causing division. For example, a collision between two vehicles causes the simultaneous division and transfer of paint.

Recognize that divisible matter does not account for a large category of evidence, that of pattern transfer evidence, such as prints and impressions. The transfer of matter requires its prior division; the transfer of *traits* may not.

C.   The Processes

At some point after the commission of a crime, evidence may be recognized as such and collected. The recognition of evidence and all of the processes that follow in a case investigation result from decisions made and actions performed by people. We, therefore, separate the practice of forensic science from the fundamental scientific principles upon which the generation of evidence rests. If the crime is never discovered or the evidence is never detected, matter has still divided and transferred, and traits have still transferred. But it is only by attempting to answer investigative questions about a crime that the processes of association through class and individualizing characteristics and of reconstruction are employed.

1. Identification

Kirk and others emphasize the process of individualization, the reduction of a class of evidence to one. It is useful to take a step back and realize that identification, defining the physicochemical nature of the evidence, can be an end in itself. For some purposes, for example, the recognition of illegal drugs, the forensic process stops with identification. The criminal justice system is not necessarily concerned with the marijuana field or methamphetamine laboratory from which the drugs originated (although sometimes they may be); simple possession of the scheduled substance fulfills the criteria of illegality. The process of identification answers the case investigation question of, "what is it?"

2. Classification and Individualization

Identification may also occur as a step leading to individualization. To distinguish it from end-point identification as discussed in the last section, we will refer to the intermediate process that may lead to individualization as classification. Several authors (DeForest et al., 1983; Tuthill, 1994; Saferstein, 1998; Cook et al., 1998a,b) have remarked on the special meaning of individualization in a forensic context as a conclusion of common source for two items. Any forensic analysis that proceeds on the path toward individualization relies on a comparison of at least two items. Physics and logic determine that any individual object is unique; this is not the question. The forensic question asks whether items share a common origin. There may be some disagreement about whether an item must be classified before it is individualized. We believe that, whether intentionally or not, the analyst will know what the item is by the time he concludes a common source. If ambiguity exists about the classification of an item, the individualization to a common source is also compromised. The process of individualization answers the questions of "which one is it?" or "whose is it?" depending on whether the item is animate or inanimate; it does this by inferring a common source or origin.

3. Association

Although the word *association* is used freely in describing the results of a forensic examination, no clear definition seems to exist, at least not in published literature. We propose that *association* be defined as an inference of contact between the "source" *of the evidence* and a "target." Such an inference is based on the detection of transfer of material or a physical match determined by complementary edges. The *source* and the *target* are relative operational terms defined by the structure of the case; if transfer is detected in both directions, for instance, each item is both a source and a target.

The association process involves the evaluation of all of the evidence for and against the inference of common source; in other words, competing hypotheses are compared. The probability of the evidence under competing hypotheses is an expression of the likelihood of the evidence given that the target and source items were in physical contact, contrasted to the likelihood of the evidence given that the target was in contact with a different unrelated source. This process requires combining the strength of the evidence established during the individualization process with additional information (such as may be provided by manufacturers of materials and empirical studies), as well as assumptions made by the analyst. Others have commented on the complexity of determining the significance of an association, including Robertson and Vignaux (1995) and Cook et al. (1998a,b).

To illustrate this concept, consider a fiber collected from the body of a deceased individual. The fiber is compared with a carpet from the floor of an automobile van. The evidence fiber from the body and the reference fibers from the van carpet are found to be the same type and to contain indistinguishable dye components. These similarities suggest that the van carpet could be the source of the evidence fiber (alternatively, the van carpet cannot be eliminated as a possible source of the evidence fiber). Next, all possible sources of the evidence fiber are considered, including the carpet from the van, all of the carpet manufactured from the fiber, and any other items manufactured from that particular fiber, and any other fiber indistinguishable from the evidence fiber by the analysis performed. From the data obtained by the laboratory analyses, combined with real-world information about the distribution of the fiber, an inference might be made that the deceased individual and the van carpet were in contact.

Note the distinction between a conclusion of common source (the evidence and reference fibers are classified or individualized as sharing a common source) and an inference of contact between a source and a target (the carpet and the deceased are associated).

4.   Reconstruction

We consider reconstruction to be the ordering of associations in space and time. Reconstruction attempts to answer the questions of "where? how? and when?" It should be stressed that the "when?" usually refers to an ordering in relative time only; was the sweater in contact with the couch before, during, or after the murder took place?

D.   Summary

We propose an organization of the forensic paradigm centered around the crime event. The principles of divisible matter and transfer interact in the generation of evidence before and during the crime. The practice of forensic science begins after the crime event with the recognition of evidence. Divisible matter and transfer are the two fundamental scientific principles upon which the forensic analysis of physical evidence is based. Identification, association through classification and individualization, and through reconstruction form the infrastructure for the practice of forensic science.

References

Cook R. et al., A model for case assessment and interpretation, *Sci. Justice,* 38(3), 151–156, 1998a.

Cook R. et al., A hierarchy of propositions: deciding which level to address in case-work, *Sci. Justice,* 38(4), 231–239, 1998b.

DeForest, P., Lee, H., and Gaensslen, R., *Forensic Science: An Introduction to Criminalistics,* McGraw Hill, New York, 1983.

Kirk, P. L., The ontogeny of criminalistics, *J. Criminal Law Criminol. Police Sci.,* 54, 235–238, 1963.

Kuhn, K. S., *The Structure of Scientific Revolutions,* 3rd ed., University of Chicago Press, Chicago, 1996.

Locard, E., Dust and its analysis, *Police J.,* 1, 177, 1928.

Locard, E., The analysis of dust traces, Part I–III, *Am. J. Police Sci.* 1, 276, 401, 496, 1930.

Osterburg, J. W., *The Crime Laboratory; Case Studies of Scientific Criminal Investigation,* Indiana University Press, Bloomington, 1968.

Robertson, B. and Vignaux, G. A., *Interpreting Evidence,* John Wiley & Sons, Chichester, 1995.

Saferstein, R., *Criminalistics: An Introduction to Forensic Science,* 6th ed., Prentice-Hall, Englewood Cliffs, NJ, 1998.

Tuthill, H., *Individualization: Principles and Procedures in Criminalistics,* Lightening Powder Company, Salem, OR, 1994.

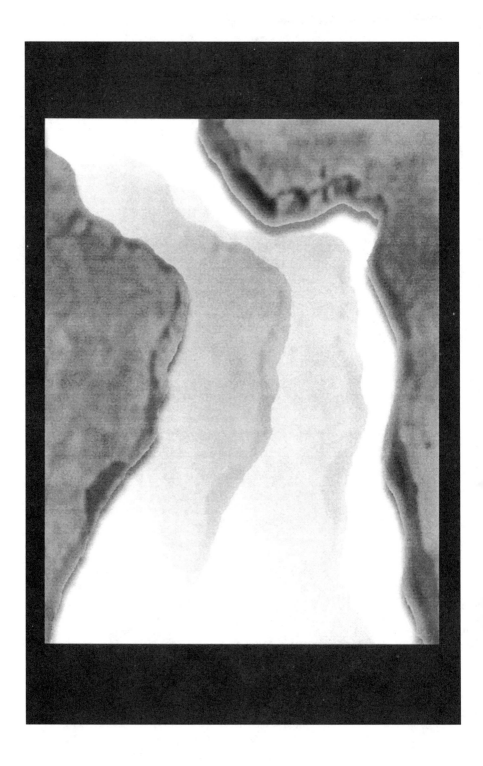

The Origin of Evidence — Divisible Matter and Transfer

4

Figure 4.1 The continents. When matter divides, some characteristics retained by the smaller pieces are unique to the division process. These traits are created at the boundary of the fracture. Boundary roughness is a natural consequence of breaking one surface into two, and these new surfaces are closely, but not completely, complementary. At the moment of division the separated fragments commence to change and become different both from each other and from the original object. At some point, it might become impossible to associate the two fragments by physical matching of their complementary edges. Do Africa and South America share a common origin? The figure allows you to make your own judgment.

> Every contact leaves a trace
> **—Anonymous**

A. In the Beginning ...

The cornerstone of forensic science since the early 1920s has been a maxim attributed to Edmund Locard. It appears in two or three permutations in his writings, but the most comprehensive statement translates as follows:

> No one can commit a crime with the intensity that the criminal act requires without leaving numerous signs of it: either the offender has left signs at the scene of the crime, or on the other hand, has taken away with him — on his person or clothes — indications of where he has been or what he has done.*

Locard himself never proffered this as a principle; his students and colleagues were the ones who transformed this simple *raison d'être* into a foundational principle of forensic science. In the process, Locard's musings were transformed into the definitive, "Every contact leaves a trace." In the same way that Quetelet's "Nature exhibits an infinite variety of forms" was adulterated to "Nature never repeats herself" (Thornton, 1986) subtle but important differences exist between Locard's original quote (1920) and the modern redux of it. Among other distinctions, the redacted version retains no mention of a crime; the reader is left with the impression (whether correct or not) that transfer is equally likely and equally important under any circumstance. Further, Locard implies that the criminal is acting under stress and with anxiety ("the intensity that the criminal act requires"). This leaves no room for the psychopathic criminal who feels no emotion whatsoever in the commission of a criminal act, and so does not experience the type of stress and anxiety implied by Locard. Nor does it allow for the serial criminal, who may perfect the crime's *modus operandi* with each new commission of it, reducing the chances of leaving traces behind. Neither Locard's original

---

* Translation courtesy of Sharon Kruzik. Alternate translations of some of the words appear later in this chapter.

writings nor current interpretations explicitly address the possibility of transfer in both directions, although one might argue that Locard implies it. Our expectations with regard to cross-transfer impact on both the search for evidence and the interpretation of that which is found. For example, an expectation that two-way transfer should occur might weaken an association for which traces of contact are not found in both directions.

After reviewing Locard's writings (1920; 1923; 1928; 1930), it seems to us far more likely that, rather than intentionally articulating a global principle, he was merely reflecting on the reasons a careful scrutiny of the crime scene, including victims, suspects, and witnesses, was worth the effort. Frequently (or perhaps, in Locard's mind, inevitably) contact between two objects will be indicated by small traces of each left on the other. Find the traces, and contact is established.

Arthur Conan Doyle had Sherlock Holmes deduce the cigarette smoked by the type of ash that it left, discern the part of London a person was from by the mud on his jacket, and even the part of the world where a tattoo was acquired by the particular delicate shade of pink (Doyle, 1891). It is difficult to know if such a simplistic view of physical evidence could be justified in the time of Locard's Lyon. However, it is reasonably certain a person's surroundings contained more individual character than they would today. The reasons for greater homogeneity in today's world, than in even the recent past, derive from the mass production of items and the worldwide distribution of these goods. Additionally, people have acquired increased mobility, hence exposure, to all parts of the globe. The disintegration of physical boundaries containing both people and things means that any individual will perennially bathe in a wide variety of materials that are ubiquitous in the world, such as white cotton, sugar, salt, and glass. Consequently, traces found on a person or in her environment may not provide any useful information to differentiate this person from the rest of the world. To take this a step farther, merely finding traces that "match" a reference material does not necessarily establish contact. A conclusion of contact is an inference, not a fact, and that inference is stronger or weaker depending on how much must be assumed about a variety of hard-to-test premises, including transferability, persistence, detectability, and the frequency of the evidence in the world.

We conclude from the foregoing that Locard hit upon an essential, but not all-inclusive, precept for the forensic scientist. For example, transfer fails to explain either impression or physical match evidence. He wrote volumes describing the kinds of traces that might be detected as a result of contact, and described the kinds of techniques that utilized the unique nature of the material to identify and classify it (Locard, 1931–1940). He therefore knew that understanding the nature of the evidence was just as important as explaining its presence through contact. It follows that understanding the nature of evidence and the mechanisms that allow it to be transferred are also useful concepts for the forensic scientist. It seems clear to us that Locard understood that the nature of the evidence comprised the central part of his work, and that it was so obvious he did not need to state it. We inch farther out on the limb and suggest that, to Locard, transfer was merely the mechanism for finding the evidence before doing the important work.

We propose that understanding the origin of evidence does not begin with transfer; it must begin with understanding the nature of the evidence and the mechanisms that make it available for transfer. In this chapter, we develop the idea that matter must first divide before it can be transferred, and that the combination of division of matter and transfer after division accounts for the origin of physical evidence in connection with criminal events.

B.   The Nature of Matter

The examination of evidence relies on an understanding of the fundamental nature of matter. When matter becomes evidence by virtue of its connection with a criminal act, this modulates to an understanding of the *nature of the evidence*. Matter (and hence physical evidence) is the "stuff" around us that is composed of the fundamental building blocks of the universe, ordered according to well-articulated chemical and physical principles. We need not concern ourselves with subatomic particles when discussing physical evidence, but rather atoms and how they are arranged to compose our physical world. Because they can only be arranged in specific ways allowed by the laws of chemistry and physics, their fundamental properties remain constant and reproducible each time we examine or analyze them. Forensic scientists take advantage of these properties of matter in forensic science by applying tests designed to reveal the underlying nature of the material so that we might draw some useful conclusions about what it is, and what the potential source of the evidence might be.

A forensic scientist is thus well grounded in the fundamentals of chemistry and physics; here is the starting place for understanding what property of an item of evidence might be examined to answer a useful legal question. Analysts must come to appreciate how the material is generated, whether by nature or by human hands; they must ascertain the characteristics that define the material, including which of those characteristics are shared with other materials, and which are unique to this material. From the synthesis of this knowledge comes the ability to determine what traits may be used to categorize or classify the material, what properties might lead to source determination, and whether that source might be unique.

For bloodstain patterns and ballistics, an understanding of the substance, combined with a grasp of its dynamic interaction with the environment, is integral to interpreting the evidence. For this kind of "dynamic" evidence, we are as interested in the process as the end result. In particular, we look to this type of evidence to assist in the final reconstruction of the event, in other words, the movement of matter through space and time. We will address this aspect in more detail in Chapter 7.

Once an appreciation is gained for the fundamental nature of matter, and consequently for physical evidence, it is necessary to describe those principles and processes that form the unique aspects of the enterprise we call forensic science.

C. Divisible Matter — A New Fundamental Principle in Forensic Science

As objects exist in our normal physical world, a variety of forces act upon them. When the input energy resulting from these forces is greater than the forces holding a piece of matter together, a small piece of the object may separate from the parent object. This is *fracture*. While there is no specific physical law defined for this phenomenon, it is important to forensic science. We therefore suggest that fracture of physical objects is a fundamental principle of forensic science, and we name it the principle of *divisible matter*.

> **Matter divides into smaller component parts when sufficient force is applied. The component parts will acquire characteristics created by the process of division itself and retain physicochemical properties of the larger piece.**

This statement leads directly to three corollaries with important consequences to the analysis and interpretation of physical evidence.

Corollary 1: Some characteristics retained by the smaller pieces are unique to the original item or to the division process. These traits are useful for individualizing all pieces to the original item.

Corollary 2: Some characteristics retained by the smaller pieces are common to the original item as well as to other items of similar manufacture. We rely on these traits to classify the item.

Corollary 3: Some characteristics of the original item will be lost or changed during or after the moment of division and subsequent dispersal; this confounds the attempt to infer a common source.

In particular, the principle of divisible matter and its logical corollaries have a profound effect on the forensic process of source determination.

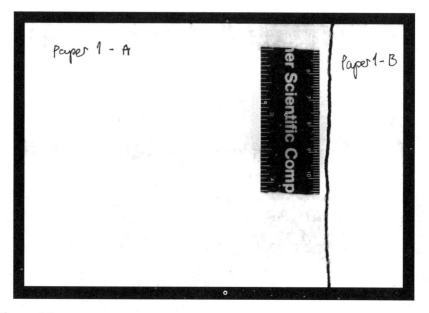

Figure 4.2 Torn paper overview. Juxtaposing the edges of pieces of torn paper reveals complementary edges. A sufficient length of such complementarity may convince the examiner that the two fragments were once one contiguous piece of paper. The reader may wish to compare this figure with Figure 6.4.

1. Properties Useful for Source Determination

The process of division creates physical traits not present in the original, and these may serve to connect the two separated items at a later time. These traits are created at the boundary of the fracture. Boundary roughness is a natural consequence of breaking one surface into two (Kalia et al., 1997), and these new surfaces are closely, but not completely, complementary. Forensic scientists use complementary edges in "physical match" comparisons to infer a common source for two items. For instance, tearing a piece of paper in half will create edges that were not present in the original piece of paper, and juxtaposing the two new edges may convince the examiner that they were once a contiguous item (Figure 4.2). This is the most immediate consequence of the division of matter.

Also, traits and characteristics present in the undivided object at the moment of division are carried with all pieces that originate from it. This includes all physicochemical traits present in the undivided object, except those that define it as intact, specifically size and shape. Examples of properties that might be inherited by the progeny fragments are color, elemental composition, and microcrystalline structure.

To some extent, the properties inherited depend on the scale of homogeneity of the original object as compared with the scale of fragmentation.

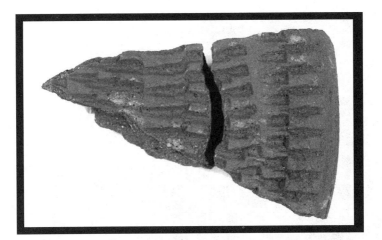

Figure 4.3 Pottery — texture. If complementary edges are insufficient to conclude a common origin for evidence and reference samples, other physicochemical traits are required to compare the two objects. In this photograph, the texture seen in both pieces narrows the possible sources to those pottery manufacturers creating such a texture.

If pottery with a characteristic texture design is broken into several large pieces, the fragments will show the characteristic texture (Figure 4.3). This texture would assist in associating a pottery fragment with the small class of pottery of similar design. If, however, the pottery is shattered into small particles, it is unlikely that any one particle will clearly exhibit the characteristic texture. The fragments are likely to be placed in the larger class of pottery with similar mineral composition (Figure 4.4), rather than the smaller class of items exhibiting the characteristic texture.

In summary, both the new complementary boundaries resulting from division and the physicochemical traits of materials are useful for individualizing an object to its source, leading to an inference of common origin.

2.   Properties Confounding Source Determination

At the moment of division, the separated fragments commence to change and become different both from each other and from the original object. We call this phenomenon *temporal instability* to indicate continuous change over time; it is, most simply, a consequence of increasing entropy. After the process of division and dispersal, each property of the newly created items will diverge from the others at some discontinuous rate, k. This temporal instability will affect the ability to assess the original values accurately at and before division. A future comparative analysis of both items might lead to the detection of different values and a potentially erroneous conclusion of different sources for the items.

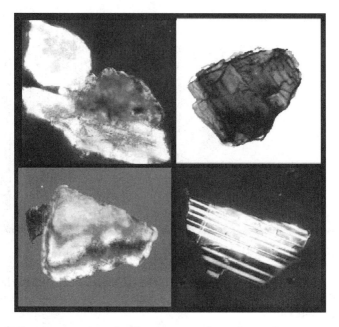

Figure 4.4 Pottery — minerals. If gross manufacturing traits are not present in either the evidence or the reference material, more common physicochemical characteristics are compared. In this circumstance, only the mineral composition is available for analysis and comparison. Pottery from many manufacturers may be included as possible sources for the evidence fragments.

Consider again the example of torn paper. As a result of nonuniform exposure to local environmental factors, the edges of each piece, as well as the physicochemical traits, will begin to diverge from their original values. At some point, it might become impossible to associate the two paper fragments by either physical matching of their complementary edges or by physicochemical traits.

In addition, the very act of division inevitably results in the loss of some characteristics that define the original material. From a consideration of a fragment of paper, one cannot infer the number of remaining pieces, nor the exact size and shape of the original item. As another example, one cannot, infer a sweater from the examination of a single fiber divided from it (Figure 4.5).

In the absence of physical matching between an evidence and reference item, *ambiguity* about the original global character of the whole item leads to the consideration of more than one possible source for the evidence. No analysis can determine which source is correct, even if the true source item is recovered and compared. Even assuming all of the physical and chemical traits from an evidence/reference pair correspond, ambiguity will preclude an inference that the source was *this* sweater, as opposed to all other sweaters manufactured at the same time, or any other item made from the precursor yarn.

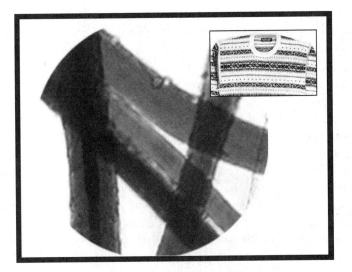

Figure 4.5 Sweater and fibers. When an object divides and the resulting fragment is transferred to another object, analysis of the fragment may not reveal the nature of the original item. One cannot infer the source sweater (inset) from analysis of the evidence fibers.

3. More on the Nature of Matter: Thermodynamics and Entropy

We briefly mentioned entropy in the preceding section. We would like to expand on the necessity of understanding thermodynamics and its impact on the nature of physical objects.

> Thermodynamics is the study of the patterns of energy change. Thermodynamics refers to energy, and "dynamics" means the patterns of change. Specifically the study of thermodynamics deals mainly with (A) energy conversion and (B) the stability of molecules and direction of change. (Thinkquest, 1996)

It is the second concept, the stability of molecules and direction of change, that interests us in the examination of physical evidence. This is addressed by the second law of thermodynamics:

> A spontaneous change is accompanied by an increase in the total entropy of the system and its surroundings. Thus, the entropy of the universe always increases. (Thinkquest, 1996)

Entropy (S) is most simply a measure of disorder. While the entropy in a closed system might decrease, the entropy of the universe never decreases. For instance, the molecules in one's body exist in great order at the expense of the ever-increasing entropy of the rest of the universe. Without specific input energy, things spontaneously move from order to randomness. Every moment that an object exists in the real universe, random forces from either energy or other matter impinge on it and drive it farther toward disorder. These random influences result in changes to an object that are neither predictable nor repeatable. The ever-increasing disorder at both the micro- and macrolevels results in the generation of random characteristics that will never be exactly repeated in another similar object.

This is a two-edged forensic sword. On one hand, disorder predicts the accumulation of random marks on an object (e.g., a shoe or gun barrel), unique complementary edges from a fracture, or unpredictable fingerprint ridge patterns arising from basal volar pads. On the other hand, once an item has fractured into more than one piece, each is also subject to the influences of this disorder that may result in the destruction of traits that might be useful in a forensic examination. The analyst benefits from this understanding both in deciding what traits might be useful for individualization and by considering the possibility of adventitious or ambiguous traits confounding the possibility of concluding a common source.

4. An Example of Divisibility

The number of "things" that can be evidence is limited to the things that exist in the physical universe! In other words, any "thing" can be evidence. To attempt an enumeration of how divisible matter might apply to every object would be ludicrous, and so we will simply provide an illustrative example and leave the reader the exercise of considering how this principle might apply to the infinite variety of matter that may be encountered.

A consideration of fibers affords an opportunity to develop some practical applications of divisible matter. Consider first a sweater made of dyed cotton. Cotton is a material that is easily fractured, and so little force is required to separate a fiber fragment from the parent piece. Once fractured, little opportunity exists to perform a physical match examination. First, finding the matching fiber on the parent piece would make it a "career case" (not a case that makes your career, but consumes it!). Second, the nature of cotton is such that very little input energy is required to change the fractured (complementary) ends, and soon they would not appear very complementary. Instead, the analyst would more likely perform some examination of the physicochemical properties of the item. Cotton is easily discerned by a polarized light microscopic exam. After that, only the dye components would be useful for further differentiating it from any other cotton fiber. The dye itself can be examined from the perspective of divisible matter, for it once was a liquid in a large vat or lot of dye that was then used to dye many pieces of cotton. It was divided from the remaining lot when absorbed onto the fiber. Its characteristics (color, chemical constituents, chemical properties) can be examined and would be indistinguishable from any other dye made with the same components. If either the sweater or the separated fiber had been exposed to some deteriorative process, such as bleaching, weathering, or washing, some chemical traits of the dye, such as its color, may have changed from the original values.

Divisible matter provides a basis for examining and interpreting similarities and differences between an evidence item and any putative source.

5.   Impression Evidence — Does Divisible Matter Apply?

Divisible matter does not account for a large category of evidence, that of pattern transfer evidence, such as prints and impressions. Although small amounts of physical matter may be transferred, it is the pattern of transfer that concerns us, not the substance. Therefore divisible matter does not apply. The transfer of matter requires its prior division; the transfer of *traits* may not.

D.   Transfer Theory (Locard)

Once matter has divided, it is "available" for transfer. Two different excerpts from Locard's writing* provide slightly different insights into his thinking on the issue of material transfer.

1.   *Il est impossible au malfaiteur d'agir, et sourtout d'agir avec l'intensite que suppose l'action criminelle sans laisser des traces de son passage.* (1920)
    It is impossible for the criminal to act, and especially to act with the force that a crime demands, without leaving behind traces of his presence.

2.   *Nul ne peut agir avec l'intensite que suppose l'action sans laisser des marques multiples de son passage, tantot le malfaiteur a laissi sur les lieux des marques de son activiti, tanto par une action inverse, il a emporti sur son corps ou sur ses vetements les indices de son sejour ou de son geste.* (1923)
    No one can act (commit a crime) with the force (intensity) that the criminal act requires without leaving behind numerous signs (marks) of it; either the wrong-doer (felon, malefactor, offender) has left signs at the scene of the crime, or on the other hand, has taken away with him — on his person (body) or clothes — indications of where he has been or what he has done.

* Translation courtesy of Sharon Kruzik.

As much as the Locard transfer theory has been invoked, no peer-reviewed literature exists that proffers it, tests it, or refutes it. It is axiomatic in forensic science; it is accepted as true without proof.

The second of the two quotes above is a more complete explication of Locard's sense of what happens during the commission of a crime. For example, he talks about transfer of material both from the criminal to the scene, as well as from the scene to the criminal. Significantly, this passage has been taken to mean that when two objects come in contact, material will be transferred in both directions *between the two objects*. That does not appear to be the plain reading of this translation. It is possible to interpret this passage to mean that different kinds of material may be transferred from the criminal to the surroundings, *or* from the surroundings to the criminal; carpet fibers may accumulate on the shoes of a criminal, yet there may be no trace of his on the carpet.

For a maxim that has been accepted as the lynchpin of forensic science for over 80 years, it is curious that no one has ever tested this theory by trying to falsify it. Of course, if it were completely false, then no physical evidence would exist to examine. Not wanting to tackle the disputatious "*Il est impossible...,*" we can say as a matter of common observation that at least some of the time, contact between two objects results in the transfer of material from one to the other. We leave as a challenge to the profession of forensic science to begin the process of testing this working hypothesis.

1.   Physical Transfer

Locard posited that when a person was engaged in the commission of a crime, the intensity of the effort dictated that traces present on the person would be left behind on anything with which he came into contact, or that he would take away something of the crime scene on his body. One alternative to the translation of the word "intensity" is "force"; the implication is that the force required to commit a crime is such that transfer of material is inevitable.

Three objects and some energy are required for transfer.

> *Object 1* — The original *source*
> *Object 2* — A *fragment* (ultimately the *evidence*) divided from the source
> *Object 3* — A *target* object onto which the fragment is transferred
> *Energy* — Some energy that facilitates movement of the fragment from the source to the target. This is typically taken to be contact between the source and the target, but it need not necessarily be so.

When the fragment is detected on the target by some responsible and authoritative person (typically but not always law enforcement), it becomes evidence. Largely unappreciated is the difference between the target and the evidence. Later we will develop a critical distinction between *individualization* (how sure we are the evidence is from a particular source) and *association* (the inference of contact between the source and the target). For now, it is important to recognize that there is more complexity to transfer than the deceptively simple statement derived from Locard.

a. Trace Evidence — Transfer of Very Small Physical Entities

Locard was particularly concerned with the transfer of trace materials, such as dust, dirt, and grime (1920; 1923; 1928; 1930; 1931–1940). In today's crime laboratory, typical trace evidence includes hairs, fibers, paint, soil, and other materials that make up the world. Trace evidence is typically characterized by the need for a microscope to characterize the material adequately, even if it can be seen by the unaided eye. These are the materials that Locard felt were most important in forensic science because the criminal would not be aware that such materials would be transferred.

b. Macroscopic Evidence — Transfer of Larger Physical Entities

Because the concept of transfer arose through the study of dusts and other microscopic material, we are used to thinking about transfer only on a microscopic scale. In fact, it is inordinately useful to consider transfer on a macroscopic scale as well. Because it is impossible to draw an arbitrary line between microscopic evidence and that which is easily visible to the naked eye, we will take the liberty of creating the term "macro-transfer" to describe this situation.

Much physical match evidence falls into this category. For instance, the scrap of paper used to write the ransom note is only one half of the original intact piece, the other half of which is still in the kidnapper's pocket. Broken glass fragments are another example of this type of evidence.

c. Factors Affecting Transfer and Detection

Several factors either promote or inhibit transfer of materials. These influence both our ability to detect crime-related materials (i.e., evidence) and our interpretation of the analytical findings. These components must be considered when assessing the strength and significance of an association:

- The *force for division* and *ease of divisibility* (fragmentation) of a material — These influence the number and size of fragments available for transfer. For example, a cotton fabric will divide much more easily than a steel door when subjected to similar forces.
- The *force for transfer* during contact and the *transferability* of the material — These determine how likely a daughter fragment will either adhere to its parent piece or be transferred to a target.

- The *abundance* of fragments transferred — The preceding factors, combined with the initial abundance, will determine how many fragments are transferred to a target.
- The *persistence* of the fragment — This refers to the ability of a fragment, once transferred from a source to a target, to adhere to the target.
- *Secondary transfer* — This refers to a fragment transferred from its source A to target B, and then transferred from target B to target C. Detecting the fragment from source A on target C leads to the inference of contact between A and C, when in fact no such contact has been made.
- *Unrelated transfer* — This refers to the possibility of fragments transferred and detected that are unrelated to the crime event.

These last two factors lead us to realize that the commission of a crime is not the only time that fragments are transferred from a source to a target. At any crime scene there is an overabundance of physical material, some related to the crime, and much that is not. Unfortunately, Locard's formulation of transfer theory ignores the consideration of objects being transferred when crimes are not being committed. This is an important limitation to be incorporated into the final inference of a putative association between a source and a target.

2.   Spatial Trait Transfer

a.   Impression Evidence

Although we are used to thinking about transfer of physical material, many criminalistic examinations deal with traits or characteristics of one item left behind on some receptive medium, rather than any transfer of actual physical material. Dermal ridge prints, shoeprints, and tire tracks all fall into this category. This may be accomplished by *impressing* the traits into the medium (e.g., a toolmark), or leaving the trait as a *print* or *track* on a substrate via yet another medium (e.g., a fingerprint left in naturals oils and perspiration from the finger). One can think of these mechanisms as transfers as well; however, in these cases traits rather than matter are transferred.

b.   Three- to Two- to One-Dimensional Transformations

In most types of trait transfer, some dimensional information is lost. For example, in a toolmark, the mechanism for producing a mark is usually the passing of a defect in the tool over some target material. This defect may be a gouge or a protrusion, and has three dimensions (Figure 4.6). When examining the mark made on the substrate, normally only one of the dimensions

Figure 4.6 Tool and mark. A toolmark is a three-dimensional impression. However, so many variables are involved in producing the mark, that only one dimension is normally used to conclude a common source between a tool and a mark left by it.

(width) is used for comparison. The length is lost in the process of producing the mark, and the depth is highly dependent on a number of factors, such as the relative hardness of the two media (source and target) and the angle between them. Thus, a three-dimensional defect is reduced to a one-dimensional mark.

In friction ridge examinations, normally only one dimension coupled with spatial information is used to compare evidence and reference prints. Some examiners will perform a more complex analysis involving the integration of pore placement and the shape of the ridges themselves. Nonetheless, the fingerprint examiner is restricted to an analysis of at most two dimensions.

Shoeprints and tire prints hold the potential for including all three dimensions, but typically this examination is done using only width and length data (two dimensions). The number of dimensions available for examination ultimately depends on whether the mark is an impression, where three-dimensional information might be retained, or a track, where some other medium (such as dust) is transferred to the target, and the dimension of depth is lost. As we have previously mentioned, some material is transferred along with the print or track, but this is usually not the item of interest. Rather, the shape of this transferred material provides more information about the source than the material itself. In the case of shoe traits transferred to a floor through the medium of dust, the medium communicates nothing about the shoe itself.

The transfer of traits does not seem to fit into Locard's writings, but we believe that this is an appropriate expansion of his philosophy. One way to think of transfer of either material or traits is at a level that unites them both, the concept that what is being transferred is *information* about the source of the evidence. Understanding the nature of the evidence allows the analyst to decide which information might be most useful in answering the relevant question(s). It may be that analysis of both the shoe print and the dust in which it is made will be useful in deciding where a particular shoe has trod. It may also occur that an incomplete fingerprint can be analyzed for its DNA content via the physiological fluids in which the print is made. When we think of transfer in terms of the information gleaned about the source of some evidence item, a new avenue of research is opened for forensic science that relies on *information theory* (Shannon, 1948). This may, for the first time, lead to some hypothesis testing of Locard's transfer theory.

E.   Summary

We reiterate that understanding the fundamental nature of matter is the essential starting point for a forensic scientist. A good grounding in chemistry and physics provides this background knowledge. This information allows for a determination of the relevant properties of a material that might be useful in answering a legal question.

In attempting to identify those principles that are unique to forensic science, we have in this chapter articulated what we believe are the two principles involved in the origin of evidence: division of matter, and transfer of the divided fragment from the source to a target. It is certainly true that division and transfer occur whether a crime is being committed or not, or whether we are aware of it or not. When applied to forensic science, however, the division and transfer of matter becomes the division and transfer of evidence. It is arguable that the amount and types of physical evidence at a crime scene are more complex now than at the turn of the century; what cannot be argued is that the simplistic view of a criminal acquiring traces from the scene and leaving some of his own behind leaves out some inherent ambiguity and complexity. Division of matter and transfer of divided material or transfer of traits provides a theoretical framework for the collection, analysis, and interpretation that occurs after a crime has been discovered.

References

Doyle, A. C., Adventures of Sherlock Holmes: The Red-headed League, *The Strand Magazine*, 1891.

Kalia, R. K. et al., Role of ultrafine microstructures in dynamic fracture in nanophase silicon nitride, *Phys. Rev. Lett.*, 78, 2144–2147, 1997.

Locard, E., *L'enquete criminelle et les methodes scientifique*, Ernest Flammarion, Paris, 1920.

Locard, E., *Manuel de Technique Policiere*, Payot, Paris, 1923.

Locard, E., Dust and its analysis, *Police J.*, 1, 177, 1928.

Locard, E., The analysis of dust traces, Part I–III, *Am. J. Police Sci.*, 1, 276, 401, 496, 1930.

Locard, E., *Traité de criminalistique*, J. Desvigne, Lyon, 1931-1940.

Shannon, C. E., A mathematical theory of communication, *Bell Syst. Tech. J.*, 27, 379–423, 623–656, 1948.

Thinkquest Chemystery page, Introduction to Thermodynamics, ref. Atkins, P., General Chemistry, 1996, available at *http://library.thinkquest.org/3659/thermodyn/intro.html*.

Thornton, J. I., The snowflake paradigm, *J. Forensic Sci.*, 31(2) 399–401, 1986.

Figure 5.1 Detection of blood with luminol. What you see depends on how you look. In this illustration, blood is invisible to the naked eye (top photograph), but searching after applying luminol in a dark room reveals both the presence and pattern of blood (bottom photograph).

Recognition of Physical Evidence

5

Contents

> The eyes see in things only what they look for, and they look only for what
> is already in the mind.
> **—Posted in the classroom of the School of Scientific Police at the Palais de
> Justice in Paris**
> **Luke S. May,** *Crime's Nemesis,* 1936

The most difficult challenge in the investigative process is the recognition of *relevant* physical evidence. Prior to any laboratory analysis, an item must be recognized as evidence in a crime or it will never be examined, much less interpreted. Ideally, the crime defines the relevant evidence. In this chapter we will explore the attributes and circumstances that combine to make something evidence and, in particular, physical evidence. We will also discuss the seemingly obvious, but sometimes complex relationship between evidence and reference. We leave a detailed discussion of the crime scene itself to Chapter 8.

A. Evidence and the Law

As discussed briefly in the Introduction to this book, forensic science has no existence outside of the law. Forensic scientists are invited by the law to assist in establishing the elements of a crime. Except for *identification evidence*, which we will meet again in Chapter 6 we do this only *indirectly* by providing *circumstantial* evidence. To reiterate part of our discussion from Chapter 1, circumstantial evidence is frequently confused with weak evidence. Attorneys, in particular, like to call any evidence that is strong and convincing *direct evidence*. For example, a quote from a recent news article reads "'There's a great deal of direct evidence,' *[the attorney] said, including DNA evidence and a confession [the suspect] made to his father and brother*" (Lavie, 1999). While the confession may or may not be true, it is still considered direct evidence. And, however rare the DNA profile is, its presence still does not prove that the suspect committed the murder, nor does it tell us when the material was deposited; it simply indicates the presence of the suspect at some time at a location connected with the crime. Depending on the circumstances of the crime, this may be very convincing, but that does not make it direct evidence.

Science may establish a fact that allows for an *inference* that the element is true, but not the fact of the element. Briefly, an inference consists of two parts, a fact and some assumptions. An inference is not a fact; it relies on facts, but it must also rely on assumptions.

> For instance, red wool fibers are found on a body dumped out in the woods. A suspect is apprehended and a red wool sweater found in his closet. The criminalist examines both items and reports to the detective that they are microscopically indistinguishable. The detective infers that the suspect is the perpetrator. Science provides the facts (indistinguishable red wool fibers); the detective provides the many assumptions (the fibers would continue to be indistinguishable by further testing, no one else has a red wool sweater with the same characteristics, the suspect wore the sweater found in his closet when he perpetrated the crime, the fibers were transferred during the commission of the crime, the fibers persisted after the crime, etc., etc., etc.) required to make the (very tenuous) inference that the fibers on the body lead to the suspect as the killer.

We discuss this important concept in more detail in Chapter 8, but for now, we emphasize that science is the only player who can contribute facts about physical evidence. Were it not for our ability to provide this service, we would quickly be uninvited to the party.

B.   The Crime, the Crime Event, and the Crime Scene

A *crime* is a violation of a statutory law. Therefore, a *crime scene* might be defined as any location or item connected with the crime. We distinguish this from the *crime event* which is the actual commission of the crime.

Recognition of evidence may occur at any time after the crime occurs. However, the interval between the crime event and securing the scene, and any further time that passes before evidence is detected, affects our ability both to recognize evidence as such and to relate it to the crime event. The simple passing of time obscures our ability to determine by whom, or in connection with what, the material was deposited in some particular location. The possibility of connecting multiple scenes also declines with time.

Additionally, the evidence item acquires a history between the crime event and the recognition of it as evidence. It is precisely during this time period that the sample is subjected to unknown and unknowable factors, creating an unbreachable void in our understanding of evidence. It defines the uncontrolled nature of case samples.

C.   What Is Evidence?

Interestingly, in the United States, at least, the law defines evidence only by its relevance. Relevant evidence is admissible; irrelevant evidence is inadmissible. The following are excerpts from Article I and Article IV of the U.S. Federal Rules of Evidence* (1999) (Figure 5.2).

Thus, it is left to science to define the conceptual nature of *physical evidence*. The material attributes of physical evidence require simply that it be detectable. This may be accomplished by human senses or enhanced by optical, physical, or chemical means. Physical evidence may be examined, compared, or analyzed by those same means. Conceptually, evidence must be associated with a crime. As interesting as it may be to examine your office conference room for fingerprints or test unknown stains in the parking lot for blood, these samples would not become evidence unless someone stole the boss's favorite coffee mug or a murder was committed outside the building. Incorporating the legal requirement, evidence must therefore provide factual information about the crime, establishing its relevance to a criminal proceeding.

> Let's take a simple example. A man walking through a park is assaulted, and a fist fight ensues. The assailant bloodies the nose of the victim. The victim reports the assault to the police, who eventually apprehend a suspect. The clothing of both are collected, and the police enlist the aid of the scientist to determine whether the suspect is in fact the assailant. The testimony of the victim, the testimony of the suspect, any eyewitness accounts, and the clothing collected from both persons involved might all be considered relevant

* The Uniform Rules of Evidence (1988) are very similar to the Federal Rules of Evidence. They have begun to be adopted by states to accomplish a goal of standardization.

United States Federal Rules of Evidence

ARTICLE I
GENERAL PROVISIONS

Rule 104(b). Relevancy conditioned on fact.

When the relevancy of evidence depends upon the fulfillment of a condition of fact, the court shall admit it upon, or subject to, the introduction of evidence sufficient to support a finding of the fulfillment of the condition.

ARTICLE IV
RELEVANCY AND ITS LIMITS

Rule 401. Definition of "Relevant Evidence"

"Relevant evidence" means evidence having any tendency to make the existence of any fact that is of consequence to the determination of the action more probable or less probable than it would be without the evidence.

Rule 402. Relevant Evidence Generally Admissible; Irrelevant Evidence Inadmissible

All relevant evidence is admissible, except as otherwise provided by the Constitution of the United States, by Act of Congress, by these rules, or by other rules prescribed by the Supreme Court pursuant to statutory authority. Evidence which is not relevant is not admissible.

Rule 403. Exclusion of Relevant Evidence on Grounds of Prejudice, Confusion, or Waste of Time

Although relevant, evidence may be excluded if its probative value is substantially outweighed by the danger of unfair prejudice, confusion of the issues, or misleading the jury, or by considerations of undue delay, waste of time, or needless presentation of cumulative evidence.

Figure 5.2 Article I and Article IV.

evidence under the law. However, only the clothing comprises physical evidence. It is tangible, so we can examine and analyze it; it is associated with a crime by virtue of being worn by the victim or assailant; its relevance can only be established after it is examined and analyzed. The simple fact of its presence on the participants probably does not help to establish any facts about the crime; the presence of bloodstains, fibers, or damage might.

1.   The Search for Evidence

Some types of evidence patently relate to the criminal event. Blood from a stabbing, bullets from a deceased person, or broken glass from a burglary, clearly derive from the crime incident and are readily discerned. The recognition of such evidence is usually accomplished simply by looking. But for other types of evidence, the connection to the crime is not necessarily obvious. We each lose hundreds of hairs a day (some of us more than others), so the finding of human hair almost anywhere is predictable. The finding of human hairs at a crime scene is therefore expected, whether or not the hairs bear any relation to the crime. The presence of hairs that appear to have been forcibly removed immediately suggests increased relevance to the crime; bloody clumps of hair increase that relevance exponentially.

> The case of *People v. Axell* involved the stabbing murder of a convenience store clerk by an unknown female. The victim was found clutching 10 anagen* hairs in his fist, a circumstance consistent with the victim having pulled the hair from someone's head during a struggle. Because anagen hairs must be forcibly removed from the scalp, it is reasonable to infer that a clump of hair clutched in the hand of a murder victim is related to the assault that killed him. DNA analysis of the hairs by RFLP** showed genetic concordance between the evidence hairs and a reference sample from Linda Axell. While the DNA analysis was vital to increasing the strength of the evidence by virtually individualizing the hairs to Linda Axell, their significance in the context of the crime was determined wholly by circumstance. The hairs were determined to be relevant to the homicide by virtue of their location (his hand) and by their apparent state as pulled hairs. If they weren't, the results of the DNA analysis would have been less significant in the context of the crime (and probably impossible at the time!).***

Remember that the law asks the relevant question. Whether it is asked by a detective, a criminalist, or an attorney, the elements of a crime must be

---

* Anagen hairs are in a growth phase and would not be expected to fall out easily.
** Restriction fragment length polymorphism, the first DNA technique to be widely used and accepted.
*** RFLP analysis requires follicular material to be present on the hair root. Fallen telogen hairs are usually not amenable to RFLP testing.

proved; this defines the purpose of the investigation and, by extension, the examination of the crime scene. The legal question also impacts what will ultimately be considered evidence. That we can ascertain all the evidence that exists just by looking runs counter to the entire evolution of detective work. Just looking does not work; *looking with purpose*, or *searching*, is central to a competent investigation. To search effectively, the investigator must discern what evidence might reasonably be relevant to the crime or he will waste inordinate amounts of time searching aimlessly.

Whether we are aware of it or not, we constantly form provisional hypotheses about life as well as about crimes. I assume that the train will arrive at the station at exactly at 8:14 A.M. Therefore, if I get there at exactly 8:13, I will even have a chance to grab a cup coffee before boarding the train. My hypothesis is based on the fact that the train always arrives on time or late, and on my assumption that this pattern will continue today. Similarly, I assume that I will find my keys hanging on the hook next to the door when I go to leave the house. This is based on the fact that I usually place the keys there upon entering, and the assumption that I did that last time I entered, and that neither I nor anyone else has moved them in the meantime. Without these provisional hypotheses, we would not be able to function in life; each decision would require starting from neutral, with all possibilities equally probable. We need not try to eliminate preconception, but to identify our hypotheses and the assumptions on which they are based. We can then use this information to guide our actions, and we can change our hypotheses when new information is presented to us.

When presented with the aftermath of a criminal event, the goal of law enforcement is to solve the crime and charge the guilty party in the most efficient and expeditious way possible. Thus, the investigator in charge of the scene must determine what crime has been committed, what are the legal elements, and what evidence he expects to find. Immediately following recognition of the crime, the investigator will learn information that will lead to a preliminary hypothesis. The challenge presented to an investigator is to determine what evidence exists. At the same time, he must consider the question of what evidence *should* exist given that this crime occurred. These complementary notions are based on the *expectation* of the investigator (or the criminalist, if given access to the scene). To harbor an expectation, we require information about the crime. In other words, we must anticipate what physical manifestations we expect as a consequence of that event.

For instance, the crime is murder, the *modus operandi* is similar to a string of other crimes, and it occurred at the known headquarters of a local gang. It is not unusual to develop a prime suspect quite early in the investigation based on information that has accumulated in police files. The investigator will then direct the search for evidence *assuming that this crime was committed by this person.* While a provisional hypothesis is necessary to process a crime scene and begin the search for evidence, the investigator must also be willing to update his hypothesis based on new information. At some point, we become convinced that no piece of information will change our hypothesis about what happened.

The scientist has tried to define her role apart from the law and usually feels some obligation to maintain the same objectivity that characterizes her other scientific work. This does not imply that she holds no preconceptions; however, she may approach the scene with competing hypotheses rather than a single hypothesis. For instance, what evidence do I expect to find assuming either (1) *this crime was committed by this person* or (2) *this crime was committed by some other person.* If it is accepted that we can and should look with purpose, then we must ensure that one of the purposes is to search for inculpatory evidence (evidence that supports our primary hypothesis) as well as exculpatory evidence (evidence that supports some other hypothesis).

The environment in which evidence is found must be taken into consideration before we determine its relevance to the crime. Like hair, fibers are ubiquitous in our environment, and their presence at a crime scene is expected. Simply detecting a particular fiber, or even finding matching fibers in reference and evidence samples does not *a priori* imply their connection to the crime. The case of *People v. Morin* (Commission on Proceedings Involving Guy Paul Morin, 1998), illustrates how easily one can become misled by failing to consider the circumstances of the case. Fibers prove particularly difficult in this respect and we must take great care to understand their relevance to a crime clearly and completely.

> In *Morin*, fibers were collected from the body of a murdered girl and also from the suspect's car and house. Thousands of fibers were collected and a few were selected that appeared to be shared between the body (a known crime scene), the car (a suspected crime scene), and the house (a reference environment for the suspect). Only after two trials and a judicial inquiry was it clarified that the two families were neighbors, were occasionally in each other's houses and cars, and used the same laundromat. The judge conducting the inquiry opined that the fibers should never have been collected as their value from the start was worthless due to the shared environments of the victim and suspect. That most of the matching fibers were later suspected to have originated from contamination in the laboratory is another matter.

We emphasize that *searching* for evidence involves a different thought process than *interpreting* evidence. The former is deductive — we formulate a theory based on previous experiences and information and use this working hypothesis to help us know where to look. The philosophy and mind-set of searching for evidence may upset some of you as it specifically transposes the conditional (we condition on the hypothesis rather than the evidence) and thus flies in the face of Bayesian thinking. But to interpret evidence, we must have some, and successful searching requires presumptions, expectations, and preliminary hypotheses. In contrast, interpreting evidence uses inductive reasoning — we synthesize all the evidence, including the results of examinations and analyses — and develop a theory of the case. We suggest that the Bayesian logic is most appropriate and helpful in the *interpretation* of evidence. We discuss this topic in gory detail in Chapters 6 and 7.

2.   The State of the Evidence

A crime scene and all of the evidence in it are subject to the effects of time and environment. We will discuss the dynamic crime scene and its implications for collection and preservation of evidence in Chapter 8. For now, we simply relate the implications of change over time to the recognition of evidence at a crime scene.

As objects were not fixed in some state before the crime event, neither do they become frozen in time for the convenience of the investigator and the analyst. In Chapter 4 we discussed how divisible matter and transfer work to generate evidence. The moment material becomes evidence as silent witness to a crime, environmental influences commence to change it from its original form. The evidence continues to change and evolve subject to biotic and nonbiotic forces; it does not discriminate between intent and happenstance.

The changes to biological evidence are most readily apparent. A bloodstain deposited on a painted wall inside a house will initially be wet and quite red. Subject to biochemical reactions within the blood itself and to a gaseous environment, it will clot and dry. Further exposure to air will provoke oxidation of the heme molecules in the blood, and the stain will turn darker and darker red, finally acquiring a brownish tinge. The same bloodstain deposited on a sidewalk will additionally be subjected to the diurnal influences of the sun and relatively large temperature fluctuations. It may go from red to black in a short period of time. Rain or a stray step may disintegrate the stain altogether, leaving no trace that it ever existed. At what point do we fail to recognize it as evidence? At what point do we fail to recognize it as blood? At what point do we fail to recognize it at all?

Nonbiological physical evidence also exhibits change due to time and physical influences. For instance, a bullet can change dramatically between its expulsion from the barrel of a gun and its excavation from a wall by a firearms expert. The bullet may have passed through a body, possibly acquiring biological material or damage as a result of deflecting off bone. Its entrance into the wall may further alter its overall shape and potentially obliterate microstriae. Alternatively, the bullet may explode or be shattered into many small pieces, or it may become lodged in the body and never exit. Both the bullet and any casings may accumulate debris if either they or the scene remain undiscovered for some time. These alterations can confound our attempts to recognize the items and relate them directly to the crime.

Similarly, a piece of colored paper left at a crime scene may become bleached by exposure to the sun, altering its color; it may get wet and dry again, altering its texture; it may blow away with the wind, challenging us to both find it and recognize it as evidence. If we are searching for the paper using the other half of an extortion letter as a reference, the writing on the paper may have become faded and smudged. If it was written in "invisible ink," it may not be visible at all until we can find it and examine it with that purpose in mind.

All of these circumstances challenge our ability to recognize and recover evidence at the scene. They also potentially confound our ability to eventually connect evidence and reference samples. We discuss the criteria we use to conclude that two items share the same source in Chapter 6. In particular we address *explainable differences*, one of the most basic tenets of forensic science, and without which we could not function as forensic analysts. We also discuss implications of the *absence of evidence* in Chapter 7.

D.   Evidence and Reference

A characteristic aspect of forensic science that differentiates it from all other applications of science is the comparison of evidence samples to reference samples. This criterion was recognized by at least one judge in attempting to determine the qualification of a defense expert to comment on forensic casework (*People v. Maclanahan*, 1998). The relationship between an evidence item and a reference item is operational. Like everything else, it depends on the question. A bloodstain on the sheet of a murder-rape victim functions as an evidence item until we verify that the source is the victim. It may be used as a secondary reference with which to compare blood on a suspect's pants 20 years later. Nevertheless, for most kinds of evidence (as used colloquially), the correlation between an evidence item and a reference item is pretty obvious. It is hard to mistake the spent cartridges at the scene of a shooting as anything other than evidence samples and the cartridges cycled through the suspect weapon's action are clearly reference samples. The paint transferred to a car's fender is clearly an evidence item and the car from which it came a reference item, regardless of who was at fault.

Less evident, perhaps, is which item, evidence or reference, one should use to define the traits on which to base a comparison. In large part, this judgment impacts decisions you will make during analysis, and a correct understanding is also crucial to the reasoned collection of evidence at the scene. In particular, the concepts are helpful to understand the connection of trace evidence both to the scene and to possible reference samples. Because hair and fibers are ubiquitous in our environment, it is often difficult to determine which, if any, relate to the crime and which are simply adventitious. In desperation, the criminalist will sometimes survey the suspect and his environment (house, car, employment) for reference material, and then look at the crime scene samples for matching evidence. Stoney (1984) has made the case that this is backward; defining the relevant hairs, particles, or fibers by looking for reference material in crime scene evidence emphasizes the reference rather than the evidence. By focusing on reference samples gathered according to a particular suspect, we ignore the possibility that the trace material may be adventitiously associated with the crime, or that some other reference is the source; worse yet, we may miss detecting some truly relevant trace evidence. The most relevant evidence is that which is patently related to the crime event. Items adjudged to be evidence by first surveying the environment of a suspect interject an element of bias into both the investigation and the analysis. Criteria for concluding the evidentiary value of trace material include abundance, rareness, and lack of representation in the victim's environment. This process is perhaps the ultimate challenge in the recognition of evidence.

E.   Summary

The law defines the relevance of physical evidence. Physical evidence that does not require an inference to establish a legal fact in the case is direct evidence; identification evidence is direct evidence. Classified and individualized evidence both require inference to establish their relevance; this is the definition of circumstantial evidence. We expand on the concept of inference in Chapter 6, and especially in Chapter 7.

The most critical aspects of any physical evidence analysis are (1) its physical detection and (2) its recognition as evidence relevant to the case. Without this starting point, any laboratory examination may be, at best, impossible, at worst, irrelevant (or maybe it is the other way around). To find relevant evidence, one must search with purpose; the articulation of competing hypotheses is a useful tool in the endeavor. Physical evidence left as a result of a crime event may not be in the same state that it was the moment the incident occurred. Those who search for evidence must be familiar with the nature of various types of evidence, and how it may change and degrade with time and exposure to the elements.

References

Commission on Proceedings Involving Guy Paul Morin, The Honourable Fred Kaufman, C.M., Q.C., Queen's Printer for Ontario, 1998, available at *http://www.attorneygeneral.jus.gov.on.ca/reports.htm*.

Federal Rules of Evidence, Legal Information Institute, Cornell Law School, 1999, available at *http://www.law.cornell.edu/rules/fre/overview.html*.

Lavie, M., The Associated Press, Tel Aviv, Israel, July 5, 1999, available at *http://abcnews.go.com/sections/world/DailyNews/sheinbein990705.html*.

May, L. S., *Crime's Nemesis*, Macmillan, New York, 1936.

People v. Axell, 235 Cal.App. 3d 836, 1991.

People v. Maclanahan, San Francisco SCN 16241, California, 1998.

Stoney, D. A., Evaluation of associative evidence: choosing the relevant question, *J. Forensic Sci. Soc.*, 24, 472–482, 1984.

Uniform Rules of Evidence, Biddle Law Library, University of Pennsylvania, 1988, available at *http://www.law.upenn.edu/bll/ulc/fnact99/ure88.htm*.

Figure 6.1 The burglar. Every criminalist yearns for evidence that yields a wealth of information with little analysis. Such appears to be the case with a photograph ascribed to either Edmund Locard or Alphonse Bertillon. Intricate details can be seen for items such as the buttons on the vest and the weapon in one hand. The missing little finger on the other hand should also provide a useful clue to the identity of the phantom. Alas, Duayne Dillon (1998) reveals that this evidence is too good to be true; he documents the appearance of this photograph in at least five books, each with differing descriptions of its provenance. According to these various accounts, an apparent burglar either fell/stumbled/leaped into clay/mud/sand/dust. The resulting impression was cast in some unknown medium. This hoax deserved some investigative work of its own, with the results presented at a "Last Word Society" meeting at an AAFS meeting.

Classification, Identification, and Individualization — Inference of Source

6

The chemical composition between the two was found to be ... **I–DENTICAL!**.

—Jim Trotter III
D.A. in the movie My Cousin Vinnie, played by Lane Smith

A. The Relationship of Evidence to Source

In *Crime Investigation* (1953), Kirk suggests that the central task of the criminal investigator is to establish personal identity. He continues to say that supplementary to this task is the identification of physical objects that may, in turn, contribute to the desired personal identification. Kirk outlines the issues and difficulties inherent in the endeavor to establish personal identity through clues provided by physical evidence. In this chapter, we continue that discussion.

In Chapter 3 we introduced the concept that identification and individualization are each legitimate goals in a forensic analysis. Historically, the word *identification* has had two meanings: one dealt with defining the nature of a substance, while another implied the failure to individualize. We think that each meaning is an important concept in forensic science and so have adopted two words to communicate these separate intentions. While acknowledging that in some instances usage may indeed overlap, we offer the following definitions:

> *Identification*: Defining the physicochemical nature of an evidence item (without a specific reference item).
> *Classification*: Inferring multiple potential common sources for an evidence item.
> *Individualization*: Concluding a singular common source for two items.

Because the objective of identification defines an end point in and of itself, we depict this route as a bifurcation from the path leading to individualization (Figure 3.2). Both identification and individualization are concepts essential to the practice of criminalistics. Which of the two is invoked depends on the legal question as well as the attributes of the evidence. Classification, on the other hand, becomes an end point by default rather than by design. We set out with a goal to individualize and because of some limitation imposed by either the evidence or the test, we fail to narrow the source item to a category of one. Although we may not succeed in individualizing, we can restrict the category to which the evidence belongs and define the characteristics of items in that category. This results in classification.

In this chapter we address that aspect of forensic science that virtually defines it, the process of comparing an evidence and reference sample and forming a conclusion about their relationship. We start with classification — a process that either results in identification or proceeds to individualization — then continue with identification, the unrecognized hero of the criminal justice system. We conclude with a discussion of individualization. But first, we make a brief digression to discuss a couple of themes common to any forensic comparison.

1. Principle, Process, or Objective

In the last chapter, we introduced the idea that classification, identification, and individualization all depend on understanding the fundamental nature of matter or, for our purposes, the *nature of the evidence*. In this chapter, we expand on the generation of material characteristics and the qualities of those characteristics that allow identification or source determination. The process of individualization leads to a conclusion of common source resulting from analytical similarities between two items, usually a reference sample and an evidence sample. Writers such as Kirk (1953; 1974) and Tuthill (1994) treat individualization as a principle, but it seems to us that individualization is a *process* that relies on the principles of chemistry and physics directed to a specific end.

2.   The Question of Source

Both classification and individualization attempt to answer the question of source. Rarely explicated, however, is the distinction between a conclusion of source for classification and a conclusion of source for individualization. Classification allows for multiple source items; the evidence may derive from source A, but it could also have come from source X, Y, or Z, all of which are indistinguishable from source A by the tests employed. The implication of multiple potential sources is perhaps underappreciated by both students and practitioners of criminalistics and often is not adequately conveyed to attorneys. It is not only that several or many items belong to the same class as the evidence and reference, it is that we cannot distinguish from which of these potential sources the evidence originated.

In addition, the *level of source* must be defined by the question. This is determined by the legal requirements necessary to satisfy an element of a crime. To clarify what we mean, let's take an example of carpet fibers.

> It may be sufficient to determine that the evidence is a carpet fiber. It may be sufficient to show that it is a polyester carpet fiber. It may be sufficient to show that it is a polyester carpet fiber manufactured by DuPont®. It may be sufficient to show that it is a green carpet fiber manufactured by DuPont in 1977. It may be sufficient to show that it is from 10,000 yards of green carpet fiber manufactured by DuPont in 1977. It may be sufficient to show that it is a green carpet fiber manufactured by DuPont in 1977 and that it was distributed to 15 vehicle carpet installers. It may be sufficient to show that it is a green carpet fiber manufactured by DuPont in 1977 that was distributed to 15 carpet manufacturers, and that one of them installed 10 square feet in a specific van in 1978. Or you may need to know that it is a green carpet fiber manufactured by DuPont in 1977, that it was installed in a specific van in 1978, and that it came from just behind the driver's seat of the van as opposed to the area by the rear door.

If the question revolves around showing that the fiber came from a carpet rather than a garment, it is only necessary to show that it is a carpet fiber, a relatively simple proposition. If, on the other hand, the case turns on whether this bloodstained carpet fiber came from just behind the driver's seat of the van as opposed to the area by the rear door, the analyst must consider whether such a determination is even possible. The circumstances and the legal needs of the case determine the level of source required.

B.   Classification — Categorization with Like Items

Before the analyst can even decide whether classification or individualization is the goal, he must have some idea of the type of material being examined.

The first level of examination involves nothing more than human sensory perception. Is it a solid, liquid, or gas? How big is it? What color is it? What shape is it? What is its texture? What are its obvious optical qualities? Does it have an odor? What does it sound like?* Although the days when scientists took a judicious whiff from a can to determine if it contained a flammable liquid or used the tactile method to detect semen stains on bedsheets are long past, a thoughtful preliminary assessment of the sample is still required.

We are reminded of a student who gave a presentation on the analysis of paint. She was so dazzled by the sophisticated, instrumental methods for paint analysis, such as pyrolysis GC-MS and FTIR, that she never even thought to simply look at it with her eyes, never mind a microscope, to determine its color. It is not necessary to do a DNA analysis to put an elephant in a different category than a turnip. In addition to human senses, simple chemical, physical, and optical tests can be very useful in delimiting the class of substances to which an item belongs. What does it look like under low-power or higher-power magnification? How much does it weigh? Is it organic or inorganic? Is it soluble or insoluble in certain solvents? How does it react to certain presumptive tests? These are all tools that help us classify unknown substances or objects.

Because the process of classification relies on our ability to place materials into categories, we must know something about the characteristics common to any particular class of objects. To do this, we must understand the properties of these *class characteristics*, their mode of creation, and the limitations of any conclusions based solely on them.

1.   Class Characteristics

We begin by reviewing several definitions of class characteristics compiled from the literature. The authors' choices of very different language to describe similar observations about the class characteristics of shoes serves as a reasonable starting point for this discussion. Osterburg (1968) describes them as obvious, gross features distinguishable in an object. Cassidy (1980) was more specific in describing them as the size, shape, style, and pattern of an object, all created during their manufacture, and Bodziak (1990) explains

---

* Although electronic evidence such as audio or video recordings are not generally processed by most crime laboratories, they frequently comprise important evidence in a case and are sent out to be examined by specialists. Because electronic playback devices are necessary to even hear or see them, they strictly involve more than just our sense of hearing. Testimonial evidence, such as a confession, would require just human senses, but is not something most analysts would encounter. Another example involving sound is the determination of whether a gunshot could have been heard at some distance under particular conditions. This might involve the use of a decibel meter.

that they are intentional or unavoidable characteristics that repeat during the manufacturing process and are shared by one or more other shoes.

Extending that thinking to other objects, items exhibiting similar characteristics, as detected by the tests performed, comprise a class defined by those characteristics. We can perform a visual test on all of the pencils in a large office. Yellow pencils form a large class, yellow #2 pencils may form a subset of that class, and yellow #2 pencils with erasers make up an even smaller category. All pencils that are some color other than yellow, a different grade from #2, or lack erasers are excluded from the third and smallest class.

We arrive at a definition of class characteristics:

> *Class Characteristics:*
> Traits that are produced by a controlled process.
> They are used to group like objects into sets.

The traits that determine class characteristics are intrinsic to the material itself; without these traits, the object or material would be something else. For example, a pencil with graphite tightly embedded into the middle of a piece of cedar is known as a wooden pencil; a pencil with reloadable graphite sticks is known as a mechanical pencil. While both might be classified on one level as pencils, we have no difficulty further refining the classification into wooden pencils and mechanical pencils. We would not confuse the two (although we might not be able to differentiate writing made with one or the other).

One consequence of classifying something as belonging to a particular group containing similar items is that we exclude it from other groups. At its most trivial, this means that by classifying something as a hair, we exclude it from the class of trucks. In other words, classification is just as important for what it excludes as for what it includes. More pragmatically, if an analyst can say that the hair belongs to the category containing cat hair, it is, by definition, excluded from the class containing human hair. Classification can answer important questions and allows some intelligent decisions to be made on the basis of the determination. The classification as a cat hair may also raise other questions that were not issues before the analysis; for instance, can the hair be traced to the victim's cat? The foregoing also suggests an analytical approach to the classification of materials; if you cannot prove what it is, prove what it is not.

a.   Class Characteristics Result from a Controlled Generation Process

Class characteristics always originate as a result of some repetitive generation process. This process can be either mechanical or biological. Because the production of the material is controlled either by nature or by humans, all items that originate as a result of this process will exhibit the same class characteristics. Cocaine produced in coca plants, shoes manufactured from a mold in a shoe plant, and gross rifling characteristics in the barrels of a particular make and model of gun, all result from processes that produce more than one item with similar traits. As they are produced or manufactured, they are indistinguishable by the traits conferred by that process. For instance, the cocaine molecules from all coca plants are easily identified as cocaine by their chemical structure; the shoes from a single mold can all be traced by their tread pattern, including any defects in the mold; and the gross rifling characteristics of a gun barrel derive directly from the tool and process used to imprint them. These reproducible traits are exploited by the analyst to classify objects and substances in the laboratory.

Scale of detection imposes an unavoidable limit on the reproducibility of class characteristics. Even items produced by the same process can be distinguished by microcharacteristics if one looks closely enough. By their nature, microcharacteristics cannot be controlled because they result from random events. These fortuitous differences in manufacture or generation are one source of the individualizing characteristics that we discuss later in this chapter. Examples include differences in the microstriae of consecutively manufactured gun barrels, bubble formation in polyurethane-blown shoe molds, and mutations during DNA replication that might produce mutant cocaine molecules.

b. *Items with the Same Class Characteristics May Have Different Origins*

Perhaps obvious, but worth exploring, are the implications of the one-evidence-from-many-possible-sources conclusion inherent in class evidence. (Figure 6.2). Because multiple source items exist, any one of them could be a potential source of some matching evidence item. For instance, millions of tires may be cast from a single mold, all having the same width and tread design. Frequently, these are the only characteristics that we can discern from a tire track. Based only on these class characteristics, any one of those millions of tires (or at least the thousands in the geographic area at the time) could be the source of the track.

We began this discussion with the class characteristics of shoes and their prints. Consider the following hypothetical:

A partial shoeprint is found in dust. The print contains some detailed characteristics from the shoe, including width (but not length), the logo of the shoe, and some tread detail. By doing some research, we find out that a shoe with these class characteristics has a polyurethane sole and was

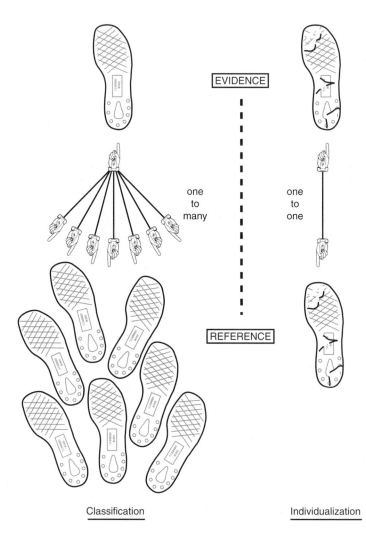

Figure 6.2 One to many; one to one. When only class characteristics are present in an evidence item, it is not possible to determine a single source for it. The evidence item could also originate from many other objects with indistinguishable class characteristics. Therefore, one evidence item could have many possible sources (classification). When an evidence item shows several individualizing traits, the analyst may conclude that only one object could be the source of the evidence. The analyst believes that only one object with indistinguishable individualizing traits exists. In this circumstance, the evidence item has only one possible source (individualization). It is interesting to note that we virtually never compare an evidence item to its putative source, but rather to a known reference from that source: a bullet from a gun, a print from a finger, a blood sample from a person.

manufactured by the Shoes-'R-Us Company for 16 months, after which the molds were destroyed. They tell us that approximately 10,000 of these shoes were made in sizes corresponding to the measured width.

A possible suspect is developed, and investigation uncovers a pair of size 14 shoes of this make and style in his closet. Comparison to the reference print made with the suspect's right shoe shows concordance with all of the class characteristics visible in the evidence print. Assuming no individualizing traits are evident, what can we say about the relationship of the suspect's shoe and the evidence print?

In this not-uncommon situation, it is incumbent upon the analyst to clarify both the hypothesis and the alternative hypothesis, and to consider the evidence in light of both. The hypothesis is that the suspect's shoe is the source of the print; an alternative hypothesis is that some other shoe bearing these class characteristics is the source of the print. Any conclusion about the relationship of the shoe and the print must communicate not only the information about the match, but its limitations, and at least an estimate of its strength. Without all of these elements, the conclusion is at best incomplete, at worst misleading.

Sometimes, we need to consider a hierarchy of class characteristics. For instance, clay mined for pottery will be distributed from the quarry to many different pottery factories. Consequently, the pottery pieces from all of the factories will exhibit similar class characteristics when analyzed for mineral composition. Mass-produced pieces from each different manufacturer may also acquire an additional set of class characteristics particular to molds or paints used at a certain location. Firearms examiners have identified these kinds of traits in certain types of barrel manufacture, and have termed them *subclass characteristics* (Nichols, 1997). Thornton has also discussed this issue and its value to the forensic examiner (Thornton, 1986b).

Determination of source depends both on the question and the state of the evidence. Suppose we have an entire pot with a very intricate relief design characteristic of a single pottery manufacturer. With this information, we could answer questions about where the pot was made and from which quarry the clay originated. In contrast, suppose we have only a small fragment of broken pottery. No other pieces of the pot are available. Although we might trace the clay back to the quarry, we would be unable to place the fragment in the smaller class of pots from one particular manufacturer.

c.   *When Is Evidence Class Evidence?*

Because a class can contain as few as two members, just about any type of evidence may be encountered as class evidence. Even potentially individualizing evidence must still be treated as class evidence if individualizing traits are not available for comparison in both the reference and evidence samples.

All types of trace evidence must frequently be treated as class evidence. Fibers, even if rare or unusual, are manufactured in quantity, and therefore are not individualizable strictly by composition. Hairs, as examined microscopically, make for some of the weakest class evidence. In fact, many analysts believe that hairs should only be used as exclusionary evidence. In the absence of a physical match or some extremely unusual characteristic, glass can only be assigned to a relatively large class. Paints and polymers are class evidence by composition; however, the presence of layers introduces the possibility of individualization. The gross rifling characteristics of firearms and fresh-from-the-factory tools only provide class evidence. Finally, serological blood grouping only provides class characteristics, although the class can be narrowed quite substantially using a combination of several markers.

C.   Identification

Because individualization is perceived as the ultimate goal of a forensic examination, the inability to individualize is sometimes equated with failure. This is unfortunate, for it overlooks aspects of criminalistics that unquestionably make up the largest volume of the forensic community's work. Recall that identification classifies materials into categories where more than one object shares the same characteristics. These could be yellow pencils, .22 caliber cartridges, size 9 shoes, or all heroin molecules. The reader can, no doubt, think of many similar examples.

We have mentioned several times that identification frequently suffices to meet a legal standard of proof. This is evident in crimes that involve illicit substances, namely, drugs, where mere possession of specified chemicals is deemed illegal; one need only demonstrate that a class of molecules known as heroin is present. Another example is the assessment of DUI (driving under the influence) where the finding of a particular concentration of alcohol in a person's blood, breath, or urine, by definition, legally prohibits the operation of a motor vehicle. The molecules of ethyl alcohol in the person's system are the same as any other molecules of ethyl alcohol; it is their presence above a predetermined concentration while driving that is illegal. Interestingly, these limited situations are the only time that physical evidence can be considered *direct evidence* as opposed to *circumstantial evidence*. The mere finding of cocaine is direct evidence of criminality; the fact-finder requires no inference or assumption to reach this conclusion.

D.   Individualization

In "The Ontogeny of Criminalistics," Kirk (1963) proffers individualization as that unique aspect of criminalistics that establishes it as a discipline in its own right. While not all evidence is either potentially or necessarily individualizable, the concept remains the hallmark of our profession. To the extent that naming a material satisfies the law, identification is invoked. When the objective is to establish the source of an object, the process of individualization must be used. We spend the remainder of this chapter exploring the questions and assumptions, the pitfalls and quagmires, that we encounter in the process of individualization.

1. A Conclusion of Common Source

Criminalists today agree that the goal of individualization is an inference of singular common source. That is, two objects are concluded to share a common origin if they were at one time contiguous (physical matching) or if they both originate from the same unique source. Examples include evidence and reference bullets fired from the same weapon, evidence and reference prints from the same shoe, and pieces of paper that were once one. Implied is the expectation that no other source could have produced both items. This defines the key difference between individualization and classification. When a substance or object is classified, multiple sources remain possible; when it is individualized, the number of possible sources is narrowed to one. The distinction between classification and individualization can be summarized as *one-to-many* vs. *one-to-one* (see Figure 6.2). Note that these phrases describe the *relationship* between source and item, not any physical attribute of an object or substance itself.

2. Individuality and Uniqueness

Before we can understand individualization, we must explore the relationship between individuality and uniqueness and address the requirements necessary to claim uniqueness. Most laypersons, and perhaps even a majority of scientists, accept the concept of uniqueness at face value. It is imperative to appreciate that this view, while eminently reasonable, constitutes a leap of faith. Our belief that uniqueness is both attainable and existent is central to our work as forensic scientists. But we must be clear that it is a belief, not a fact. Not only has it not been proved, it is unprovable. In the language of science, the theory of uniqueness is not falsifiable (Popper, 1962). Nevertheless, because we rely on certain corollaries that follow from a presumption of uniqueness, it is worth clarifying both our assumptions and the relationship of individuality to uniqueness.

a. Existent Objects Are Unique

What do we really mean when we say an item is unique? Basic physics tells us that two objects cannot occupy the same space at the same time. Hayakawa

(1939) said it more whimsically as "Cow 1 is not cow 2." Thus, by definition all objects in the universe are subject to different local microenvironments. Even two objects that were once one and then separated, such as torn pieces of fabric or broken pieces of glass, now each occupy exclusive space and may undergo independent changes rendering them dissimilar to any other object. From this standpoint, all existent objects qualify as unique.

b. The Generation of Individual Characteristics

Another aspect of uniqueness concerns the generation of physical objects. We have previously introduced the idea that objects may be produced by nature or manufactured by the hand of man.

i.   Generation by nature.   The Belgian statistician Quetelet is acknowledged as one of the first to comment on the diversity exhibited by nature. His aphorism that "Nature exhibits an infinite variety of forms" (Thornton, 1986a) supports the cornerstone of our belief in human individuality. As we reviewed in Chapter 2, Bertillon based the first organized system of personal identification on Quetelet's theories. Thornton (1986a) points out that Quetelet's original remark has been transmogrified through the years into "Nature never repeats herself." This takes the concept one step farther and may or may not have been Quetelet's original intent. Nevertheless, it is clear that nature's factory generates both class characteristics, as we discussed above, and individual characteristics. Individual characteristics result from random variation. In living organisms this is constrained to nondetrimental alterations; in abiotic material, no such constraints apply. Examples of random patterns resulting from biological processes include grain and coloration in wood,* DNA mutations,** and fingerprint minutiae*** (Figure 6.3). Examples of random patterns resulting from purely chemical or mechanical processes include the deposition of layers in sedimentary rock, erosion of ice by water, and the often-mentioned formation of individual snowflakes.

---

* The growth of "tree rings," which ultimately determine wood grain, occurs on a seasonal basis, but is highly dependent on climactic conditions, nutrition, and other factors. Although it was once thought that one could tell the age of a tree just from counting the rings, this is no longer considered reliable. The myriad of factors influencing the number, width, and color of the rings, and the asymmetric nature of tree trunks in general, combine to make wood grain a highly random characteristic. The Lindbergh case is an excellent example of how this individualizing characteristic was used to good advantage (Koehler, 1973; Palenik in Saferstein, 1998).

** Both sequence and length mutations accumulate freely in the "non-coding" regions of any genome (Lewin, 1997).

*** Although the gross pattern of a fingerprint is determined genetically, the minutiae, upon which fingerprint comparison is based, appear to form randomly during embryological development (Ashbaugh, 1996).

ii.   Generation by man.   Uniqueness in manmade items is acquired in a slightly different manner. The first objects crafted by human hands were all different from each other. As hard as a craftsperson might try to produce 10 clay pots of the same size and shape, limitations in hand production will always preclude absolute uniformity. Because hand-formed objects have become increasingly rare, they are now more expensive than their machine counterparts, and we value their uniqueness. Over the last century, machine production of all types of things has become both common and expected. Items produced by machine are more uniform and mass production has reduced their cost. However, for the criminalist, this means that it is becoming harder and harder to, for example, identify individualizing characteristics in two synthetic fibers that have just come through the holes of a spinneret, or two screwdrivers that have just come out of a forge or stamp. For mass-produced items, individualizing characteristics are acquired mostly by use, wear, or exposure to different environmental conditions. For example, shoe soles acquire unique gouges and cuts as they are worn; the screwdriver may acquire indentations and deformations from both intended and unintended use.

iii.   Entropy and disorder.   In Chapter 4, we introduced the idea that individual traits are a direct consequence of entropy, the tendency of the universe to move toward disorder. Order is imparted during the manufacture of an object, whether it is a plant making cocaine or a machine making a gun barrel. Objects made in the same way will acquire comparable characteristics; these are *class characteristics*. The level of similarity depends on the amount of control exerted during manufacture. The less control that is exerted over the manufacturing process, the greater the dissimilarity allowed, and on a larger scale. Tool machining is a good example. A slotted screwdriver need only be flat and fit into the head of a slotted screw. Fairly large tolerances are acceptable for this purpose. The existence of microstriae does not affect its primary performance as a screwdriver, nor do even minor imperfections in the edge. For this reason, no attempt is made to control the microappearance of the edge or the number or placement of microstriae. Because of mass production, lots of screwdrivers will initially look quite similar, even at the level of microcharacteristics (Murdock and Biasotti, 1997). However, the moment the tool is machined, it begins to diverge from all other similar screwdrivers. Unless it is a magical self-repairing screwdriver that can violate the second law of thermodynamics, disorder begins to result from use (gauges and dents) or even simple existence (rust and dirt). This disorder manifests as individual characteristics.

Let's take this a step farther and consider the fate of this same screwdriver and a pry mark made with it in a door frame. The moment the pry mark is

made, the characteristics of the screwdriver and the pry mark each begin to diverge as entropy takes its toll. This relates directly to our ability to match the screwdriver to the pry mark. If the mark was made recently, a reference mark made by the same screwdriver will look quite similar to the evidence mark, allowing ready assignment of both to the same source, the screwdriver. If the mark is only detected after a year has passed, its relation to a reference mark made by the same screwdriver may be less readily concluded. Not only has the pry mark been subject to change, but, depending on the circumstances, so has the screwdriver. After a year, it might only be possible to compare class characteristics, expanding the possible sources of the pry mark. In extreme cases, even the class characteristics may have changed, resulting in either an inconclusive determination or a false exclusion.

c. The Scale of Detection Is Determined by the Scale of Manufacture

What we see depends on how we look. From space, the shorelines of the continents on Earth appear as smooth outlines. Standing on the coastline, we can see that they are actually composed of jagged racks. The edges of the rocks may again appear fairly smooth to the naked eye, but examined more closely with a hand magnifier, we begin to detect roughness.

In examining forensic evidence and deciding which traits are significant, we must be aware of how the scale we choose for detection may influence our final conclusion. Take, for instance, a bullet. With the naked eye, the manufacturing characteristics of diameter, shape, and the number of lands and grooves are apparent. Depending on the condition of the bullet we may be able to tell something about other characteristics such as jacketing and nose construction. Were we to stop at this level of detection, we might conclude that two bullets that were indistinguishable in all of these characteristics could have been fired from the same barrel. If we then examine both bullets under a comparison microscope, microstriae become visible. From these characteristics, we might decide that the two bullets were still indistinguishable, even at the magnification offered by the comparison microscope. We might now decide to examine the bullets under a comparison scanning

---

Figure 6.3 Random patterns in nature. Nature exhibits an infinite variety of forms. These unique patterns appear anywhere one cares to look. Can you guess where in nature these forms were produced? (Clockwise from upper right: zebra from Ngorogoro Crater, Tanzania; rock formation from Death Valley, CA; Moreno glacier in Patagonia; fingerprint from an unknown person; sand dunes in Death Valley, CA; Bristlecone pine, White Mountains, CA).

electron microscope (SEM).* Lo and behold, we find that if we compare the edges of analogous striae, the two bullets that were previously indistinguishable in the comparison microscope now look radically different. Does this mean we have negated our previous conclusion of common origin? No, because we do not expect this level of reproduction of detail from one firing to the next. The scale of detection is a choice made by the examiner, and knowledge about the nature of the evidence and the scale of significant traits is critical in deciding which scale to employ.

We can confound ourselves from at least two different directions. Either we could use too low a magnification, and fail to detect individual differences, or we could employ too high a magnification and detect differences that constitute noise in the system. The correct scale of detection is determined by the scale of production of the unique trait, the origin of the evidence, to some extent the history of the evidence, and the question. In fingerprint comparison, one might use a stereomicroscope to enlarge the pattern to a comfortable viewing size, but it would not be helpful to look under power high enough to start resolving the grain of the paper or the texture of the ink. However, when the question is whether the fingerprint is counterfeit rather than if the pattern matches the reference, the microcharacteristics of the paper and the ink suddenly assume greater importance, and a different scale of detection is required.

i.   Signal vs. noise.   Closely related to the scale of detection is the issue of signal vs. noise. This type of problem manifests itself more in analyses involving chemical interactions or instrumental data output than in strict visual comparison. Although noise may certainly be present in visual images, it is more likely to result simply in a loss of data or resolution rather than be misinterpreted as a true trait. The distinction of signal from noise, when an instrument or process stands between the evidence and our eyes, requires an additional level of consideration.

Most people are familiar with the blue dots that represent the final result of one kind of DNA typing using PCR. These blue dots are the culmination of a chain reaction of chemical interactions instigated by the hybridization of specific DNA sequences. It is a well-known fact among practitioners that, shortly after representative results are achieved, nonspecific background color begins to appear. It would be very easy for someone unfamiliar with the test system to be misled and become concerned about whether the faint signals represent DNA types actually present in the sample. For this reason it is standard practice to document the dot pattern with a high-quality photograph

---

* Although such an instrument does exist, we acknowledge that this would be an unusual endeavor.

immediately after optimal development and to discard the original strips which, over time, no longer represent the true genetic result.

Similar decisions must be made for any kind of chromatographic or electrophoretic analysis. Are the blips along the baseline random fluctuations inherent in the system or do they represent a minor component that could be of interest? The ability to distinguish signal from noise depends on understanding both the nature of the evidence and the nature of the test system. To make these crucial decisions reliably, the analyst relies on extensive validation of both the test system and instrumentation, as well as her own education, training, and experience. This is particularly critical for samples of a forensic nature.

3. Individualizing Characteristics

We have now established several points.

1. All physical objects are unique by virtue of their existence in space and time.
2. Class characteristics are created by repetitive, controlled processes.
3. Individual characteristics are created by random, uncontrolled processes.
4. Both the source and any items originating from it commence to change the moment they each begin an independent existence in space and time. You should recognize this as one of the corollaries of divisible matter from Chapter 4.

Thus, we can define an individualizing characteristic as

> *Individualizing Characteristics:*
> Traits that are produced by a random, uncontrolled process.
> They are used to individualize items to a common source.

4. Physical Evidence with Individualizing Potential

Over the years, both by default and design, analysts have collected large amounts of empirical data about individualizing traits (e.g., Biasotti, 1959; Pounds and Smalldon, 1975; Gaudette, 1978; 1982; Bodziak, 1990; Stoney and Thornton, 1986a,b; 1987; Murdock and Biasotti, 1997; Nichols, 1997; Grieve and Bermann, 1997; Houck and Siegal, 1999).* From these data, criteria have emerged regarding the number and kind of traits required for

---

* These references represent only a small sampling of the accumulated body of work addressing individualizing traits. The population studies of serological and DNA traits in biological evidence are too numerous to even begin to enumerate here.

a conclusion of common source. The formality of organization, breadth of dissemination, and rigor of testing of these criteria have varied historically for different disciplines. Nevertheless, criminalists agree that certain categories of evidence contain inherently individualizing potential:

- Physical match evidence
- Print and impression evidence
    - Toolmarks of all kinds, including firearms
    - Shoeprints (as opposed to footprints)
    - Biological prints including fingerprints, footprints, and those from other body parts, such as ears (van der Lugt, 1997; Burge and Burger, 1999) and lips (Moenssons, 1999).
- Handwriting evidence
- DNA analysis of biological evidence

Although comprehensive numerical databases are only available for DNA,* a large amount of qualitative data exists upon which examiners of comparison evidence currently base their opinions.

5.   The Conceptual Process of Individualization

From our knowledge about the nature of the evidence and its potential for individualization, a conceptual process for examining evidence emerges. This process directs our actual examination and analysis. The following points summarize various factors that may affect the individualizing potential of an item and any evidence generated from it:

1. How the traits were generated (controlled or random);
2. The level of control exerted over the generation of the traits (size and nature of controlled vs. uncontrolled traits);
3. The scale of manufacture (size of the trait compared with the size of object);
4. The scale of detection (resolution of the test compared to the size of the trait and the size of the object);
5. Whether these traits are transferred to other targets for detection as evidence material.

We emphasize the need to search actively for both concordant traits between the evidence and the reference that could lead to a conclusion of common source, and for differences that might limit our final conclusion. The major

---

* Oddly, the existence of statistical data for biological evidence has served only to make an opinion of individuality more contentious.

steps of a prototypical examination are outlined below, and each is developed in a subsequent section of this chapter.

a. Analysis of Evidence for Class and Individualizing Characteristics

The following depicts a general scheme for analyzing an item of evidence to determine its potential source(s):

1. Collection and preservation of the evidence item
2. Collection of putative reference source material(s)
3. Selection of class and individualizing traits from the evidence item
4. Comparison of evidence and reference
5. Conclusion:
    Common source for evidence and reference
        or
    Different sources for evidence and reference

i. Collection and preservation.   We cover the proper collection of evidence in Chapter 8. We emphasize here simply that, after its detection and recognition, evidentiary material must be collected with an eye toward discerning and preserving any potentially individualizing traits. The TV private detective who pokes his pen into the barrel of a weapon to preserve the fingerprints is a caricature of the more subtle problems inherent in recognizing, collecting, and preserving evidence. A generalist approach that considers which types of evidence may be most relevant and helpful in answering the questions posed in the case is clearly superior. Eventually, suitable reference materials must also be collected to complete the comparison.

ii. Examination

Selection of class and individualizing traits from the evidence item
Selection of traits for comparison may be the most challenging aspect of the examination of evidence, for it incorporates the education, training, and experience of the examiner into a *gestalt*. It involves careful examination and observation of the item for those traits that may classify it and potentially individualize it (Nordby, 1992; Smith et al., 1993).

Under ideal circumstances, the analyst will examine the evidence for classifying or individualizing traits before examining the reference item (Smith et al., 1993). This mitigates prejudgment on the part of the examiner, forcing her to consider the uncertainty of the origin of any trait found in the evidence prior to comparison with a putative source. While some may argue with this contention, it surely decreases the value of a trait if it is detected first in the reference and then found in the evidence. Detecting a trait first in the reference might instill a subconscious expectation of finding that trait in the evidence, especially if we already harbor some belief that they should match. Thus, prior examination of the reference introduces the risk that we might simply complete a pattern to fit our expectation when we examine the evidence (Nordby, 1992).

Evidence traits may certainly be defined even in the absence of a specific reference. Sexual assault samples are routinely examined in suspectless cases, resulting in DNA profiles of the semen donor. These traits are used to search a data bank of previous offenders with the aim of linking the evidence to a source. Similar databases also exist for firearms and fingerprint evidence. In all cases, the analyst is forced to determine relevant traits from the evidence before searching a reference database, demonstrating the feasibility of this procedure.

How many traits?

This is one of the magic questions in forensic science. A single randomly acquired trait is rarely sufficient to individualize a particular type of evidence. In firearms examinations, for example, one can find two or three matching striae in a row from different weapons (Biassotti, 1959; Murdock and Biasotti, 1997; Nichols, 1997). Similarly, one can readily find two or three matching fingerprint minutiae from different fingers. Therefore, it is important to accumulate a body of work that determines the expected characteristics and limits of the evidence type.* In firearms examinations, consensus criteria exist regarding the number and quality of traits required to convince the examiner of a common source (Murdock and Biasotti, 1997; Nichols, 1997). For shoeprints on the other hand, greater emphasis is placed on the analyst's judgment regarding the kind of traits that are present rather than the number of traits (Cassidy, 1980; Bodziak, 1990). A dichotomy exists in the fingerprint community whether more emphasis should be placed on an absolute number

---

* Although the wording differs, criteria for individualization offered by practitioners in a wide variety of disciplines share a common thread. Some examples are as follows. *Fingerprints*: Characteristics of such number and significance as to preclude the possibility of their having occurred by mere coincidence (Tuthill, 1994; Ashbaugh, 1996). *Shoeprints*: Confirmed random characteristics that could not be repeated on another outsole (Bodziak, 1990). *Handwriting*: A sufficient number of uniquely identifying characteristics with an absence of unexplainable variations (Homewood et al., 1999). *Toolmarks (including firearms)*: When quality and quantity of consecutive striae (characteristics) exceeds that of known nonmatch bullets. This is generally conceded to be a minimum of three to four high-quality striae (Nichols, 1997; Murdock and Biasotti, 1997). For biological evidence, where quantitative data are both expected and available, the criteria take a different turn. The FBI was the first to proffer a quantitative limit, beyond which it accepts a DNA profile as individual (unpublished). Many other DNA analysts are reluctant to take this leap, and continue to treat DNA as very rare class evidence, simply proffering a population frequency of likelihood ratio and passing the buck to the jury. In the following section we explore some mathematical approaches to expressing the strength of the evidence.

of matching points or on analyst judgment (Ashbaugh, 1996; Cole, 1998; 1999). For genetic analysis, the population frequency of a profile, rather than the number of loci examined, is usually considered the more useful criterion.

Comparison of evidence and reference
Once the examiner has chosen potentially individualizing traits in one item, she compares them to the other item. The examiner looks for patterns — sizes, shapes, colors, or other measurements — that are indistinguishable from each other. Traits are indistinguishable if they fall within the range of variation that has been determined to exist for traits of that evidence type. This is typically accomplished by repeated analyses of the same known trait. For quantifiable data, the range of variation ideally reflects the results of formal validation studies; for qualitative evidence, it is often left to the experience and judgment of the individual analyst.

At the same time, the analyst must actively seek out differences between the two items that might disqualify them as originating from a common source (Smith et al., 1993). This is the heart of our attempt to rigorously falsify the null hypothesis, that the items derive from a common source. The analyst may decide that such occurrences are explainable or unexplainable, and this decision will determine, in part, her conclusion. Even one *unexplainable* difference is sufficient to prove the null hypothesis and negate a potential individualization.

Because of the nature of forensic evidence, the task of deciding whether traits are similar or dissimilar is less than straightforward. How hard should we look? On what scale? At some level, every item will appear different from its true source. These are some of the issues over which two qualified analysts might reasonably disagree. Because any differences seen (significant or not) may be inherent in the evidence (*intrinsic differences*) or may result from external factors, such as the way the evidence is transferred or detected (*extrinsic differences*), the analyst must not only be cognizant of the *nature of the evidence*, but the *nature of the test*. In fact, the factors most likely to confound the analyst's ability to determine the authenticity of similarities or differences between evidence and reference traits are external to the evidence. It is beyond the scope of this book to explore the specifics of these issues for every type of evidence. We present a few representative examples here and leave the reader to extend the underlying concepts to her own work.

Physical match evidence. Consider two pieces of paper that share a border of the same general shape (Figure 6.4). To the naked eye, they appear to fit together, and most would agree that they were once one. Upon closer examination with a hand magnifier, regions of apparent mismatch are detected at various locations along the border. When the border is examined under a high-power microscope, many discontinuities are apparent along the length of the border. The examiner must first decide which scale of detection is

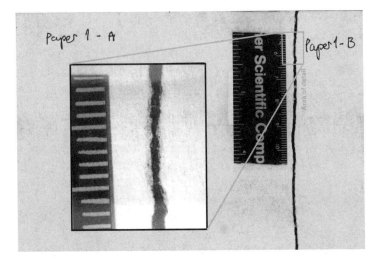

Figure 6.4 Paper enlargment. The education of the examiner, knowledge of the nature of the evidence (acquired through research and validation by the profession), and experience analyzing the particular evidence type are all necessary for a competent comparison of evidence and reference samples. In this example, examination of the complementary borders requires a decision about the scale of magnification. Too little magnification results in insufficient resolution to detect important differences; too much magnification shows only differences, and little complementarity. The truth is that these two pieces of paper each represent one half of two different pieces of paper held together and torn simultaneously.

appropriate for the evidence. Note that the scale of detection is a factor extrinsic to the actual evidence. For example, if experiments have previously shown that two halves of the same piece of paper always appear noncomplementary under high power, this scale of detection may be too high relative to the scale of the evidence and the scale of the characteristics. Conversely, if experiments have shown that two pieces of paper representing halves of different sheets in the same stack torn simultaneously are indistinguishable to the naked eye, the scale of detection may be too low relative to the scale of the evidence and the scale of the characteristics. Selection of the examination procedure depends both on previous experimentation and the experience of the field as a whole and the individual examiner. If the examiner decides that discontinuities seen along the boundary of the paper fragments are both real and significant, he must attempt to discern whether the explanation is trivial or consequential. Two possibilities exist. Either the two pieces were once one and conditions since their separation have conspired to degrade or obliterate the detail along one or both edges. The analyst might adopt this explanation for any differences noted. Conversely, degradation might fail to explain the differences (for example, if protrusions existed at the analogous location on each piece rather than a potentially complementary protrusion and recess), forcing the examiner to conclude that the paper fragments must originate from different sources. The examiner bases the decision on his knowledge of paper, information about this particular kind of paper and its fragmentation qualities, experiments with tearing paper in general and this paper specifically, how paper degrades under various environmental conditions, and information about the history of this sample. He might try to recreate conditions that led to the kind of degradation seen. Using all of this information in conjunction with his own personal experience, the analyst will either decide that the pieces of paper were once one and any discontinuities are explainable or he will conclude that no reasonable explanation exists for the boundary differences and that the paper fragments originated from different intact sheets of paper. Similar considerations apply to any physical match problem.

Biological evidence. Some of the most physically fragile evidence is biological evidence. Once parted from a living system, biological material quickly begins to lose integrity. In a short period of time, even DNA, the most hardy of physiological substances, degrades in both quality and quantity under nonoptimal conditions. Because of this, the DNA profile from an evidence sample may show intrinsic differences from a reference sample even if they have a common origin. Fortunately, because of the scrutiny forensic DNA typing has received, extensive validation studies have been performed, allowing analysts to judge from a highly informed position whether the differences are explainable or unexplainable. For instance, the analyst may assess the average size of the DNA in the sample before performing any analysis to get an idea of what might be expected, and also to choose an analysis system intelligently. If data for the largest locus are missing from an otherwise clear evidence profile, and the assessment data predict that no DNA of a sufficient size is present, then the absence of that particular datum is explainable. Although its absence may conflict with a reference profile, this finding would not by itself be cause to eliminate a common origin. Sometimes the method used to detect the evidence traits (an extrinsic factor) introduces apparent differences in samples that do, in fact, originate from the same source. For example, in DNA typing, differences in electrophoretic systems, such as the presence or absence of denaturants, can produce apparently discrepant typing results for the same sample (Fregeau and Fourney, 1993; Gill et al., 1994).[*] Similarly, different PCR primer sets for the same STR locus may occasionally

---

[*] Differences in the resolution of an electrophoretic gel system may cause a locus that is resolved as a heterozygote in one system to appear as a homozygote in another system. Denaturants such as formamide or urea are used to increase the resolution of certain electrophoretic systems.

produce different results for the same sample (Kline and Jenkins, 1998; Walsh, 1998).*

Print and impression evidence. It is interesting to note that almost every aspect of print and impression evidence is extrinsic to the actual source pattern. The transfer medium influences the fidelity of trait transfer and also adds its own characteristics. The nature of the substrate onto which a two-dimensional print is deposited, or the substance through which it is deposited, may either obscure or reveal details of the source. For latent prints, the substrate also affects the choice of detection method, which adds yet another layer to the visualization and resolution of the traits. Because the deposition of any print or impression occurs in three-dimensional space, the angle of its deposition will affect trait transfer, as will the force with which the impression is made. When examining an evidence impression or print, the criminalist must decide which traits are faithful to the source and which are ambiguous as a result of these many possible extrinsic influences. Even two reference dermal ridge prints, for example, rolled under the most optimal conditions, will show clear differences. Yet everyone agrees that differences due to ink quality, ink quantity, transfer pressure, and transfer angle are not genuine differences. In a bloody shoeprint, for example, three components interact to create the print: the sole of the shoe, the blood, and the substrate (a floor or some other surface). Each will contribute elements to the final quality of the evidence print. Uneven distribution of blood on the shoe sole might mean that some traits are not transferred. A large volume of blood on parts of the sole might push blood into the recesses of the shoe sole, producing a featureless deposition in that area and obliterating potentially individualizing traits. An uneven substrate, such as floor tile, will likely take the shoe impression on the peaks of the surface but not in the valleys. Given a nice even reference print with lots of detail, and an uneven, partial evidence print, the two items are clearly distinguishable. Yet, a shoeprint examiner might be perfectly justified in concluding that they originate from the same source. This is one of the more extreme examples where determining which differences are explainable and which are not dominates the final conclusion.

Both the known characteristics and limits of the evidence and the capabilities and limitations of the method, and any other factors extrinsic to the evidence, must be acknowledged so that both concordant and discordant traits can be accorded the proper relative weight. However, when a single

* A sample may contain a primer binding site mutation that affects a primer in one amplification system but not another. The result for this particular sample is that in one PCR amplification system, the sample appears homozygous for that locus, while in a second system it appears heterozygous.

difference between an evidence and reference item is seen that cannot be explained by the nature of the evidence or the nature of the test, then the two items must be concluded to have a different source.

E.   Inferring a Common or Different Source

At the termination of the analysis and comparison processes, the examiner considers three questions:

1. Do unexplainable differences exist that convince me that the items compared* originate from different sources?

    If not,

2. Do the quantity and quality of the class characteristics convince me that the items could originate from the same source?

    If so,

3. Do a sufficient number and quality of individualizing traits exist to convince me that they originate from the same unique source?

This opinion is the culmination of all of the collection, preservation, and analytical work, and it relies on information accumulated by the field as well as the knowledge, education, and experience of the analyst. A formal consideration of all of the data requires the examiner to contemplate each of the above two questions in turn. It should be clear what criteria were used, what data were gathered to satisfy the criteria, and how they support the final conclusion.

1.   Conclusion, Inference, or Opinion of Common Source

The analyst must now express the results of his formal consideration of the relationship between the evidence and reference items. He started the examination by formulating (explicitly or not) a source determination question in the form of the null hypothesis: "I will prove that this reference is the source of the evidence." Failure to disprove the null hypothesis means that the analyst *hasn't* shown that the evidence and reference *do not* share a common origin. In other words, the analyst is forced to admit that they may share a common source, and, in the case of classified evidence, that the evidence may also have other potential sources. A way of expressing this in

* Most often, the items are an evidence sample and a reference sample, but they could also be two evidence items.

a few words is that the analysis leads to an *inference of common source between the evidence and reference samples*. Note that both classified and individualized evidence may lead to an inference of common source; the difference is in the number of sources, one for individualization, or more than one for classification.

Throughout this chapter, we have referred to an *inference* of common source, rather than a *conclusion* of common source. We have also used the term *opinion* to summarize the individualization process. *Webster's* (1996) defines these terms as follows:

Inference:	to conclude from something known or assumed.
Opinion:	a judgment not based on absolute certainty or positive knowledge, but on what seems true, valid, or probable to one's own mind.
Conclusion:	the last ... division of a discourse, usually containing a summing up of the points and a statement of opinion or decisions reached

We believe the term *inference* is best suited to communicating our belief of common source. For our purposes, an inference is more appropriately defined as a conclusion derived from both facts *and* assumptions. An inference is not fact per se; it is only as strong as the limitations of the combination of evidence, test, and test results. An expression of these limitations will be different for classified evidence than it is for individualized evidence. We develop these ideas in the Section F of this chapter.

2. Three Inferences

Assuming the evidence is of sufficient quality,* three inferences are possible:

1. The items originate from difference sources.
2. The items may be classified but cannot be individualized due to a limitation of the evidence or the test.
3. The items share a unique common origin.

a. The Items Originate from Different Sources

We have already explained that differences will always exist between an evidence and a reference item, even if they share a common source. When differences are found, the examiner must determine if they are explainable

---

* It is assumed that both items have traits of sufficient quality and quantity for a legitimate comparison. Otherwise no result or an inconclusive result might be obtained.

or unexplainable. When a single *unexplainable* difference is found, then the analyst must conclude that the two items originate from different sources.

b.   The Items May Be Classified, but Cannot Be Individualized Due to a Limitation of the Evidence or the Test

Classification results when ambiguity is present in potentially individualizable evidence. Ambiguity regarding the source of the evidence derives from at least two circumstances. If the characteristics used for comparison are clear, but are either too few in number or too common to convince the analyst that the source is unique, then the inference falls short of individualization and we are left with a *classification*; the items may have originated from more than one source. If potentially individualizing characteristics are present on one of the items (usually the reference), but details are obscured on the other (usually the evidence), it also may not be possible to infer a single common source.

The latter situation is a direct consequence of the origin of forensic evidence. Fingerprints are smudged, DNA is degraded, and bullets fragment into tiny pieces. When such evidence is compared with a pristine reference sample, only a portion of the pattern may be available for comparison. That portion that is discernible may be indistinguishable from the reference, and no data suggest that the reference is not the source of the evidence. However, the comparison is based on partial information, and does not reach the level of specificity required by the analyst to infer a single source. In this case, the reference cannot be excluded as a possible source of the evidence, but the analyst believes that other sources could also show these limited characteristics, thereby allowing for multiple common sources. Additionally, clearer traits in the evidence might reveal differences sufficient to eliminate the possibility of a source in common with this reference.

c.   The Items Share a Unique Common Origin

The third possible outcome, that the items share a unique common origin, represents the culmination of the individualization process. Individualization provides information about the relationship of the evidence to a source. If the two items exhibit the same individualizing traits in sufficient number or quality, the analyst infers that they share a common origin to the exclusion of all others. The evidence and reference items have been individualized to a unique source. Always bear in mind that the analyst becomes *convinced* of individuality (Stoney, 1991a). The characteristics seen are so rare that it is unreasonable to believe that they could be duplicated by chance in another similar object. No evidence to the contrary would change the mind of the examiner about the source of the item.

d. The Conclusion

The analyst must provide a *conclusion* that summarizes the strength of the evidence so that the full import of the inference is communicated. This will include (1) a statement inferring a common source, (2) a qualifying statement that portrays whether the analyst believes that common source to be, in his opinion, the only possible source, or whether multiple potential sources exist, and (3) the likelihood of encountering other potential sources in this case as a random chance.

F. Mathematical Approaches to Expressing the Strength of the Inference

In the first part of this chapter, we discussed different possible inferences about the relationship of evidence and reference samples. If an evidence sample cannot be excluded as originating from the same source as a reference sample, we infer either that multiple sources are possible (*classification*) or that they share a single common source (*individualization*). We spend the rest of this chapter exploring the quantitative expression of this relationship of evidence to source.

   In the preceding chapters, we have alluded to the discrepancy both in the availability and expectation of quantitative data for different evidence types. We make no secret of our proclivity toward the use of quantitative data to assess the link between evidence and reference for class evidence, and to support an opinion of a single common source for individualizing evidence. However, we also acknowledge the difficulties inherent in acquiring and applying frequency data for nonbiological evidence, some of which we discuss later in this chapter. At the very least, however, we feel that all forensic scientists should familiarize themselves with the various mathematical tools available to help assess the strength of the evidence. The rest of this chapter is devoted to introducing some of these tools.

1. The Necessity of Providing an Assessment of the Strength of the Inference

Without some expression of the strength of the source determination, the results of an examination are virtually worthless and potentially misleading. This was expressed most emphatically about DNA evidence in the first report of the National Research Council (1992), and can be generalized to all forensic evidence.

   Some practitioners argue that a mere description of the tests performed and the results obtained fulfills the responsibility of the forensic scientist. For instance, some reports on biological evidence merely list the results of a battery of genetic marker tests performed on a physiological fluid stain and a reference sample, leaving it to the reader to see that the results are the same. Even if this similarity is highlighted in the report, a discussion of its meaning is frequently lacking. This leaves the lay reader in the unenviable position of having to determine the meaning of the similarity. This, we contend, is a disservice to the public. The forensic scientist is in the best position to comment on the strength of the evidence. For potentially individualizing evidence, this is simple. In fingerprint, toolmark, and physical match examinations, the strength is typically expressed as an *opinion* that the evidence and reference share a singular common source. Because the strength of class evidence is more difficult to determine and support, such an expression is less commonly provided. Results of an evidence examination presented without a statement about the strength of the relationship of the evidence to the putative source is an abdication of the responsibilities of the competent examiner. No one is better able to comment on the strength than the forensic scientist.

2. Tools for Estimating the Strength of the Inference

We turn now to methods used to describe the strength of the relationship between evidence and reference when a conclusion of individualization is not possible. These methods are tools that help us decide for ourselves the strength of the relationship, as well as to communicate this strength to interested parties. Several tools exist that can assist us in our evaluation of the results. To determine which tool is best suited to the specific evidence under consideration, the competent analyst must possess at least basic skills in mathematics and statistics. These subjects should be an integral part of the education and training of every forensic scientist.

It is useful to understand the concept of probability as our *degree of belief* in a proposition. Another way of saying this is that we need tools to quantitate the uncertainty or lack of knowledge about our conclusion. This mind-set allows us to think more clearly about our task, to include both the capabilities and limitations of our test into an expression of strength, and to communicate more clearly our opinions, and the basis for them, to interested parties.

Two basic fields of study in statistics provide information about the strength of evidence. One is *frequency estimates*, where the number of times the evidence is found in some defined population is used to relate the probability of finding the evidence as a random occurrence. The second is *likelihood ratios* (LRs) (usually in the context of Bayesian reasoning), where the probability of competing hypotheses is compared, and the results are expressed as how much more likely the evidence would be under one scenario compared with another.

a. Frequency Estimates

The simplest and most common method of expressing the strength of the evidence is through frequency estimates. Information is gathered about how common any item or trait might be in the population of possible sources. This frequency is then used to convey how unusual it might be to encounter this evidence by chance alone. In biological evidence, this has been called the random match probability. It simply estimates the probability of seeing this evidence if it were from a source other than the reference in the instant case. For biological evidence this is rather simple, while for other evidence types, such as trace, it has been called impossible.

For any biological evidence, surveys of various populations are performed, and the results tabulated and tested according to standard genetic theory. This procedure provides reasonable estimates for the probability of encountering a biological evidence profile at random (Griffiths et al., 1993). Population studies performed on human populations rely on the relative stability of human populations, our knowledge about their distribution, and our ability to acquire a representative sampling. Using the laws of genetics, we can also test for the independence of traits.

However, for inanimate evidence, in particular trace evidence, frequency studies provide much more ephemeral data. Populations of manufactured materials change both quickly and unpredictably; a frequency survey represents a snapshot in time. The composition of these populations also depends greatly on geographical location and may be extremely localized. Therefore, it is difficult to know if the sample fairly represents the population (Horrocks et al., 1999) or if the population is the correct one to estimate the strength of some evidence found at another time or location. Because of this uncertainty, errors associated with frequency estimates could be higher than the estimates themselves. It is difficult to answer such a question as "What is the probability of seeing this evidence by chance alone?" when the frequency is a moving target. Finally, and as a direct consequence of the preceding issues, it is difficult to imagine how to test for independence between two inanimate objects because no physical laws govern their distribution or dispersal. When is it appropriate to multiply traits in estimating the frequency of a particular type of evidence (Gaudette, 1978; 1982; Bodziak, 1990)? Can we derive a combined estimate of the strength of the class of evidence using different types of the same class of evidence (Deadman, 1984a,b; Deadman *in* Saferstein, 1998), or even two different traits from the same evidence such as mitochondrial DNA and microscopic traits (Shields, 1998)?

b. Likelihood Ratios

We discussed in Chapter 5 how a scientist will approach the crime scene and evidence with at least two hypotheses in mind: one that the suspect did commit the crime, and the other that someone else committed the crime. This mind-set leads to searching for both inculpatory and exculpatory evidence. In addition, *it leads to an evaluation of each item of recovered evidence in light of at least two possibilities.*

Hypothesis 1: The suspected source is the true source of the evidence.
or
Hypothesis 2: Another source is the true source of the evidence.

At the conclusion of testing, the analyst evaluates the strength of the evidence in light of these alternative hypotheses. Likelihood ratios (LRs) are particularly suited to this logic. While the use of LRs is common in many fields, it is only within the last 25 to 30 years that careful study and development of mathematical models have emerged for evaluating forensic evidence (Taroni et al., 1998). It is our view that LRs offer a more elegant and complete picture of the strength of the evidence than frequency estimates alone.*

A likelihood ratio is typically written in the following way:

$$LR = \frac{P(E|H_1,I)}{P(E|H_2,I)}$$

where P = probability
E = evidence of common source.
H = hypothesis (H_1 and H_2 are the two hypotheses under consideration)
I = information (which refers to other knowledge we have about circumstances surrounding the analysis)

The symbol | means "given that," or "assuming"; the parentheses are translated as "of." Under the hypothesis proposed above, the numerator of the likelihood ratio is read, "The probability of *evidence of a common source*, assuming that the putative source is the true source." In the same way, the denominator is read, "The probability of *evidence of a common source* assuming that an alternate source is the true source."

When examining physical evidence, we cannot know the probability of common source given the evidence that we see, but we can calculate the probability of finding this evidence if we assume the proposition to be either true or false. If we assume that the evidence is from the putative source, then the probability of our test showing similar results to the reference is 1 (one); that is, we are certain that the test results of the evidence and the reference

---

* We caution the reader to remember that this approach should be viewed as a tool, not a religion.

will be concordant. If we assume that the evidence is from some other source, then the probability of seeing concordant results is the chance of encountering this evidence at random. In this situation, a frequency calculation provides a useful approximation of this probability.

By convention, LRs used in forensic science have been presented with H_1 as the "prosecution hypothesis" (H_p) and H_2 as the "defense hypothesis" (H_d). This nomenclature has had the unfortunate consequence of alienating many criminalists at first blush. The scientist immediately recoils at the thought of proposing adversarial hypotheses, and some dismiss the utility of LRs without exploring them further. In fact, this nomenclature is completely extraneous to the mathematical reasoning. The scientist may simply use the LR as a tool to compare any number of reasonable hypotheses, without considering which side might advance them. A simple change in nomenclature to $[H_1, H_2, ...]$ makes LRs much more palatable to the scientist.

i. Likelihood ratios in Bayes' theorem.   From the foregoing discussion, we have learned that LRs answer the question of the probability of the evidence assuming, alternatively, this source or another source. This will be a good time to step back and consider LRs in the context of Bayes' theorem. Bayes' theorem provides a general model for updating our certainty about any proposition.

Using words, the expression of Bayes' theorem looks like this:

$$\text{Prior odds} \times \text{LR} = \text{Posterior odds}$$

This may be read: "However likely you think a proposition (prior odds), change your judgment (posterior odds) by this additional evidence (LR)."

Using symbols, the expression takes this form:

$$\frac{P(H_1|I)}{P(H_2|I)} \times \frac{P(E|H_1,I)}{P(E|H_2,I)} = \frac{P(H_1|E,I)}{P(H_2|E,I)}$$

Note several important points. The prior odds are simply the *hypothesis* given some *information*. We have some idea about the probability of an event or hypothesis. Ideally, this is supported by numerical data, but it could also be speculative. Either way, it must be expressed as a quantity. This initial estimate is updated by multiplying it by the LR. Calculation of an LR in light of new *evidence* provides a way to modify the prior odds. This results in posterior odds. The addition of the E term to the expression of posterior odds reflects the integration of the new evidence.

Analysts are sometimes concerned about expressing their results in terms of an LR because they believe they will be forced to define prior odds. In fact, at the level of source determination, the analytical results can be expressed using only the LR term. Any information about the samples that directly affects analytical results can be incorporated into either the numerator or denominator of the LR, as appropriate. The strength of the inference about the source of the evidence can be expressed wholly by the LR. Any interested party can then pose prior odds to be modified by the inference resulting from the physical evidence examination. In some cases, the criminalist may wish to assist by pointing out information to be considered as part of the prior odds; in any case, prior odds provide a perfect vehicle for each advocate to proffer the hypothesis that best supports her case. The Bayesian framework provides a way for integrating the physical evidence results into the rest of the case.

3. Classification

We will not attempt a lengthy mathematical treatment of classified evidence. The breadth and the depth of such a discussion precludes its inclusion here, and several excellent treatises cover the subject (Robertson and Vignaux, 1995; National Research Council, 1996; Cook et al., 1998a,b; Evett and Weir, 1998). However, one example using likelihood ratios will illustrate the usefulness of the method.

> The evidence involved is DNA. A woman relates that she and her boyfriend engaged in consensual sex early in the morning and, as she was seeing him off to work, she was attacked from behind as she stood on her porch. The assailant dragged her back into the house and raped her. The victim immediately reported the rape, and was examined at the local hospital. A vaginal swab was taken, and DNA analysis was performed. Results of the RFLP analysis showed a mixture of DNA in the sperm fraction. Either three or four bands were seen at each locus, implying two donors. Reference samples from the boyfriend and the suspect showed that all of the bands in the evidence profile could be attributed to a combination of their separate profiles. Thus, the suspect could not be eliminated as a potential donor to the sperm fraction. This leads to the inference that the suspect was one of the semen donors.

The task is now to assess the strength of the inference. Some analysts insist that a calculation summing all of the possible contributors (sometimes called random man not excluded, or RMNE) is the most relevant expression. This calculation does address the concerns of the defendant (perhaps a single suspect arrested in a case of multiple rapists) who wants to know, "What is the probability of picking one person at random from the population who would not be eliminated as a potential donor?" However, the RMNE approach ignores the fact that two donors are present, and once the types of one donor are identified, the types of the other are fixed. Merely summing the frequency of every potential donor ignores information we have about the data and fails to represent the complexity of the evidence adequately.

Alternatively we can use an LR to compare competing hypotheses. In our example, the most relevant and reasonable hypotheses are:

- The mixture was left by the boyfriend (B) and the suspect (S).
- The mixture was left by the boyfriend (B) and an unknown random unrelated person (X).
- The mixture was left by the suspect and an unrelated person (X) (i.e., not accepting the victim's story at face value).
- The mixture was left by two unknown random unrelated individuals (X) and (Y) (i.e., not accepting the victim's story at face value).

We first evaluate the probability of each hypotheses separately,* then compare them using likelihood ratios as follows:

LR 1. Assuming the presence of Boyfriend in both hypotheses

$$\frac{P(E|\text{Boyfriend} + \text{Suspect})}{P(E|\text{Boyfriend} + \text{random man})} = 1.5 \text{ billion}$$

LR 2. Assuming the absence of the Boyfriend

$$\frac{P(E|\text{Suspect} + \text{random man})}{P(E|\text{two}(2)\text{random men})} = 45,000,000$$

The results can be summarized as follows: The probability of the evidence under Hypothesis 1, the boyfriend and the suspect, is many orders of magnitude greater than any of the others. How should this be expressed? We take LR 1 as an example. We could say either of the following:

- The evidence profile is at least 1.5 billion times more likely to be of the type seen if the boyfriend and the suspect are the donors, than if the boyfriend and any other random man are the donors.
- The probability of someone other than the suspect having the requisite profile to complete the observed mixture, assuming the boyfriend is present, is 1 in 1.5 billion.

---

* The details of these calculations are given in Appendix E. We use the Caucasian population frequencies for the example.

To illustrate the value of this approach, the RMNE is also calculated in Appendix E. By ignoring the additional evidence (E) provided by the analysis, that two and only two donors are present, and the information (I) about the case, that is, that the victim indicates a consenting intercourse with a named donor whose sample is available, at least three orders of magnitude of information are lost.

a. Hypothesis Testing vs. Bayes' Theorem — Which One?

We have discussed two logical frameworks for the consideration of forensic science data, hypothesis testing, and likelihood ratios in the context of Bayes' theorem. In hypothesis testing, one proposition at a time is considered; failing to falsify the proposition, the uncertainty associated with the truth of the proposition is usually expressed as a frequency. In an LR, alternative hypotheses are compared and the relative uncertainty associated with the truth of the propositions is calculated. Frequencies are incorporated with other information in this calculation.

Perhaps these logical frameworks are not as antithetical as extremists of both persuasions might have us believe. Stoney (1991) wrote that "The likelihood ratio is a generalization of the more generally used 'match frequencies.'" We believe that it is useful to study and understand the ideas inherent in both of these schools of scientific philosophy. Considerable research and refinement will be necessary before the profession of forensic science evolves a unified understanding and application of the various tools available to express the strength of forensic evidence. Certainly, the Bayesian model is more sophisticated and allows for the logical consideration of more complex situations. However, we believe that the concept of hypothesis falsification is still fundamental to the applied sciences. We are not willing to discard one set of ideas wholesale; rather, we take from both as the situation demands. We continue to draw from both schools of thought throughout the rest of this volume.

4. Individualization

Neither the Bayesian model using likelihood ratios nor hypothesis testing is very helpful in expressing an individualization. Strict Bayesians exclude the possibility that one alternative is ever completely wrong, allowing us to accept the other one as true; strict frequentists insist that a number must always be proffered, however irrational such a number might be in the context of an actual population.

Although it may seem irrelevant to discuss probabilities for evidence that has been individualized to a single source, we must remember that an opinion of unique common source still relies on a body of data. Consciously or not, the data convince the analyst to make the leap. No evidence to the contrary would change the analyst's belief that the evidence and reference share a common source. The state of the practice of forensic science is that examiners do provide opinions of individualization.

a. Individualization and Opinion — A Special Case

How do we reconcile an opinion of individualization with the hypothesis testing model, in which we accept a hypothesis only by failing to disprove it?* By definition, we are left with only a provisional explanation which, at any time, may be disproved by further work. This presents an interesting dilemma for any applied science, including forensic science. If no hypothesis is ever proved, merely disproved, how can an analyst ever draw any firm conclusions from the data? Scientists understand that no fact is ever proved, yet the criminal justice system looks to science for help in establishing facts. The lawyers roll their eyes at the inability of the scientist to make up her mind, for the attorney's life is made up of practical events that require practical decisions. In its purest form, science is of no value to the judicial system.

However, as a hypothesis continues to be tested, repeated failure to disprove it strengthens our conviction that it is correct and weakens our skepticism that it is wrong. Another way to say this is that, with each piece of additional information, our uncertainty regarding the truth of the hypothesis decreases. Finally, the analyst judges that no other potential reference source could possess the observed traits. Therefore, the chance of encountering a different reference with these characteristics by chance alone is zero.

Using LRs, the analyst judges the denominator (the probability of the evidence assuming a different source) to be zero. Dividing by zero drives the LR to infinity and, consequently also, the posterior odds. Purists, of course, contend that the denominator can never be zero. Robertson and Vignaux (1995), of the Bayesian persuasion, recognize this dilemma and suggest an interim solution.

> In these cases it seems that the expert is giving evidence of identity when, and only when, in his judgment the probability of getting the evidence assuming the alternative hypothesis is so small that it does not matter what the numerator or even the prior are. At what point this is reached seems to be a matter of judgment and experience and there most writers on expert evidence are content to let the matter rest. This may have had the unfortunate effect of removing the incentive to carry out the basic research necessary to build appropriate models. Intellectually, this is unsatisfactory and further

---

* This must be an intelligent failure to disprove the hypothesis using discriminating tests. For instance, failure to prove that an individual is not the donor of a stain using secretor status (80% of the population are secretors) is virtually meaningless and would not alter our certainty very much one way or the other.

work is required in order to understand the processes involved in making these decisions. In the meantime the proposal that all forms of scientific evidence be given in the form of a likelihood ratio is a counsel of perfection.

As a practical matter, we suggest that:

At some *subjective* point, *most* qualified *authorities* would agree that, for *practical applications*, the likelihood that the hypothesis is untrue is so *small* that it can be ignored.

This concept is critical to moving forward in any applied science. Before we continue discussing its implications, let's clarify the meaning of several key concepts.

Subjective.   This implies a criteria that is personal and, as such, may be different for each individual. It is important to understand that any endeavor in which humans participate involves a subjective component; it is the nature of human existence that we each operate from a slightly different perspective, and all of our decisions are shaped by our cumulative experiences. Science is no different and the subjective element makes our conclusions no less valid. According to Popper, "We must distinguish between truth, which is objective and absolute, and certainty, which is subjective."* (Horgan, 1996).

One fingerprint expert may be "certain" when she can find 9 points of comparison between two prints; another expert may require 10 points of comparison to be "certain." Even if the two experts agree that 9 points of comparison exist, they may come to different conclusions based on their subjective uncertainty. The chromatogram of a suspected ignitable liquid is an objective piece of data. Everyone can agree on the number of peaks and their size. Two qualified analysts might disagree about whether they are comfortable concluding that the chromatogram represents a highly evaporated sample of gasoline.

Most.   Not all qualified observers might agree with the assessment. This derives in part from the subjective nature of the evaluation, and in part from the nature of our culture, which seems to require disagreement to instigate progress.** However, if you are hanging in the wind all by yourself with a conclusion of singular common source, and none of your lab-mates is willing to brave the storm with you, you might wish to reconsider your conclusion.

---

* Popper believed that a theory *could* be absolutely true, but rejected the belief that we could ever *know* that a theory is true (Horgan, 1996).
** "The reasonable man adapts himself to the world. The unreasonable man persists in trying to adapt the world to himself. Therefore all progress depends upon the unreasonable man" — George Bernard Shaw.

Qualified authority.   One who has undertaken a formal study of the subject or who has extensive experience with it, has communicated with others on the topic, and can speak to the majority and minority opinions. To proffer an opinion on a particular case, one must also have reviewed the evidence and data relevant to that case, and synthesized an *independent* conclusion. Simply criticizing another's conclusion is insufficient.

Small.   How small does small need to be for the likelihood of untruth to be ignored? The uncomfortable part of this is that there is no absolute answer because "small" is necessarily relative. One is always *comparing* hypotheses rather than considering any hypothesis in a vacuum solely on its own merits. We've discussed likelihood ratios as a means for comparing hypotheses in this chapter.

Practical application.   This brings us back around to the idea of subjective certainty. Although we have beat to death the idea that a hypothesis can only be disproved, never proved, we also embrace the reality that forensic science is an applied science whose purpose is to supply facts to the trier of the same.

When we analyze the evidence and reference samples and see no differences, we conclude from this analysis that the two items could share a common source. For individualizable evidence, the inference may be so strong that we believe it to be true, even though we could not prove it with absolute certainty. We state this conclusion of common singular source as an *opinion*. Based on the experience and knowledge of both the forensic community and the individual, we may reasonably accept a properly qualified conclusion as fact.

G.   Summary

Charles Sanders Peirce, the founder of the *Philosophy of Pragmatism*, defined absolute truth as: "whatever scientists say it is when they come to the end of their labors" (Horgan, 1996). This is a particularly appealing bit of philosophy for those of us working in the applied sciences, particularly one such as forensic science where an entirely unrelated discipline depends on us to provide it with "facts." Although we govern ourselves by the rules of science, we also embrace the practical nature of our endeavor. Pragmatism provides the philosophical foundation for Stoney's clarification that individualization cannot be proved, we can only become convinced of it (Stoney, 1991).

However, to become convinced of an individualization, one must first be convinced that such a possibility exists. This conviction grows from an understanding of the nature of the evidence, including its inherent possibilities and limitations. This is rarely accomplished by a single person. A communal effort is needed to produce a body of empirical work that can support that pragmatic leap of faith to a conclusion of a single common source. In addition, each practitioner must rely on an individual body of education, training, and most of all experience, to justify his conclusion of individuality. The greater the common wisdom and the more extensive the individual experience, the more confidence we have that the leap of faith is both appropriate and justified. Equally important are the checks and balances that a working community provides in helping the individual analyst determine when the limitations of the evidence or the tests prevent individualization as a reasonable conclusion in any specific case.

When individualization is not legally necessary, and identification is sufficient, no further information is required. However, when individualization is desirable, but not possible, we default to classification. In this situation, more than one source could have produced the evidence, and we must provide an estimate of how many more than one this might be.

Lest we lose sight of why we care, remember that at this point in the paradigm (Figure 3.1) we are attempting to infer the source of a piece of evidence. Classification establishes a nonexclusive relationship between some evidence and its source; individualization establishes a singular relationship between a piece of evidence and its source. Whether we arrive at a classification or an individualization, that information will be used as a link to infer *associations* between objects (for instance, a suspect and the crime scene). The processes of *association* and *reconstruction* will be the topic of the next chapter.

References

Ashbaugh, D. R., *Quantitative-Qualitative Friction Ridge Analysis: An Introduction to Basic and Advanced Ridgeology*, CRC Press, Boca Raton, FL, 2000.

Biasotti, A., A statistical study of the individual characteristics of fired bullets, *J. Forensic Sci.*, 4(1), 133–140, 1959.

Bodziak, W. J., *Footwear Impression Evidence*, Elsevier, New York, 1990.

Burge, M., and Burger, W., Ear biometrics, in *Biometrics: Personal Identification in a Networked Society*, Jain, A. K., Bolle, R., and Pankanti, S., Eds., Kluwer Academic Publishers, Boston, 1999.

Cassidy, M. J., *Footwear Identification*, Canadian Government Printing Center, Quebec, 1980.

Cole, S., Witnessing identification: latent fingerprinting evidence and expert knowledge, *Soc. Stud. Sci.*, 28(5–6), 687, 1998.

Cole, S., What counts for identity? The historical origins of the methodology of latent fingerprint identification, *Sci. Context*, 12(1), 139, 1999.

Cook, R. et al., A model for case assessment and interpretation, *Sci. Justice*, 38(3), 151–156, 1998a.

Cook, R. et al., A hierarchy of propositions: deciding which level to address in casework, *Sci. Justice*, 38(4), 231–239, 1998b.

Deadman, H. A., Fiber evidence and the Wayne Williams trial: Part I, *FBI Law Enforcement Bull.*, 53(3), 12–20, 1984a.

Deadman, H. A., Fiber evidence and the Wayne Williams trial: Conclusion, *FBI Law Enforcement Bull.*, 53(5), 10–19, 1984b.

Evett, I. W. and Weir, B. S., *Interpreting DNA Evidence*, Sinauer Associates, Inc., Sunderland, MA, 1998.

Fregeau, C. J. and Fourney, R. M., DNA typing with fluorescently tagged short tandem repeats: a sensitive and accurate approach to human identification, *Biotechniques*, 15(1), 1993.

Gaudette, B. D., Some further thoughts on probabilities and human hair comparisons, *J. Forensic Sci.*, 23, 758, 1978.

Gaudette, B. D., A supplementary discussion of probabilities and human hair comparisons, *J. Forensic Sci.*, 27(2), 279–289, 1982.

Gill P. et al., Report of the European DNA Profiling Group (EDNAP) towards standardization of short tandem repeat loci, *Forensic Sci. Int.*, 65, 1994.

Grieve, M. C. and Biermann, T. W., The population of coloured textile fibres on outdoor surfaces, *Sci. Justice*, 37(4), 231–239, 1997.

Griffiths, A. J. F., Miller, J. H., Suzuki, D. T., Lewontin, R. C., and Gelbart, W. M., *An Introduction to Genetic Analysis*, 5th ed., W. H. Freeman, New York, 1993.

Hayakawa, S. I., *Language in Thought and Action*, Harcourt, Brace and Co., New York, 1939.

Homewood, S. L., Oleksow, D. L., and Leaver, W. L., Questioned document evidence, in *Forensic Evidence*, California District Attorneys Association, Sacramento, 1999.

Horgan, J., *The End of Science*, Addison-Wesley, New York, 1996.

Horrocks, M., Coulson S. A., and Walsh K. A. J., Forensic palynology: variation in the pollen content of soil on shoes and in shoeprints in soil, *J. Forensic Sci.*, 44(1), 119–122, 1999.

Houck, M. and Siegal, J., A large scale fiber transfer study, paper presented at the American Academy of Forensic Sciences, Orlando, FL, February, 1999.

Kirk, P. L., *Crime Investigation*, 1st ed., Interscience, John Wiley & Sons, New York, 1953.

Kirk, P. L., *Crime Investigation*, 2nd ed., Thornton, J., Ed., Krieger Publishing (by arrangement with John Wiley & Sons), Malabar, FL, 1974.

Kirk, P. L., The ontogeny of criminalistics, *J. Criminal Law Criminol. Police Sci.*, 54, 235–238, 1963.

Kline, M. C. and Jenkins, B., Non-amplification of a vWA allele, *J. Forensic Sci.*, 43(1), 250, 1998.

Koehler, A., Techniques used in tracing of the Lindbergh kidnapping ladder, *Police Science*, 27(5), 1937.

Lewin, B., *Genes VI*, Oxford University Press, New York, 1997.

Moenssons, A., Lip Print Identification Anyone? (on *People v. Davis* — Ill), 1999, available at *http://www.forensic-evidence.com/site/ID00004_10.html*.

Murdock, J. E. and Biasotti, A. A., The scientific basis of firearms and Toolmark Identification, in Firearms and toolmark identification, in *Modern Scientific Evidence*, Faigman, D. L. et al., Eds., West Law, San Francisco, 1997.

National Research Council, Committee on DNA Technology in Forensic Science, *DNA Technology in Forensic Science,* National Academy Press, Washington, D.C., 1992.

National Research Council, Committee on DNA Technology in Forensic Science, *The Evaluation of Forensic DNA Evidence*, National Academy Press, Washington, D.C., 1996.

Nichols, R. G., Firearm and toolmark identification criteria: a review of the literature, *J. Forensic Sci.*, 42(3), 466–474, 1997.

Nordby, J. J., Can we believe what we see, if we see what we believe? — Expert disagreement, *J. Forensic Sci.*, 37(4), 1115–1124, 1992.

Osterburg, J. W., *The Crime Laboratory; Case Studies of Scientific Criminal Investigation*, Indiana University Press, Bloomington, 1968.

Popper, K. R., *Conjectures and Refutations: The Growth of Scientific Knowledge*, Basic Books, New York, 1962.

Pounds, C. A. and Smalldon, K. W., The transfer of fibers between clothing materials during simulated contacts and their persistence during wear: part I: fiber transference, *HOCRE Report*, Home Office Central Research Establishment, Aldermaston, 1975a.

Pounds, C. A. and Smalldon, K. W., The transfer of fibers between clothing materials during simulated contacts and their persistence during wear: part II: fiber persistence, *HOCRE Report*, Home Office Central Research Establishment, Aldermaston, 1975b.

Pounds, C. A. and Smalldon, K. W., The transfer of fibers between clothing materials during simulated contacts and their persistence during wear: part III: a preliminary investigation of the mechanisms involved, *HOCRE Report*, Home Office Central Research Establishment, Aldermaston, 1975c.

Robertson, B. and Vignaux, G. A., *Interpreting Evidence*, John Wiley & Sons, Chichester, 1995.

Saferstein, R., *Criminalistics: An Introduction to Forensic Science*, 6th ed., Prentice-Hall, Englewood Cliffs, NJ, 1998.

Shields, W. M., The validation of novel DNA typing techniques for forensic use: peer review and validity of the FBI's validation studies of PCR amplification and automated sequencing of mitochondrial DNA, Unpublished draft, 1998.

Smith, W. C., Kinney, R., and Departee, D., Latent fingerprints — a forensic approach, *J. Forensic Identification*, 43(6), 563–570, 1993.

Stoney, D. A., What made us ever think we could individualize using statistics? *J. Forensic Sci. Soc.*, 3(2), 197–199, 1991a.

Stoney, D. A., Transfer evidence, in *The Use of Statistics in Forensic Science*, Aitken, C. and Stoney, D., Eds., Ellis Horwood, 1991b.

Stoney, D. A. and Thornton, J. I., A critical analysis of quantitative fingerprint individuality models, *J. Forensic Sci.*, 31(4), 1187–1216, 1986a.

Stoney, D. A. and Thornton, J. I., A method for the description of minutia pairs in epidermal ridge patterns, *J. Forensic Sci.*, 31(4), 1217–1234, 1986b.

Stoney, D. A. and Thornton, J. I., A systematic study of epidermal ridge minutiae, *J. Forensic Sci.*, 32(5), 1182–1203, 1987.

Taroni, F., Champod, C., and Margot, P., Forerunners of Bayesianism in early forensic science, *Jurimetrics* J., 38, 183–200, 1998.

Thornton, J. I., The snowflake paradigm, *J. Forensic Sci.*, 31(2), 399–401, 1986a.

Thornton, J. I., Ensembles of class characteristics in physical evidence examination, *J. Forensic Sci.*, 31(2), 501–503, 1986b.

Tuthill, H., *Individualization: Principles and Procedures in Criminalistics*, Lightening Powder Company, Salem, OR, 1994.

van der Lugt, C., Ear Identification: State of the Art, paper presented at the Conference for Shoe Print and Tool Mark Examiners, Noordwijkerhout, the Netherlands, 1997, Crime & Clues, available at *http://crimeandclues.com/earprint.html*.

Walsh, S., Commentary on Kline MC, Jenkins B, Rogers S., Non-amplification of a vWA allele, *J. Forensic Sci.*, 43(5), 1103, 1998.

Webster's Encyclopedic Unabridged Dictionary of the English Language, Gramercy Books, New York, 1996.

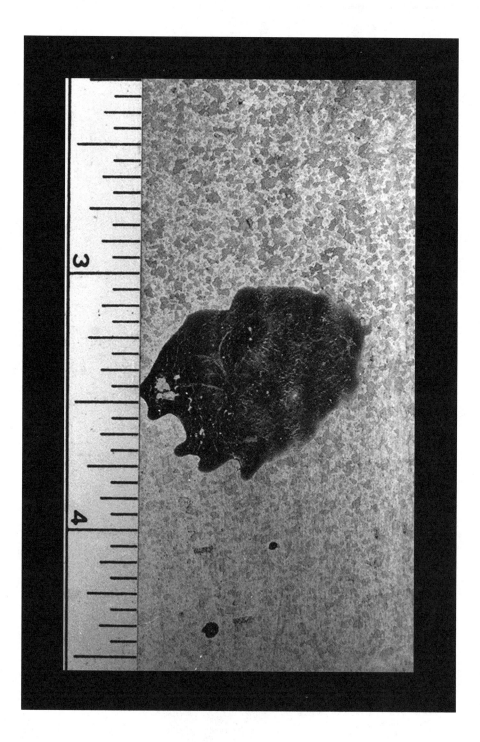

Association and Reconstruction — Inference of Contact

7

Figure 7.1 Stain A. This bloodstain was found on the wardrobe door in the bedroom in which Marilyn Sheppard was murdered. In Dr. Paul Kirk's reconstruction of this homicide, he determined that Stain A was created through a different mechanism of blood deposition than the one responsible for the main pattern of relatively fine blood spatter on the door. This was a key discovery, and led him to conclude that the assailant was himself injured during the incident.

"Circumstantial evidence is a very tricky thing," answered Holmes thought-fully. "It may seem to point very straight to one thing, but if you shift your own point of view a little, you may find it pointing in an equally uncompromising manner to something entirely different."

—Arthur Conan Doyle
Boscombe Valley Mystery, The Strand Magazine, 1891

A.   Association

1.   Evidence and the Law Revisited

As we have seen, much of the research and analytical effort of the criminal-istics community is devoted to source determination. The next step of our paradigm, *association* (inferring contact between two objects), bridges the laboratory work product of the scientist and the needs of the law by making a statement about the meaning of the physical evidence in light of the specific case circumstances. A great amount of misunderstanding between scientists themselves, as well as between scientists and lawyers, results from a failure to appreciate this essential role of associating two objects, and the factors involved in the inferential process used to effect the association.

a.   The Lawyer, the Scientist, and Relevance

As always, we must return to the purpose of the law and the invitation extended to science to enter the legal arena. The law requires that the court determine whether the accused has committed a crime, by hearing evidence for and against the proposition. While we have covered the topic of legal evidence in Chapter 5, its definition is crucial to the discussion of association, and so we briefly repeat it here.

> Relevant evidence means evidence having any tendency to make the existence of any fact that is of consequence to the determination of the action more probable or less probable than it would be without the evidence.

The law places physical evidence in the category of circumstantial evidence.* One characteristic of circumstantial evidence is that it requires an inference to connect the evidentiary fact with a principal fact in the case. For physical evidence, this means connecting the results of an analysis for source determination, by means of an inference, with the proposition that the defendant committed the crime. We have previously distinguished between identification evidence (e.g., drug possession, blood alcohol concentration) and potentially individualizing evidence. Because identification evidence is, in effect, direct evidence, it does not require an inference of association to establish its relevance. Therefore, any further reference to physical evidence in this chapter will be, by definition, to potentially individualizing evidence for which we have established a common source between an evidence sample and a reference sample.

Science, on the other hand, perceives physical evidence primarily as tangible evidence that we can detect with one of our five senses, and that is amenable to some analytical technique. Because a court will not admit irrelevant evidence to be heard by the fact finder, however, the results of a physical evidence examination must lead to an inference that makes the existence of a legal fact (Is the suspect guilty?) more or less probable than it would be without the physical evidence. Without a showing of relevance, the physical evidence may not be admitted. We assert that mere source determination per se is not relevant to a legal proceeding. While Cook et al. (1998b) briefly highlight this contention, it is not widely appreciated in scientific circles. If you are not yet convinced, consider the following scenario:

- A fingerprint at the scene of a burglary is found and submitted to an examiner. The examiner eliminates the current residents as a source of the print, and determines from a search of the national fingerprint database that it is from Fred Flintstone.

---

* Circumstantial evidence is that which is applied to the principal fact indirectly or through the medium of other facts, from which the principal fact is inferred. The characteristics of circumstantial evidence, as distinguished from that which is direct, are (1) the existence and presentation of one or more evidentiary facts and (2) a process of inference, by which these facts are connected with the facts sought, tending to produce a persuasion of their truth (Haight, 1996).

This information is provided to the detective, who heaves a sigh of thanks to the crime scene technician, the fingerprint examiner, and St. Paul of Kirk, and sets out to locate the burglar. The detective stops short when she discovers that:

- Fred Flintstone died 10 years before the crime was committed.

At first doubting the competency of the examination, she asks another fingerprint analyst to compare the evidence and reference prints. The second analyst confirms the source determination, concluding that Fred Flintstone left the print. The detective must now reconsider her theory of the case. Some interesting possibilities occur to her, including:

1. The print was deposited at least 10 years ago, and is unrelated to the current crime.
2. The print is a coincidental match.
3. The print was planted as a forgery.

As esoteric and unusual as these explanations might be, one of them must be true, because it is impossible for Fred Flintstone to be implicated in the current crime (unless, of course, Fred faked his death, and he is still out there committing crimes). We note that fingerprint examiners will resist alternative 2, while the detective might be willing to consider it. From this example, it is clear that the mere existence of facts derived from an analysis of physical evidence is insufficient to make it relevant. No one says it better than author Conan Doyle, in the quote at the beginning of this chapter; a slight shift in viewpoint and, all of a sudden, evidence that seemed immutably inculpatory is suddenly irrelevant.

2.   Inferential Reasoning in Science

a.   *Science and Inductive Inference*

Evett (1996) has argued that the central activity of science is inductive inference. This concept is foreign to many forensic scientists and to most laypersons, yet the ramifications of it profoundly influence the answers that science provides to relevant legal questions. Inferences derived from inductive thinking will be perceived, interpreted, and used differently by the fact finder than conclusions presented under the guise of "facts."

As we outlined in Chapter 1, Karl Popper summarized his understanding of modern scientific philosophy in arguing that we can never conclusively prove a hypothesis. Jeffreys (1983) adds that scientific progress, resulting from the application of the scientific method, is not merely describing what we see, but also making inferences from past experiences to predict future experience. If the prediction is wrong, then the inference upon which it was predicated is wrong. Science seeks not merely to catalog what is observed, but to predict what might be seen if we look in another place or another way. It hopes ultimately to uncover the *reasons* things are the way they are, and along the way to develop rules to explain the underlying causes of what we see. These rules, determined from a large number of observations, are derived by reasoning from the specific measurements to a general theory. As we explained in Chapter 1, generalizing from numerous observations is known as induction. The generalization itself is called an inference.

A trivial example:

I see the sun rise every morning. I speak with my friends and they also see the sun rise every morning. From these specific observations, I infer that the sun will rise after the passage of approximately 24 hours. Because my observation has been invariant my whole life, I feel quite strongly that my inference is correct.

A more speculative example:

The sun comes up on one side of my world, traverses the sky, and sets on the other side. I wonder how it gets from the side on which it sets to the side on which it rises. I infer either that the land on which I stand could be fixed, allowing for the sun to move around it, or that the land on which I am standing rotates, with the sun being fixed. Both of these inferences are possible and reasonable based on the observations that I have made. I do not have any specific reason to believe one over the other. Both are derived from specific observations and lead to a general statement that could explain the cause of the phenomenon. Without more information, I cannot choose between the alternatives.

We refer you at this point to a children's story featuring Sherlock Hemlock, the text of which is reproduced in Sidebar 4. If this volume has been too serious up to now, take the time to get this story and read it in the children's format. To appreciate it fully, you must have the illustrations.

In this story, Sherlock Hemlock makes many observations while examining the "crime scene." From his examination of specific items of evidence, he makes inferences about what happened in the past. All of us readers were sure he was wrong, listing as he did one improbable cause after another to explain the evidence. Clearly, we thought, there is a more plausible explanation for all of the evidence than the one he proffered, that a birthday party had just taken place! This is directly related to our past experience with candles, cakes, and wrapping paper. In the end, however, Sherlock's inference proved correct. This brings us to two key characteristics of inductive inference

Sidebar 4

Sherlock Hemlock — The Falsification of Occam's Razor

One day, as I walked past my friend's house, I spied a terrible mess in his front yard.

"What a terrible mess!" I cried. "What on earth has happened here?"

Just then a man in a checked hat and coat appeared carrying a magnifying glass.

"Sherlock Hemlock here the world's greatest detective," the man announced. "Sherlock Hemlock sees all!"

"Hello!", I said.

He leaped three feet into the air.

"Zounds!" he cried. "I did not see you!"

"I'm glad you're here, Mr. Hemlock," I said. "Maybe you can tell me what on earth has been happening here."

"Aha!" said the man. "Has something been happening here?"

"Indeed it has," I answered. "There's a terrible mess in my friend's front yard."

"A terrible mess!" said the man. "That sounds like a job for Sherlock Hemlock."

"Look!" I said, pointing. "There are some little horns and paper hats. Perhaps they will help us guess what happened here."

Sherlock Hemlock frowned.

"Now let me see," he said. "You probably haven't noticed this, but in the front yard there are some horns and paper hats. I've got it! The Twiddlebugs were doing their famous jellybean dance."

"What?" I exclaimed.

"Once every seven years, the Twiddlebugs appear and play their horns in the hope that it will rain jellybeans. When the jellybeans start raining down, the Twiddlebugs take off their hats and try to catch them."

Now, it seemed to me that there might be a simpler way to explain what those horns and paper hats were doing there. Do you think Sherlock Hemlock was right?

"I think there might be a simpler way to explain what those horns and paper hats are doing there," I said. "That piece of cake in the yard tells me something."

"Quiet!" replied the great detective. "Do you see that piece of cake there? When the Twiddlebugs did their jellybean dance, and jellybeans fell from the sky, the Twiddlebugs got very hungry. They began to eat that piece of cake."

"But how do you explain the candle in the piece of cake?" I asked.

"Egad!" said Sherlock Hemlock. "There is a candle in that piece of cake! That can mean only one thing. While the Twiddlebugs were doing their dance, along came a big, scary monster who threw candles at them. One of the candles stuck in that piece of cake."

I thought about it. Horns and paper hats, and a piece of cake with a candle in it. Where had I seen those things together before? It certainly was not at a Twiddlebug dance!

I was absolutely sure now that I knew what had happened in my friend's front yard. Can you guess what it was?

Then Sherlock Hemlock pointed to some crumpled paper on the grass.

"Aha!' he cried. "Then the Twiddlebugs discovered that a big, scary monster was throwing candles at them, one of them wrote a message on that paper. Something like: 'Dear Sherlock Hemlock, please help! A big scary monster is throwing candles at us!'"

"But Mr. Hemlock," I said, "that's wrapping paper — the kind you wrap birthday presents in."

"Don't be silly, young lady," said Sherlock Hemlock. "The big scary monster grabbed that paper and crumpled it up. And he chased all the Twiddlebugs into that house. That's it! The remarkable brain of Sherlock Hemlock has solved another mystery!"

"You may be a great detective," I said to Sherlock Hemlock, "but I think you are wrong about why those horns and hats and that piece of cake with a candle in it and the crumpled wrapping paper are in my friend's front yard. I think that what happened here was a birthday party! And I think most people would agree with me!"

"You believe the great Sherlock Hemlock has made a mistake!" exclaimed Sherlock Hemlock. "Amazing! But look, there's your friend coming out of his house. Why don't you ask him what happened here?

I waved to my friend.

"Friend," I shouted, "this gentleman and I have been having a little argument. You can settle it if you tell us what has been happening in your front yard."

"Oh," said my friend, "it's very simple. Today's my birthday, and I had a party here."

Sherlock Hemlock shook his head.

"Impossible!" he cried. "No Twiddlebugs doing the jellybean dance? No monster throwing candles? Sherlock Hemlock has never been wrong before!… Oh, well, there's always a first time." And, with a sigh, the great detective moved on down the sidewalk.

"Well," I said to my friend, "let's go inside and look at your presents!"

"I'd love to invite you in," said my friend, "but I cannot. You see, we were having the party when all of a sudden all these little bugs came and started doing a dance, and then a monster ran up and threw candles at everyone and chased us into the house. You cannot possibly go in there now."

"So Sherlock Hemlock was right after all!" I said.

Just then the door to the house flew open and out ran hundreds of screaming Twiddlebugs, followed by a big scary monster throwing candles at everyone.

"Well, look at that!" I said, thrilled at the fact that I had been there to listen while Sherlock Hemlock, the world's greatest detective, solved perhaps his greatest case — the mystery of the terrible mess in my friend's front yard!

Source: By Betty Lou as told to Sir Arthur Conan Rubberducque, *Sherlock Hemlock and the Great Twiddlebug Mystery*, Western Publishing Company, 1972.

in science: (1) more than one possible underlying cause always exists to explain an observed effect and (2) each inference of cause carries some risk of being wrong.

i. The alternate explanation. In hypothesis testing, we are often satisfied simply to falsify the null hypothesis without proposing a specific alternative. In trying to solve a crime, however, it is preferable to articulate what we call the "competing hypothesis," some other *specific* explanation for the observations we have recorded. In our example using the sun, the observations lead to at least two explanations, or hypotheses, for how the sun could move from the west to the east to rise once again in 24 hours. To progress in understanding the cause of the observed phenomenon, the scientist, whether cognitively or subconsciously, must weigh the relative merits of at least two explanations.

We read with amusement the inferences drawn by Sherlock Hemlock, and automatically compared them with our own assessment of the meaning of the evidence. His implausible inferences seemed so much weaker than our own that we were sure he was wrong and we were correct. This provides a lucid example where two competing hypotheses for a set of observed facts were compared and, finally, one disproved, leaving us to accept the alternative explanation as current fact.

Similarly, a scientist must weigh two or more causes for the effect that she is seeing. To do otherwise invites bias by failing to see and account for other possible explanations. If I am convinced that only one cause is responsible for the effect, then I am blinded to evidence that may point in another direction, and also tend to look only for evidence that supports my hypothesis. Objectivity in science emanates from vigorously searching for different explanations, and evaluating how likely each is to lead to the observed effect.

ii. Uncertainty. By nature, uncertainty is associated with the inference that results from inductive reasoning. When additional observations are made of the same phenomenon, our uncertainty about the generalization changes. If the new information does not falsify our previous hypothesis, it may increase or decrease our confidence in it. A (preferably quantitative) statement of this uncertainty is crucial to communicate how new work should be incorporated with previous observations of the same phenomenon. According to at least one community of experts in this field, this uncertainty is properly measured by probability (Lindley, 1991).

Unlike *academic* science, which makes predictions about future events, *applied* science is concerned with solving practical everyday problems, often involving inferences about events that have occurred in the past. Archaeologists try to infer whole cultures and languages from remnants left behind, while art conservationists examine works of art in an attempt to establish provenance. Similarly, in forensic science we make inductive inferences about criminal events that have occurred in the past. We examine a piece of physical evidence and want to know if it has anything to tell us about a particular event of concern. It will not tell us *everything*, because every event has more than one potential cause, even if some of the potential causes are extremely unlikely. This is one source of uncertainty in inferential thinking in forensic science.

In the Sherlock Hemlock tale, it is interesting to note that the additional information provided at the end of the story by the occupant of the house caused us to reject our first hypothesis of the birthday party in favor of the alternate hypothesis, the Twiddlebug dance. Without this information, we would still be convinced of the birthday party hypothesis.

This awareness that inferences are not absolute truths or immutable facts is crucial for the forensic scientist. The scientist almost never possesses all of the information about an event, if for no other reason than the physical evidence represents only one small effect of the incident. For an inference to be accepted by either the scientist or a fact finder, each is forced to make some assumptions about the remaining information. The scientist may change her assumptions based on new information and, when she does, her inference may also change. Another scientist or fact finder may make different assumptions, resulting in yet different inferences. It is invariably the assumptions about which people disagree, not the facts.

3. Inferential Reasoning in Forensic Science

Based on our discussion so far, we propose the following as a basic tenet of forensic science:

> **Inductive inference is a primary tool for evaluating physical evidence gathered from a criminal event.**

We have already encountered one process used by the forensic scientist that ends in an inference, that of source determination. We have also established that the law requires another inference to make this source determination relevant evidence. We now explore further the misunderstandings and debates about this latter process of associating two or more objects through an inference of contact.

a. Association and Interpretation — A Divergence of Understanding

It is noteworthy that so little has been written using the term *association* in the forensic science literature. The few references that one can find among textbooks consist of short fragments that are incomplete and rarely help to uncover what is meant by the term.

Osterburg (1968) asserts that associative evidence is "linking a person to a crime scene." Stoney (1984) describes it as "linking a suspect with an offense" (not exactly the same meaning as Osterburg's). DeForest et al. (1983) talk about the "association between people and the physical evidence." Without using the word association, Kirk (1953; 1974) offers that the "identification of a murder weapon may lead to its possessor at the time of the crime," a clear attempt at connecting an item of physical evidence with a perpetrator.

Absent from any of these meager attempts to define association is a discussion of how one proceeds from linking evidence and reference to a connection between people, places, and things. The implication is that once the source of the evidence has been determined, the association follows without question. No mention is made of the assumptions that must undergird the inferences of various associations, or of alternative possibilities that might also explain the recovered evidence.

Another body of forensic literature emphasizes understanding the nature of the factors leading to deposition of the evidence, and how, after analysis, evidence should be interpreted in the context of the case. In these writings, the word *interpretation* appears frequently. For example, Cook et al. (1998a) contend that the process of interpretation is "drawing rational and balanced inferences from observations, test results, and measurements." Taroni (1998) asserts that "appropriate interpretive procedures ... need to be applied ... to aid in the correct interpretation of scientific evidence."

The difference between association as an adjunct to individualization and interpretation as a separate process amounts to more than a mere contrast in emphasis; it is a divergence in understanding the fundamental role of science in legal matters. This leads to confusion among practitioners of forensic science and between the service provider and the client; it raises the decibel levels during debates and hearings, and hinders progress in the incorporation of science into law.

Two well-known figures serve to draw a sharp contrast between the two schools of thought:

> Paul Kirk — "The criminalist does not attempt identification except as a prelude to his real function — *that of individualization*" [emphasis added] (1953; 1975).
>
> Henri Poincaré — "An effect may be the product of either cause A or cause B. The effect has already been observed; one wants to know the probability that *it is the result of cause A*" [emphasis added] (Taroni, 1998).

These two quotes reveal a clear difference in the perceived role of the scientist in legal matters. Kirk believes that the scientist is to determine the *source* of the evidence; Poincaré believes that the scientist is to assist the fact finder in establishing the *cause* of the evidence.* This divergence forms the central theme of a continuing debate between jurists and scientists over the function of science in the legal arena.

b. Inference and Association

The weak and limited definitions of association found in the forensic literature reveal the mistaken notion that the step from individualization to an inference of contact is inexorably easy and obvious. The reasoning behind this belief stems from our experience with strong personal individualizing evidence (fingerprints and physiological fluids), where the presence of the "mark" virtually "proves" the presence of the individual; how else could the evidence have been deposited if not by the individual to whom it belongs?

---

* Note that he does not want to *determine* the cause, but rather to *assist the fact finder in determining the cause*. The distinction is crucial, as we hope to make clear in the remainder of the chapter.

As our example with Fred Flintstone's fingerprint illustrates, however, this is still an inference.

When considering other potentially individualizing evidence, such as tool-mark or shoeprint evidence, the inference is less immediate, and requires additional assumptions before intimating contact. At the very least, we need to connect the person with the tool that made the mark, and place the person with the tool at the scene at the time the crime was committed. Even in this simple example, we have named several assumptions external to the conclusion that the tool made the mark, necessary to associate the person with the crime.

In the phrase from Kirk quoted earlier, he links an item of evidence with a perpetrator by suggesting that:

> identification of a murder weapon *may* lead to its possessor at the time of the crime [emphasis added].

He clearly understood that individualizing a bullet to a firearm also might *not* lead to the perpetrator, and that other evidence would be needed to establish this fact more convincingly. An expansion of the previous comment from DeForest et al. (1983) seems particularly applicable to evidence limited for whatever reason to classification:

> Depending on the degree of individuality exhibited by the samples, various conclusions can be drawn about the association between people and the physical evidence in the case... These kinds of considerations need to be kept in mind when evaluating the value of *associative* physical evidence comparisons.

Here, "various conclusions" can be construed as different explanations for the occurrence of the physical evidence, including multiple sources or multiple possibilities for the transfer of the evidence from the source to the target. In this situation, numerous assumptions must be accepted to sustain an inference of common source, and even more assumptions to support an inference of contact. Any discussion of "association" generally defaults to a plea for better methods of individualization, completely missing the conceptual point. Most authors fail to detail any approach that would describe the relationship between the evidence and the crime or criminal besides the useless admonition that these considerations "need to be kept in mind."

Stoney (1991) comes the closest when he says:

> Association is an inference of contact between two objects, and is the only way in which legally relevant evidence can be generated by a scientist. Mere source determination is not legally relevant, *per se.*

The field would benefit from further development of this important thesis.

c. *Inference and Interpretation*

While those espousing interpretation as the primary goal of a forensic examination use inference as the basis for communicating that interpretation, they
also frequently fail to distinguish clearly between source determination and
an inference of contact. Sometimes it is difficult even to determine which of
these ideas a writer has in mind. Early in their book, Robertson and Vignaux
(1995, p. 34), articulate a global "prosecution hypothesis" as "The accused
was present at the scene." This clearly encompasses an inference of contact.
Later they describe the alternative (defense) hypothesis as "obtaining a match
by chance," (p. 58) a clear reference to source determination. They then make
the point that "the match could not have occurred unless the prosecution
hypothesis was true." Their prosecution hypothesis is predicated on contact
and transfer (the accused was present at the scene), while their defense or
alternate hypothesis relies only on source determination (obtaining a match
by chance).

Oddly, the distinction between source determination and inference of
contact becomes increasingly clear with more ambiguous evidence. In such
instances, the leap from source determination to an inference of contact
requires more assumptions, hence is more evident. Rarely, for example,
would an analyst argue that a physicochemical correspondence between a
brown cotton evidence fiber and a brown pullover sweatshirt is strong evidence supporting an inference of contact.

d. *The Source of the Confusion*

We have outlined some of the intellectual confusion that we perceive exists
in criminalistics today. Perhaps the first step toward clarification is to look
backward in an attempt to discern the origin of the confusion. Both anthropometry and fingerprints were popularized as direct personal identification
evidence. Notwithstanding attempts by Galton, and later by others, to quan-
tify the likelihood of a coincidental match, the inference of source was generally accepted without much question. And because few or no inferences
need be made to connect a person with this type of evidence, the subtle
distinction between personal identification and inference of contact went
essentially unrecognized. Even Locard's work with trace evidence focused on
the *identification* of the dusts that he was convinced could provide information about a person's occupation and whereabouts. Although he was the first
to articulate the concept of transfer, if he appreciated the assumptions needed
to strongly infer the source of a relatively common fiber, or the further
inferences needed to conclude, from the discovery of a fiber at the scene, that
a person committed a crime, it is not prominent in his writings.

Relatively little documented work exists that explores a formal scientific
framework for extending a source determination to an inference of contact.

Taroni (1998) summarizes some of the early efforts. Perhaps, in part, because of our 20th century love affair with technology, the focus in criminalistics has been to develop more efficient, more sensitive, and more highly discriminating tests, all directed toward increasing a random match probability in support of an opinion of individualization. This has cast source determination as the central, or even sole, player in the use of physical evidence to help solve crimes. Ironically, Kirk must accept much of the responsibility for fomenting the very thing that he decried. For in declaring *individualization* as the primary function of criminalistics, he placed the focus squarely on the physicochemical analysis of objects, and shifted emphasis away from the interpretation of data in the context of the crime. By focusing on individualization, the field was doomed to progress that Kirk describes as "technical rather than fundamental, practical rather than theoretical, transient rather than permanent."

Source determination depends on technology and our knowledge of the nature of the evidence; scientific logic furnishes the means to summarize the possibilities that could have produced the physical evidence. As we have seen, the application of science consists of forming inductive inferences from the analytical results, and making a statement about the likelihood of encountering the evidence under competing hypotheses. The truly scientific aspect of our work lies not in the technical minutiae of the analysis itself, but rather in the way that the analysis is constructed and interpreted (Evett, 1996). We spend the rest of this chapter exploring some of these relatively undeveloped ideas about inference and association.

4.   Definition of Association

In attempting to refine our understanding of association in forensic science, we have established several points:

1. The law requires that evidence be relevant; the existence of the evidence must make the actuality of some principal fact more or less probable than it would be without the evidence.
2. Potentially individualizing physical evidence is circumstantial evidence; an inference is required to connect the evidentiary fact with the principal fact in question.
3. Source determination is usually not relevant per se; an inference is required to make it relevant.
4. The inference required to render a source determination relevant is that of contact between two objects.
5. Inferences depend on assumptions and other information; the same physical evidence may support several competing inferences, depending on the assumptions and available information.

We summarize these points into a definition of association:

> *Association:*
> **An inference of contact between two objects, the source of the**
> **evidence, and the target on which it was found.**

Although the term *association* has, up to now, been poorly defined, it is potentially more descriptive than the term *interpretation*. We choose to retain association to characterize this aspect of the paradigm. We also define the phrase *inference of contact* as a synonym for association.

5. Associating Two Objects through an Inference of Contact

Criminalists examine potentially individualizing evidence with the (usually unarticulated) goal of providing information about the proposition of contact. Source determination is only the first step in the inferential chain that leads to an inference of association. Keeping this thought in mind during examination will help the analyst define the limitations of the evidence, and will force an explication of the assumptions that must be made to support an inference of contact.

a. *A Bayesian Framework for Inferential Thinking — Principle or Practice*

The literature written over the last two decades that addresses inference of contact is almost exclusively Bayesian in outlook. We do not attempt here to review all of the various arguments in favor of the Bayesian framework as a tool for inferential thinking, nor do we attempt a rigorous mathematical treatment. We acknowledge the pivotal role played by Evett in pioneering its use, and recognize the valuable contributions made by scientists Buckleton, Taroni, Margot, Champod, Aitken, Stoney, Walsh, Curran, and Weir and by jurists Robertson, Vignaux, Kaye, and Thompson. We refer the interested reader to the various publications by these and other authors, some of which are listed in the references at the end of this chapter. The best one-stop, overall reference is Aitken and Stoney (1991), whereas a specific application to DNA evidence is found in Evett and Weir (1998).

Although most of the literature on inference in forensic science is decidedly Bayesian-centric, a major dichotomy exists between that literature and current practice. Common practice in forensic science is to present a report and testimony regarding source determination. When asked to define the significance of an examination, practicing criminalists usually respond with frequencies if they have them, or general word descriptions that amount to the same thing if they don't (notwithstanding the criticisms that have rained down on that practice). Even when likelihood ratios (LRs) are used, they are generally restricted to comparing hypotheses regarding the source of the evidence. We rarely encounter a report that formally evaluates an inference of contact between source and target. This has presented a major difficulty in writing this chapter. While we are convinced that these ideas are both legitimate and useful, they have not been generally embraced by the practicing community of criminalists,* nor have they undergone the refinement that only comes with use over time. We present them here as a tool for the community to consider, while acknowledging that they have not gained widespread use in practice. The remainder of this discussion will focus on how a criminalist might contribute to the proposition of contact using a Bayesian framework. We will assume here that you have read the introduction to Bayesian thinking offered in Chapter 6.

b.   Hypothesis Testing and Likelihood Ratios

Consideration of more than one hypothesis to account for the physical evidence forces the criminalist to think more rigorously and discourages bias in evaluating the results of analyses. LRs not only allow, but specifically require the simultaneous evaluation of the competing hypotheses. If the analyst has been considering alternate causes from the inception of the analysis, it is natural to continue this comparison using LRs as a tool. This brings us to a subtle distinction between hypothesis testing and Bayesian statistics.

In classical hypothesis testing, we attempt to falsify the null hypothesis. Only two outcomes are possible from this predicate. Failing to falsify it, we accept the null hypothesis, or, disproving the null hypothesis, we must accept an alternate hypothesis. However, in the common scheme where no specific alternate hypothesis is defined, the analyst is left with the unsatisfying and unhelpful conclusion merely that the null hypothesis is incorrect. For events connected to a crime, however, this is rarely satisfactory. If cause A did not effect the event, then some other specific cause must have. While a defendant might appreciate the conclusion that he did not cause the event, the detective who wants to solve the crime needs not only to figure out what did not happen, but what did happen. Even if a specific alternate explanation for the evidence is proposed, we can, again, only falsify or fail to falsify it. The statistics are all directed at the null hypothesis. No quantitative information is gathered about any alternatives, so we have no idea if yet another explanation might be more likely. In falsifying a null hypothesis, we must blindly accept the alternate hypothesis, and we are essentially blindsided into accepting it as the "right" answer. Thinking stops.

---

* We are aware of some jurisdictions, such as New Zealand, where criminalists typically present testimony in Bayesian terms.

Construction of LRs in Bayesian statistics encourages the comparison of uncertainty for specific competing hypotheses. This allows for the simultaneous evaluation of different causes of an event, and results in a quantitative statement about which cause the physical evidence favors. We still do not know for sure which one is "right," but the quantitative information resulting from the comparison helps us determine which might be more likely. Because the physical evidence is not the only evidence used to determine the cause of an event, it, in and of itself, does not equate to the probability of the event. A full Bayesian treatment forces an explication of assumptions and inferences before the fact finder incorporates the physical evidence into a comment on the ultimate issue. Whatever new information is proffered is used to update our certainty about the cause of an event. We reiterate the mathematical form of this verbal expression:

$$\text{Prior odds} \times \text{LR} = \text{posterior odds}$$

The use of Bayes' theorem recognizes the circumstantial, and therefore inferential, nature of physical evidence. It does not usurp the fact-finding role, but contributes information to a specific proposition. It is a natural fit with the purposes of evidence in law.

c. The Analyst and the Evidence — Articulating Hypotheses

Regardless of which statistical framework one chooses, some person must articulate the hypothesis or hypotheses to be tested. The statistics are only a tool to evaluate the hypotheses. If stupid or irrelevant hypotheses are proposed, the statistics will evaluate those just as easily as they will intelligent and useful hypotheses. If the correct hypothesis is never proffered, no statistical or logical framework can rescue the examination from defeat.

To formulate relevant hypotheses, the analyst must have as many case details as will assist in this effort, and he may consult any number and variety of individuals and sources to achieve this goal. This is one of the primary reasons that a criminalist should respond to crime scenes: to gain firsthand knowledge of the problem. Provisional hypotheses can be made on the spot, and relevant evidence collected. In addition, reading police reports, discussions with detectives and attorneys, and knowledge of other physical evidence results all contribute to a thoughtful framing of hypotheses. Creativity is also useful in imagining what might have happened. Most important, each hypothesis must be falsifiable, and some means of evaluating a failure to falsify must exist. All hypotheses should be directed to answering some legal fact in dispute, whether it be the contact of the suspect with the scene, contact between victim and suspect, or even contact of the victim with a crime scene.

d.   Absence of Evidence

We include a discussion of absence of evidence in this chapter because this question usually applies at the level of *association* — did contact occur between the putative target and a suspected source? For example, a rape victim describes a green wool jacket that the perpetrator was wearing during the incident. A jacket of that description is found in the suspect's car; however, no green wool fibers were recovered from the victim, her clothing, or the immediate crime scene. Does the failure to find "expected" evidence support a hypothesis that the jacket (*source*) and the victim (*target*) were not in contact? Strictly speaking, the failure to find evidence does not necessarily lead to a conclusion that no contact occurred. This is a difficult problem in hypothesis testing. The null hypothesis is, "the source and target were in contact." The scientific question is, can a negative result falsify a hypothesis? This depends heavily on our knowledge about certain properties of the item in question, such as transferability, persistence, and detectability. As we discussed in the previous chapter, what knowledge we have of these attributes may be limited and neither accurate nor precise.

Nevertheless, the bottom-line question remains whether we would ever accept an absence of evidence as evidence of absence. Many analysts do not believe a lack of evidence to be strong evidence that no contact occurred. They have adopted a more specific application of the general maxim, "Absence of evidence is not evidence of absence." How do we evaluate evidence when there isn't any? Scientists are accustomed to analyzing material things; they are not accustomed to evaluating the absence of something. One way of looking at this problem is that although nothing may not *be* something, it may still *mean* something. One way of thinking about a problem such as this is to take it to a logical extreme.

> Suppose a man attacks a woman. She is able to describe him as wearing a white shirt and jeans. She sprays him with ortho-chlorobenzilidinemalanonitrile (tear gas) with an orange dye mixed in. A man wearing a white shirt and jeans is picked up running from the scene. An examination of his shirt shows no traces of dye.*

Under this scenario, the failure to find the orange dye (in other words, a finding of nothing) provides substantial evidence supporting the hypothesis that the arrestee is not the attacker. We have a very high *a priori* expectation that orange dye will be present on the shirt of the attacker.

---

* This example was offered by Dr. John Buckleton during an exchange on an Internet e-mail list.

A Bayesian framework allows us to compare the likelihood of contact vs. no contact rather than depending on the unsatisfying exercise of trying to nullify a hypothesis using a negative result. In Bayesian terms, the evidence (lack of orange dye on the suspect) is so much more likely if he were not the person sprayed, than if he were; this evaluation overcomes almost any prior odds that we have identified the correct suspect. The resulting posterior odds tell us we have the wrong guy. Note also, that the assumptions necessary to associate a non-orange shirt with an innocent suspect under this scenario are relatively few. We must assume he did not have time to change the shirt, as appears likely from the scenario, we must assume that the woman's aim at point-blank range was good enough to hit the attacker, and we must assume that she is in fact telling the truth. That we have a reasonable expectation in this circumstance about what an absence of evidence reveals suggests that we might also have expectations in more ambiguous cases. However, the more assumptions we must make about why no evidence exists, the weaker will be any inferences that explain the evidence.

An interesting example using absence of evidence to infer one kind of contact rather than another can be found in Sidebar 5. In this example, the behavioral analyst (profiler) suggests that, based on a lack of transfer of Marilyn Sheppard's blood to Sam Sheppard, and subsequently to items he may have touched, he must have been her killer. It is interesting to note the unarticulated assumptions in this analysis. They include:

1. That he successfully washed all the blood away after killing her,
2. That he couldn't have washed all the blood away after touching her to take her pulse,
3. That all the blood was hers,
4. That the blood on the watch is hers, and
5. That the bloodstain on his pants knee is irrelevant.

The final *coup de grace* that makes the entire exercise absolutely worthless is the *assumption* that Sam Sheppard was the killer. We encourage readers to examine the entire analysis (McCrary, 1999) and reach their own conclusions.

The temptation in evaluating negative results is to dismiss the failure to find evidence as insignificant, and therefore of no consequence to the case. The two examples provided above represent opposite ends of the spectrum when considering the implication of an absence of evidence. As for all associative evidence, the relevance and strength of the inference rests entirely on the facts and assumptions from which it is formed. The fewer facts we have and the more assumptions we are then forced to make, the weaker the inference. Situations involving an absence of evidence frequently offer fewer facts and necessitate more assumptions. As long as this is explicated, there is nothing inherently wrong about offering a conclusion.

An inference stemming from absence of evidence necessarily relies heavily on the experience of the examiner. Some practitioners are uncomfortable with this. They also believe that the variables involved cannot be adequately enumerated, controlled, and quantified. We suggest that an experienced examiner might give an opinion that he would have expected to detect traces of the source on the target, and that their absence, therefore, provides useful information. Such an opinion should be based on as much supporting data as possible, and the assumptions should be explicated. Obviously, no consensus exists in the field regarding this issue. The challenge to the forensic community is to address this question, both from a research and intellectual perspective, and to continue the discussion.

e.   Combining Source Determination and Inference of Contact

We have outlined two processes in forensic science that require inference — source determination and contact. We are left with the question of how we are to incorporate the inference of common source into our inference about contact. Because of the constant confusion in the literature about association and interpretation, this issue has not been addressed with clarity. Clearly, a Bayesian framework provides the most explicit and quantitative approach. However, perhaps because the process is so case specific, no general suggestions or guidelines have been set forth in the literature about how to do this. We challenge the field to consider this problem in applying the results of a physical evidence analysis to a case.

f.   O. J. and Inference — Is the Tube Half Full or Half Empty?

The *Simpson* case provides an interesting example of inferential thinking. One noteworthy example (math not required) of LRs in (intuitive) action is found in the criminal trial of O. J. Simpson. In that case the formulation of competing hypotheses was crucial to the verdict. The prosecution hypothesis was that the defendant had committed a double-homicide, and when considering the physical evidence, this translated into the hypothesis that Simpson was present at the crime scene. Multiple biological evidence samples were collected from at least three different locations (Rockingham, Bundy, the Bronco). DNA analysis provided overwhelming correspondence frequencies in favor of the prosecution hypothesis. The alternate hypothesis posed by the defense was not merely that Simpson was not present, but that the police had planted evidence from which we could would infer his presence at the various locations. The competing hypotheses are translated into an LR as follows:

$$LR = \frac{P(E|\text{Simpson present})}{P(E|\text{Blood planted})} = 1$$

Under this set of hypotheses, the LR = 1, because we would expect to find the defendant's blood in either case. The jury could then ignore the DNA evidence, because it did not provide compelling evidence in favor of either proposition. This left the determination of the probability of his presence at the scene dependent wholly on the prior odds. In this case, the prior odds are directly concerned with the juror's belief that the police were both capable and willing to plant evidence, compared with their belief that the defendant would murder two people.

$$\text{Prior odds} = \frac{P(\text{the defendant murdered two people})}{P(\text{the police planted the blood})} = \frac{\text{Small number}}{\text{Big number}}$$

The defense then had to demonstrate that the opportunity existed for the planting to take place, and also had to rely on the jurors' subjective prior belief in the proposition that the police were willing to plant evidence. The ratio of these beliefs would have to rise above the standard of "beyond a reasonable doubt" in favor of the prosecution hypothesis in order to convict. The verdict of "not guilty" says that their evaluation of the prior odds of the police planting blood was very high. In mathematical notation:

$$\frac{\text{Small number}}{\text{Big number}} \times 1 = \frac{P(\text{the defendant murdered two people})}{P(\text{the police planted the blood})} = \text{Posterior odds}$$

$$\therefore$$

Posterior odds = Prior odds

In other words, the results of the physical evidence were essentially not considered because the jurors believed they had no relevance to the case. Thus, the prior odds completely determined the posterior odds. This reiterates the point that physical evidence merely updates our belief in a proposition; it does not substitute for the belief. Different assumptions or facts will change our acceptance of an inference.

6. Who Makes the Inference?

A significant and reoccurring issue is, who makes the inference of contact, the scientist or the fact finder? It is the purview of the fact finder to draw inferences from circumstantial evidence, and, of course, potentially individualizing physical evidence is circumstantial evidence. However, there are pieces of information that only science can legitimately provide to the fact finder, such as population frequencies, transfer and persistence data, and limitations of the evidence and the test. These clearly are of assistance to the fact finder in drawing inferences about physical evidence. We assert that the scientist is in the best position to provide this information and to place it within the context of the case. When communicated to the fact finder in a manner that clearly establishes the limits of the information, the scientist can and should talk about an inference of contact. The scientist must avoid statements about guilt or innocence, and should clarify the assumptions upon which the inference relies. As assumptions change, the inference may also change, and the scientist must be willing to adjust her inferences as information changes.

B.   Reconstruction

The commission of a crime involves the interaction of numerous objects, including at least one person, the criminal. Up to this point in constructing the principles of criminalistics, we have been concerned with the relationship of three objects, the evidence, the source of the evidence, and the target on which the evidence is found. We now consider the relationship of multiple objects that may contact each other during commission of a crime. With this concept, we arrive at the final process in a criminalistics examination, that of *reconstruction*.

1.   The State of the Practice

Very little formal literature has been written about reconstruction as an autonomous process. Almost no scientific research has been performed, and no universal principles have been articulated. Further, the age of specialization in criminalistics has decreased the number of criminalists that are both competent and willing to undertake a true reconstruction. The state of the practice today is such that this area is the least-understood procedure in forensic science.

Perhaps because of this continually diminishing field of qualified scientists, nonscientific professionals, such as detectives, attorneys, and profilers, have eagerly stepped in to fill the perceived void. Although properly trained and educated profilers can clearly make a valuable contribution to the psychological aspects of a reconstruction, they are ill-equipped to appreciate and integrate the result of physical evidence examinations. We provide an example below of at least one behavioral analyst who has superseded the limits of his expertise. Similarly, attorneys and detectives should not be put in the position of intepreting scientific evidence. We suggest that it would be appropriate for criminalists to provide a reconstruction to one of the professionals described above, in the same way that they would provide the results of an analysis of source determination. Each would then have that information to assist in, variously, investigating the case, prosecuting the case, or establishing a motivation or psychological profile for the perpetrator.

Two major subcategories of reconstruction exist, almost certainly because of the frequency with which they are encountered, bloodstain pattern interpretation and shooting reconstruction. A body of literature and research does exist regarding the dynamics of both blood spatter (Eckert and James, 1989; Bevel et al., 1997), the ballistics of bullets (Garrison, 1993, *AFTE Journal**), and how they might pertain to a crime scene reconstruction. However, there is a dearth (although not a complete absence; Chisum, 1991) of material detailing general principles and guidelines of reconstruction.** We attempt here to at least categorize the current state of the practice of reconstruction, as it exists in the literature and in practice.

a. Definition of Reconstruction

Earlier, we reviewed two definitions of reconstruction by DeForest et al. (1983) and Saferstein (1998). We combine and paraphrase slightly to provide the following definition:

> *Reconstruction*:
> **The ordering of events in relative space and time based on the physical evidence**

We will use the following nomenclature:

Event   The interaction of two objects
Incident The compilation of all of the individual *events* comprising the activity of interest

2.   Capabilities of Reconstruction

Virtually nothing has been written in the scientific literature about the specific steps involved in reconstructing an incident, that is, ordering the events in space and time. For the most part, this is a logical process that involves thinking about which event must have occurred before some other event. The criminalist will combine facts about the crime scene with the results of physical evidence examinations to propose a path through time and space linking each individual contact. Assumptions, and other information not

---

* The *Association of Firearms and Toolmark Examiners (AFTE) Journal* is dedicated in part to publishing articles about ballistics in the context of crime scene reconstruction.
** We do not consider here accident reconstruction, which is the most common type of reconstruction in civil cases.

strictly related to the physical evidence, must also be incorporated into a reconstruction. Because of this, if the assumptions or information change, the reconstruction may also change.

Clues, in the form of physical evidence, will inevitably be left as a result of every crime, especially violent crime. When the evidence is recognized, collected, and analyzed properly, there exists the possibility of not only associating two of the objects through an inference of contact, but of ordering several such associations in time and space. As with all endeavors in criminalistics, it is imperative to keep the relevant questions clearly in mind. One can spend inordinate amounts of time reconstructing an incident, only to have the work ignored because it is irrelevant. Before attempting a reconstruction, the analyst should have in mind what dispute needs to be resolved, and whether the physical evidence is capable of providing information to the fact finder that will assist in that resolution. To continue a theme repeated throughout this book, the analyst must also form more than one hypothesis for how an event occurred. This tempers any unconscious bias that we might have, and reminds us that there is always more than one possible cause for each event that contributes to an incident.

Consider a simple incident where someone is shot, and the victim's blood is subsequently found on some other person's clothing. The question is whether the transfer of blood occurred in connection with the shooting. Two hypotheses can be considered.

1. Blood from the victim's gunshot wounds was contemporaneously transferred to the other person's clothing.
2. The blood of the victim was transferred to the other person's clothing during an unrelated incident.

A variety of other facts, information, and assumptions will assist in differentiating between these two competing hypotheses. This information can and should be considered when attempting a reconstruction of this incident. A non-exhaustive list includes:

1. The location of the wound on the victim;
2. The volume of blood exuding from the wound;
3. The volume and location of blood on the clothing;
4. Whether the wearer and the owner of the clothing are the same person;
5. When the clothing was collected relative to the incident.

If, for example, an insufficient amount of blood is coming from the wound to account for the amount of blood on the clothing, then an inference that the blood is not related to the incident is appropriate. Note, also, that the person could have acquired the victim's blood on her clothing in connection with the shooting, but as a result of some completely innocent activity, such as assisting the victim. This simple example demonstrates the complexity of any attempt at reconstruction. Trying to incorporate more events will increase the intricacy even further, providing opportunities for overinterpretation.

a.   Predictive Value of a Simulation

It is common, particularly when attempting a reconstruction, for the criminalist to try to recreate or simulate the circumstances he thinks led to the scenario found at the crime scene. This kind of experimentation can be informative, but its limits must be well understood. All too often, having set up conditions that appear to duplicate the physical observations, the investigator will then conclude that he has discerned what happened. Doing an experiment is a good idea, but it is crucial to understand that an experiment can only tell you that the evidence *could* have been produced using your simulated conditions. It does *not* tell you either that this is the only way to produce the evidence, or that the incident happened in the way you envision. However, failure to recreate an expected result can be helpful in eliminating that set of circumstances and actions from consideration, thus reducing the number of possibilities. A simulation supports a reconstruction, it does not prove one.

> In one case, it was suggested that fine blood spatter found in a particular pattern was produced by a contact gunshot wound with the victim and suspects in particular positions. The analyst simulated the circumstances that he thought had led to the scene as it was first found. Sure enough, he reproduced what he was looking for, including particular sizes of blood spatter drops at a specific distance from the victim and in a similar pattern. He then testified that his simulation proved his reconstruction, and that the events happened in exactly the way he envisioned.

This criminalist could not conceive that an alternate explanation for the evidence might exist; he was caught in his own expectations and prejudices about how the crime could have occurred.

b.   Corroboration or Refutation of Statements

Frequently detectives will elicit statements from victims, suspects, and witnesses about an incident. One way to establish the veracity of these accounts is via a reconstruction. If the physical evidence fails to support a particular statement, then the detective can use this information in further questioning. This type of reconstruction can also be used during testimony to corroborate or refute statements made during the investigation, or in previous testimony by other witnesses. Corroborative reconstruction is generally easier because it is, by definition, focused on a specific proposition or hypothesis that has been proposed by someone else. In this context, the expert is asked to comment on whether an event could have happened as it was related by the witness, and examination of the physical evidence is directed toward answering this question.

A typical example is a suspect relating that he was acting in self-defense.

One such case involved a shooting death, where the suspect insisted that he was simply defending himself from the victim. He described a scenario where the victim was attacking him with a hatchet poised over his head, ready to strike. In fact, a hatchet was found on a small table next to where the victim was shot, so a real possibility existed that the suspect was telling the truth. The table was covered in fine blood droplets obviously resulting from the fatal shot to the victim's head. The question related to whether the hatchet was on the table or in the victim's hand when he was shot. The criminalists first sprayed the area with luminol with the hatchet still in place. Fine blood spatter could be seen on the table and hatchet. They then removed the hatchet and repeated the luminol test. A dark shadow (indicating the absence of blood) appeared in the shape of the hatchet, surrounded by the glow of fine blood spatter on the rest of the table. This convincingly demonstrated that the victim did not have the hatchet in his hand when the shot was fired, refuting the suspect's story of self-defense.

This case provides an effective demonstration of how a thoughtful analysis of physical evidence, performed with the specific reconstruction question in mind, successfully assisted in establishing a factual element of the case.

3.   Limitations of Reconstruction

Before attempting a reconstruction, the criminalist is well advised to recall one of our favorite aphorisms:
Unless we have articulated competing hypotheses, it is much too easy to see

> **We see what we expect to see.**

the evidence and information that supports one hypothesis without subjecting it to rigorous criticism. It becomes easy to dismiss evidence that does not fit and emphasize evidence that does. This leads to two common problems in reconstruction, overinterpretation of the evidence and attempting to re-create the incident.

The farther we travel from source determination, the greater the number of assumptions we incorporate into our inferences. At the level of reconstruction, all of the previous assumptions are implicitly incorporated, and more assumptions are added. Sometimes, the assumptions may outweigh the facts; change any in the complex web of assumptions, and the conclusion may change. Many reconstructions simply reflect one person's view of how the events transpired. Because neither the facts nor the assumptions on which reconstructions stand are often challenged, it is both easy and tempting to allow our personal biases and expectations to drive our conclusions.

a. Bias and Expectation

The temptation to overinterpret evidence or create reenactments results from a generally unconscious expectation on the part of the analyst, that a particular cause is responsible for a specific effect. Common phrases revealing this bias are typically encountered when reconstructing suicides. Such phrases as "no one would do that," "it's too hard that way," or (our favorite) "no one in their right mind would do that," are frequently heard. These reveal a subtle bias; how would I perform this act, or how would I react to it? How one person might contemplate suicide is of no consequence to how anyone else might try to accomplish it. In particular, people committing suicide may or may not be in their right mind, so this may not be taken as a limitation on how the incident was accomplished. Frequently, this bias is revealed in reports with expressions that include "it is reasonable," "it is probable," or "it is likely," with absolutely no reference to any facts or information to support them.

An analyst's experience is a second source of expectation; when I see that an action results in a particular consequence once, I expect that the next time I see the effect, it will have resulted from the same cause. This is less serious if the analyst uses the expectation as one hypothesis, but it is bias if it becomes the only hypothesis. Experience should widen the analyst's expectation, not narrow it.

The end result of expectation based on personal bias and experience is the introduction into the reconstruction of nuance and emotion that is not supported by the physical evidence. A criminalistics examination may not always, or not even frequently, culminate in a reconstruction. But when it does, the role of the forensic scientist is to provide scientifically defensible information about the sequence of events. Other speculative elements reveal bias based on personal expectations, and reduce the credibility of the scientist and the reconstruction itself.

b. Overinterpretation

The criminalist must resist the temptation to overinterpret by providing more detail than the evidence will support. Overinterpretation occurs when inferences are drawn based on what the *examiner* thinks is *most likely*, as opposed to expositing the alternative possibilities and evaluating the evidence in light of them.

One example of such an overinterpretation occurred in a case involving two suspects accused of torturing and shooting the clerk at a *Stop 'N Rob* convenience store. A detective from another jurisdiction, who had attended several bloodstain pattern interpretation workshops, was retained to prepare a reconstruction based on the blood patterns at the scene. He wrote an 11-page report, including every movement of the victim and suspects over a 30- to 45-minute time period. He included in his reconstruction a 5-minute time period where all activity ceased for the three individuals, basing this on a photograph of what he interpreted as a blood clot. He concluded that the victim was shot, bled for a period of 5 minutes on the floor, and then was beaten by the assailants. How did he arrive at his detailed reconstruction? He was given one suspect's confession, who indicated that they had shot the victim, sat around eating sandwiches and mocking him for 5 minutes, and then beat him for good measure. The detective used this as a starting point for his reconstruction, and picked out stains from the crime scene photographs that appeared to him to be clotted blood. As a nonscientist, he couldn't quite comprehend the criticism that it was not possible to distinguish between a blood clot and a bloodstain based on a photograph. Happily, he did not include a reconstruction of the suspect's meal, although perhaps only because no blood was involved in it.

The numerous reconstructions of the Marilyn Sheppard murder provide a classic example of how completely antithetical conclusions can apparently be reached from the same evidence. We contrast two examples, one from Paul Kirk (1955) a criminalist, the other from Gregg McCrary (1999) a behavioral scientist (profiler). Although these individuals come from completely different backgrounds, resulting in varying perspectives, the preambles to each of their conclusions sound eerily similar:

Kirk — "... the facts are clear, and the conclusions inescapable."
McCrary — "The ... evidence allows for only one logical conclusion, ..."

Both men worked from essentially the same physical evidence results, except that McCrary had the benefit of DNA evidence that only became available several decades after Kirk worked on the case. Kirk's inescapable conclusion was that Sam Sheppard *did not* murder Marilyn Sheppard; McCrary's one logical conclusion was that Sam Sheppard *did* murder Marilyn Sheppard. That both would reach mutually exclusive conclusions from the same evidence accents the dual dangers of ignoring inconvenient evidence and emphasizing only evidence that tends to corroborate one's hypothesis. Both reconstructions are highly subjective and speculative. We highlight sections of each to illustrate the seduction of overinterpretation and the dangers of ignoring evidence that does not fit your theory.

We start with McCrary on the issue of a sexually motivated attack*:

> The body of Marilyn Sheppard was found on her bed in the early morning hours of July 4, 1954. Subsequent investigation revealed that her pajama top had been unbuttoned and pushed up exposing her breasts and that one pant leg of her pajama bottoms had been pulled off of her leg. The victim's knees were at the foot of the bed with her lower legs hanging vertically from the end of the bed. Her legs were slightly spread. Blood smears on her ankles along with the blood pattern higher on the bed sheet suggest that the killer pulled her down toward the foot of the bed into that position...
>
> With her breasts exposed, one pant leg removed, her legs slightly spread and hanging off the foot of the bed, one would have to consider the potential that this was a sexually motivated crime. However, the evidence does not support this hypothesis. Having manipulated the victim as described above, the offender positioned her so that a large horizontal wooden bedpost is over her pelvic and vaginal area thus presenting a physical obstruction which would prevent anyone from sexually assaulting the victim in that position. In fact the evidence shows that the victim was not sexually assaulted...
>
> An examination of the vaginal smears taken from the victim during the autopsy found no spermatozoa present.

It is odd that McCrary assumes that if Marilyn Sheppard was sexually assaulted, it would only have been in the final position in which she was found. What eliminates the very reasonable possibility that she was raped in another position on the bed and then killed? This is but one of many examples of failing to entertain an alternate hypothesis. Further, McCrary misrepresents available facts when he states that "the evidence shows that the victim was not sexually assaulted." In examining vaginal swab slides taken at autopsy in preparation for DNA analysis in 1997, Mohammed Tahir states explicitly that he observed sperm. Because that work was performed for the plaintiff in the civil case, it is inconceivable that McCary did not have access to it. One might legitimately ask if this is simply an example of ignoring evidence that is inconvenient to the proffered theory of the incident.

Later in the report, McCary states that:

> There is also inconsistent behavioral evidence in that if this was a sexually violent offender who engaged in overkill to subdue his victim it is most likely that the sexually violent behavior would have continued unabated and he would have ripped the victim's clothing off, and brutally raped her leaving clear evidence of vaginal and anal trauma.

* Excerpts reproduced here and in Sidebar 5 with all typographical and grammatical errors intact.

Sidebar 5

The Case of Marilyn Sheppard — Is Absence of Evidence, Evidence of Absence?

Forensic Inconsistencies
Inconsistencies Regarding the Location of Blood:
Dr. Sheppard had no blood on his hands or body following the homicide and denies having washed or cleaned himself. As the killer certainly would have been stained with the victim's blood after bludgeoning her to death, one might consider this lack of blood on Dr. Sheppard's person to be consistent with his testimony as well as the physical evidence at the crime scene sets forth several compelling reasons to believe that not only should Dr. Sheppard have had blood on his person but there also should have been blood on items that had none.

Dr. Sheppard testified that he touched his wife and took her pulse on at least two different occasions by placing his fingers on her neck and throat.

A. I looked at her and I felt her (Trial testimony 12/13/54 Pg. 4971).

B. I felt her. I took her pulse at the neck.

Q. You took her pulse at the neck?

A Yes, sir. (Trial testimony 12/13/54 Pg. 4973).

Q. Did you touch Marilyn's body?

A. I believe I did, sire.

Q. And what part of the body did you touch?

A. I'm not sure. I believe I touched the neck, the face, possibly the wrists.

I touched her, I feel that I touched around the face and neck. (Trial testimony 12/13/54, Pg. 4957–4958).

Touching his wife's face and taking her pulse by placing his fingers on her bloodstained neck and/or wrist on at least two separate occasions would have undoubtedly resulted in a primary transfer of blood from the victim to fingers and hands of Dr. Sheppard. After checking his wife's pulse a final time, Dr. Sheppard testified that he went downstairs and called the Houks on the telephone. It would be logical to expect a secondary transfer of blood from his fingers and hands to the telephone. No blood was detected on either the telephone or on Dr. Sheppard's fingers, hands or person in spite of the fact that Dr. Sheppard testified that he did not wash or clean up.

It is important to note that Dr. Richard Sheppard, brother of Dr. Samuel Sheppard, who arrived at the scene later that morning observed wet blood on Marilyn Sheppard's face. If the blood on Marilyn's Sheppard's face was wet when Dr. Richard Sheppard observed the body later that morning, then it was even wetter and more likely to have been transferred to Dr. Samuel Sheppard's hands and fingers as he took her pulse and touched her face.

Other reasons to expect Dr. Sheppard to have blood on his person is his testimony that he "grappled" with the killer on two separate occasions the night of his wife's murder. Since the killer would have been covered with the victim's blood, it would be expected that there would have been a secondary transfer of blood from the offender to Dr. Sheppard having "grappled" twice, yet Dr. Sheppard had no blood on his person. Secondly there would have been blood transferred to Dr. Sheppard's hand and fingers by the bloody-handed killer as he removed Dr. Sheppard's wristwatch and ring.

In addition, there is the issue of the blood found on Dr. Sheppard's wristwatch, which was found in a green bag with his ring and a set of keys. The bag was recovered outdoors, a short distance from his house. The crime scene photographs depict blood spots or spatter (as opposed to smears) on his wristwatch. These would be consistent with impact blood stains and it would indicate that the watch was near the victim while she was being attacked. It would be expected that similar blood spots or spatter would be found on Dr. Sheppard's wrist, forearm or hand, immediately adjacent to the location of his watch. No such blood was found.

A transfer bloodstain on his watch would be consistent with a scenario in which either the watch brushed against the victim or a bloody-handed killer removed the watch from Dr. Sheppard's wrist as it implied the watch having been recovered in the green bag. There was no such stain on the watch. One might have expect to find evidence of sand from the beach in his watchband as he reported he "grappled" with the killer and was rendered unconscious while on the beach, but there was no evidence of sand in the watchband.

Additionally, it would be expected that there would be evidence of blood on the green bag in which the killer placed the watch as well as indications of blood on the ring and set of keys that were also placed in the bag by the killer. No blood was detected on the green bag or any of the items inside the green bag.

Dr. Sheppard testified that as he regained consciousness in the bedroom, he saw light reflecting off of the badge that he had in his wallet. He later indicated that about between thirty and fifty dollars was missing from the wallet, but that a check and about 60 dollars in cash were under a flap in the wallet were apparently overlooked by the killer. The implication being that the offender, after murdering Marilyn Sheppard and rendering Dr. Sheppard unconscious, removed the wallet from Dr. Sheppard's pants, opened it, stole some money, left other money and then discarded the wallet near Dr. Sheppard with the badge displayed. With fresh blood on the killer's hands, it would be expected that there would be a secondary transfer of blood from the offender's hands to Dr. Sheppard not only as they "grappled" but also on Dr. Sheppard" pants and wallet. This would have occurred as the bloody-handed killer removed Dr. Sheppard's wallet from his pants and then searched the wallet for money. There was no blood on Dr. Sheppard's wallet or pants.

One must conclude that the most logical explanation for the lack of blood on Dr. Sheppard's pants and wallet, as well as on his watch, keys and ring and the green bag in which these three items were found ins that these items were not handled by anyone with bloody hands. The most logical explanation for the lack of blood on Dr. Sheppard" person is that he washed himself thoroughly after the murder and before using the telephone to call the Houks. He did not, however, clean the blood spots or spatter from his watch which present compelling evidence that the watch was in close proximity to the victim as she was being attacked. The only blood on Dr. Sheppard's pants was one diffuse stain around the knee, which is not really proof of anything.

Also of importance in analyzing this crime and crime scene is to consider the amount of time it took for the offender to stage this scene. Crime scenes are high-risk environments and none more so then a homicide scene. Offenders typically spend no more time than necessary at a crime scene for fear of being interrupted or caught. Consequently there is high degree of correlation between the amount of time an offender spends at a crime scene and the offender's familiarity and comfortability at that scene. The more time an offender spends at a crime scene the higher the probability that the offender is comfortable and familiar with that scene. Offender who spend a great deal of time at a crime scene often have a legitimate reason for being at the scene and therefore are not worried about being interrupted or found at the scene.

In his statements and testimony, Dr. Sheppard alluded to the possibility that more than one offender was involved. This is unlikely for a number of reasons. In multiple offender cases where a female victim is vulnerable it is common for one or more the offenders to sexually assault that victim. Secondly there is much more activity both criminal and non-criminal observable at the scene then there is in this scene. There likely would have been more destructive ransacking of the house and general pillaging and plunder than happened in this case. Finally It would be uncommon to leave any potential witnesses alive in the wake of a homicide. This would be especially true with a killer as enraged as the one who killed Marilyn Sheppard. In my opinion there was only one killer in the Sheppard house that evening.

The totality of this evidence reveals that this crime was, in all probability, not a "for-profit" or drug-related burglary, nor a sexually motivated crime. It was a crime in which the offender took a good deal of time to stage the scene to imply these motives. The amount of time spent staging this scene not only reveals how comfortable and familiar the offender was, but also indicates how important it was for the offender to mast the true motive for the crime. As in all staged homicides, this offender realized that if he did not stage the scene in some way he would immediately become a primary suspect. The offender displayed his lack of criminal sophistication by offering multiple, feebly staged pseudo-motives for this crime.

Source: Excerpted from Gregg O. McCrary's December, 1999 report for the State of Ohio in the civil suit of *The Estate of Samuel H. Sheppard v. The State of Ohio.* The full report may be found at *http://www.courttv.com/national/2000/0131/mccrary_ctv.html.* All typos and errors as in original.

This statement exemplifies a very unscientific and biased attitude toward the reconstruction. What verifiable scientific research has been performed to demonstrate that someone "engaged in overkill" always rips the clothing off of his victim, brutally rapes her, and leaves clear evidence of vaginal and anal trauma. Perhaps that is how Mr. McCrary would imagine the commission the crime, but to impose that prejudice on all cases is absurd.

In an excerpt from Kirk's 1955 affidavit, detailing his reconstruction of the incident, he states:

> The original motive of the crime was sexual. Examination of the slacks in which the victim was sleeping shows that they were lowered to their approximate final position at the time the blood spatters were made, as discussed above. Leaving the victim in the near nude condition in which she was first found is highly characteristic of the sex crime. The probable absence of serious outcry may well have been because her mouth was covered with attackers hand.

Kirk makes frequent use of words like "probable," "it follows," "presumably," and "instinctively" to describe his inferences based on assumptions. It is conjecture that the victim's mouth was covered with the attacker's hand. This is an example of Kirk projecting his expectation into the reconstruction, rather than drawing inferences based strictly on the physical evidence.

After recounting how the victim must have bitten the assailant, Kirk continues:

> Presumably inflamed by the resistance and pain, the attacker utilized some available weapon to strike the victim down. She instinctively turned her head (probably to her right) and shielded it with her hands which were in turn severely injured in the beating that ensued. She may also have grabbed a pillow as a shield, pressing it in front of her head, and depositing much blood on it.

Kirk uses the phrase "Presumably inflamed…" to indicate the assumptions upon which he builds the remaining reconstruction. He is inferring what seems reasonable to him, rather than evaluating the many causes that might have resulted in the evidence. The remainder of the paragraph uses words that are either subjective or suppositional ("instinctively" and "may have"). He fails to consider, for example, what effect striking the pillow with the purported weapon would have on the pillowcase. Would it have been ripped? Would there be a more definitive imprint of the weapon in blood? With the exception of the obvious fact that the assailant struck the victim, none of the reconstruction in this paragraph is based on the scientific evaluation of the physical evidence.

To be sure, Kirk's examination of this case is far more scientific than is McCrary's, but neither respects the limitations of the evidence, physical or "behavioral." The result is overinterpretation leading to seriously flawed and easily dismissed reconstructions.

c.   *Reconstruction or Reenactment*

A reconstruction should not be an attempt to reenact the incident (Garrison, 1993). The portrayal of exactly what happened during the event, including emotional elements, activities of people, facial features, and other speculative elements, rarely contains any factual elements. Although it is only human nature to try to fill in the details of any event, especially a crime, an acute awareness of this tendency should be enough to deter it in the professional. We know of one such "reconstruction" that included a reference to the victim looking at himself in the mirror before turning away to commit suicide. Of course, no piece of physical evidence would allow the analyst to infer this action; it was pure conjecture on the part of the criminalist. A re-creation, then, is a reconstruction to which is added subjective elements such as emotion and nuance that results in a "videotape" replay of the incident. The criminalist must only provide information on the sequence of events, and avoid guessing what any person "must have been thinking" under the circumstances of the event.

C.   Summary

In this chapter, we have concluded our discussion of the principles of criminalistics. The profession's understanding of the processes of association and reconstruction, and their implications, remains underdeveloped. We have outlined a number of areas that require greater thought and refinement by the forensic science community. Nevertheless, we can articulate a couple of points with which most analysts would agree. First, association is an inference of contact between two objects, and is the only way in which legally relevant evidence can be generated by a scientist. Mere source determination is not legally relevant per se. Second, the analyst requires a broad case context to most thoughtfully formulate the competing hypotheses and articulate the accompanying assumptions.

Although not all practitioners would agree that an inference of contact is best expressed using likelihood ratios, a growing community is learning the benefits of interpreting the results of forensic examinations in a Bayesian framework. Almost a decade ago, Stoney (1991) wrote, "The likelihood ratio is a generalization of the more generally used 'match frequencies,' providing a logical and theoretical framework for supporting the inference of contact. The likelihood ratio incorporates quantitative data from the factors deemed relevant from the broad case context (including databases needed for evidence evaluation, and the incorporation of properly constructed match and correspondence frequencies)." It is our opinion that this is the direction in which forensic science should continue.

Reconstruction is an attempt to order several events from an incident in time and space based on physical evidence. Although reconstruction has been practiced by criminalists for as long as physical evidence has been examined, the discipline as a whole has never been systematized and no general or guiding principles have been articulated. A reconstruction builds on the facts established by source determination and association, and, by default, also incorporates all of the assumptions that were made in those previous determinations. Although reconstruction can be a valuable tool for both the investigation and solution of crime, it must be performed by someone with the requisite expertise to understand the physical evidence and the limitations of the process.

References

Aitken, L. and Stoney, D., Eds., *The Use of Statistics in Forensic Science*, Ellis Horwood, Chichester, West Sussex, U.K., 1991.

Bevel, T., Gardner, R. M., Bevel, V. T., *Bloodstain Pattern Analysis: With an Introduction to Crime Scene Reconstruction*, CRC Press, Boca Raton, FL, 1997.

Chisum, W.J., Crime Scene Reconstruction, "California Department of Justice Firearm/Toolmark Training Syllabus," reprinted in the *AFTE Journal*, 23(2), 1991.

Cook R. et al., A model for case assessment and interpretation, *Sci. Justice*, 38(3), 151–156, 1998a.

Cook R. et al., A hierarchy of propositions: deciding which level to address in casework, *Sci. Justice*, 38(4), 231–239, 1998b.

Curran, J. M., Triggs, C. M., and Buckleton, J. S., Sampling in forensic comparison problems, *Sci. Justice* 38(2), 101–107, 1998.

DeForest, P., Lee, H., and Gaensslen, R., *Forensic Science: An Introduction to Criminalistics*, McGraw Hill, New York, 1983.

Doyle, A. C., Boscombe valley mystery, *The Strand Magazine*, 1891.

Eckert, W. G. and James S. H., *Interpretation of Bloodstain Evidence at Crime Scenes*, CRC Press, Boca Raton, FL, 1989.

Evett, I., Expert evidence and forensic misconceptions of the nature of exact science, *Sci. Justice*, 36(2), 118–122, 1996.

Evett, I. W. and Weir, B. S., *Interpreting DNA Evidence*, Sinauer Associates, Inc., Sunderland, MA, 1998.

Garrison, D. H., Jr., Shooting Reconstruction vs. Shooting Reenactment (Originally published in the *AFTE Journal*, 1993, available at *http://www.chem.vt.edu/ethics/garrison/shooting.html*.

Haight, F., *California Courtroom Evidence*, 4th ed., Parker Publications Division, Carlsbad, CA, 1996.

Jeffreys, H. *Theory of Probability*. Oxford University Press, 1983.

Kaye, D. H., What is Bayesianism? in *Probability and Inference in the Law of Evidence: The Limits of Bayesianism*, P. Tillers and E. Green, Eds., D. Reidel Publishing Co., Boston, 1988.

Kirk, P. L., *Crime Investigation*, 1st ed., Interscience, John Wiley & Sons, New York, 1953.

Kirk, P., *Affidavit in the matter of Marilyn Sheppard*, 1955.

Kirk, P. L., *Crime Investigation*, 2nd ed., Thornton, J., Ed., Krieger Publishing Co. (by arrangement with John Wiley & Sons), FL, 1974.

Lindley, D. V., Probability, in *The Use of Statistics in Forensic Science*, Aitken, C. and Stoney, D., Eds., Ellis Horwood, Chichester, West Sussex, U.K., 1991.

McCrary, G. O., Report for the State of Ohio in the civil suit of *The Estate of Samuel H. Sheppard v. The State of Ohio*, December, 1999, available at *http://www.courttv.com/national/2000/0131/mccrary_ctv.html*.

Osterburg, J. W., *The Crime Laboratory; Case Studies of Scientific Criminal Investigation*, Indiana University Press, Bloomington, 1968.

Robertson B. and Vignaux, G. A., *Interpreting Evidence*, John Wiley & Sons, Chichester, 1995.

Saferstein, R., *Criminalistics: An Introduction to Forensic Science*, 6th ed., Prentice-Hall, Englewood Cliffs, NJ, 1998.

Stoney, D. A., Evaluation of associative evidence: choosing the relevant question, *J. Forensic Sci. Soc.*, 24, 472–482, 1984.

Stoney, D. A., Transfer evidence, in *The Use of Statistics in Forensic Science*, Aitken, C. and Stoney, D., Eds., Ellis Horwood, Chichester, West Sussex, U.K., 1991.

Tahir, M., Laboratory Examination Reports, Case #76629, 1997, 1999, available at *http://www.courttv.com/trials/sheppard/DNA_ctv.html*.

Taroni, F., Probalistic reasoning in the law. Part 2: Assessment of probabilities and explanation of the value of trace evidence other than DNA, *Sci. Justice*, 38, 179–188, 1998.

Taroni, F. Champod, C., and Margot, P., Forerunners of Bayesianism in early forensic science, *Jurimetrics*, 38, 183–200, 1998.

Thompson, W. C. and Schumann, E. L., Interpretation of statistical evidence in criminal trials: the prosecutor's fallacy and the defense attorney's fallacy, *Law Human Behav.*, 11, 167–187, 1987.

Section III
The Practice of Forensic Science

Figure 8.1 Cigarette butt in the toilet. When found at a crime scene, it is hoped that one of the responding officers did not deposit this evidence.

Good Field Practice — Processing a Crime Scene

8

Always look up.
—Keith Inman

A. The Questions

Although this discussion is not intended to provide a step-by-step protocol for processing a scene, it's worth thinking about what we wish to accomplish at any crime scene, and how we can at least not sabotage the end result before we even collect a piece of evidence. To do that we need take a step backward and consider the big picture. You should not be surprised at this point to hear a reiteration of **"What is the question?"**

What is the ultimate purpose of a crime scene investigation? The kinds of information we seek to solve the commission of a crime inevitably fall under the umbrella of the six "W" questions:

1. What happened?
2. When did it happen?
3. Where did it happen?
4. Who was involved?
5. How was it done?
6. Why was it done?

Not all questions are relevant to all crimes, and the relevant question is determined by the law. The examination of physical evidence may be useful in answering the first five questions. The question of "why" is not a question science can answer; therefore it is irrelevant to the laboratory analysis. We leave the establishment of motive to the criminologists, the profilers, and the courts.

B. The Crime Scene

The crime scene is the apex of an inverted pyramid (Figure 8.2) that expands to encompass the investigation of a crime, the recognition, analysis, and interpretation of evidence, and finally a court trial. As such, it bears the full weight of all that is to come. Any mistakes made in processing the crime scene are impossible to rectify. In fact, they are only magnified at each subsequent step. To make things worse, both errors of omission and commission made in processing a crime scene can confound the final resolution. Although we provide some general guidelines for processing a crime scene, it would be counterproductive to distill the exercise in the form of a check sheet or other hard-and-fast document. Forms, check sheets, and lists can be useful to keep track of repetitive but necessary tasks, and to provide

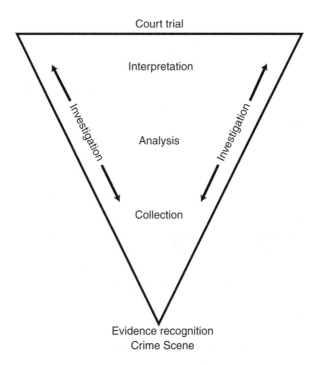

Figure 8.2 Crime scene pyramid. The crime scene is the apex of an inverted pyramid that expands to encompass the investigation of a crime, the recognition, analysis, and interpretation of evidence; and finally a court trial. As such, it bears the full weight of all that is to come. Any mistakes made in processing the crime scene are impossible to rectify.

templates for search and examination results. They should be used as a tool to free the investigator to concentrate on the details of a particular crime scene, not as a substitute for thinking. Each crime scene is unique, and must be approached with the knowledge, education, and experience of the investigator. Thinking is allowed (even encouraged!).

1. What Is a Crime Scene?

It is crucial to understand that, like many other aspects of forensic science, we look to the law for the definition of a crime scene. For practical purposes, a crime scene is the aftermath of an event that is considered, by law, to be illegal. Only if good reason exists to suspect that an illegal action has occurred is law enforcement called to the scene. Before we get too far into any investigation, we must first establish that a crime has, in fact, been committed. Many interesting events may occur that could make for fascinating analyses, but unless such an event results from an illegal act, a forensic analysis performs no useful function. For example, sexual intercourse between two consenting adults is not a crime; if force is involved, the crime of rape has been committed.

The question of criminality must always be answered when a dead body is discovered. Was foul play involved or was it a natural death? We once had a student ask us if it was necessary to continue with an investigation if a death appeared to be an "obvious suicide." We suggested that what appears "obvious" might not be the truth. Given the number of homicides that are set up to look like suicides, or even natural deaths, to the casual observer, it's clearly important to establish both *what* caused the death and *who* caused the death.

> A woman found her boyfriend lying unconscious and bleeding. She immediately called 911 and an ambulance arrived to whisk him away to the hospital. Because the man was unconscious when he was found, he couldn't say what had happened to him. Two detectives and a criminalist couldn't determine from the crime scene alone whether his injuries were self-inflicted or caused by another person, or whether they were accidental or malicious. The blood patterns could have resulted from either scenario and no other evidence presented itself. It was not clear that a crime had, in fact, been committed until the victim regained consciousness and was able to relate that he had been attacked.

a.   What Is the Scope of a Crime Scene?

Another, more subtle aspect of "What is a crime scene?" is "What is the scope of a crime scene?" For example, the site where a dead body was dumped is frequently not the place where the person was killed. A good example of this is found in the case of the Freeway Killer, where William Bonin and his accomplice, Vernon Butts, preyed on young boys in the Los Angeles area in the late 1970s. The mutilated bodies of the boys were dumped at locations scattered throughout the area but the scene of most of the killings was Bonin's van, and, secondarily, Butts' house (see Sidebar 6).

2.   Processing the Scene

The following discussion encompasses the main activities that are performed at many crime scenes.

a.   Check for Survivors

Even paramount to securing the scene for investigation is the identification of any persons that may need immediate medical attention. These may be victims (intended or not) of the crime, but could also be the perpetrator. This duty is always performed by the responding officer. Saving life and limb unquestionably supersedes any consequential disruption of the crime scene; however, it is crucial to understand that the scene will inexorably be altered by these activities. For example, the heroic efforts of paramedics to save lives invariably results in the introduction of medical debris into the scene, and

Sidebar 6

The Freeway Killer — Butt for a Videotape

During the late 1970s, a string of homicides occurred that attracted very little attention until the last few victims were recovered. This was due in part to the location of the victims; they were spread across Southern California over several counties. The victims all were found nude and showed evidence of sexual assault. Many were abandoned near freeway off-ramps, leading the press to dub the perpetrator "The Freeway Killer." By the time the Freeway Killer was arrested, he was a suspect in almost 20 homicides of young men. William George Bonin was ultimately charged and convicted of nine homicides in two counties. He was executed in California by lethal injection in 1996.

Bonin had previously been convicted of assaulting a young male, and even though genetic marker typing was then only in its infancy, Bonin knew that it had played a crucial role in this initial conviction. He vowed not to be caught by science again, and so part of his MO (*modus operandi*) was to perpetrate these crimes with accomplices, little more than teenage punks of low IQ whom Bonin could easily manipulate and control. If he raped one of his murder victims, he would make sure that one of his accompanying pals would also have intercourse with the victim. In his mind, this would ensure that the police would not have his genetic marker profile as evidence of his presence.

People are occasionally (although rarely!) more eloquent than evidence, however, and this was Bonin's undoing. For some reason, now consigned to oblivion with his police file, one of these accomplices attracted the attention of the multijurisdictional task force that had finally been formed. As they staked out the house of Vernon Butts, they were able to engage him in conversation, and succeeded in obtaining his agreement to do a consent search of his rented house. Several criminalists were brought in to search primarily for blood.

Because the house contained lots of "stuff," the search moved slowly and methodically from room to room, and consisted principally of looking at clothing for traces of blood (one of the victim's had been stabbed in the ear with an icepick). As late evening turned to early morning, the rooms of the house were sprayed with luminol. In the bathroom, right next to the bathtub on the floor tile, an outline of a hand developed as the luminol was applied. Up to now, Butts had been cooperative but noncommittal, consistently denying his involvement in anything illegal. After a discussion with the detectives, he was brought into the bathroom and the luminol reapplied. The outline once again appeared, glowing up at him out the dark. The criminalists explained to him that this chemical reacted with blood, and he was viewing the result of a bloody hand in contact with the floor. According to detectives, when he left the bathroom, he went to the couch, sat down, and confessed completely to his role in the murder, as well as Bonin's direction of it.

As Butts began his confession, the detectives asked if he would allow them to videotape the event. He agreed, and the cameras were summoned. Recall that this incident took place in 1980, and camcorders were not even a Sony dream yet. It took several hours for the video section of one of the jurisdictions to respond and set up its equipment. But this decision to document the scene via videotape paid big rewards.

As the accomplice started to talk about his involvement on tape, and to narrate the details of the crime, it was clear that he was enjoying the stardom. Sensing this, the detectives asked if he would walk through the inside and outside of the house, pointing to various locations and discussing how they were involved in the homicide. To this the (now) suspect agreed, and he gave a thorough and energetic performance for the camera. At one point, when the detectives asked him about chloral hydrate (one victim had been poisoned with the substance), he replied that he had thrown the plastic bottle containing the drug into some bushes around the house. He walked outside, camera following, and calmly reached into a tall bush and extracted the empty bottle. Detectives gratefully accepted the gift, and immediately placed it into an evidence bag.

As the on-tape interview was ending, one detective asked what they had done with this particular victim's personal belongings. The suspect responded that they had thrown away the clothing, but that Bonin had given him the school ID card of the victim and told him to dispose of it. When detectives asked where he had dumped it, the suspect replied that he had thrown it through the floorboards of the shed on the back of his property. Remembering the chloral hydrate bottle, they asked him to show them exactly where he had disposed of the ID. Once in the shed, and always talking, the suspect said that he had simply slipped it down into one of the cracks in the floor. "In fact," he said, leaning down and placing his fingers into a crack, "Here it is!" As he stood up, he held the card in his hands, and the camera zoomed in on the name and face of one of the victims in the case. Detectives were practically fainting at this *ad lib* on-camera demonstration by the suspect.

This would have made fabulous press in Los Angeles, but it never got to that point. The suspect committed suicide in jail, and the videotape was ruled inadmissible at Bonin's trial. It does, however, highlight an interesting use of videotape to document a crime scene.

the pattern of physiological fluids and human tissue that represented the original crime may also be altered. While we accept these activities as obligatory and humane, we must also recognize their impact on the original scene.

b.   Secure the Scene

Once it has been established that human life is not in danger, the officer in charge must *secure the scene*. The immediate goal is to *do no harm*. However compromised the evidence might be at the start of an investigation, responsible personnel must take all precautions to protect it from further deterioration. A primary tenet in the collection of crime scene evidence is to prevent any further compromise of the evidence beyond what has already resulted from the crime and its aftermath.

We frequently refer to the catchall expression of *responsible personnel*, but who does this really include? The short answer is anyone with authority connected, however remotely, to the scene or the evidence. "It is not my job" is simply not acceptable from anyone at any point in the investigation.

Defining a physical domain within which an illegal act occurred is the first step in processing a crime scene. Securing the area usually involves demarcating some reasonable vicinity surrounding the immediate crime scene to preserve it as well as possible until evidence can be recognized and collected. The functional perimeter of the scene or scenes must be established, and only essential personnel should be allowed inside the scene perimeter. The fewer people in the scene, the less chance of accidental contamination or destruction of potentially important evidence.

But how do we determine the physical boundaries of a crime scene? In actuality, practicality plays a large role. The detective may find it convenient to tow a vehicle, tape off a house and its yard, or maybe even a city block, for a short time. But evidence does not recognize natural or urban borders. A person might be murdered in one house and the body dragged across several lots to be dumped in another yard, the obvious crime scene. It is not uncommon for a crime to encompass more than one geographic area. For example, in *People v. Simpson*,* at least three scenes were identified: his house (on Rockingham Drive), her house (on Bundy Drive), and his white Ford Bronco.

Not only may multiple scenes be associated with the crime, we must consider their relationship in time and space. The original crime scene where the murder took place may be located and secured in fairly short order, but the path between the two crime scenes (e.g., *People v. Simpson*, the drive between the two houses in the Bronco), which may hold valuable blood, fiber, or print evidence, may never be recognized, much less secured. Even if the connection between the two crime scenes is finally established, the path between them may have already been so compromised that any evidence collected cannot be presumed to relate to the crime (e.g., in *People vs. Simpson*, credit card receipts from the Bronco were stolen by the tow truck driver, potentially compromising blood evidence eventually recognized in the vehicle (*People v. Simpson*, July 19). Multiple scenes, and boundaries defined out of practicality, are only two of the limitations of crime scene work that must be understood and acknowledged. In these days of easy mobility, a crime may encompass several different scenes of varying environments, which may easily cross interstate or even international borders.

Once the commission of a crime has been established and the scene secured, the criminalist must look toward eventually translating the legal questions into science questions. The goal is always to establish links between evidence and reference items (*classification* or *individualization*), *associations* between different source and target items, and sometimes a *reconstruction* of the events. Because association is prerequisite to reconstruction, procedures at the crime scene aim to preserve the integrity of evidence items and information about their relationships to each other. Remember that reconstruction does not mean generating a moment-by-moment videotape; rather, it refers to ordering items and events in space and time. Any number or manner of circumstances may confound any step in this process. Crime scene personnel are charged with preserving the scene and the evidence so that, no matter what may have occurred previous to recognition of the scene as a crime scene, any further deterioration or compromise of the evidence is minimized. The reconstruction will almost never be concluded at the scene. It will often not be completed until months or, not uncommonly, years later, when all of the analyses have been completed, the hypotheses articulated,

---

* We refer to the case of *People v. Simpson* throughout this chapter because the circumstances are well known and the transcripts readily available. Certainly, similar situations are represented in other less well-documented cases.

and the assumptions identified. This is only one of the reasons documentation must be carried out extensively and compulsively.

c. The Dynamic Crime Scene

A crime scene is a dynamic environment. The evidence begins to change literally the instant after the action has taken place.* The longer it has been since the crime was committed, the less the scene will resemble the original. Often, one of the largest holes in our understanding of a case is what happened between the commission of a crime and its recognition by responsible personnel. A crime scene always exists in some form, but the more distant in time from the *crime event*, the less resemblance it may have to its state at the moment the crime was committed.

There is nothing anyone can do to halt the continual changes to a scene, but we can at least minimize the human contribution to that alteration. To do that we must become part of the *crime scene gestalt*. It is essential to recognize that the moment you enter a scene, *you* become a part of the scene. To understand this, it's useful to paraphrase the *Heisenberg uncertainty principle*** on a macrolevel; you change the scene simply by being in it. Furthermore, the very act of processing the scene will change it. You will walk around the area, you will examine and record it in various ways, you will take things from it by the very act of collecting evidence. The alterations you introduce can either be minimal or egregious, deliberate or unconscious, depending on how you proceed.

For example, let's say a murder has taken place on a Friday evening in an abandoned warehouse. Blood evidence is deposited on the floor of the warehouse. However, gaping holes in the roof allow rain to enter later that night. By Saturday morning, when the investigators have finally realized that a murder has taken place, no *obvious* blood evidence may remain. This is an extreme, although not uncommon, example. Forces that may act to alter a crime scene may be inanimate (e.g., the weather), living (e.g., microorganisms or animals), or human (e.g., attempted cover-up). Although we cannot know or control how the crime scene was altered before the arrival of investigating officers, we can act to minimize the inevitable disruption caused by

---

* The only unchanging element in a crime scene is the obligatory cold coffee and stale doughnuts needed by the investigators to sustain them on the job, these days required to be consumed outside of the secured area.

** The *Uncertainty Principle*, published by Werner Heisenberg in 1927 states that, for subatomic particles, "The more precisely the position is determined, the less precisely the momentum is known in this instant, and vice versa. In other words, we can't simultaneously know the location and velocity of a quantum-scale particle, because the act of measuring either disturbs the other. We take the liberty of stretching the concept to a macro level to make the point that our very entrance into the crime scene disturbs it; however, we can't know what's in it without being in it.

our entrance into the scene. An example of how a crime scene was unintentionally disrupted by assuming too small a scope is given in Sidebar 7.

d. The Team Approach

In order for the scene to be secured, access limited, and the evidence protected, someone must be in charge. This is usually the first officer on the scene, or the detective who has been assigned responsibility for the investigation. A team approach is the most successful. To process a crime scene competently, all involved must understand the specific role they play and cooperate with each other and the person in charge. In turn, the person in command must understand the roles of all of the other players and facilitate, or at least not impede, their work. The roles of various individuals are described in numerous books that specifically address crime scene investigation (e.g., Svensson and Wendel, 1955; Goddard, 1977; Fisher, 2000; Ogle, 1995; Geberth, 1996).

e. Assess the Scene

Before stepping foot into the crime scene, much less collecting the first item of evidence, everyone on the team must obtain an overall perspective from outside the perimeter and, collectively, devise a logical approach. The detective should apprise everyone of any initial impressions and what is thought to have occurred. The detective should provide at least an initial idea of what questions need answering. An important duty of the scientific representative who is present at the crime scene is to help the detective understand the scientific questions generated from the legal questions.

After discussing the question, the hypotheses, and how they may influence the evidence to be collected, a coordinated plan must be formulated and followed to collect the most relevant evidence with the least compromise to the scene or specific items of evidence. In particular, the team must decide which areas to search, the order of the search, and what further specialists or equipment may be needed. The collection of evidence should be prioritized. Especially where a piece of evidence might be submitted for more than one type of analysis, methods of collection and preservation should be discussed before proceeding. Sometimes the collection and preservation procedures preferred for one kind of analysis may jeopardize the evidence for another type of analysis. An informed compromise must then be agreed upon by those involved.

For example, in *Crime Scene*, Ragle (1995) presents a case in which a gasoline-soaked (as determined by smell) bedspread recovered from a car also contained bloodstains and brain tissue. Three types of evidence were present, biological (blood and brains), chemical (ignitable fluid), and physical (the

---

Sidebar 7

How Big Is the Crime Scene? — The Little Bullet that Could

She was suffering from a severe case of post-partum blues, and the Fourth of July celebration just seemed to make it worse. Her husband had invited all of his friends over to the house, and they partied all day long. When they finally left, she felt overwhelmed. She knew her husband kept a gun underneath their bed, and she sought relief from the short cold blue-steel muzzle.

He caught her just in time. Standing in the living room, he grabbed the hand holding the gun, and they struggled back and forth, she looking to squeeze off the end of her misery, he to wrest death from her hands. One shot rang in his ears, and she slumped forward, blood pouring from her mouth. He half-dragged, half-carried her into the bathroom, leaning her over the bathtub to catch the never-ending river of crimson that flowed from her mouth. Not able to staunch the tide, he called 911. Paramedics arrived within minutes, and quickly whisked her out of the house, baby and father both crying in the wake of a gurney wheeling away their woman. She died on the way to the hospital.

This was the story that greeted homicide detectives when they arrived at the scene. All they had was the husband's story and whatever physical evidence was left behind. Setting up in the kitchen/dining area, photograph and latent print specialists spread out to work the scene. How could they distinguish between the story the husband told and the possibility of a homicide? A criminalist was summoned to assist in the investigation.

When he arrived at the scene, detectives had just learned that the victim had died of a single near-contact gunshot wound that entered from just below the jaw, severing a major blood vessel. The bullet was not in the victim, according to the hospital. Detectives wanted some confirmation that his story was true.

The criminalist suggested that if the husband was in close proximity to the victim when the shot was fired, then his shirt should be full of fine spatter as a result of blow-back from the shot. The shirt of the husband was collected, but because it was a dark color, no blood could be discerned from a visual inspection. The rest of the time was spent examining the remainder of the scene, including the blood patterns, and searching for the spent bullet.

Nothing found in the bloodstain patterns contradicted the story of the husband; they led from the living room to the bathroom, increasing in volume in that direction. A large volume of blood was evident in the bathroom and bathtub, again consistent with his story. Even his story that he had used the phone to call the police after touching the bloody victim was confirmed by smears of blood on the instrument.

The puzzle came in searching for the expended bullet. The hospital had confirmed an entrance and exit wound, yet a thorough search of the living room yielded no trace of a bullet or bullet hole anywhere. Every inch of the walls, ceilings, and floor were scoured for traces of an entrance hole, and none were found. The drapes were examined, not just for holes, but for the bullet itself, with no luck. As puzzled searchers scratched their heads, one sharp-eyed inspector spied a small hole in a kitchen chair. As luck would have it, the kitchen had been chosen as the setup area, and the table and chairs were chock-a-block with detective stuff, including crime scene kits, photograph kits, latent print kits, and the trash bag. When the chair was examined closely, the expended bullet was indeed lodged in the back of the chair. Needless to say, no one had a clue as to the original configuration of the chairs and tables, so it was impossible to reconstruct the direction from which the bullet had come.

Examination of the shirt in the laboratory under low-power stereomicroscopy showed thousands of submillimeter blood particles on the front of the shirt, which confirmed the close proximity of the husband when the shot was fired. Given the totality of the evidence (or rather the lack thereof), including the inability to reconstruct the shot from the misplaced chair, detectives declined to file charges against the husband.

This case illustrates just how difficult it is to choose a working perimeter for the scene.

bedspread itself). The methods for collecting and preserving each of these are quite different. Which evidence was most important and was there a way to preserve all of them? According to Ragle, the origin of the biological material was really not in question because a victim missing lots of blood and brains was also recovered from the interior of the car. However, confirmation of the solvent as gasoline (suggesting intent to destroy the evidence) and determination of the origin of the bedspread could potentially provide information crucial to associating the perpetrator with the scene.

The investigation team in that case made the decision to remove the loose chunks of brain to a glass jar for temporary storage. The rest of the bedspread was then sealed in a plastic bag, a procedure appropriate for preserving ignitable liquids, but potentially destructive to biological evidence. This decision may sound obvious and trivial to you as you read this, but put yourself out on a dark road in the middle of the night with a gasoline-soaked car full of blood, guts, and a dead victim. Our first instinct is often to give top priority to biological evidence because of its individualizing potential. The gasoline (although not the bedspread) turned out to be one of several critical pieces of evidence that helped solve the case. We suggest that you refer back to Mr. Ragle's book for a detailed rendition of this instructive case.

It is a fact that those who initially respond to a crime scene will virtually always be agents of the prosecution. This includes the police officers and any crime laboratory personnel. Because these individuals have the first, and sometimes the only, access to the scene and any physical evidence within it, they have a special responsibility to consider the crime scene in terms of alternative hypotheses. There are no second chances; crucial evidence, whether inculpatory or exculpatory, must be recognized the first time around or its value immediately begins to depreciate. A perfect example of this is the blood on the back gate of Nicole Brown Simpson's Bundy residence that was not collected until 2 weeks after the crime event (*People v. Simpson*, February 15). The laboratory results eventually obtained from that evidence appeared highly inculpatory, but its value to the case was significantly reduced because of questions about its origin that arose because it was not collected during the initial crime scene search.

Always remember that the speculations and hypotheses about what *might* have occurred are just that. They are useful for coordinating a plan of action and collection of evidence, but the true story may turn out to be completely different. Be willing to change your hypothesis as the evidence changes; listen to what the evidence has to tell you and keep an open mind.

f. Documentation

Both the scene(s) and the evidence must be documented rigorously throughout the process. This serves a number of functions. First, the condition of the scene as it was initially found is recorded. It is also important to document the scene as it is altered by the search for and collection of evidence. Finally, pictorial documentation, in particular, may record details that were overlooked when the scene was initially processed. It is not unusual for some feature of the evidence or an element of the scene to become important at a later date.

i. Chain of custody.   The whereabouts and handling of each item of evidence must be documented from the time it was collected through the time it is tested, consumed, or destroyed. Inattention to detail in the *chain of custody* or *chain of evidence* may disqualify otherwise good work from admission at trial. More importantly, from a scientific perspective, a break in the "chain" inescapably weakens any potential association between that evidence item and another. It leaves open the possibility of malicious or adventitious alteration of the evidence during the gap.

For example, in one case, a malicious alteration of the "chain" prevented admission of a large amount of otherwise perfectly good DNA results.

> In one such case, all of the DNA evidence was excluded because of a completely unnecessary break in the chain. A reference blood sample was taken from a suspect accused of murder to compare with evidence in the case. By comparing the dates on the paperwork, an inconsistency was detected between when the suspect was taken to have the reference sample drawn and when it was logged as evidence. When confronted with this conundrum, the detective admitted on the stand that he had inserted an expedient date into a report written only after the fact. Although he probably never intended to mislead anyone, he also failed to appreciate the purpose of a chain of custody. The suspect was convicted without the DNA evidence, but it needn't necessarily have been so.

Confusion, fatigue, or haste may also lead to inadvertent breaches of written documentation. We are all familiar with the doubt created when Dennis Fung and Andrea Mazzola collected samples as a "team" at the *Simpson* crime scenes and neglected to mark sample envelopes properly with the initials of the person who physically collected the sample (*People v. Simpson*, April 27).

A criminalist found himself in an odd chain-of-custody predicament created by changing jobs. While employed at a city crime laboratory, he received a case that could only be analyzed at the state crime laboratory, where he had previously been employed. At one point, he checked out evidence to himself from the jurisdiction of origin, the city, where he was then employed, and took it to the state laboratory where he analyzed it. The analyst did not consider the movement of the evidence to be external to the city jurisdiction because he was the one analyzing it. Through some accident of logic, he properly documented the "external" chain of custody on the envelope containing the reference stain, but not in his notes. This created, in the documents that the defense received at least, a breach of the chain of custody. By the time the case went to trial, the analyst had already transferred back to the state laboratory, further confusing the issue. The circumstances were successfully explained at trial, but this story emphasizes that one can never be too meticulous about documentation. The details count.

C. The Evidence

If you don't recognize it, you cannot collect it; if you don't collect it, you cannot analyze it; if you don't analyze it, you cannot interpret it.

1. Recognition

We spent a large part of Chapter 5 discussing the recognition of evidence. Recall that this involves more than just a mindless visual scan. Recognizing evidence that is actually relevant to a crime requires looking with purpose. One must have in mind a putative scenario, a preliminary hypothesis, and some plausible alternative hypothesis. Might this cause you to miss evidence that could point to a different scenario? Perhaps, but it is still preferable to searching blindly. The key to recovering evidence is to consider alternative hypotheses. Because it is impossible to search everywhere, a directed search provides the best chance of finding enough relevant evidence to assist in solving the crime. Accept that you will always miss something; it's the nature of the business. No crime scene search is perfect. The job of the crime scene team is to minimize egregious oversights by processing the scene with thoughtful intelligence.

2. Detection

Not all evidence will be in plain sight. Some will be blocked from normal view, for example, fingerprints underneath a table; some will be physically obstructed, for example, a body buried in the crawl space. Not infrequently, evidence will be in plain sight, but out of our normal field of view, for example, on a ceiling or roof. One of the more productive tenets of crime scene investigation is always to look up. Other evidence will require special methods of detection to visualize it. This aspect of criminalistics, in particular, has captured the imagination of both mystery writers and practitioners. Methods for making the invisible visible, and for instantly determining the nature of a substance, feed our compulsion for immediate gratification and satisfy our curiosity. Note that to discover latent evidence, one must have some idea of what to look for and where to look.

a.   Presumptive Testing

Sometimes, even if a stain is visible, it's not clear whether or not it is worth collecting. Is it blood or shoe polish? Is it semen or hair gel?* An initial determination may be made at the scene for the sole purpose of determining whether an item deserves further testing. Because the tests that are simple enough to use in the field do not provide conclusive results, the identity of the item must always be verified by more discriminating testing in the laboratory.

3.   Collection and Preservation

About the worst *faux pas* one can make at a crime scene is failing to collect vital evidence or, almost as bad, failing to collect it in a timely fashion. This was manifest in *Simpson* when it was revealed that a bloodstain on the back gate was missed the first time around and only recognized and collected weeks later (*People v. Simpson*, February 15). Everyone then got to argue about whether the DNA from the gate was planted, because it appeared to be in better shape than that from samples that had been collected immediately but stored in plastic bags in a hot van. As we mentioned in a previous section, this is an example of depreciation of evidence that was not recognized during the initial scene search and promptly collected. This led directly to an attempt to determine if EDTA (a preservative used in tubes used for collecting blood) was present, which in turn led to questions about the reliability and validity of testing for EDTA in blood and blood stains (*People v. Simpson*, June 20, July 24).

Almost as bad as missing a crucial item of evidence is failing to discern what is relevant and what is gratuitous. Collecting "everything" may result in losing track of critical evidence under a mountain of extraneous stuff. This only creates problems in tracking, storage, and decision making when it comes time for the crime laboratory to actually examine the evidence. There are limits to all good things, and knowing what to leave as well as what to collect is one of the finer points of crime scene processing.

> A criminalist was called to a scene in which the victim had been shot in the
> head in the back seat of a car. This resulted in the deposition of hundreds

---

* *There's Something About Mary*, movie directed by Bobby and Peter Farrelly, 1998.

of drops of fine blood spatter on the back of the front seat. The spatter pattern was obviously the result of a single event; this was not the question. However, the body had been dumped elsewhere. The blood was to be collected to answer the question, "Was it the victim's blood?" The criminalist meticulously collected each and every drop of the fine spatter separately. Not one of the stains by itself was large enough to provide reliable biological testing results. This time-consuming and thoughtless exercise could have been avoided if the criminalist had simply formulated the relevant question before beginning to collect evidence.

Collection and short-term preservation of the sample or item are inseparable. The moment one lifts a print or collects a stain, the evidence is altered from its original form. Ideally, preservation issues will be considered in determining the collection method. Probably the greatest distinction in collection and preservation methods is determined by whether the evidence is biological or nonbiological. The next section is divided into collection and preservation suggestions determined by the type of evidence. The subsequent discussion of contamination issues follows the same pattern, additionally exploring the consequences of cross-contamination between biological and nonbiological evidence.

A number of techniques have been developed to collect otherwise immovable evidence. The collective (pun optional) goal of these techniques is to:

Goals of Evidence Collection

1. Maintain physical integrity
2. Limit degradation
3. Prevent contamination

---

a. Collection Procedures

Although this is not intended to be a crime scene manual, it's worth briefly reviewing the collection and preservation of evidence. As in medicine, the first rule of evidence collection is to *do no further harm*. In general, any item of evidence should be transported to the laboratory in as intact a form as possible. Any piece of physical evidence that is small enough is simply packaged appropriately, clearly labeled, and removed to the laboratory environment where it can be processed under controlled conditions. This may be more practical in some cases than others. For example, bloodstains on a cement wall must be separated from the wall because the wall is unlikely to come to the laboratory. Indirect methods, such as tape lifts, vacuum sweeping, scraping, swabbing, casting, and photography may be used to collect evidence that is difficult to pick up and move. The specifics of these methods are reviewed elsewhere (e.g., Svensson and Wendel, 1955; Fisher, 1993; Ogle, 1995; Geberth, 1996).

b. Preservation

We take a moment to highlight the different considerations in the preservation of biological and nonbiological evidence.

i. Nonbiological evidence.   For larger items such as weapons, tools, and vehicles, the greatest danger is in introducing prints, fibers, or particles not originally present. The worst possible consequence of such adventitious contamination is the possibility of a false association between the evidence and a putative, inculpatory, source. Wearing gloves is becoming appropriately more common at crime scenes even for the collection of nonbiological evidence. It is crucial to recognize that for gloves to protect both the analyst from the evidence and the evidence from the analyst effectively, they must not only be worn but changed intelligently. For objects that may hold impressions such as toolmarks, it is important to limit mechanical contact so the impressions don't become altered. Please do not try to fit the screwdriver the burglar left at the scene into the pry mark in the door. Trace evidence on either object would be compromised and the impression could be altered. The collection of possible arson evidence is a special case. Because ignitable fluids are extremely volatile, even at ambient temperature, they must be collected in airtight cans such as unused paint cans.

ii. Biological evidence.   Once the fluid or stain is collected, the goal is to preserve it in the laboratory both to prevent degradation and contamination. The two most important elements needed to accomplish this are the reduction of both moisture and temperature. Any item collected in liquid or wet form is quickly dried. Evidence should be placed in a non-frostfree freezer for long-term storage.

4. Contamination

Although the specter of contamination is frequently used as a weapon, the subject is rarely discussed from a serious and neutral standpoint. We therefore include a relatively extended treatment here.

a. Definition of Contamination

Contamination, which we fondly refer to as the C-word, is in actual fact a catchall buzzword for a number of different situations. Like the proverbial "weeds are plants where they are not wanted", contaminating material seems to be anything that anybody deems confounding to a forensic analysis. Each situation has different consequences for handling and interpretation. As with all forensic issues, the interpretation of "contamination" depends on — *The Question.*

For example, it is discovered that bedsheets show the genetic type of more than one person. One could ask, who was the last person to leave evidence on the sheet? Some might argue that, should multiple types be detected, the ones they don't like or don't think should be present should be considered contamination, or at least an interfering element in the analysis. Another question one could ask would be, who are all the persons that ever left evidence on the sheet? In this case, all the types that might be found on the sheet are integral to answering the question. Either way, the material contributing to the types was all present before a crime scene was ever identified.

A contrary example is found in the *Simpson* case (*People v. Simpson*, April 5). A blanket from Nicole's house was reportedly used to cover her body in an effort to provide privacy from the media. The intention was commendable, but it rendered any examination for trace evidence on the body completely useless. What was relevant to the crime? What came from the blanket? The difference between this example and the previous one is that material known to be extraneous to the crime was introduced by responsible personnel.

Because the word *contamination* is widely co-opted to describe so many situations, no widely accepted definition exists. *Webster's* (1996) defines contaminate as "to make impure or unsuitable by contact or mixture with something unclean, bad, etc." Because all evidentiary material is by nature impure (it's always in contact or mixed with something), the question becomes, which impurities would render the sample unsuitable for analysis and correct interpretation?

Just as misleading as the dictionary definition, the term has acquired a negative connotation among the public, namely, that a contaminated sample is inherently an untrustworthy sample. Raising the specter of *contamination* is a convenient and simplistic way of dismissing the results of an analysis. This is both disingenuous and misleading. We reserve the word "contamination" for those circumstances where improper or careless handling by those responsible for collection, preservation, or analysis has accidentally introduced extraneous substances into the evidence sample. A good working definition might be:

> *Contamination:*
> **Any substance inadvertently introduced into or onto an item of evidence after its recognition by a responsible party.**

Using this definition, our prior illustration of multiple genetic types found on a bedsheet would actually be considered an example of a *mixed sample*. The multiple types might or might not confound the analysis and interpretation, but they are an integral part of the evidence. It is then the task of the analyst to sort out the particulars as they relate to the commission of the crime. Still using the bedsheet example, suppose an evidence technician collected the sheet and placed it into a plastic bag, where it was stored for several months at room temperature. During this time, microorganisms grew and destroyed much of the biological evidence. We would consider the evidence contaminated by the growth of bacteria because it was introduced as a consequence of improper preservation. In this instance, the contamination would likely produce no result or a partial result, but would be highly unlikely to produce an incorrect result, especially a false match to the suspect.

The concept of contamination was not invented to describe the condition of certain forensic samples. Any physical or biological sample may be associated with extraneous substances. However, the consequences hold a greater significance for forensic evidence samples for the following reasons:

Consequences of Contamination for Forensic Samples

- The true nature of the sample is unknown and unknowable. The contaminant might be mistaken for the true sample.
- Even with the adequate and proper use of controls, no independent way exists to prove conclusively that the result obtained is the one relevant to the incident.
- It is often impossible to obtain additional material if it is suspected that a sample may have been contaminated.
- The sample is often present in limited quantity. Thus a contaminant could potentially overwhelm the evidence, producing a false result. For this to be so, the contaminant would have to actually be detectable by the test and mimic or fall into the expected range for the results.

---

b. Sources of Contamination

The source of adventitious extraneous material may contribute to its classification as integral (mixed) or contaminating. Extraneous material may be introduced into a sample by normal activities of humans prior to, during, or after the commission of a crime. Because the world is a dirty place, we have termed this the *Dirty World Syndrome* or DWS. Substances acquired through DWS are classified as impurities integral to the evidence. After recognition as evidence by some responsible party, extraneous material may be introduced either at the scene or in the laboratory (including during transportation). We define substances acquired in this way as contaminants. The most egregious type of contamination is introduction of material from a reference sample either at the scene or in the laboratory; this would be the scenario most likely to confound the interpretation. Contamination with a reference sample from the suspect could lead to the worst possible consequence of contamination, a false association between crime scene evidence and an individual. Fortunately, when good collection, documentation, and laboratory practices are employed, this possibility is significantly curtailed.

c.   Types of impurities and their consequences

We need to differentiate among chemical, biological, and human impurities. All of these may have different consequences for the interpretation and significance of the evidence, and the consequences will differ depending on the nature of the evidence. In the following section, we summarize some general consequences of various types of impurities for biological and nonbiological evidence and provide a few examples. Obviously this discussion is nowhere near exhaustive and each case must be considered on its own merits.

i.   Nonbiological impurities

For nonbiological samples
Chemical substances unrelated to the crime certainly have the potential to influence the results obtained from various types of nonbiological evidence. Generally, a contaminant that causes a problem in nonbiological evidence will be of like nature to the evidence and has the potential to produce a false-positive result.

A mundane example might be a crime scene investigator tracking soil from outside a crime scene into one, or worse yet, from one crime scene to another. In a more inflammatory example (as it were), it has been suggested that improperly stored explosives evidence was responsible for false positives in the Oklahoma City bombing case. The allegation involved storing improperly sealed volatiles from numerous cases in the same physical space, thus introducing the potential for cross-contamination (*United States v. Terry Nichols*, December 1).

Historically, one of the most infamous examples of a test that routinely gave false-positive results was the paraffin (diphenylamine, dermal nitrate) test used to detect gunpowder on a suspect's hands. Detection of nitrate residue was meant to suggest recent discharge of a firearm. Unfortunately, many other substances, such as tobacco, fertilizer, and some plastics, also produce positive results with this test. The test long ago fell out of favor with forensic scientists everywhere. It was certainly responsible for a number of miscarriages of justice (Mullin, 1986); (see Sidebar 1 in Chapter 2).

For biological samples
Although nonbiologicals won't produce false-positive results in biological evidence, they may interfere with an analysis by preventing the various biochemical components from working properly. Chemicals such as dyes, oils, soaps, and others are commonly encountered in forensic samples. Part of the sample preparation is to remove or mitigate these potentially interfering agents.

Chemical impurities might also be introduced by an analyst or technician in an attempt to locate evidence, including biological evidence. For example, a crime scene will be routinely dusted for fingerprints or blood-detecting reagents such as luminol will be used to detect latent bloodstains. Because the analyst knows of the existence of these impurities, accommodations to the analysis or interpretation can be made as appropriate (Gross et al., 1999).

ii. *Biological impurities*

For nonbiological samples
The presence of biological substances normally does not cause much of a problem in the analysis and interpretation of nonbiological evidence.

For biological samples
The impact of biological impurities on biological evidence depends on the organism from which the material comes, whether the organism itself is present or just material from it, and the nature of the test being conducted. In some cases, a problem may be created by the presence of live organisms, in other cases from genetic material deposited by the organism. We'll examine each situation in turn.

Microorganisms: Microorganisms such as bacteria and fungi grow well in warm, moist conditions — conditions found at many a crime scene. They literally feed off physiological fluids that are a rich source of nutrients for them. Microorganismal spores are ubiquitous in our environment. All they need is the right conditions to grow and multiply. Microorganismal contamination can destroy a sample almost overnight. This underscores the need for proper storage of both evidentiary and reference samples as soon as possible. Material such as soil contains large numbers of microorganisms, and may well destroy a sample before it can be collected and preserved. There is nothing we can do about the growth and action of microorganisms before the crime scene is discovered. However, once the samples are collected, drying them as quickly as possible, and then freezing, can limit the destructive potential of any inherent microorganisms. Because microorganisms are ubiquitous in nature, they can also contaminate a sample during analysis in the laboratory. The analyst must adhere to good laboratory practice to avoid this circumstance. Because blood antigens or molecules similar to them are practically ubiquitous throughout living organisms, false positives in, for example, ABO typing, might be produced by certain types of bacteria (Gaensslen, 1983), or in one known case, by ants (Sidebar 8). This potential problem has abated as DNA testing, which is generally much more specific, has replaced serological typing systems. DNA typing systems are generally specific for at least primate DNA, but occasionally a bacterial result may fall within the read region (Fernandez-Rodriguez et al., 1996; Fregeau et al., 1999). However, the experienced analyst who is familiar with the specifics of a typing system should be able to distinguish a microorganismal result using a variety of indicators.

Nonhuman physiological substances. Similarly, addition of animal, but nonhuman, physiological fluids generally has no effect on the successful and correct DNA typing of a sample. Although higher organisms may share some serological similarities with humans, this usually has no consequence because the dog, cat, or even gorilla is unlikely to have committed the crime or even contributed to the sample. But the analyst must be aware of any known cross-reaction that might produce results from nonhuman DNA sources, thereby complicating interpretation of the results. This provides yet another reason for the analyst to know something about the history of the sample; in the unusual circumstance where blood or other body fluids from higher organisms other than human might be part of the sample, this information helps the analyst to interpret correctly any anomalies that might be present in the results.

Human physiological substances. The presence of more than one source of human tissue or fluid in a sample is not uncommon, and is a consequence of ordinary living. Clothing will routinely acquire perspiration, saliva, urine, or small spots of blood (Stoney, 1991). Some fluids, such as blood, are obvious because they have color. Others, such as saliva or perspiration, are less obvious. Some evidence, most notably vaginal samples, will always have material from the vaginal donor in addition to the evidence fluid (with or without sperm). A thorough analysis of the item is essential to detect these impurities, and their presence must be incorporated into the interpretation of the evidence. The type of contamination that sends serologists and DNA analysts running for cover is physiological material from another human being. To put this in perspective, however, it must be stressed that unless the introduced material shows exactly the same marker pattern as one of the principals in the crime, it would still not produce a false positive. That is, the wrong guy is unlikely to be falsely implicated. One caveat to this involves the laboratory contamination of an evidence sample with material from a reference sample. This type of mistake is devastating.

d.   Prevention and Detection

That crime scene samples are not pristine, and that laboratory analysts are human beings who occasionally make errors is inevitable. More to the point

Sidebar 8

The Hillside Stranglers — "A" is for Ant

When journalists dubbed the killer of several prostitutes in the late 1970s as the Hillside Strangler, little did they realize that they were actually writing about *two* killers. Forensic science played its role in providing information about the case, including one small aside that did not figure prominently in the outcome of the trial, but illustrates the necessity of knowing as much about the case as possible.

The origin of the infamous moniker arose from the proclivity of the killers to dump the nude, strangled bodies onto inaccessible hillsides, presumably in hopes that the bodies would not be found. One such victim was a woman who was discovered early one morning. A sharp-eyed detective noticed a trail of ants streaming to one of her breasts. He naively suggested that this might be due to the presence of saliva on the breast, which the ants were consuming as food. He insisted that the criminalist at the scene collect a nipple swab to collect any saliva that might be present.

At the laboratory, the analyst examined the swab for amylase, a component of saliva. He detected "moderate" amounts of amylase in a semiquantitative spot test. No control samples had been collected from other locations on the skin of the deceased, so the meaning of this result was problematic from the beginning. However, the analyst then performed an absorption–inhibition test for ABH antigens. He detected type B (no H) activity. The report indicated the presence of moderate amounts of amylase and the presence of B antigenic activity. The reader was left with the impression that saliva from a type B-secretor was present. The victim in the case was an type O nonsecretor, and so the antigenic activity could not have been from her.

Research from a previous case had indicated that ants possess some ABH activity, and so, even assuming saliva was present (which is not necessarily supported by the amylase finding), some question existed regarding the source of the antigenic activity. In an effort to find out more about this possibility, the analyst consulted with Dr. Roy Snelling, a leading entomologist from the California Museum of Science and Industry. The expert readily identified the ants on the body as a species of fire ants. He also agreed to assist the analyst in collecting a sample of these ants. They went to the scene of the body dump, and laid ingenious traps containing raw bacon to lure and trap only the carnivorous fire ants. Other species of ants at the location would either ignore the traps or be driven away by the aggressive and warrior-like fire ants. Sure enough, when they returned the following day, the traps contained several hundred fire ants for the analyst to take back to the laboratory. Additionally, Snelling was able to provide numerous references to the gustatory habits of ants, revealing poor table manners and the tendency to slobber. This research also revealed that previous assays for amylase were, indeed, positive.

In the laboratory, the ants were tested for both amylase activity and ABO. Not surprisingly, these ants had amylase activity, as indicated by the past research. Further, these fire ants had type B antigenic activity. The analyst was unwilling to assume that the ants were in fact the source of the amylase and antigenic activity on the breast swab, but at least these findings created a reasonable alternative hypothesis for the evidence. The attorney prosecuting the defendants decided to hold this evidence for rebuttal, rather than use it in the case in chief.

Because he was a type AB non-secretor, the defendant immediately seized on the report implying a saliva donor that was a type B secretor. After seeing the prosecution's report detailing the results of the ant analysis, the defendant retained its own forensic expert to assess the evidence. This expert also retained an entomologist, and the two of them toddled off to the crime scene to collect some ants. For some unknown reason, the entomologist never thought to identify the type of ants present on the body (a photograph was available). Therefore, at the scene they merely collected ants that were present and visible. In a curious twist, they also consulted the entomologist retained by the prosecution, Dr. Snelling. The defense expert's only question to Snelling, however, was to identify the ants that they had collected *in the field* from the crime scene. The entomologist easily identified them as ubiquitous Argentine ants.

The defense expert then carried out some of his own experiments. He discovered (to his surprise) that ants do have ABH-like substances. In his case, the Argentine ants showed type A antigenic activity. He further demonstrated that the ants could deposit this activity simply by walking around on a substrate such as a piece of paper. While this expert had previously questioned the possibility that ants could contribute ABH-like substances, for this case he was satisfied with his results showing they could; they failed to explain the type B antigen found on the nipple of the deceased victim.

At trial, the defense attorney presented only one piece of physical evidence supporting his client's innocence, that of the nipple swab containing type B antigenic activity. His expert argued that amylase was found, consistent with the presence of saliva, and further that type B antigen was present. He argued that together, these supported the hypothesis that saliva from a type B secretor individual was present. He further testified that both the defendant and his previously convicted accomplice were type AB non-secretors. During direct and cross-examination, the expert presented his findings regarding the ants. At one point he identified the ants that he tested as Argentine ants, and concluded that, while they did exhibit A antigen activity, they did not exhibit B antigen activity, so they could not be the source of the B activity found on the nipple of the victim. Thus, in his opinion, neither the ants nor the defendant(s) could be the source of the B antigen.

On rebuttal, the prosecutor decided to put up only the entomologist from the Museum of Science and Industry. After qualifying him, the prosecutor asked if he could identify the ants on the breast area of the deceased. When he responded that they were fire ants, one of the jurors was reportedly seen to clasp his forehead and mutter *sotto voce*, "They tested the wrong ants!"

The jury did convict the defendant of murdering this victim, and so could not have given the defense theory, the only possible exculpatory evidence, much weight.

This scenario illustrates the importance of knowing as much about a case as possible to formulate relevant hypotheses and design experiments that address the specific circumstances of the crime.

is the implementation of measures designed both to prevent negligent contamination and to detect it in the rare event that it occurs. Prevention of contamination introduced by law enforcement, crime laboratory personnel, or any extraneous human beings starts at the crime scene. We'll address the prevention and detection of contamination in the laboratory in Chapter 10.

e. *Explainable Differences*

It can be tempting to consider any and all perturbations to a sample as originating from negligent causes such as contamination or analyst incompetence. The fact remains that all samples are unique (see Chapter 6), even samples that originate from a common source. They have accumulated differences as a result of their separate local environments in space and time and will never exactly resemble another in all respects. The analyst must use her knowledge, education, and experience to discern which elements differentiate two samples as having different origins and which are merely explainable differences. This, more than any other single attribute, differentiates the criminalist from the technician.

D. Summary

In this chapter, we have begun to connect the principles we articulated in the Section 2 to the practical day-to-day work of the criminalist or crime scene technician. The recognition and collection of evidence is the first human intervention after a crime event takes place. A thoughtful and complete processing of the crime scene(s) is the best foundation that can be laid for the examinations, analyses, and interpretations that will follow. Asking the right question forms a solid beginning. Formulating not only a hypothesis, but competing hypotheses is vital to a thorough search for evidence. Finally, it is incumbent on responsible personnel to make sure that the evidence and the scene are properly documented, and to collect and preserve the evidence in a way that minimizes the possibility of adventitious contamination. The main point is that *thinking is allowed*.

References

Fernandez-Rodriguez, A. et al., Microbial DNA challenge studies of PCR-based systems used in forensic genetics, *Adv. Forensic Haemogenet.*, 6, 177–179, 1996.

Fisher, B. J. A., *Techniques of Crime Scene Investigation*, 6th ed., CRC Press, Boca Raton, FL, 2000.

Fregeau, C. J., Bowen, K. L., and Fourney, R. M., Validation of highly polymorphic fluorescent multiplex short tandem repeat systems using two generations of DNA sequencers, *J. Forensic Sci.*, 44(1), 133, 1999.

Gaensslen, R. E., *Sourcebook in Forensic Serology*, U.S. Government Printing Office, Washington, D.C., 1983.

Geberth, V. J., Ed., *Practical Homicide Investigation: Tactics, Procedures and Forensic Techniques*, 3rd ed., CRC Press, Boca Raton, FL, 1996.

Goddard, K. W., *Crime Scene Investigation*, Reston Publishing Company, Reston, VA, 1977.

Gross, A. M., Harris, K. A., and Kaldun, G. L., The effect of luminol on presumptive tests and DNA analysis using the polymerase chain reaction, *J. Forensic Sci.*, 44(4), 837, 1999.

Mullin, C., *Error of Judgment: The Truth about the Birmingham bombings*, Chatto & Windus, London, 1986.

Ogle, R. R., Jr., *Crime Scene Investigation and Physical Evidence Manual*, 1995.

People v. Simpson, CNN trial transcripts, available at *http://www.cnn.com/US/OJ/trial/*.

Ragle, L., *Crime Scene*, Avon Books, New York, 1995.

Saferstein, R., *Forensic Science Handbook*, Vol. 1, Prentice-Hall, Englewood Cliffs, NJ, 1981.

Saferstein, R., *Criminalistics: An Introduction to Forensic Science*, 6th ed., Prentice-Hall, Englewood Cliffs, NJ, 1998.

Stoney, D. A., *The Use of Statistics in Forensic Science*, Aitken, C. and Stoney, D., Eds., Ellis Horwood, Chichester, West Sussex, U.K., 1991.

Svensson, A. and Wendel, O., *Crime Detection*, Elsevier, New York, 1955.

United States of America v. Terry Nichols, CNN trial transcripts, 1997, available at *http://europe.cnn.com/US/9703/okc.trial/transcripts/*.

Webster's Encyclopedic Unabridged Dictionary of the English Language, Gramercy Books, New York, 1996.

Figure 9.1 Handwriting exam. Pattern recognition is a mandatory skill in the practice of criminalistics. Document examiners who perform handwriting analysis are asked to discern subtle pattern similarities and differences in tests like the one illustrated here. This is one way in which they demonstrate proficiency in correctly concluding whether two samples originate from the same writer or not. Which rows have matching shapes and which rows have no repeated figures?

Good Laboratory Practice — Establishing Validity and Reliability

9

If you get to think, you have to think

—Norah Rudin

A forensic examination is not a controlled experiment. In fact, it is not an experiment at all. By definition, a scientific experiment requires not only known conditions, but also controlled conditions. Ideally, one variable at a time is altered while the others are held constant. This allows the scientist to determine specifically what is causing the change, if any, in the final results.

Case samples have a whole history of which we are unaware. They are the element in the analysis over which we have no control. We test them for certain attributes, but a controlled experiment is not an option and, contrary to NASA directive, failure is frequently an option. We accept this as a limitation of the testing and interpret our results accordingly. Because of this, however, all of the other elements of the test system must be both *optimized* and *validated* to establish maximum reliability. *Standards* and *controls* must also be used when appropriate.

It is important to realize that optimization, validation, standards, and controls may apply differently to analytical testing than to comparison testing. These concepts first arose from test systems in which a reaction occurs between the sample and the test reagents, or some instrumentation is used to probe the nature of a sample. It is more difficult to understand how these ideas might be useful for comparison evidence where the examination is a simple visual exercise, perhaps with the aid of a microscope at most, and any interaction or analysis takes place in the head of the analyst.

Nonetheless, particularly in the current climate of intense scrutiny, it is necessary to demonstrate that any test system is working as expected and providing reliable results. It is also good scientific practice to do so. Historically, this has neither been offered nor expected with any consistency. In some cases, a great amount of knowledge has been amassed, but never systematized For any particular test system, we must either address these concerns or show that they are not concerns.

A.   Optimization

Optimization might be defined as relating to the test system itself. Optimization establishes that the test system is working properly so that any variation seen is due to the samples themselves. For example, for latent fingerprints, optimization might include testing visualization reagents with known prints, or surveying different inks, ink pads, and paper for taking reference prints to see which gives the clearest, most reproducible results. Optimization for shoe impressions might involve testing various casting materials to see which is the most durable and retains the most detail. Optimization of microscopic techniques would center on testing the quality of various lenses alone and in combination, and in determining which lens, filter, aperture, and light combination might work best for a specific application.

For strictly visual comparisons, optimization of the data comparison process itself is a bit hard to conceive because the instrument used is the human brain. Perhaps it is best analogized to sensitizing and calibrating one's brain to discern the characteristics upon which various comparisons depend. To extend the analogy, directed training, practice, and experience allow the skilled examiner to determine useful characteristics reliably and to differentiate between optically encoded signal and noise. The way in which we can determine if an individual brain is optimized is by proficiency testing.

For instrumental systems, such as Fourier Transform Infrared Spectroscopy, Gas Chromotography, or Capillary Electrophoresis, optimization might include establishing calibration tolerances for the instrument, deciding what settings give the best balance between signal and noise, and verifying that known samples reproducibly give correct results. Any sample preparation techniques, such as DNA amplification or chemical derivitization, must also be optimized so that the cleanest results are obtained and sample differences cannot be attributed to a preparation process needed before instrumental analysis can be employed. Interestingly, although an instrument is used to translate chemical data into a visual form that humans can understand, and the visuals are usually accompanied by quantitative data, in the end, we are left comparing visual patterns. Each analyst's individual experience at discerning the significant aspects of those patterns contributes to the quality of the analysis as a whole.

The foregoing are only a few examples of the type of work involved in establishing that a particular test system is optimized for a particular application. The reader might like to think through various forensic test systems and consider what might constitute optimization. Note that, in the process of optimizing the system to produce the highest quality and most reliable results, a body of work is accumulated that begins to address both the capabilities and limitations of the system.

B. Validation

In contrast to optimization, which concentrates on the test system, *validation* concentrates on the samples themselves. In performing validation studies, we ask what quantitative and qualitative properties of the samples themselves might confound our ability to get reliable results or to get results at all. We intentionally perturb the samples to determine at what point no result, an ambiguous result, or even an incorrect result might be produced. Because of this, validation is particularly critical for systems intended for forensic use where the samples tested will not be of uniform quality and quantity.

The purpose of validation is to establish limits within which we are confident of the results obtained. Validation also helps us to establish the variance inherent in the system as a whole, and to gain a further understanding of one kind of explainable difference. For example, if a sample is tested 100 times, the results will look similar, but small differences will undoubtedly manifest. We learn how much variation may exist between tests, so that we may determine criteria within which we can either conclude that two different samples may share a common origin or exclude them as having a common origin. How sensitive is the system to the quantity of sample? What are the lowest and highest quantities that can reliably be analyzed? What artifacts begin to appear at the extreme ends of the spectrum and can we use them as diagnostics? What do mixtures of similar substances look like in a particular test system, and are there indicators that might alert us to the presence of a mixture? How might various environmental factors to which forensic samples are commonly subjected influence the ability to analyze the samples and to interpret the results obtained? These are the kinds of questions that validation studies attempt to answer.

1. Levels of Validation

Validation can occur at several levels. The top level is that of validating a new technique when it is first introduced. This may involve efforts of multiple laboratories and extremely broad and comprehensive testing. One of the advantages of interlaboratory validation studies is the opportunity for sample exchange. This helps establish the limits not only for intralaboratory variation, but interlaboratory variation, using the same samples. These mammoth studies are usually only necessary during the initial development or technology transfer of a substantively new method. The rest of the field can then rely, in large part, on the initial body of data that will ideally be peer reviewed and published. Of course, when substantive changes are introduced into the original protocol, it must be revalidated in a more-limited fashion to understand the full impact of those changes.

The next level of validation is sometimes called in-house or internal validation. Although reliability for the general system has been established, it is still incumbent on those in each individual laboratory to document that the test works as expected in their hands, and to establish laboratory-specific limits imposed by the overall system (e.g., protocols, instruments, reagents). These studies are usually much more limited, but also serve to familiarize laboratory personnel with the test and what compromised samples might look like. Regardless of how long a method has been in use and generally accepted, internal validation must always be performed when setting up a new program.

What one might call "personal" validation translates as training and proficiency. Even though the field and the laboratory may have great confidence and experience in a particular method, each individual must also build a foundation of personal experience and familiarity. This is accomplished by a directed program in which the analyst first tests or compares pristine samples, then practices with various compromised samples. New examiners might then practice on some adjudicated case samples before taking a formal proficiency test to demonstrate their competency to work cases. ⟵

2.   Validation of Methods for Comparison Evidence

In the previous section on optimization, we alluded to some of the fundamental differences between techniques in which the evidence interacts chemically or physically with some substance or instrument to produce a detectable basis for comparison and techniques in which the comparison is based on strict visual observation (with or without magnification). Because validation addresses the interaction between the samples and the test system, we are left with somewhat of a void when we ask what might constitute validation for comparison evidence. For all kinds of comparison evidence where visual and optical methods are used directly (including microscopy), the instrument with which the evidence interacts is the human brain. This is, by definition, personal to each examiner. The nature of this kind of evidence demands, first of all, that a high level of training and experience ("optimization") be required of each individual examiner.

Nevertheless, although the data can only strictly pertain to the individual doing the testing, most aspects of validation can be explored for comparison evidence. For example, simulating the consequences of intentional environmental exposure of various materials can be very useful in helping the examiner appreciate explainable differences in two items that may, in fact, share a common origin. Can the faded red cotton evidence fiber and the bright red cotton reference fiber be classified as originating from a common source? For impression evidence, "minima" and "maxima" of detectable characteristics might be explored by taking an item with known characteristics and impressing it in various substrates with a variety of known pressures. In Sidebar 9, we refer to one example of a validation experiment involving dermal ridge prints and blood spatter. The creative criminalist can certainly think of many more such examples.

3.   Validity vs. Reliability

We are reminded of a piece of court testimony where the expert witness spent several hours vacillating about whether the laboratory's methods were valid, reliable, neither, or both (*People v. Morganti*, 1996). Probably his most fundamental mistake was to use the terms as weapons rather than tools. Nevertheless, it is worth clarifying the difference between these two concepts which are so often used interchangeably. It will be helpful to relate each back to one of two concepts all of us learned back in basic chemistry. Validity may be ⟵ conveniently understood as an extension of *accuracy* — a valid result is a

Sidebar 9

The Blood or the Print — Which Came First?

In the mid-1980s, in a motel in Oklahoma City, a young woman was found dead in the bathtub. It appeared that she had been bludgeoned where she lay and left to die. Blood was everywhere. Forensic experts from the Oklahoma City laboratory were called to the scene. One of the things they did was to dust for prints. A palm print was developed amid a few spatters of blood at the end of the ceramic tub opposite the victim's head. In particular, the print overlapped a blood drop about 1 mm square. The crime scene technician lifted the print as potentially incriminating evidence, and along with it the blood spot.

The palm print was eventually matched to an employee of the motel. According to the work schedule, the man had cleaned the room just that morning. Thus, the question became, which was deposited first, the print or the blood? This was obviously crucial in determining the order of events, as the print could have been left quite innocently by someone cleaning the room before the blood was deposited. The answer to this question was particularly critical as the print was essentially the only evidence in the case; without it, they had no evidence against the suspect.

The technician who lifted the print immediately formed the opinion that the print was left after the blood was deposited. However, it was left to a more senior fingerprint analyst to make the final determination. The examiner formed the same opinion, based on criteria that he believed to be common knowledge. These criteria included (1) the blood was "cracked," indicating that significant pressure had been placed on it; (2) ridge detail started over the stain (although it did not apparently traverse the entire 1 mm stain); (3) the presence of fingerprint powder in the cracks of the blood drop indicated the presence of oils on the stain. When challenged, the analyst could provide no supporting literature in which these criteria were established, but said they were taught at an FBI class.

For some poorly articulated reason, the lift, including the bloodstain, was sent to serology. There, a well-meaning but unthinking analyst consumed the blood spot to determine that it was of human origin. This, of course, was never in dispute. Fortunately, someone had thought to preserve the print itself in an excellent photomicrograph before the blood was sampled.

A defense expert was brought in to review the case. He was not convinced that the print was necessarily deposited after the blood spatter, and he performed some experiments to test his hypothesis. He spattered some blood on a ceramic surface and watched it dry. Without any disturbance whatsoever, it developed a cracked and crazed pattern just as a consequence of drying on this particular surface. Next, he dusted the spattered bloodstains with fingerprint powder. Without any prints, either underneath or on top of the blood spatter, he was able to reproduce a pattern with the same characteristics as that from the case.

To complete the experiment, the criminalist then spattered blood on top of previously deposited prints and also applied prints on top of a fresh spatter pattern. In both instances he could find drops that either did or did not show the apparently distinguishing characteristics of that in the case. The experiment clearly demonstrated that one could not reliably determine which came first, the blood or the print, using the criteria proffered by the Oklahoma examiner. Two examples are shown in the figure.

From the results of the experiments, he devised a test that he challenged several of his colleagues to take. All who agreed to take the test felt that they could tell whether blood or a print had been deposited first. He chose several examples that represented each of the possible test situations, and included instances in which the appearance of the spatter either supported or did not support (according to the "generally accepted" criteria) what he knew to be the order of deposition. Of the five certified fingerprint examiners who took the test, no one had fewer than 10 years of experience, and the most senior examiner boasted 25 years of experience in fingerprint examination and comparison. The best score was only 80% right, while the worst was 80% wrong — worse than guessing!

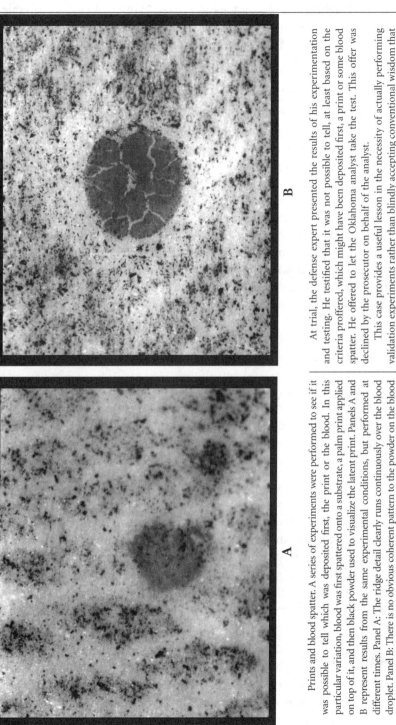

A

B

Prints and blood spatter. A series of experiments were performed to see if it was possible to tell which was deposited first, the print or the blood. In this particular variation, blood was first spattered onto a substrate, a palm print applied on top of it, and then black powder used to visualize the latent print. Panels A and B represent results from the same experimental conditions, but performed at different times. Panel A: The ridge detail clearly runs continuously over the blood droplet. Panel B: There is no obvious coherent pattern to the powder on the blood drop. Experienced analysts who believed that they could reliably determine whether the blood or the print was deposited first incorrectly concluded that, for the example in Panel B, the print was deposited before the blood.

At trial, the defense expert presented the results of his experimentation and testing. He testified that it was not possible to tell, at least based on the criteria proffered, which might have been deposited first, a print or some blood spatter. He offered to let the Oklahoma analyst take the test. This offer was declined by the prosecutor on behalf of the analyst.

This case provides a useful lesson in the necessity of actually performing validation experiments rather than blindly accepting conventional wisdom that has been passed down through oral tradition — even if it is taught in a class at the FBI.

correct result. Reliability can be understood in terms of *precision* — a reliable result is one that can be reproduced within defined quantitative or qualitative limits. The term *validation* is commonly understood to pertain to studies that help us ascertain both the validity and reliability of our results. ⟵

4. Is Validation Required?

We cannot leave the subject of validation without emphasizing that its primary utility is to the analyst and the laboratory that is performing the work. Validation establishes the capabilities and limitations of the system, and builds a body of work from which practitioners can learn when variations are explainable and when they indicate a real difference. The greatest utility of validation studies is in providing the practitioner doing the work with information that will assist in the interpretation of difficult samples. Validation studies are essential — for the field, for individual laboratories, and, in the form of proficiency testing, for individuals. This is simply good science and contributes to a solid foundation for performing work and interpreting the results. Nevertheless, a lack of validation on some level does not, *a priori*, invalidate a particular analysis. However, the fewer challenges to which a particular system has been subjected, the more assumptions that must be made about the result of a particular test, and the weaker any conclusions about the results must be.

C. Quality Assurance and Quality Control

A list of references that address general scientific and also forensic-specific quality assurance issues are provided following the general reference list for this chapter.

1. Quality Assurance

Quality assurance guidelines, usually found in a *quality manual*, define all the aspects of a program that are necessary to ensure a minimum standard of operation. These guidelines encompass everything from laboratory safety, to personnel requirements, to documentation of method reliability. Both fieldwide and in-house validation studies contribute specific information upon which the procedures and protocols portion of the quality assurance program is based.

2. Quality Control

Quality control refers to the specific ways of implementing various points of the quality assurance program. This includes all aspects of day-to-day laboratory operation such as instrument maintenance, reagent preparation, and the proper use of standards and controls. The latter is the only aspect that we will address in detail at this point.

a.   Standards and Controls

For the science in forensic science to be taken seriously, each analytical test must be accompanied by the appropriate standards and controls. These will differ depending on the kind of analysis, but their conspicuous absence is unacceptable. Again, for strictly comparison evidence, there is usually no system to test, so standards and controls, in the sense that we discuss them here, are not relevant.*

More than a few analysts include standards and controls in their examinations only to meet some new-fangled post-modern standard, but fail to truly understand their utility and necessity. No academician would be caught dead publishing the results of an experiment without including both verification that the test system was working as expected (positive controls) and confirmation that no extraneous material had been introduced into the system that would skew the results (negative controls). Because we have relinquished full control over the conditions in a forensic test by acknowledging the limits of the sample, it is even more crucial that we confirm that the test system is functioning as expected.

We should probably start by defining the terms *standard* and *control*. These terms are typically used rather loosely and interchangeably. While it's true that their functions can overlap, and sometimes the same sample can fulfill both requirements, it will be useful for the purposes of this discussion to give you our working definitions.

Standard: A measurement system against which an unknown sample is compared. It can be numerical, generating a quantitative result, or comparative, giving a qualitative result. An example of a numerical standard would be a simple ruler. An example of a qualitative standard would an element with which an unknown substance is compared.

Control: A sample whose result is known. This assures the user that the test system is functioning as expected. An example of a positive

---

* The ASCLAD-LAB report resulting from the inspection of one particular laboratory decried the absence of a "positive control" for footwear analysis. This is one of those instances where a no doubt well-meaning inspector applied a general quality criterion without thinking about it very hard. Perhaps a vision test of the analyst would show that he could see within proscribed parameters on the day the comparison was done.

control is a sample containing a known percentage of alcohol that is used to calibrate a breathalyzer. A negative control contains all the reagents in a test system but no sample.*

When we are training new analysts, or worse yet, old supervisors and managers, the question inevitably arises regarding when it might be acceptable to omit the proper controls and standards. Gee, my runs are only 5 minutes apart; I just have to rerun this one sample that I diluted improperly. Gee my runs are only 1 hour apart; I haven't changed any of my reagents between this run and the last one; my runs are only a day apart.... Well, you get the idea — when do you draw the line? Good laboratory practice is like the religion of science; the philosophical generalization always wins over any situation in which one might like to manipulate an exception. It is not up to us to figure out ways to circumvent good laboratory practice. Like the "do it right or do it again" dilemma, one soon learns that it is not worth trying to eliminate a sample or two, because this attitude will inevitably backfire. The run in which it turns out you have a marginal evidence sample will be exactly the one in which you have decided it's just too much trouble to include the calibration controls that assure you that the instrument is operating at peak sensitivity.

Quality assurance guidelines and quality control procedures are neither merely an encumbrance nor a panacea. When implemented thoughtfully and with intelligence, they are simply another tool used to demonstrate the high quality of a work product.

D.   Standardization

Unlike other industrial and clinical manifestations of applied science, forensic science has traditionally shied away from any kind of oversight, including standardization. This has begun to change radically over the last decade, in large part because of the attention focused on the field by the advent of DNA

---

* Particularly for biological analyses, two types of "control" samples have evolved that don't control for anything, but do serve other important functions. The so-called *substrate control* — a sample taken from an apparently unstained area adjacent to a suspected physiological fluid stain — is more appropriately called a *substrate sample*. It provides important information about what might be lurking in the background that might confuse results from the observed stain; because the answer is previously unknown, it does not meet the criterion of a control. The second example concerns the threshold "controls" used in the reverse dot-blot detection of PCR products in DNA typing. These "C" and "S" dots simply give information about the amount of amplified sample introduced into the test system (and for the "S" dot even further caveats exist). As such, they do not meet the criterion for a control that indicates that the test system (in this case, amplification and hybridization) is functioning properly. This role is fulfilled by a known DNA sample that is run as a positive amplification control.

testing. Efforts at standardization ideally emerge from the initial cross-laboratory validation effort. Sometimes it is necessary to backtrack if laboratories have developed similar protocols independently. Methods may be standardized against a protocol or a sample. In other words, laboratories can agree to use exactly the same protocol to ensure that comparable results are obtained. Or control samples can establish that two slightly different protocols still produce the same results. In forensic science, it is often more practical to employ the latter method as it allows for greater flexibility while still demonstrating reliability.

Several organizations have developed complementary programs that address these different approaches. The American Society for Testing and Materials (ASTM) is a well-established organization that provides a framework for any discipline wishing to develop a nucleus of standards. The ASTM blueprint, developed initially for use in industry, focuses on methods and protocols. For industrial and clinical applications, a goal is to institute absolutely standardized protocols throughout the industry. The ASTM Committee E-30 on Forensic Sciences was created in 1970 to address the process of standardizing the methods and terminology that are particular to the field. ASTM E-30 is split into a number of subcommittees, one of which is criminalistics. Although some material has been developed (ASTM, 2000) and those standards have been incorporated by some laboratories as part of their in-house protocols, no forensic discipline has formally adopted ASTM standards.

The complement to standardizing against protocols is standardizing against known samples. The National Institute of Standards and Technology (NIST) develops and distributes standard materials for a myriad of testing procedures. NIST materials are used regularly in various forensic disciplines to establish that a particular instrument or method is giving the expected results. Other accessory devices, such as NIST-traceable thermometers, also assist the forensic laboratory in standardizing its methods.

In 1989, in response to the increased scrutiny that came with DNA testing, the FBI sponsored a pioneer working group, then called Technical Working Group in DNA Analysis Methods (TWGDAM). This group, comprising representatives from public laboratories throughout the country, compiled a document outlining guidelines for qualifications, training, validation, testing, and report writing. Shortly thereafter additional "TWGs" were formed in an effort to address similar issues in the other forensic disciplines. The adjective "scientific" has now replaced the word "technical," and all the acronyms begin with "SWG" in stead of "TWG." Most are works in progress, although just this year SWGMAT released several documents addressing trace analysis, fibers, hair, and paint. The SWG guidelines do not attempt to provide specific methods or protocols. Rather they direct that validated protocols be implemented, and that standard materials be used to verify the proper working of any methods employed. For whatever reason, the community has directed its resources toward the SWGs rather than the ASTM groups. It is possible that at some future point, those efforts may be merged.

E.   Review

The review of work product may take several different forms, each for a different purpose. The first level of review is performed within the laboratory, before a case is formally signed and released. This laboratory is most frequently the one retained by the prosecution, but it could also be a laboratory performing analysis or reanalysis at the request of the defense. Another type of review may be performed by an independent expert on behalf of opposing counsel. Finally, case review is also performed as part of laboratory accreditation. Although the mechanics of the process and the material examined are virtually the same for all these types of review, the reviewer may look at the material with different questions in mind. Below, we discuss the sometimes contrary perspectives of an internal reviewer and an independent reviewer. A review in the context of accreditation is similar to an internal review except that the inspectors are drawn from other working laboratories. We follow with a brief description of the review process and some specific case examples.

1.   Internal Review

It is to the analyst's advantage for a qualified peer or supervisor to review the entire case file, including the notes and report, before it leaves the laboratory. The main objective of this technical review is to confirm that the data support the conclusions. It also provides a last-ditch opportunity to verify that the data were recorded correctly, that the controls worked as expected, that any calculations or statistics are correct, and to check for clerical errors. Because only someone with technical expertise is likely to catch a clerical error involving data, this is actually part of the technical review. Sometimes laboratories separate an administrative review — are all the pieces of the report present and are the pages numbered and in order? — from the technical review. An administrative review could also be done by someone without specific technical expertise.

An internal review is to be welcomed, not avoided. Wouldn't you rather have your conclusion and its basis questioned by your colleague, whose intention is to help you put out the best work product possible, than challenged for the first time by opposing counsel on the stand? In our collective experience in performing technical reviews, we frequently find careless errors that are easily corrected. No reason exists for a report to go out with that kind of ammunition readily available. More important, however, we invariably find that discussing the data and proposing alternative hypotheses leads to a more complete understanding of the case and provides the analyst with the confidence that no obvious errors were missed. A forensic analysis is not a closed book exam; the more people you talk to and the more opinions you solicit, the better job you will be doing. As we discussed in Chapters 1 and 2, the criminalist has traditionally been both territorial and fiercely independent. This attitude does not foster a position of strength for either the individual or the community. We support and encourage the positive trend toward discussion and review.

2. Independent Review

In academic science, the results of an experiment are generally not considered conclusive until they have been published in a peer-reviewed journal and reproduced independently by another investigator. Forensic science can approach this model in the optimization and validation phases of developing a new technique. However, because of the limitations inherent in testing actual evidence, both independent verification and publication become problematic. The adversarial nature of the court system and the expectation of a certain degree of confidentially prevent formal publication until after a case is adjudicated. Sometimes the opposing side will reexamine a sample, but this may be precluded if the sample is consumed in the initial analysis. In this situation, if an independent expert has already been retained, he might witness the testing of the sample. This is less of a problem for comparison evidence in which the sample is not altered or consumed in the examination process. Nevertheless, because the legal burden of proof is on the prosecution, it may not necessarily be advantageous to the defense to reexamine any evidence. Finally, except in a small number of high-profile cases, the defense is notoriously underfunded and has access to far fewer resources than the prosecution. Even in a case where retesting is desirable and possible, it may be unfeasible because of a lack of monetary resources. For all of these reasons, independent review of the entire case file must often suffice to determine if the work is reliable and the data support the conclusions drawn.

We emphasize here that a truly competent review should be performed by a qualified expert — someone who has experience in a forensic laboratory, and fully appreciates the peculiarities and limitations of forensic samples. In spite of the fact that "experts" with fancy academic degrees abound, and many have been consecrated by the courts, we do not sanction the representation that a Ph.D. automatically qualifies one as a forensic expert. An interesting litmus test is whether the expert works only for the defense. It is hard to imagine how one can truly understand a discipline if one's persistent and enduring goal is to discredit its work product. The mate to this pair is that scientists who have only worked in government laboratories, despite their best intentions, may fail to appreciate both the necessity and, frequently, the difficulty of performing an independent review. In our ideal world, the well-rounded forensic scientist would be required to experience both environments; in reality, this may be impractical.

A competent review is comprehensive and covers not only the specifics of the analysis, but also the forensic context within which the analysis is set. The independent expert will address all the same questions the analyst and internal reviewer have, bringing to the effort a fresh mind and perhaps a different perspective.

3.   Elements of Review

You will not be surprised to see the same concepts that we have discussed throughout this book return in this section. Because review is part of establishing validity and reliability, we include it in this chapter. In the next chapter, we will backtrack and discuss some of the same issues in the context of the actual analysis. Consider this a preview. In the following summary, we highlight aspects of the work product that the internal reviewer or independent expert might approach differently.

a.   What's the Question?

This juncture provides yet another opportunity to review *the Question*. Does the scientific question follow from the legal question? Were the appropriate tests performed? In particular, the internal reviewer should ask if the analyses performed reasonably address the questions asked, or if more work needs to be done.

The independent expert may have questions different from those posed by the original analyst. The defense may have an alternate hypothesis in mind and, consequently, may consider the results of the analysis with a different scenario in mind. They may have information that the prosecution does not have, and they certainly have a different goal. For example, the defendant may have named an accomplice or alternative suspect to the defense attorney, but the prosecution may not have this information. Consider the following real-life scenario:

> An individual (Suspect 1) had confessed and been tried and convicted for the murder of a woman. Afterward, he named the woman's ex-boyfriend as an accomplice (Suspect 2), claiming he had committed the crime under duress from the ex-boyfriend. Several others close to the case named yet another suspect (Suspect 3). Suspect 3 claimed to know nothing of the crime and to have no relationship with the woman. Physical evidence had been

collected in the case, but very little of it had been analyzed after the original suspect confessed. Suspect 2 was subsequently charged, and the attorney representing him was interested in whether the physical evidence might put Suspect 3 at the scene of the crime. Because the prosecution had never heard of Suspect 3, they couldn't have even asked this question, nor would they have had the reference samples with which to answer it.

Either reviewer will also consider if pertinent questions exist that the tests did not or couldn't answer.

b.   Documentation

Any kind of review becomes an exercise in diminishing returns if the documentation is incomplete or unclear. One of our common observations is the seemingly ubiquitous lack of good scientific practice in the area of documentation. When the details of the test or analysis are not recorded, that information is quickly lost to the distant recesses of the analyst's brain, rarely to be recovered. If it was not recorded, it was not done, or at best we are left guessing exactly how it was done. It is not uncommon for information that would be of great help in answering questions about the interpretation to be unavailable. This is unfortunate because all it does is weaken our confidence in any one interpretation. Ambiguity is rarely anyone's goal in solving a crime.

The documentation that started with the collection and preservation of evidence in the field must continue through the examination and analysis in the laboratory. There is nothing worse than receiving a case file for review in which the total documentation consists of one page listing the case number, the results, and the dreaded acronym, SOP — Standard Operating Procedure. By definition, every case is different and each sample is novel — how can exactly the same procedures have been used in any two cases? Although it is certainly necessary for the laboratory to maintain SOPs as a starting place for different analyses, each sample provides its own challenges and intrigues. We've insisted that the analyst gets to think; she can use her education, knowledge, and experience to process each sample for maximum informativness. For the privilege of getting to think, the criminalist is also required to think, and to record that thought process both for posterity and review.

As trivial as it sounds, an internal reviewer should check that the case notes and report are complete and legible so that any other experts can readily see what was done and when. The analyst must have carefully and clearly documented not only which items were tested, but what areas on the items were tested. A bullet hole in the back of the victim's jacket means something completely different than a bullet hole in the front, especially if the victim claims he was shot in the back. An internal reviewer should also examine the chain of custody from the time the evidence has entered the laboratory.

The independent reviewer should request the complete chain of custody, starting with evidence collection. Frequently, no one else may review it on behalf of the defendant. We mentioned a couple of examples of chain-of-custody problems in the previous chapter.

The internal reviewer should also check that each item has a unique identifier. If not, there may be ambiguity about which item was actually tested. We know of one case where the suspect and a boyfriend of the victim were both labeled as "K2" and a second reference sample from the suspect was later labeled as "K3." This led to some interesting gyrations throughout the analysis and interpretation in the attempt to identify which was which, and ultimately, to a mistake in labeling.

c.   What Evidence Was Tested?

The internal reviewer should check the evidence received against the evidence tested to make sure nothing major was missed, at least from his perspective. Obviously an analyst's choice of evidence, perhaps as suggested by the investigator, will influence the results. The independent reviewer might like to see other items tested. This, of course, assumes he actually knows about them. With the advent of specialty laboratories, such as DNA and drugs, which may receive only selected items of evidence in a case to test, the independent reviewer might have to look back to the originating laboratory or even the detective's report to find a complete listing of evidence collected in a particular case.

d.   Data and Results

The most obvious function of the internal reviewer is to check the veracity and integrity of the results and to verify that they support the conclusions. This includes checking for clerical errors as well as confirming judgment calls. The reviewer will also check a second reader's calls against the primary analyst's and verify that no substantive differences exist.

Because the independent reviewer must verify (or disagree) that the data support the final results, the original data must be available for inspection. It is not unreasonable to expect the reviewer (usually through an attorney) to ask for the primary data, but he should not have to ask three times. Occasionally, the data may be difficult or expensive to reproduce, or the original item may be needed for independent verification. In these instances, the reviewer should be willing to travel to the laboratory where the original work was done to view these items. The data and results should be accompanied by a complete and detailed documentation of the work as performed.

i.   Standards and controls.   Any reviewer should check that all controls have performed as expected, and that no spurious results were obtained. This includes verifying the results from known samples and confirming that negative controls have failed to give reportable results.

ii.   Second blind read.   The reviewer should verify that no significant discrepancies exist between the results recorded by the primary analyst and a second reader. This assumes that the second reader has independently read and recorded the results rather than simply signing-off on the primary analyst's read. Minor subjective differences that do not alter the interpretation or conclusions would generally not be considered significant.

Although many DNA laboratories have now incorporated blind second reads as part of their standard protocol, other disciplines have been slower to jump on this particular bandwagon. The absence of a second intralaboratory blind read exacerbates the need for the outside reviewer to have access to the original data. If weak or ambiguous data are relied upon to form a conclusion, lack of verification by a second qualified analyst would weaken any conclusions drawn from those data.

e.   Calculations

Calculations are perhaps the most fertile ground in a report for errors. Nobody likes to recheck numbers and, even if the rest of the report has been critically reviewed, the last residuum for errors may be in the calculations. The reviewer should, if possible, check the source of any numbers used in the calculation and independently verify the calculations themselves.

> One of our students brought into class a report from a private DNA laboratory as part of a presentation (Figure 9.2). The work had been performed for the prosecution. The student, one of the attorneys for the case, put a copy of the page detailing the population statistics on an overhead projector. It was immediately obvious to us that each alternating "total" row was a cut-and-paste replica of the one just before it and had no relationship whatsoever to the actual sum of the numbers in the column. The final calculations at the bottom of each column were, in fact, correct, but could not be derived from the intermediate sums. Not only did the laboratory technical reviewer (if there was one) fail to catch the error, so did anyone from the defense team. The trial had long since concluded with a conviction of the defendant and apparently no one the wiser.

f.   Interpretation and Conclusions

The internal reviewer should independently form his own conclusions from the data and compare them with the analyst's. Any differences in interpretation make for useful discussion. If the analyst or examiner and the reviewer cannot, in good faith, resolve any differences in interpretation, they should

Generic Marker	Penile swab	Reference	Possible types of second contributor	Second party frequency		
				Caucasian	African American	Hispanic
DQA1	1.3,2,3 < 1.2 >	1.2,2	1.3,3	0.024	0.015	0.015
LDLR	AB	AB	AA AB BB	0.192 0.492 0.322	0.039 0.313 0.651	0.221 0.499 0.288
			Combined Frequency:	1.00	1.00	1.00
GYBA	AB	AB	AB BB	0.498 0.221	0.499 0.277	0.464 0.136
			Combined Frequency	1.00	1.00	1.00
HBGG	AB	AA	AB BB	0.500 0.268	0.205 0.058	0.432 0.421
			Combined Frequency:	0.768	0.263	0.853
D758	AA	AA	AA	0.327	0.462	0.347
GC	ABC	BC	AA AB AC	0.096 0.094 0.332	0.008 0.131 0.028	0.044 0.111 0.217
			Combined Frequency:	0.768	0.263	0.853
Cumulative Frequency %				0.22%	0.022%	0.099%
Reciprocal Frequency:				1/440	1/4400	1/1000

Figure 9.2 Calculations. Which columns don't add up? Careful inspection by both the analyst and recalculation by a reviewing analyst will minimize the opportunities for such an oversight to emerge from the laboratory in a report.

consider whether the results are sufficiently reliable to be presented in a report or a court of law.

Another point that is not always highlighted in the laboratory report is any inherent weaknesses in the case or the data. These may have nothing to do with the laboratory or the analysis. Rather they are integral to the evidence, the test, or the case. For example, the evidence may be quite common, or the evidence may be of poor quality such that a comparison is difficult, or it may be unclear how the evidence relates to the case.

The reviewer's most important role is to determine if the conclusions are supported by the data. This is difficult to do if the laboratory has not supplied a conclusion. One of the most annoying things an independent reviewer will encounter is a report that stops with a simple listing of the results. WHAT

DOES IT MEAN? Either by design or default, the analyst has failed in his ultimate obligation — to provide his best interpretation of the results to the client as well as opposing counsel, the judicial system, and anyone else who reads his report. Sometimes this is a game played by certain laboratories to facilitate ambush in court; other times it is simply entrenched, institutional policy. There is usually little a reviewer can do to extract conclusion from a laboratory not used to providing one.

In a more subtle and also more common variation, the laboratory will report only one out of several equally possible conclusions. For example, the attorney has asked the question of whether a particular suspect is included as a contributor to the results. It may not be untrue to include the suspect, but neither may it always be complete. It is up to the reviewer to expose all reasonable interpretations of the data, and to predicate various conclusions on the appropriate assumptions. We will talk more about the analyst's obligations in this area in the Chapter 12.

An independent reviewer, looking at the same data as the analyst, may interpret the data differently and may come to a different conclusion about its meaning. One way in which this can happen is when the two scientists use different assumptions to modify the facts. For this reason, both should articulate any assumptions to help clarify the basis of any differing conclusions

g.   *Validation*

Validation studies should be in place for procedures that the laboratory performs on a day-to-day basis. The internal reviewer should verify that the analyst's interpretation of the results falls within the limitations of the data and is supported by the validation data. For new techniques, or substantive adaptations of established techniques, the reviewer should ascertain that sufficient validation has taken place to support the reliability of the test for the purpose used in the case.

The independent reviewer will also be interested in whether sufficient validation has taken place. Sometimes this can be accomplished by reviewing a literature of published articles. However, for new or obscure methods, published studies may not be available. In these cases, the reviewer must depend on studies performed by the laboratory, the field, or increasingly, a commercial supplier of reagents or equipment. In these cases, he should attempt to obtain this information through discovery. This is not always possible. Although laboratories are becoming increasingly open about making this information available to independent experts, the privilege has also been abused by certain of those experts, causing some laboratories to establish strict policy restrictions regarding access. An additional hurdle concerns commercial companies who claim proprietary rights over certain patented elements of a product, or refuse to disclose internal studies validating its reliability. This practice seriously undermines the scientific basis of the testing procedure. Without full information, the scientist is limited in investigating the cause of anomalous results and must rely on the company to troubleshoot the procedure. Extensive empirical validation by the client laboratory can counter these concerns to some extent, but does not substitute for complete disclosure.

h.   The Big Picture

The scope of the report will depend in part on the breadth of the laboratory. A specialty laboratory may only receive a few items of one evidence type to analyze, and may be totally unaware of the results of other types of evidence or even similar evidence analyzed in another laboratory. Analysts in the same laboratory have been known to produce separate reports for similar analyses of different cuttings from the same garment. It seems obvious that, at least within the same specialty laboratory, or the same section of a full-service laboratory, a single report should compile all the results. This then allows the internal reviewer to note any glaring discrepancies before the report leaves the laboratory. Someone with a general criminalistics background should review all of the reports generated from the evidence in a single case, regardless of discipline or jurisdiction. It would be useful for this person to write a comprehensive overview report that would assist the detective and attorneys in understanding how all of the physical evidence fits together. Although this was common practice in the 1960s and 1970s when most criminalists were generalists, and most laboratories were full-service laboratories, it is now unusual. Some laboratories are attempting to reinstitute this valuable practice and one has proffered a modern prototype of this model (Zeppa, 1999).

The independent reviewer has a slightly different responsibility in that he may be the only scientific expert with which a defense attorney has contact. Especially when funding is tight, the independent reviewer may be asked to look at several reports, both within and outside of his specialty, to help the attorney understand their meaning. The reviewer may assist the attorney by summarizing the totality of the physical evidence in the case, relating its import, and clarifying its limitations. He may also proffer alternative hypotheses and suggest further defense testing. To be of maximum assistance to the attorney client, the independent expert should have at least a working familiarity with forensic specialties outside of his own discipline.

F.   Summary

In this chapter we have begun to address some of the practical aspects of forensic laboratory work. In particular we discussed some of the steps that may be taken to demonstrate that the data are valid and reliable. Before evidence is examined or analyzed, the system must be optimized and validation studies performed. These efforts ensure, respectively, that the maximum information can be obtained from the evidence and that interpretation is performed within the limits established for the system. We also reviewed the ongoing efforts at standardization in forensic science. Finally, we discussed the review process that occurs after the initial report has been issued. In particular, we contrasted the potentially different perspectives of an internal reviewer and an independent reviewer. In the next chapter, we explore the process of examination and analysis.

References

ASTM, *Annual Book of ASTM Standards, Volume 14.0*, American Society for Testing and Materials, West Conshohocken, PA, 2000.

People v. Morganti, 43 Cal. App. 4th 643, 1996.

Technical Working Group on DNA Analysis Methods, Guidelines for a Quality Assurance Program for DNA Analysis, *Crime Lab. Dig.*, 22 (2), 21–43, 1995.

Zeppa, Z. E., The primary examiner, paper presented at the Spring meeting of the California Association of Criminalists, 1999.

Reproduced from:
Guidelines for a Quality Assurance Program for DNA Analysis, 1995

AABB Standards Committee (1990). P7.000 DNA polymorphism testing, in *Standards for Parentage Testing Laboratories*, 1st ed., American Association of Blood Banks, Arlington, VA.

Alwan, L. C. and Bissell, M. G. (1988). Time series modeling for quality control in clinical chemistry, *Clin. Chem.*, 34, 1396–1406.

American National Standard ANSI/ASQC Q90-1987 (1987). *Definitions, Symbols, Formulas, and Tables for Control Charts*, American Society for Quality Control, Milwaukee, WI.

American National Standard ANSI/ASQC Q90-1987 (1987a). *Quality Management and Quality Assurance Standards — Guidelines for Selection and Use*, American Society for Quality Control, Milwaukee, WI.

American National Standard ANSI/ASQC Q90-1987 (1987b). *Quality Management and Quality System Elements — Guidelines*, American Society for Quality Control, Milwaukee, WI.

American National Standard ANSI/ASQC ZI.2-1985 (1985). *Guide for Quality Control Charts*, American Society for Quality Control, Milwaukee, WI.

American National Standard ANSI/ASQC ZI.2-1985 (1985). *Control Chart Method of Analyzing Data*, American Society for Quality Control, Milwaukee, WI.

American National Standard ANSI/ASQC ZI.3-1985 (1985). *Control Chart Method of Controlling Quality during Production,* American Society for Quality Control, Milwaukee, WI.

American National Standard ANSI/ASQC Z1.15-1979 (1979). *Generic Guidelines for Quality Systems,* American Society for Quality Control, Milwaukee, WI.

American National Standard ANSI/ASQC A3-1978 (1978). *Quality Systems Terminology,* American Society for Quality Control, Milwaukee, WI.

American National Standard ASQC Standard C1-1968 (1968). *Specification of General Requirements of a Quality Program,* American Society for Quality Control, Milwaukee, WI.

AmpliType User Guide for the HLA DQa Forensic DNA Amplification and Typing Kit, 1990, Section — Laboratory Setup, Cetus Corporation, Emeryville, CA.

ASCLD (1986). *Guidelines for Forensic Laboratory Management Practices,* American Society of Crime Laboratory Directors, September.

ASCLD (1985). *ASCLD Accreditation Manual,* American Society of Crime Laboratory Directors, Laboratory Accreditation Board, February.

AT&T Technologies (1985). *Statistical Quality Control Handbook,* AT&T Technologies, Indianapolis, May.

Baird, M. (1989). Quality control and American association of blood bank standards, presented at the American Association of Blood Banks National Conference, April 17–19, Leesburg, VA.

Bicking, C. A. and Gryna, F. M. (1979). Process control by statistical methods, in *Quality Control Handbook.* 3d ed., J. M. Juran, Ed., McGraw-Hill, New York.

Bond, W. W. (1987). Safety in the forensic immunology laboratory, in *Proceedings of the International Symposium on Forensic Immunology,* U.S. Government Printing Office, Washington, D.C.

Box, G. E. P. and Bisaard, S. (1987). The scientific context of quality improvement, *Quality Progress,* 20(6), 54–61.

Bradford, L. W. (1980). Barriers to quality achievement in crime laboratory operations, *J. Forensic Sci.,* 25, 902–907.

Brunelle, R. L., Garner, D. D., and Wineman, P. L. (1982). A quality assurance program for the laboratory examination of arson and explosive cases, *J. Forensic Sci.,* 27, 774–782.

Budowle, B., Deadman, H. A., Murch, R. S., and Baechtel, F. S. (1988). An introduction to the methods of DNA analysis under investigation in the FBI Laboratory, *Crime Lab. Dig.,* 15, 8–21.

Bussolini, P. L., Davis, A. H., and Geoffrion, R. R. (1988). A new approach to quality for national research laboratories, *Quality Progress,* 21(1), 24–27.

Code of Federal Regulations (1988a). Title 10, Part 19 — Notices, Instructions, and Reports to Workers; Inspections, U.S. Government Printing Office, Washington, D.C.

Code of Federal Regulations (1988b). Title 10, Part 20 — Standards for Protection against radiation, U.S. Government Printing Office, Washington, D.C.

Ford, D. J. (1988). Good laboratory practice, *Lab. Practice,* 37(9), 29–33.

Gautier, M. A. and Gladney, E. S. (1987). A quality assurance program for health and environmental chemistry, *Am. Lab.,* July, 17–22.

Gibbs, F. L. and Kasprisin, C. A. (1987). *Environmental Safety in the Blood Bank,* American Association of Blood Banks, Arlington, VA.

Gryna, F. M. (1979). Basic statistical methods, in *Quality Control Handbook.* 3d ed., J. M. Juran, Ed., McGraw-Hill, New York.

Hay, R. J. (1988). The seed stock concept and quality control for cell lines, *Anal. Biochem.,* 171, 225–237.

Juran, J. M. (1979). Quality policies and objectives, in *Quality Control Handbook,* 3d ed., J. M. Juran, Ed., McGraw-Hill, New York.

Kenney, M. L. (1987). Quality assurance in changing times: proposals for reform and research in the clinical laboratory field, *Clin. Chem.,* 33, 328–336.

Kidd, G. J. (1987). What quality means to an R&D organization, in *41st Annual Quality Congress Transactions,* May 4–6, American Society for Quality Control, Milwaukee, WI.

Kilshaw, D. (1986). Quality assurance. 1. Philosophy and basic principles, *Med. Lab. Sci.,* 43, 377–381.

Kilshaw, D. (1987a). Quality assurance. 2. Internal quality control, *Med. Lab. Sci.,* 44, 73–93.

Kilshaw, D. (1987b). Quality assurance. 3. External quality assessment, *Med. Lab. Sci.,* 44, 178–186.

Mills, C. A. (1989). *The Quality Audit — A Management Evaluation Tool,* American Society for Quality Control, Milwaukee, WI.

National Bureau of Standards (1966). The place of control charts in experimental work, in *Experimental Statistics,* National Bureau of Standards Handbook 91, U.S. Government Printing Office, Washington, D.C.

National Fire Protection Association (1986). *Standard on Fire Protection for Laboratories Using Chemicals,* National Fire Protection Association, Quincy, MA.

Good Forensic Practice — Obligations of the Analyst

10

Figure 10.1 Evidence room. This represents job security. With too many cases and too much evidence, it is tempting to cut corners or stop thinking. One obligation of the professional is to maintain the integrity of the evidence, the analysis, and the results, in the process safeguarding the overall integrity of the profession.

> It does not matter if you're looking through a bucket of barf, or at a questioned document, the examination is the same
>
> **—David Crown**
> *AAFS meeting, San Diego, 1977, at a joint session of the criminalistics and documents sections*

We have finally arrived at the point in a case investigation that criminalists are most familiar with — the laboratory analysis or comparison. For a complex analysis, a good analyst may spend more time thinking about it than analyzing it. Failure to do so may result in an incorrect or suboptimal analysis, rendering useless all the good work that may have preceded it. The events and decisions surrounding the physical act of analysis share equal importance with sample processing and data collection. In this chapter we will discuss the decision-making process that occurs between the time the evidence is collected and the time the analysis is performed.

A. Asking the Right Question

At the beginning of this book, we warned you that we would continually be returning to a consideration of *The Question*. This chapter is no exception.

> **If you don't ask the right question,
> you won't get the right answer,
> no matter how brilliant your analysis.**

1. Translating the Legal Question into a Science Question

When the evidence arrives at the door to the laboratory, the first duty of the analyst is to find out from the detective or attorney what he expects from the laboratory analysis. What pertinent question does he hope you can help him answer? Let's first take a very straightforward example. Fibers are found adhering to a broken window at the scene of a burglary. A suspect was apprehended as he was apparently fleeing from the incident on foot. The jacket he was wearing was confiscated as evidence, and fibers from the jacket have been submitted as reference samples along with the evidence fibers from the window glass. The detective wants to know if the suspect was at the scene. The analyst translates this question as, can the evidence fibers collected from the window glass be distinguished from reference fibers collected from the suspect's jacket? She will also advise the detective that, to link the suspect to the scene, he needs to link not only the jacket to the scene, but also the jacket to the suspect at the time of the burglary.

Helping the attorney or detective understand the question is not as trivial as one might think. The following request in Figure 10.2 was received by the crime laboratory serving a major metropolitan city. The most obvious gaff in this note is the request by the district attorney for a particular result ostensibly beneficial to his case — the "matching" of some blood on a piece of evidence to the suspect. Perhaps the attorney can be forgiven this particular slip in his role as an advocate. Regardless, the analyst should explain to the attorney that the test will determine *if* the evidence and reference could share

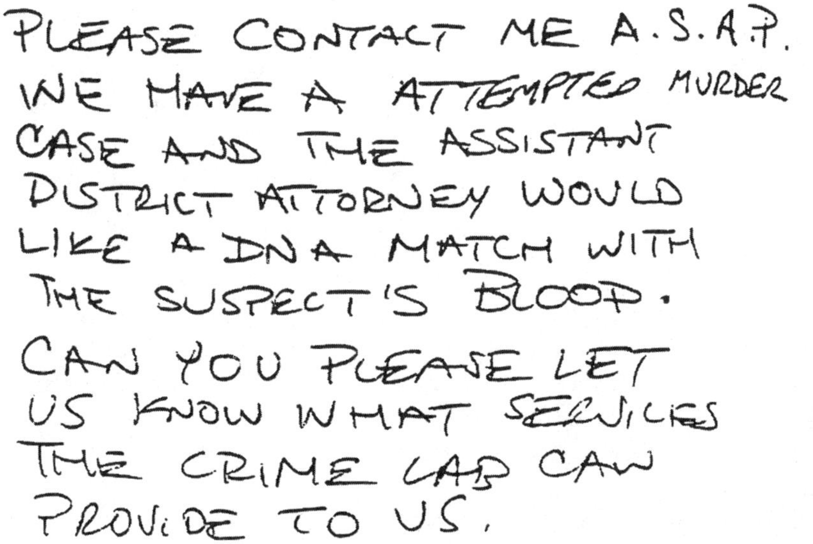

PLEASE CONTACT ME A.S.A.P.
WE HAVE A ATTEMPTED MURDER
CASE AND THE ASSISTANT
DISTRICT ATTORNEY WOULD
LIKE A DNA MATCH WITH
THE SUSPECT'S BLOOD.
CAN YOU PLEASE LET
US KNOW WHAT SERVICES
THE CRIME LAB CAN
PROVIDE TO US,

Figure 10.2 Analysis request. Who determines the analyses to be performed? The analyst is in the best position to determine which evidence might assist in answering a legal question, but only if he has knowledge of the case circumstances. An investigator or attorney will sometimes ask for results that would be useful to his case, rather than asking for an analysis to resolve some specific issue. In this example, if the results obtained were as the attorney requested, the prosecutor would have to dismiss the charges against the defendant, because the shoes were found in the suspect's closet.

a common source. At this point you are probably thinking that what has been described so far is really not that big a deal. However, a quick look at the original police report reveals that the shoe was collected from the suspect's closet, and the person who was bleeding was the victim! While this would not have changed the final analytical results, failure to discover the misunderstanding before any analysis took place could, at the very least, result in wasted time. Although it is generally prudent to obtain reference samples from all of the principals potentially involved in a crime, this same attorney might decide that, in this case, the victim's reference sample is not relevant, and therefore fail to obtain it and provide it to the analyst. The analyst's predictable failure to link the evidence to the suspect's reference sample might result in a correct analytical exclusion that would fail to address the relevant question in the case. Unless someone thinks to get a reference sample from the victim at this point, the case is over and justice has not been served.

2.   Formulating Hypotheses

To reiterate, hypothesis testing is the cornerstone of classical science, and one operational model for forensic science. This would seem to obligate the scientist to state a null hypothesis that can be tested and potentially falsified. Interestingly, in forensic science, the hypothesis being tested is rarely explicated. We believe that it should be. Carefully formulating alternative hypotheses can save countless hours on useless analyses and prevent immeasurable aggravation in attempting to interpret an analysis that might have been organized differently.

Probably the biggest favor most analysts could do for themselves and our profession would be to start formulating and explicating the scientific hypotheses that they will be testing with their analyses. To formulate a useful scientific hypothesis to test, the analyst must have some idea of the circumstances of the crime. This brings us to one of the more contentious points of argument between lawyers and scientists. How much should an analyst know about a case, and does that knowledge precipitate bias?

3.   How Much Should an Analyst Know?

The singular act of laboratory analysis or comparison is set against the greater backdrop of the events and decisions surrounding it. In many ways, the analysis itself can have less effect on the final outcome of a case than the decisions leading to which evidence is tested, how it is tested, and how the results are interpreted and communicated. Typically, the analyst knows something about the history of the evidence up until the time it enters the laboratory, and will interpret the results based on that history. Forensic scientists are generally familiar with the need to interpret evidence in the context of the history of the sample prior to its collection and preservation. But before the results are interpreted, and even before any analysis occurs, the criminalist must define the relevant questions. The more the analyst knows about the case, the better she can direct and refine the questions so that the answers are both useful and relevant.

The argument, made mostly by attorneys, against the analyst knowing the circumstances of a case, is that such knowledge may introduce subconscious, or worse yet malicious, bias, leading to prejudiced interpretation of the results. Superficially, this would seem to be a credible thesis. However, we believe that the advantages gained as a result of an informed analysis substantially outweigh the concerns. Furthermore, a series of checks and balances can and should be employed to ensure that alternate explanations for the data are duly considered. Moreover, we submit that bias is most likely to enter a case and do the most damage at the level of the question being asked, rather than in the interpretation of results. Because the hypotheses (however unconscious), and the assumptions that generate the questions, virtually always initiate with law enforcement, the criminalist is indeed in an excellent position to question accepted notions about a case and provide counterpoint suggestions.

Criminalists are experts in the possibilities inherent in physical evidence and also in the limitations of the various tests employed. Because of this specialized knowledge, we are in a unique position to offer the criminal justice system guidance on the best way to elicit information about a disputed or unknown fact. One of the greatest unrecognized contributions that a criminalist can provide is in framing the correct question about the physical evidence in the context of the particular case. Both the law enforcement and defense communities should be exploiting this resource to a much greater extent than has historically taken place. In Chapter 11 we'll discuss the education and communication that must take place for the criminalist to provide optimal assistance to their clients.

Although not documented in any systematic fashion, conventional wisdom says that the first suspect identified by the detectives working a case is frequently the one convicted, or at least arrested. Perhaps no compelling evidence may point to another individual, but neither have alternative possibilities necessarily been fully explored. Especially in the case of highly publicized crimes or protracted investigations, law enforcement is under great pressure to apprehend and convict someone, anyone, for the crime. In the effort to assign responsibility and assure society that the bad guys are off the streets, objectivity may become an inadvertent victim. When individuals with a stake in the outcome or a hunch as to the culprit (e.g., the detective or prosecutor) are allowed solely to determine what analysis is done by requesting some specific examination, there is potential, not necessarily for a bad analysis, but for an irrelevant one. With access to vital case information, the analyst has a chance to retrieve a useful analysis from obscurity. The participation of the analyst in determining both the kinds of evidence that will be examined and the types of examinations to be performed is a vital prerequisite to a competent analysis. In Sidebar 10, we present a case in which the independent analyst's understanding of the crime was the key to uncovering a valuable piece of evidence.

All of the preceding assumes that the forensic analyst in fact possesses the knowledge, education, and experience required to consider the evidence intelligently and thoughtfully in light of the case circumstances. In this day and age of specialization and automation, it is sometimes left to the detective or attorney to fill the role of coordinator and generalist, simply by default. We will address the issue of education in forensic science more specifically in Chapter 12.

a. Analyst Bias

Although we strongly believe that more knowledge can only lead to a better analysis, we also feel obliged to entertain legitimate concerns about bias and prejudice that might result from an analyst's awareness of the details of a case. Questions about objectivity come into play on a number of levels, and stem from different roots. We'll address each of these in turn and suggest different solutions to satisfy the various concerns.

Let's first tackle the distinction between malicious intent and unconscious bias. Because we are all human, we cannot help but have our own personal and professional prejudices. With or without knowledge about a case, we must constantly be on guard both to identify and to put aside any inclination to prejudge the evidence. Understanding one's own limitations and biases, and taking them into consideration in one's work, is key to a competent professional life. Nevertheless, we will detail some checks and balances external to the analyst that may be introduced at various points in the process to detect unconscious bias. Malicious intent is a different animal. Individuals whose goal is something different from a competent, objective analysis will not be stopped by simply denying them access to case information. Interestingly, neither law enforcement nor the legal participants are under any injunction to display objectivity. In particular, the attorneys on both sides are not only allowed, but required to advocate strongly for one side or the other. This is not the arena from which objective interpretation is expected to emanate.

The assumptions of the individual tasked with analyzing the evidence can affect the choice of which pieces of evidence to analyze and how to analyze them. For example, in the example of the facial tissue detailed in Sidebar 10, the assumption of the original analyst, based on information from the submitter, was that the tissue was evidence from a rape. She blindly followed the

The Seminal Bloodstain — What's the Question?

The key to the case was reconstructing the movements of the assailant as specifically as possible.

The point of entry was obvious; the screen material on the screen door was cut with a knife. Immediately inside of the point of entry, the phone cord was also cut through to prevent outside communication. From there, the assailant's movements were much more difficult to reconstruct.

This much was clear. He had ransacked much of the house, overturning drawers and belongings in most of the rooms. Debris was strewn everywhere. The victim was found facedown in the upstairs hallway, nude, with numerous blunt-force blows to the head. Large blood drops were obvious on her bedspread and on the floor leading to the hallway, indicating that she had been beaten in the bedroom. Her pantyhose was tied tightly around her neck, a clue to the cause of death.

Detectives collected the bedspread from the bed, surmising that the sexual assault had occurred there. They also found a semen stain on the carpet of the room, but this was long before DNA and DNA databases, so they would have to wait for a suspect before they could do any comparisons. The latent print examiner was able to lift some prints from several places in the house, including an ornate money bank from one of the ransacked rooms.

The exit point, however, remained a puzzle. Detectives were not clear if the assailant had exited through the same cut in the screen door, or used another door. On a concrete pad outside one of the doors they found a piece of facial tissue. Knowing that the victim was nude, and suspecting a sexual assault at the scene, one detective surmised that the assailant may have wiped his penis with the tissue, and later discarded it. If this were true, then the egress would be established. Of course, this door faced an alley, and the tissue could also easily have been dropped by one of the occupants of the house, or could simply have been random detritus from the alley.

➔ A primary source of bias in any analysis stems from the person asking the question. This bias is not, as is commonly thought, geared toward implicating any one person, but rather in too narrowly circumscribing the possible outcomes of the examination. That is the reason detectives should provide the crime scene circumstances and the question they are trying to resolve, rather than ask for specific analyses. In this case, detectives submitted the facial tissue with the request to examine it for semen. The analyst examined the tissue for semen and, detecting none, dutifully wrote a report saying that "semen was not detected."

There the case stood for several years, with no suspect in view. While routinely running unsolved cases through the fingerprint database, a hit was obtained from a latent lifted from the money bank. Detectives determined that the suspect was currently in prison for homicide, but that he had been out at the time of their murder. They went directly to Folsom Prison and arrested him.

As the district attorney was preparing the case, she was puzzled about the facial tissue. She thought that the door would be a natural exit for the suspect, and suspected that this piece of evidence might have more to offer. She resubmitted it to the laboratory, this time providing all of the details of the case. Armed with more information, a different criminalist easily detected a light smear of blood on the tissue. He performed some blood typing and also determined that the blood showed genetic types corresponding to those of the victim. With this piece of information, the district attorney had a more complete case to offer the jury.

While the facial tissue was a small bit of evidence in the overall reconstruction of the crime, the detective's preconceived idea that rapists wipe their penises following a rape unnecessarily narrowed the scope of the examination by the initial criminalist. The more criminalists know about the case, the greater assistance they can provide in the form of intelligent analyses addressing relevant legal questions.

detective's lead and tested the tissue for semen. Only after studying the case circumstances and determining that the crime was a violent sexual assault, did the independent analyst think to test for blood. Information about the case can only assist in choosing appropriate samples to analyze and informative tests with which to analyze them. Education, training, and experience provide the analyst with the tools to make good choices.

4. What Can Science Contribute?

Assuming the basic questions are heading in the right direction, the analyst must still help the client understand what a laboratory analysis can contribute to the understanding of a case. Can the question be answered by science? Even if some analysis can be performed on a particular piece of evidence, is it the best analysis? Is it a useful analysis? Should it be the first analysis? If that specific analysis is performed, how would a positive association, a negative association, no result, or an inconclusive result influence the understanding of events?

a.   Can the Question Be Answered by Science?

As we've related several times already, the question of motive, the *why* question, can *never* be answered by science. This can be quite frustrating to all involved, as human nature prompts us to try to understand why someone would commit a violent act. In spite of the best efforts of the profilers and the criminologists, the question can often only be answered by the perpetrator, and sometimes not even by him. Because motive is one of the legal elements that must be proved to convict someone of a crime, however, the arranged and sometimes uneasy marriage between science and law is called to the fore. It can be tempting for the criminalist, as well as the detective or attorney, to read intent into the story told by the physical evidence.

> In one case, the defendant was accused of firing the shot that killed an officer. In contention was the position of the officer when the shot was fired (standing, prone, or somewhere in between), his condition (was he incapacitated), and how far the gun was from the officer's head. The expert acting on behalf of the defense testified that "the gunshot wound was not reminiscent of a 'classical *coup de grace* execution wound.'" He further defined this as "… a person is incapacitated and another person with a firearm wants them dead and approaches the body of that individual and deliberately places the muzzle of the firearm in very close proximity to the head to ensure a particular placement of the bullet.…" Not surprisingly, the prosecuting attorney objected to the statement. Later in the same testimony the expert discussed physical traits that he might expect to see in a "classical execution wound." The facts in evidence were the presence of stippling around the wound and a lack of smoke deposition, indicating that the shot was not a contact or near-contact shot. While the term *coup de*

grace may simply indicate the last shot that killed someone, the term *execution* carries with it an implication of premeditation. With the translation of the physical evidence into a comment about "execution-style killing," indicating intent, the expert, in our opinion, crossed the line.

Another question for which a satisfactory answer is rarely obtained is *when*. Frequently, it would be useful to know when the bloodstain was left on the gate, if the semen was deposited in the vagina before or after death (in many jurisdictions, intercourse with a dead body is not rape), or when the fibers from the victim's house were transferred to the suspect's van (before or after the victim bought the new drapes).

This concept is exemplified in the infamous historical crime of the murder of Marilyn Sheppard (Holmes, 1961; 1966; S. A. Sheppard, 1964; Cooper and Sheppard, 1995; S. H. Sheppard, 1966). Richard Eberling, their handyman and perennial suspect in the crime, early on voluntarily mentioned bleeding in the house as a result of a cut acquired in removing a storm window. The relevant evidence was a blood trail in the house that may have been left by the killer. It is difficult to know whether this was a preemptive strike or a legitimate explanation, as Eberling alternately confessed to the crime and retracted that confession throughout the years. The ability to tell when stains comprising the blood trail were deposited would answer the question of whether it was connected with the crime or was deposited previously. Unfortunately, this was not possible then (1954), nor is it even now. Any possibility of elucidating that particular secret died with Eberling in 1998.

b.   Is the Evidence Useful?

Sometimes, especially if laboratory facilities are easily accessible to law enforcement, evidence is submitted for testing simply because it can be. Similarly, evidence is not infrequently collected from the scene with little thought about its relation to the alleged crime.

> An instance where the evidence may or may not be useful is a pool of blood in which a stabbing victim is found. This, of course, depends on the question. It would be superfluous to ask whose blood it is, although it might be collected as a secondary reference sample. On the other hand, the pattern of the blood might be useful in reconstructing the crime — was the person killed in that spot or was the body dragged? Additionally, if anything about the bloodstain pattern suggested the contribution of a second person, that portion might provide genetic information about a possible perpetrator or second victim.

A good litmus test of whether evidence is useful is if some piece of information about it could settle a fact that is actually in dispute. Does it answer a question that has been posed, or has the analysis been requested merely because it is technically possible? It is a good idea to ask if the evidence is expected to be present whether or not its contributor committed a crime. Fingerprints in the suspect's residence or workplace, semen on his own or his girlfriend's sheets, gunpowder residue on an officer's hands, hypodermic syringes in a doctor's medical bag — these are all example of evidence that might be damning under other circumstances, but in these circumstances are utterly useless. In Sidebar 11, we present a case that illustrates this point.

Sidebar 11

The Hair That Cried Uncle — An Inference of Association

A 12-year-old girl accused her 18-year-old uncle of rape. To the detective's questions, she related that after the assault, she had taken a shower and dried herself with a towel. Detectives seized the towel, and also transported the victim to the hospital for collection of physical evidence. They also learned that the uncle lived in the same house as the little girl.

Analysts at the crime laboratory first examined the sexual assault kit; however, no semen or other evidence of sexual assault was found. The towel, however, yielded a pubic hair. The victim was clearly eliminated as a possible donor of the hair as she was in the early stages of puberty and still lacked any pubic hair. Reference pubic hairs were duly collected from the suspect. After a microscopic comparison, the laboratory was unable to eliminate him as a potential donor of the evidence hair collected from the towel.

The district attorney in the case had little evidence besides the story of the victim, and so requested DNA analysis of the hair. She was cautioned that any finding would have little meaning, but she persisted, and the laboratory acquiesced to the examination. This was in the early days of DNA typing, and only one locus, DQα using the reverse dot-blot procedure, was available to test small amounts of DNA such as might be found on a hair root. The DQα test showed no differences between the type of the suspect and of the evidence hair. Although some number of other people in the world could have contributed the hair, probably none of them, other than the uncle, had access to the bathroom where the towel resided.

However, the fact that the uncle couldn't be eliminated as a donor of the hair on the towel misses the point completely. In point of fact, the uncle's pubic hair on the girl's towel established precisely nothing useful pertaining to the accusation. Many alternate explanations existed for the presence of his hair on the towel, including transfer from anywhere in the bathroom to the victim and then to the towel, or transfer to the towel from anywhere in the bathroom. Further, when considering the mechanism of purported transfer, the hypothesis would have to include the hair surviving the shower to be transferred during the drying action.

Even if we accept that the hair was from the uncle, no clear connection existed between the presence of the hair on the towel and the crime event. The evidence was simply not useful in establishing intimate contact between the girl and her uncle, and hence was only marginally relevant to the case. Far too many assumptions were needed to sustain an inference of contact related to the crime event. This is an excellent example of a piece of evidence that could not settle a fact in dispute. In the language of law, the physical evidence was simply not relevant.

In spite of this, the defendant pled guilty!

It is interesting to note in this example, that, although source determination was the original question, answering it did not further an understanding of the case. Too many alternatives existed for how the hair came to be associated with the towel, with no clear way to decide among them.

It is interesting to note that the inability of science to determine *when* frequently underlies the lack of utility of the evidence. This is particularly true when the evidence is not necessarily the result of violent activity. For example, fibers from a suspect's clothing would be expected in his vehicle; large bloodstains are less likely to result from normal daily activity even if they occur in an area frequented by their donor.

c.   Is the Test Useful?

Frequently, evidence is submitted to the laboratory with a request for a specific test. The detective has made some assumption, either consciously or not, about what might have occurred. The evidence is submitted with this particular scenario in mind and without having considered alternative possibilities. Similarly, an analyst who has received a piece of evidence absent any case information may simply perform the easiest or most obvious test without considering if it is the best test to answer a question in the case. We presented such an example in Sidebar 9 in Chapter 9, where an analyst consumed a bloodstain found on the bathtub containing the murder victim to determine that it was of human origin.

These types of situations occur in different guises. The print in blood spatter detailed in Sidebar 9 is a specific example of the more general decision-making process that is invoked when several different kinds of evidence, each requiring different tests, are present. Choices involving *collection* of biological or chemical evidence and *documentation* of print or impression evidence require the most careful thought. Good communication, not only between the detective and the analyst, but between the various experts, is crucial to eliciting the greatest amount of useful information from a single item of evidence. The tests more likely to yield helpful information should be given priority, while still preserving the possibility of doing other kinds of analyses.

Another common situation in which both the collection of *analytical* evidence and the documentation of *comparison* evidence need to be considered is in the instance of bloodstain pattern analysis. Which test will be most useful in light of the question, at least as currently understood? Should the area be treated with chemicals to enhance visualization of the blood, potentially limiting biological analyses?* Is it more important to establish the pattern to help with a later reconstruction of events, or to establish if the

---

* Historically, some of the presumptive tests for blood inhibited the ability to type antigenic or biochemical genetic markers. Fortunately, DNA typing has proved much more resilient (Gross et al., 1999).

blood is human and whose is it? Fortunately, with a little planning, the evidence can usually be preserved for both kinds of analyses. The spatter pattern is optimally first studied at the scene, in relation to its true three-dimensional environment. It should then, of course, be photographed and perhaps videotaped. The question is, at what point does the criminalist sacrifice the pattern to collect samples for potential biological analysis? How much of the pattern is collected? Are individual stains kept separate, or might they be combined if one concludes they were deposited as a result of the same event from the same source? Does every single last stain need to be collected, or can a representative sample be collected? (See Chapter 8 for an example of this conundrum.) The answers, of course, depend on the individual circumstances in each case.

For example, because mitochondrial DNA (mtDNA) analysis can never (except in rare cases of mutation) distinguish between siblings, the test would not be useful for answering this particular question. Similarly, it is of no use in answering a question about paternity because no genetic link exists between a father and his children through mtDNA.* In a slightly different way, even the most specific and reliable test for GSR, SEM-EDX, is limited by its ability to establish an association between the shooter and a weapon. Because GSR has the apparently conflicting properties of being both persistent and ephemeral, the significance of its presence can rarely be determined with any degree of reliability.**,***

It is the consideration of the relative advantages and limitations of the various analyses, as related to the question, that remains constant.

d. What Further Questions Arise as a Result of Analysis?

The question frequently arises regarding the analyst's prerogative or even obligation to suggest additional tests based on the result of those already performed. In some laboratories it is stated policy never to suggest further tests that might clarify lingering questions about the case. This verges on

---

* mtDNA analysis, as it is currently performed, differs from nuclear DNA typing in a number of ways. For the purposes of this discussion, we emphasize one particular difference, the fact that mtDNA is maternally inherited. Thus, a mother and her biological children will have the same mtDNA type and siblings sharing the same mother should have the same mtDNA type. A frequent consideration in DNA cases is whether the stain could have been left by the suspect's sibling, his closest genetic relative. Because of the laws of genetic inheritance, siblings can readily be distinguished using nuclear DNA testing (the caveat being that the sibling must be found and tested).

** Depending on such circumstances as whether the suspect legally handles and shoots weapons on a regular basis, say, for hunting or sport, and whether he washed his hands or his clothes immediately after firing the fatal shot in a homicide, the presence or absence of GSR can be interpreted differently.

*** The presence and pattern of gunpowder residue on a shooting *target* remains useful evidence. It is the presence or absence of either gunpowder residue or primer residue on a suspected shooter's hands that is difficult to interpret reliably.

incompetence. It might even be considered unethical if the original results are ambiguous and the ambiguity is used to implicate a suspect. The following case illustrates such a situation.

In this case, bloodstains from a murder scene had been analyzed by a state laboratory. Three different stains, apparently from the same source, as inferred from the bloodstain pattern, were tested using two different kinds of genetic analyses. The testing gave internally inconsistent results. Seven PCR-based DNA markers exhibited the same type as the victim. One blood protein marker, *PGM*, exhibited the same type as the defendant. The laboratory interpreted these results to mean that in each of three separate stains, bloods from both the victim and the defendant were present as a mixture. The fact that neither marker system showed any evidence of being a mixture, such as extra types or uneven intensities of dots or bands, did not seem to bother them too much. Neither did the observation that the relative intensities of the types were similar to each other both within and between the stains. From the work performed, no satisfactory interpretation explained all the data. Although the three analysts that testified in this case all agreed that no evidence of a mixture was apparent, the "party line" was that the only explanation for the data was a mixture. One possibility was that the evidence was contributed by a close relative of the victim. The possibility of siblings sharing both alleles at seven loci, but distinguishable at the eighth is remote but not impossible (generally, siblings are distinguishable using only a few genetic markers). However, the laboratory failed to inform the prosecution team of this possibility and to request reference samples from any close relatives. They argued that it was "not their job" to supply alternative hypotheses to the prosecution.

We take this opportunity to emphasize, yet again, that, although case counsel can and, in fact, is obligated to work from a position of advocacy, the scientist must maintain a neutral stance. It is all too easy to follow the detective down a path leading to a named suspect and approach the evidence with this in mind. As we will see just a bit later, a series of checks and balances incorporated into the system counter the possibility of a single analyst working alone to become unduly influenced by the advocates for whom she is working.

B.   Examination and Analysis

Finally, in one of the last chapters of this book, we get to build a house on the foundation we have so carefully laid. In this chapter we discuss some of the considerations pertinent to actually performing and interpreting an examination or analysis. This is the part you all know how to do very well; it is your day-to-day work. And it is the foundation of the work product you will eventually present in the form of a written report and possibly testimony.

As such, it should be performed and documented with meticulous care. The following suggestions are based on our collective experience of doing case-work and performing both internal and independent reviews of casework.

1. Documentation

In Chapter 8, we emphasized the need to document evidence adequately as it is recognized and collected at the crime scene. In this section we will concentrate on providing a good record of what has happened to the evidence between the time it enters the laboratory and the submission of a final report. The report itself, we deal with in Chapter 11.

a. Documentation Standards

Forensic laboratories have frequently been content to issue reports containing the results from some test or examination and a vague reference to a standard operating procedure (SOP) as the only confirmation of the procedures that were actually performed. Aside from the fact that the report is rarely accom-panied even by a copy of the SOP, this level of documentation is unacceptable for a serious scientific endeavor.

The SOP method of documentation derives directly from the clinical model, where most samples are identical in state, if not in content. In clinical laboratories, most or all of the samples are of similar quality and quantity, and their history is known. No questions exist as to their source or nature of the material, and they are usually received in a pristine state. The tests ordinarily address very limited questions. Samples are generally processed in a batch mode and submitted to exactly the same procedures. These days, much of the process may well be automated. In this sort of situation, when the processing protocol truly never varies, a reference to SOP is acceptable.

None of these conditions holds for samples received by a crime labora-tory. By definition, each case is different, each sample presents unique chal-lenges, and we usually have less rather than more information about a sample. The academic model for documentation is preferred for situations encoun-tered by the forensic laboratory. In any research endeavor, it is expected that the worker will *contemporaneously document the work as performed*. Certainly a general protocol will be used as an initial guide, but because details of the procedure will invariably depend on the exact samples and conditions, these should be accurately documented. The standard for notes in the academic community is that another researcher should be able to duplicate your results from your notes. The forensic community should hold to no less a standard. Because of the additional considerations specific to forensic work, such as potentially limited quantity and quality of the sample, and legal confidenti-ality, complete and adequate documentation is even more crucial than in any other scientific discipline.

If you need another reason to support a detailed documentation of your examination, remember this: if you did not write it down, you did not do it. This is a basic tenet of quality control. A written record is the analyst's best tool of confidence and the first line of defense. "How do you know for sure, Dr. Analyst, that you added 10 microliters of hydrochloric acid to your reaction?" "See, it's right here in this line in my notes." Why depend on your "best recollection" of what you did when you can know for sure.

2. Preserving the Integrity of the Evidence

For all evidence, it is imperative that evidence and reference be clearly marked in such a way that they cannot be confused. For prints and impressions, this is usually a sufficient precaution. Because of their nature as cohesive visual patterns, their proximity to each other does not present the kind of danger for cross-contamination as it does with other kinds of samples where a small portion of the sample could give the same pattern as the main portion. For identification evidence, no case-specific reference samples are usually collected, but bulk samples of common evidence types present a similar danger for cross-contamination within and among cases.

a. Prevention of Contamination

For any sample type where contamination is an issue, more stringent precautions should be taken. This would include liquids (biological or chemical), gases, or solids that might flake or sublime. Remember that contamination can be defined as "any substance inadvertently introduced into or onto an item of evidence after its recognition by a responsible party" (see Chapter 8). The general philosophy behind preventing contamination, in particular of evidence samples with reference samples from the same case, is separation in time or space. If this philosophy is followed during the reception, processing, and storage of case samples, the possibility of contamination is greatly minimized. We leave it to the individual analyst or laboratory to determine how this might work for a particular evidence type or laboratory situation.

b. Detection of Contamination

For analyses that present an inherent potential for contamination, the analytical protocol should provide a way to detect instances of it. The most straightforward way to accomplish this is through the proper use of controls. As we discussed in Chapter 9, most analytical protocols benefit from the inclusion of both positive and negative controls. In particular, a negative control, that is, a sample that includes all laboratory reagents but no sample expected to yield detectable results, is useful in detecting positive results where there should be none. Both positive and negative controls may be used in various combinations to monitor the appearance of any unexpected results. The results of the controls, together with the complete set of results from the case samples, can be used to assess the validity of the particular run or test. Artifactual or unexpected results should be thoughtfully interpreted in the context of the case.

3. Results

We will not be discussing specific methods of analysis here. Rather we outline general categories of results, and mention situations in which each might arise. In general, five possible outcomes may result from any examination or analysis:

1. **The true result** — A result is obtained that reflects the true nature of the sample. It correctly indicates that an evidence sample and reference sample share a common origin if, in fact, they do, or that a substance has been correctly identified.
2. **A false negative result** — A result is obtained that fails to reflect the true nature of the sample and instead falsely reflects the nature of sample. It incorrectly fails to indicate that an evidence sample and a reference sample share a common origin when, in fact, they do, a substance that is present fails to be detected.
3. **A false positive result** — A result is obtained that fails to reflect the true nature of the sample and instead falsely reflects the nature of sample. It incorrectly indicates that an evidence sample and reference sample share a common origin when, in fact, they do not, or that a particular substance appears to be present when, in fact, it was not present in the original sample. This is the most egregious error that can occur.
4. **An inconclusive result** — A result is obtained but no conclusion can be reached. This may be due to the nature of the sample or limitations of the test. Information is present but cannot reliably be interpreted to discern the relationship of an evidence sample to a reference sample, or whether a substance is present. Insufficient sensitivity or resolution are examples of situations that may lead to inconclusive results.
5. **No result** — No result is obtained. This is often due to the nature of the sample or limitations of the test. No information is present, so no clarification regarding the relationship of an evidence sample to a reference sample is obtained. For identification evidence, this means that the substance is not present or is present below the detection limits of the test.

When the analyst makes wise evidence choices and uses reliable methods to examine or analyze the evidence, the most frequent result should be *the true result*. The proper use of controls and standards, when relevant, will support the reliability of the result as true. However, because of the nature of forensic evidence, it is not uncommon for an analyst to obtain *an inconclusive result* or *no result*. If things are working properly, this should rarely be due to a failure of the test. If some aspect of the test itself has completely failed, this should be immediately evident by inspection of the positive control (one of the very good reasons for including one every time the test is performed).

A result should be reported as *inconclusive* only after all other avenues of analysis or interpretation have been exhausted. This choice of reporting nomenclature has sometimes been misused as a crutch for the analyst to avoid interpreting difficult results. The more complicated the result, the more important it is for the forensic scientist to explain as clearly and simply as possible what the results mean and what they do not mean. Transferring this burden to nonscientists even less qualified to understand the meaning of the data is irresponsible. The decision to call results inconclusive should be the rare exception and employed judiciously only in those cases in which it is truly warranted. Sometimes, when, after lengthy discussion in good faith, two qualified analysts cannot agree on the meaning of a result, it might properly be reported as inconclusive. One way to think of an inconclusive result is that the analysis has provided no new information. In Bayesian terms, the likelihood ratio is 1. A brief explanation of why no reliable conclusion can be reached should always accompany a result reported as inconclusive.

For evidence types in which the goal is source determination, a failure to properly include a reference as sharing a common origin with an item of evidence (false exclusion) can simply be a consequence of the state of the evidence. Evidence that has been exposed to the environment and become degraded, evaporated, faded, or otherwise obscured may retain some characteristics of the original and may also exhibit newly acquired characteristics. At some point, it may be impossible to conclude a common origin, or even a common classification when, in fact, this should be the true result.* A good understanding of the state of the sample, and the appropriate use of diagnostic tools, can greatly reduce the risk of falsely excluding the source of a sample due to divergence of sample traits. A sample switch could also result in a false exclusion. Although good laboratory practice can help prevent a sample switch, detecting one can be more problematic. Something like a permutation of the order of all samples might be obvious to the alert analyst, but a switch of adjacent samples might not reveal itself so easily, depending on exactly which samples were switched. One advantage of including a known positive control sample in each test is the presence of an immediate diagnostic of a global sample permutation. Regardless, an error leading to a false exclusion is not usually as serious in the context of a case as a false inclusion, as it would generally not be expected to implicate an innocent suspect.

---

* These are examples of the corollaries of divisible matter in action.

For all evidence types, the most serious error, a false positive result, is more likely to arise from human error than as a consequence of any limitations inherent in the evidence or the test. Although the latter is not impossible, a thorough understanding of the state of the evidence, and good use of diagnostic tools, can minimize any possibility of falsely including a source for an evidence sample, no matter how compromised. The two greatest risks for false inclusion are contamination and a sample switch, both human errors. Gross contamination, of the sort that might lead to an incorrect pattern match of a reference item with an evidence item, is largely preventable, and certainly detectable. This kind of wholesale contamination would be expected to permeate the analysis, revealing itself in the negative control and in multiple samples. This presents a difficult problem for trace evidence because, like the shoeprint example we described earlier, it's hard to conceive of a useful negative control. For example, in the case of *People v. Morin*, an independent review suggested that the numerous red fibers used to link several evidence samples actually originated from the examiner's sweater.

For class evidence and identification evidence, random contamination is more of an issue than for individualizing evidence. An improperly stored reference sample of volatile explosive could potentially cause false positives in several cases. However, only contamination with the reference sample in the case at hand would be likely to cause a false positive in DNA evidence. Similarly, a sample switch between cases involving class evidence would be of more concern than for potentially individualizing evidence. Just about the worst mistake that can happen is a switch or mislabeling of two different reference samples in a case involving individualizing evidence. If there is reason to believe such a switch could have occurred, this may be resolved by retesting or even reacquiring the reference samples.

a. Analyst Judgment

Even in the most objective analysis, an element of subjectivity is introduced by human involvement. Subjectivity should not, however, be considered a dirty word. Introduction of a human brain allows common sense to be overlaid onto numeric or graphic results from some piece of sophisticated, automated instrumentation. It allows the recognition of results that are nonsensical because someone forgot to plug in the heating element or add the sample. It prevents us from subjugating our best judgment to the stupidity of a machine or allowing results to stand that are not reflective of the actual sample for any of a variety of reasons, including human error or instrument malfunction. And yes, it also allows for the expert judgment of the analyst in recording marginal results.

All forensic examinations and analyses can be distilled into an exercise in pattern recognition. Print and impression evidence requires little in the way of help from instrumentation or chemistry to produce patterns that the human visual system can compare. Chemical and biological evidence depend on chemical reactions and instrumental output to display patterns detectable by human beings. Ultimately, however, whether the final pattern takes the form of a fingerprint, an FTIR spectrum, a bullet comparison, or a DNA electropherogram, the instrumentation and chemistry are the means, not the end. They are tools we use to get to the point where a trained, experienced individual can make intelligent conclusions about the results.

4.   Verification of Results

a.   Blind Second Read

Because we recognize that even two qualified scientists might make slightly different subjective judgments when examining the same data, it is useful for a second examiner to verify the results independently. The interpretation of these results will ultimately lead to some conclusion about identification or source determination. However, understand that, at this point in the analysis, we are simply talking about recording data, not its interpretation. Nevertheless, the examiner is frequently called upon to make decisions about whether a data point reflects signal or noise, and whether it meets reporting guidelines. Because we are all subject to subconscious bias, it is desirable for a second qualified analyst to read the data independently.

This second analyst should be ignorant of the case circumstances and the read should be completely independent. Simply signing off on the first analyst's read may meet the letter, but fails to meet the spirit, of a blind second read. The former may catch blatant malicious attempts to record incorrect data; only the second acts as a check on the recording of weak or ambiguous results when both analysts are well intentioned, but human. The incorporation of a blind read by a second analyst goes a long way toward addressing concerns about analyst bias. If both analysts make the same judgment calls then confidence in the results is enhanced. If the reads are different, then that forms the basis of a discussion. Wouldn't you rather have that discussion with your colleague at the next bench than with opposing counsel in court?

b.   Technical Review

Review of the entire case file by another qualified analyst in the laboratory provides the next level of scrutiny. The main job of the technical reviewer is to confirm that the conclusions are supported by the data. Among other things, this requires yet another check of the actual results, and, most importantly, an independent interpretation of their meaning *in the context of the case*.

The last level of technical review frequently comes in the form of an expert hired by opposing counsel. In addition to providing the opportunity for yet another check of the data and its interpretation, the outside reviewer brings to the table different questions, different assumptions, and sometimes additional information perhaps not available to the prosecution. Independent review is the most effective tool available for identifying either subconscious or malicious bias. For a lengthy discussion of review, please see Chapter 9.

5. Interpretation and Conclusions

A criminalist must provide an interpretation of the evidence and a conclusion about it. Not only is this role appropriate, it is obligatory. Above all, we must remember that our aim is to present the scientific truth. The rendering of an interpretation and the formation of a conclusion in a written report is our last best chance to provide an understanding of the data outside of an adversarial forum.

It is at this juncture that principles of criminalistics and the practice of criminalistics intersect to become one and the same. The hypotheses have been articulated, the evidence has been chosen, the laboratory work performed, and the results recorded. What does it all mean? This brings us full circle to a discussion of the very same issues we explored in detail in Chapters 6 and 7. We will review some of these concepts briefly.

a. Defining Facts and Assumptions

Earlier, we introduced you to the idea that an inference is based on both assumptions and facts. This can be conveniently summarized as:

$$(A)\text{ssumptions} + (F)\text{acts} = (I)\text{nference}$$

Some inferences rely on virtually no assumptions or very well grounded assumptions; some may depend on less solid assumptions. Because changing the assumptions might lead to a different inference, hence conclusion, the underlying assumptions must be explicitly stated. Facts are rarely in dispute; it is the assumptions about which experts argue, whether or not they realize it. This model can be applied at any level of interpretation. It works as well for an inference of association between two or more items as it does for an inference of source.

If competing hypotheses are proffered, the assumptions leading to each should also be clearly defined. For example, a common assumption made in interpreting DNA profiles involves the number of donors who could have contributed the evidence. Analysts rarely disagree about whether two profiles exhibit matching patterns, it is the interpretation of complex patterns, especially profiles to which two or more individuals may have contributed, that engenders lively debates. A complete approach would be to state competing hypotheses based on different (reasonable) assumptions regarding how many individuals, or which of the principals, might have contributed to the sample, and follow each through to a logical conclusion. An example from *Simpson*, detailed in Sidebar 12 illustrates this process very well.

b.   Explainable Differences

In Chapter 6, we discussed at great length the idea of explainable differences, and mechanistically, how evidence and reference samples might diverge once they are separated. Briefly, any differences seen might be due to actual differences inherent in the evidence (*intrinsic differences*) or they might be a consequence of the imprecision of the test system (*extrinsic differences*). First, the forensic scientist must evaluate any differences between evidence and reference to determine if they are significant and how they might be explained. Differences will virtually always exist; it is the job of the criminalist to decide how to interpret them. The role of the expert is to use all of information to make an informed judgment. Without apology, we note that this is a subjective process, and should only be undertaken by a scientist with the proper education, training, and experience. Qualified experts may disagree. It is crucial to appreciate that reference and evidence items need not be, nor are expected to be, absolutely identical in every detectable characteristic for a conclusion of common source. As Kirk (1953) cogently points out:

> Moreover, the finger is not actually identical from moment to moment, but its significant features that are useful for practical fingerprinting remain permanent and unchanged.

c.   Inference of Source vs. Inference of Contact

As we discussed in Chapters 6 and 7, we find it helpful to distinguish between an *inference of the source* of the evidence and an *inference of contact between two items of evidence*. The mental compartmentalization of these two ideas provides a sequential structure for the interpretation of case results. It also helps to clarify at which point experts disagree, so provides a useful framework for discussion.

i.   Inference of source.   Recall that the strength of an inference of source, as we define it, tells us something only about the relationship of *evidence to source*. An evidence profile* that is relatively common provides an inherently weaker link between evidence and source, while a very rare or individual

---

* We use *profile* here to denote the composite of traits for any kind of evidence, not just DNA.

Sidebar 12

The Simpson Saga — The Blood in the Bronco

On June 12, 1994 Nicole Brown (NB) and Ronald Goldman (RG) were brutally murdered. O. J. Simpson (OS) was charged with the commission of the crime, and among the evidentiary items confiscated was his white Ford Bronco. A bloody smear on the passenger side of the center console was initially noted and sampled on June 14, 1994. At least three relevant forensic questions can be asked about this evidence.

1. How was the stain deposited?
2. When was the stain deposited?
3. Who may have contributed to this stain?

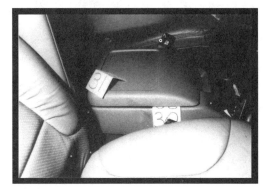

For the purposes of this exercise we will not attempt to address how and when the stain was deposited. We will concentrate on what the evidence can tell us about who contributed to the stain.

DNA testing was used to investigate the source(s) of the stain. Both DQα and D1S80 tests were performed on the two evidence samples collected in June 1994. From the results, it was concluded that one stain included Simpson as a donor, while excluding NB and RG. The other showed a mixture consistent with OS and RG. A larger sample was collected on September 1, 1994. It should be noted that in the intervening time period, the Bronco was burglarized. Although the items taken were themselves of no evidentiary value, the integrity of the bloodstain evidence could no longer be guaranteed. Three separate swatches were collected that more nearly covered the large area of the smear. These samples were also analyzed for DQα and D1S80. Let's examine the data from two of these swatches in detail.

	1	2	3	4	C	1.1	1.2 1.3 4	1.3	All but 1.3	AMPLITY DQ-Alph
EVIDENCE 1	1●	2	3	4●	C	1.1●	1.3●	1.3	●	AMPLITY DQ-Alph
substrate sample	1	2	3	4	C	1.1	1.2 1.3 4	1.3	All but 1.3	AMPLITY DQ-Alph
EVIDENCE 2	1●	2	3	4●	C	1.1●	1.2 1.3● 4	1.3●	All but 1.3●	AMPLITY DQ-Alph
substrate sample	1	2	3	4	C	1.1	1.2 1.3 4	1.3	All but 1.3	AMPLITYF DQ-Alph

Above is a set of DQα strips showing the results from two of the later samplings, along with their substrate samples. (A substrate sample is collected from an apparently clean area near an evidentiary stain. It is a way of assessing which, if any, genetic types might be present in the background.) One of the ways an analyst avoids even an unconscious bias is to analyze the evidence before comparing it with the reference samples. In this case, both evidence strips show the same pattern of dots, and even the intensities are similar. In both samples, all the dots, with the exception of 2 and 3, are positive, so we can safely eliminate anyone with a 2 or 3 allele from having contributed to this sample. The next step is to note that more than two alleles are manifest. Because any normal individual has, at most, two alleles at any one genetic locus, this is a clear indication of multiple contributors.

From an examination of the nominal dots to the left of "C," we note the presence a 4 allele and a 1 allele. The 1.1 and 1.3 dots are both positive and, although the 1.3 dot is substantially lighter, both are stronger than the "C" dot. The 1.1 and 1.3 subtypes, at least, are represented. Is the 1.2 allele also present? Consider the more difficult "trio" and "all but 1.3" dots, both of which are positive and greater than "C." The "trio" dot may be positive due to the presence of the 1.2 allele, the 1.3 allele, or the 4 allele individually, or any combination of them. Because we can confirm the presence of both the 4 allele and the 1.3 allele, the "trio" would be positive regardless of the presence of a 1.2 allele, and so cannot be used to determine its presence. This consequently makes the "all but 1.3" dot useless in determining, along with the "trio," the presence of a 1.2 allele. In short, from the pattern of dots on these strips, it is impossible to tell if a 1.2 allele is present in the sample or not.

At this point in the interpretation, the analyst would normally draw up a chart of alleles excluded (2, 3), those positively present (1.1, 1.3, 4), and those about which we have insufficient information to determine presence or absence (1.2). The analyst would also list possible pairwise associations of the alleles into genotypes of the possible contributors (we will spare you this exercise). Enumeration of the types in the DQα system depends in part on compound dots which together determine a type. Because of this, the analysis of mixtures becomes a bit complex. In addition, a mixture of bloodstains is often more difficult to interpret than a sexual assault mixture, in which at least one of the contributing types (the victim's) is often known.

Now let's take a look at the DQα types of the three principals in this crime. OS is a 1.1,1.2; NB a 1.1,1.1; and RG, a 1.3,4. Because none of them possesses a 2 or 3 allele, none is excluded on that basis from having contributed to the samples.

Both these samples were also analyzed using the D1S80 system. The advantage of D1S80 is that the interpretation of alleles present is straightforward — there are no hidden alleles. The disadvantage is that two D1S80 alleles, 18 and 24, are quite common in the population. The D1S80 results from both swatches showed bands at 18, 24, and 25. (One of them is shown below as CS.) This is, again, clearly indicative of a mixture. Can genotypes be assigned? It depends on what can be assumed. If it can be assumed that there are only two donors, then clearly the 24 and 25 alleles are present as a genotype based on the similar intensities of the bands as compared with the 18 band. If two or more donors are assumed, then the alleles cannot be paired into genotypes with confidence. No information is gleaned from either the DQα or D1S80 results that supports one assumption over the other.

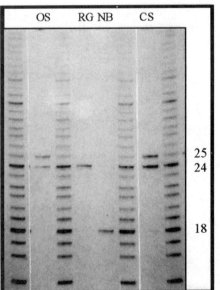

25
24

18

The final interpretation might be summarized as follows:

1. More than one individual contributed to the blood samples collected from the console of the Bronco.
2. All individuals carrying the 2 and 3 DQα alleles are eliminated as contributors to the detected DNA. All others are included as possible donors.
3. Individuals included in the evaluation in step 2 are eliminated if they do not have some combination of the D1S80 18, 24, and/or 25 alleles. The remainder are included as possible donors.

The genotypes of the three reference samples each contain some combination of the DQα 1.1, 1.2, 1.3, and/or 4 alleles. Each also contains at least one of D1S80 18, 24, and/or 25 alleles. Thus, none of the three principals is eliminated as a possible contributor to this sample.

Another way of evaluating the results would be to examine combinations of types from the reference samples to see if any combination could produce the pattern seen in the evidence stain. The Bronco console stain(s) cannot be just a mix of NB and OS, they both lack the DQα 1.3 and 4 alleles. All other combinations are possible (NB/RG; OS/RG; NB/OS/RG). Similarly, the stain(s) cannot be a mix of only OS and RG; neither carries the D1S80 18 allele. The stain(s) also cannot be a mix of only NB and RG; neither has the D1S80 25 allele. Other combinations cannot be eliminated (NB/OS; NB/OS/RG).

Thus all pairwise combinations of the reference genotypes are eliminated by the results from either one or the other marker system. Only a mixture of all three could account for the evidentiary pattern. Therefore, the stain was either contributed by a mixture of all three principals, or by two or more unknown individuals. Likelihood ratios would assist in determining which of these hypotheses was a more likely cause of the evidence.

profile indicates a strong link. The probability of the evidence given alternate sources can be expressed as a likelihood ratio. For some types of evidence, it can be difficult to obtain a reliable estimate of the frequency of the characteristic or characteristics exhibited by the evidence. Our confidence in the frequency estimate (or lack of it) must also be revealed as a limitation of the test, and factored into the inference of common source.

ii. Inference of contact. The strength of an inference of contact concerns the relationship of different items of evidence to each other. It incorporates information about the evidence in the context of the case. With a consideration of contact, we consider the relationship of *source to target* (association). An inference of contact starts with the forensic scientist in the laboratory and extends to involve eventually others connected with the case, including the investigators and attorneys. Note that, for an association, the strength can only be as good as the strength of the inference of source upon which it is built.

d. A Statement of Conclusion

Finally, the analyst must provide a conclusion that will communicate the meaning of the physical evidence results to any interested party who reads the report. A conclusion is an inference (of either source or contact) accompanied by a statement of assumptions and limitations. For identification evidence, the assumptions and limitations are usually trivial and the conclusion is simply a statement regarding the nature and quantity of the substance detected. For individualized evidence, a statement of conclusion about source determination is also straightforward; the analyst simply states her opinion that the evidence and reference could only originate from a unique common source. The assumptions and limitations are usually summarized in the words "in my opinion." It is for classified evidence where the formulation and wording of a conclusion make a real difference in how a reader will understand the import of your results.

The field has not agreed on consistent standards or wording for conclusions about classified evidence. The following conclusions are commonly encountered in reports about classified evidence:

- The reference cannot be excluded as the source of the evidence.
- The reference is included as a possible source for the evidence.
- The reference is a possible source of the evidence.
- The evidence could have come from the reference.
- The evidence is consistent with coming from the reference.
- The evidence and reference have matching class characteristics; therefore, they could have a common origin.
- The evidence and reference are consistent with originating from a common source.

Although none of these statements contains any blatantly false conclusions, the strength of the conclusion is conveyed slightly differently in each. First, none of these statements addresses the possibility of the evidence originating from a source other than the reference. In addition, they all lack any quantitative or semiquantitative information that would assist the reader to understand the strength of the source determination. The omission of any statement of strength renders all of the above statements incomplete. A statement that incorporates an estimate of the number of possible sources of the evidence would provide a much better understanding to readers of the import of the findings.

Also lacking from any of the above statements is an articulation of any alternative hypotheses. This is incomplete at best, misleading at worst. A likelihood ratio provides a vehicle to compare the simplest alternative hypothesis, that the evidence derives from another source with similar characteristics, and also to consider more complex scenarios.

We leave you with our favorite comment on classified evidence by Jim Trotter III, the district attorney played by Lane Smith in the movie *My Cousin Vinnie*. A portion of the text can be found in Figure 10.3.

C. Summary

Because we provide results and information to parties who lack the expertise to independently understand their meaning and implications, it is up to us

Expert witness: I am a special automotive instructor of forensic studies for the Federal Bureau of Investigation.

> *(snip)*

Expert witness: We compared the tire marks outside the convenience store with the rear tires of the defendant's car. They are the same model and size tire - Michelin XGV size 75R 14" wheel.

Prosecutor: They are the same size and model tire! – Anything else?

Expert witness: Yes indeed. The car leaving the convenience store spun its wheels dramatically and left a residue of rubber on the asphalt. We took a sample of that rubber and analyzed it and also took a sample of the rubber form the rear tires of the defendant's Buick and analyzed that too.

Prosecutor: What kind of equipment did you use to find this out?

Expert witness: A Hewlett Packard 57-10A dual column gas chromatograph with flame analyzation detectors.

Prosecutor: What was the result of your analysis?

Expert witness: The chemical composition between the two was found to be – identical.

Prosecutor: *I – DENTICAL!*

Defense attorney: Is it possible that two separate cars could be driving Michelin model XGV size 75R 14" wheel?

Expert witness: Of course.

Defense attorney: What is the best selling single model tire being sold in the US today.

Expert witness: The Michelin XGV.

Defense attorney: What's the most popular size?

Expert witness: 75R14

Defense attorney: The same size on the defendant's car.

Expert witness: Well, yes, but two faded green 1964 Buick skylarks?

Defense attorney: Excuse me, but what I'm asking you is the most popular size of the most popular tire is on the defendant's car.

Expert witness: well....yeah.

Of course, the defense attorney's point is that tens of millions of XGV 75R14 tires are made in the U.S. each year; the significance of making a tire track to this model and size are virtually nil. The GC analysis of tire rubber is no better.

Source: My Cousin Vinnie, Producer, Paul Schiff; Director Jonathan Lynn; lawyer Vincent La Guardia Gambini, Joe Pesci; Bill Gambini, Ralph Macchio; Stan Rothenstein, Mitchell Whitfield; Chamberlain Haller, Fred Gwynne; district attorney Jim Trotter, III, Lane Smith; Mona Lisa Vito, Marisa Tomei, Fox Picture, 1992.

Figure 10.3 My Cousin Vinnie. Excerpt from the courtroom scene.

to furnish an accurate and complete interpretation of our results. If we do not do this, our conclusions are at best incomplete, at worst potentially misleading. We should clearly state the limitations of the test and the evidence, our inferences, our assumptions, and the conclusions that follow from them. We should explicate both what the results mean and what they do not mean. We should resist the temptation to proffer only a conclusion that the client wants to hear if there are other equally valid conclusions, perhaps based on other assumptions. And yes, we do require access to case information to do this in the most helpful and truthful fashion.

References

Commission on Proceedings Involving Guy Paul Morin, The Honourable Fred Kaufman, C.M., Q.C., Queen's Printer for Ontario, 1998, available at *http://www.attorneygeneral.jus.gov.on.ca/reports.html.*

Cooper, C. L. and Sheppard, S. R., *Mockery of Justice: The True Story of the Sheppard Murder Case,* Northeastern University Press, Boston, 1995.

Gross, A. M., Harris, K. A., and Kaldun, G. L., The effect of luminol on presumptive tests and DNA analysis using the polymerase chain reaction, *J. Forensic Sci.,* 44(4), 837, 1999.

Holmes, P. A., *The Sheppard Murder Case,* McKay, New York, 1961.

Holmes, P. A., *Retrial; Murder and Dr. Sam Sheppard,* Bantam Books, New York, 1966.

Kirk, P. L., *Crime Investigation,* 1st ed., Interscience, John Wiley & Sons, New York, 1953.

Sheppard, S. A. with Holmes, P., *My Brother's Keeper,* McKay, New York, 1964.

Sheppard, S. H. with Holmes, P., *Endure and Conquer,* World Pub. Co., Cleveland, 1966.

Figure 11.1 Jail painting. An inmate painted his recollection of his trial for one of the authors. The judge's demeanor says it all. An expert witness should endeavor to avoid producing this kind of ennui in his listeners when giving technical testimony.

Communicating Your
Results — Where
Science Meets the Law

11

"That house on the hilltop — can you see what color they've painted it?" ....
"It is white on this side"
Robert Heinlein
—Anne, the Fair Witness. *Stranger in a Strange Land*

A. Communicating Your Results

Forensic science is an applied science, and it is the legal arena to which the science is applied. Because of this, the way in which we communicate our results is just as important as the results themselves. Incomplete, misleading, or simply poor representation of the results from a forensic analysis can be just as deadly as a sample switch. Just as a brilliant analysis fails to save you from asking the wrong question, a poorly written report or unclear testimony can instantly obscure your otherwise convincing results. In this section, we'll concentrate mostly on the mechanics of clear communication. However, by its very nature, the subtle variations in how a set of results are presented begins to verge on a discussion of ethics. We'll save most of that for Chapter 12, but will make a few comments here when the material requires it.

1. Writing a Report

A report should clearly and completely convey your conclusions about the evidence in a case. Your report is the work product that will reach more people than any other aspect of your work. Most scientists possess notoriously poor communications skills, particularly technical writing skills. The scientist must take responsibility for communicating his results and conclusions, using thoughtful wording that clearly conveys the intended meaning of the data. The report should be organized, easy to read, and written in grammatically correct English. In other words, the burden should be on the scientist, not the reader, to ensure that written communication is effective in disseminating the scientist's opinion.

a. Is a Written Report Obligatory?*

Probably the first question to ask about report writing is, does one have to? Most government laboratories write some sort of report as a matter of course, even if it's just a one-line summary of the results. If the case goes to court, the defense is always entitled to discover the results of any examinations, and the results are invariably provided in the form of a written report.

---

* Again, we are most familiar with the rules governing expert reports and testimony in the United States. You should check with the attorney for whom you are working for the exact law governing your jurisdiction.

Private laboratories, which frequently provide services to both prosecution and defense, find themselves in a slightly different situation. Depending on the legal "Rules of Discovery" in a particular jurisdiction, and whether the case is criminal or civil, the defense may not be required to disclose forensic results.* In civil proceedings, full discovery is almost always required of both plaintiff and defendant. However, in criminal trials, the defense commonly retains limited rights to keep certain materials confidential. If the defense attorney does not request a report, or specifically asks that one not be written, what is the obligation of the criminalist? Currently, conflicting views exist regarding this dilemma. First of all, because we participate in the legal system, we must abide by its rules and regulations. In other words, we don't get to decide. However, assuming your *defense attorney* client is acting legally and ethically, in most cases you should respect a request not to forward a report. We acknowledge that not all practitioners agree with this view. We also emphasize that this would never be acceptable if your client is the prosecution. Although the extent of required discovery varies by jurisdiction and, for that matter by case, the defendant (and his experts and attorney) usually (at least in the United States) have the right to review potentially inculpatory evidence, and the prosecution has the obligation to disclose exculpatory evidence.

Whether or not your report is disclosed, you nevertheless have a scientific obligation to document your results formally. Presumably, you have a detailed and accurate set of bench notes from your examination or analysis. You should also have some case information to assist you in your interpretation of those notes. You could simply write a report to the file in preparation for saving your own sanity if you ever have to go back to it. Or you could pull your notes out 25 years later when the case is rediscovered by a persistent investigator and resurrect your interpretation and conclusions from scratch. If you are at all like us, 25 minutes is almost as bad as 25 years; we make sure to keep copious notes and close out each case with at least a written, if unformatted, summary of our interpretation of the data and the conclusions to which it led.

What about private consultants who do not generate data, but simply review the work of others and render an opinion about it? Should they be required to provide a written report, to be disclosed to the other side at the attorney's discretion? We believe that a reviewer has the same obligations as the individual or agency who performed the work. Within the bounds of legal obligation, the consultant should provide a detailed and explicit report that clearly states her opinion and the data and other information upon which that opinion rests. General lists of possible problems with a procedure

---

* Because we are not legal experts and our familiarity with the legal system stems only from our interaction with it as forensic scientists, we'll confine any legal references to U.S. law. We hope that those of you reading this in other countries will be able to take the philosophical points and apply them to your own legal system.

and nonspecific comments about the reliability and interpretation of results are no more acceptable from this quadrant than would be an incomplete report from the primary analyst.

Unfortunately, some of the defense-only consultants who insist on invading the laboratory anew with each subsequent case to scrutinize the same validation studies and the same proficiency test results don't seem to feel a reciprocal obligation to document their opinions. Figure 11.2 contains a reproduction of one such consultant's report that was finally written only after a direct order from the judge. Although several pages of typing were generated, the report contains only generalities, some unsubstantiated, some blatantly incorrect. It provides no hint whatsoever of the "expert's" interpretation of the specific data from the actual case other than that it might be different than the laboratory's interpretation. In our opinion, this expert did both the court and her own client a disservice with this immaterial work product.

b. What Information Should Be in a Report?

As the final work product of the criminalist's effort, a written report is frequently the sole source from which others will understand the evidence and the analyst's opinion of it. The analyst should carefully consider for whom the report is being written. Different readers require different levels of technical discussion and summaries with different emphases. A forensic report should be useful and accessible to a layperson, such as the detective or attorney, and should also provide enough information for another expert to understand what was done and what it means. Your report is basically the means by which you publish your data. Remember that people may make decisions based solely on the content of your report. We suggest a structure similar to the following:

1. **Summary**

   The summary should be directed to the layperson who may never get past the first page of the report. For a forensic report, the summary should encapsulate the salient elements of the rest of the report. At the very least, it should contain the *conclusion* derived from the results of the tests. The conclusion is not the results. It is the analyst's best interpretation of what the results mean. The conclusion should always contain any information relating to the strength or reliability of the test. Without this information, the lay reader, in particular, could be seriously misled regarding the import of your results.

2. **Purpose**

    The purpose is where you have a chance to translate the legal question into a scientific question. Why are you bothering to perform scientific examinations on this evidence? What are you hoping to learn? Inclusion of a purpose is standard practice in scientific articles.

3. **List of evidence received and examined**

    All of the evidence received by the analyst should be listed, and the evidence that was examined or analyzed should be specified.

4. **Examination and results**

    In this section, you should briefly describe the tests or comparisons that were performed (the gory details should be in your notes), and the results you obtained. If frequencies or statistics are used in assessing the strength of the data, the data and their sources should be explicated.

5. **Interpretation and conclusion**

    In this section, you should summarize the reasoning behind your conclusion. Depending on the particular evidence, this section might be very brief or quite lengthy. At the end you should provide a *conclusion* — in other words, your *opinion* of what the results mean in the context of the case. This statement will be recycled in the initial summary section, perhaps with slightly different wording intended for a lay audience.

The information detailed above can be presented in a variety of formats; the names of the sections are less important than the information contained therein. One example of a complete report may be found in Figure 11.3.

These suggestions are generally supported by the DNA Advisory Board (DAB) standards but there is no reason that they should be specific to DNA analysis. We expect that groups now working to develop guidelines in other disciplines will arrive at similar conclusions. The relevant section of the DAB guidelines is reproduced in Figure 11.4.

The results of all examinations should be included in the report; the analyst does not have the option of excluding a result because he thinks it is irrelevant, or worse yet, inconvenient. His opinion may not be, and should not be, the final filter regarding the usefulness of a particular result. Raw data generated from the case need not be available in the body of the report, but should be immediately and cooperatively made available to a qualified analyst acting (usually through an attorney) on behalf of opposing counsel. This is the only way the original work product can be effectively reviewed by an independent expert.

_____, Ph.D., Expert Witness Summary:

Pursuant to your request for a formal report, I have put together the following points, based on the provided information from [State] v. [Suspect] and the following protocols:

       _____ Crime Lab bench notes
STR results from GeneScan and GenoTyper Software programs
Photographs of DQA1/PM results from _____ Crime Lab
Evidence receipt and Property report dated 5/21/98
Evidence receipt and Property report dated 6/04/98
Evidence receipt and Property report dated 6/9/98
Evidence receipt and Property report dated 7/15/98
Evidence receipt and Property report dated 7/16/98
Evidence receipt and Property report dated 10/09/98
Criminalistic Analysis Report – SEROLGY dated 7/13/98
Criminalistic Analysis Report – SEROLGY dated 10/21/98
Criminalistic Analysis Report – DNA dated 9/30/98
Criminalistic Analysis Report –DNA-STR dated 11/12/98
Criminalistic Analysis Report – DNA-PCR 11/17/98
       _____ Crime Lab Protocols
Perkin-Elmer Profiler Plus Amplification Manual
Perkin-Elmer ABI Prism 310 Genetic Analyzer Manual
Perkin-Elmer GeneScan Software Manual
Perkin-Elmer GenoTyper Software Manual

1. Issues regarding reliability of use of STRs on crime scene samples.
    I will opine that because of problems that arise during the amplification process, STR genotyping can be problematic for crime scene samples.
2. Issues regarding reliability of use of the ABI Prism 310 Genetic Analyzer on crime scene samples.
    Perkin-Elmer has withheld developmental validation studies from view by the scientific community, which makes evaluation of this machine difficult. With the addition of amplification problems enhanced by the complexity of the Profiler Plus kit, I will opine that use of the machine is questionable for crime scene samples.
3. Opinion of test result obtained from known and questioned samples examined at PM/DQA1 and D1S80
    I will opine that samples evaluated in this case can be interpreted differently than the _____ Crime Lab chose to do.
4. Opinion of test result obtained from known and questioned samples examined at the STR and amelogenin loci present in the Profiler Plus amplification kit.
    I will opine that samples evaluated in this case can be interpreted differently than the _____ Crime Lab chose to do.

_____ , Ph.D.
[State] v. [Suspect]

Figure 11.2 Example of a poor report. This report was received by a state laboratory from an independent consultant only after an order by the judge. It has been retyped for clarity, following the format as closely as possible within the confines of space and legibility. All identifying information has been omitted or generalized. Note that the report fails to mention which, if any, of the stated potential "inherent problems in STR testing" pertains to the case at hand, and how that problem might affect the interpretation of the results. Note, also, that the report fails to provide an independent interpretation of the results, stating only that they "can be interpreted differently."

The following is an example of a situation in which a laboratory abused its discretion regarding the contents of a report.

In the previous chapter, we presented a case in which a state DNA laboratory interpreted the collective results from several genetic analyses to mean that,

PROBLEMS WHICH ARISE DURING STR AMPLIFICATION	PROBLEMS WHICH ARISE FROM THE MACHINE
1) Allelic Dropout	1) Dye Blobs
	2) Pull-ups
	3) Electronic Spikes
2) Stutter (frequent and unpredictable)	4) Baseline Problems
	a. High Baseline
3) Preferential Amplification	b. Formamide
	c. Insufficient Polymer
4) Plus –A Anomalies	5) Saturation Problems
	6) Bad Matrix File
5) Inhibition	7) Non-stutter / non-pull-up
	8) One Color Non-reproducible Peak
	9) Spurious Peaks
	10) Saturated Peaks

Figure 11.2 (continued)   Inherent problems in STR Testing.

in each of three separate stains, blood from both the victim and the defendant was present as a mixture. Recall that seven PCR-based DNA markers exhibited the same types as the victim. One serological marker, *PGM*, exhibited the same type as the defendant. Their report consisted of a table of results. No conclusions were drawn about the inclusion or exclusion of various principals, and no interpretive prose was to be found. The analysts testified in court that, although no evidence of a mixture was apparent, their conclusion was that the data resulted from a mixture of the victim and defendant. The data were clearly inconsistent with their testimony. Likely, they had only constructed the explanation after receiving a written report from an independent expert detailing a different opinion.

If the analyst is convinced that the data support a particular conclusion, this should be stated in the written report; if the data are uninterpretable or inconclusive, this information is just as important and should also be stated.

c. *Language*

One of the most hotly debated topics among forensic science professionals is the use of language, both in testimony and reports. The dilemma stems from the fact that data composed of numbers, patterns, or images must be expressed in words. By definition, this involves a translation of sorts, and not everyone agrees on the correct translation. Language is simply an imprecise way to express scientific and mathematical concepts. But, without it, we have

The headings for a report vary according to jurisdiction, and will not be including here.

SUMMARY

Sexual assault evidence collected from the victim had been previously examined by a criminalist at another laboratory. She had examined the vaginal swabs and a skirt , and performed DNA testing in the DQA1 and D1S80 typing systems. Results showed that the DNA from the suspect was different from the results obtained from the skirt in the D1S80 system. This laboratory was requested to examine DNA from these samples using RFLP methodology to confirm the elimination of the suspect as the semen donor. If the elimination is confirmed, then we are requested to search the unknown profile from the skirt against the state felon database.

DNA from the sperm fractions of two stains from the skirt was subjected to RFLP testing at 5 independent loci, and the results compared to DNA extracted from a reference blood from the suspect. Results show that the suspect is eliminated as a source of the DNA found in these sperm fractions from the skirt.

On October 31, the DNA profile of the semen donor from this evidence was submitted for search against 25,000 felons and 200 cases. A hit was obtained at 4 independent RFLP loci with a felon identified as Doit Agen, at 4 independent RFLP loci.

EVIDENCE

On September 18, the following items were received from....

    1.   Reference sample from the victim

    2.   Reference sample from the suspect

    3.   One skirt.

EXAMINATION AND RESULTS

Two semen stains were detected on the skirt (Item 3). DNA extracted from these samples[1] and from the reference samples from the victim (Item 1) and the suspect (Item 2) were prepared for RFLP analysis according to a standard protocol using the restriction enzyme *Hae*III, and subsequently examined at 5 independent genetic loci.

Results of the analysis are summarized in Table 1.

Several conclusions can be drawn from the data. First, the non-sperm fractions from the skirt (3A and 3B) are concordant with the reference sample from the victim (Item 2). This is expected, and serves as a quality control check on some of the analytical process. Second, the sperm fractions from both stains show similar semen donor profiles, indicating a common source for the semen in both samples.

Finally, the RFLP profile from the sperm fraction of both stains is dissimilar to the profile from the suspect. He is eliminated as the semen donor for the stains on the skirt.

On October 31, the DNA profile of the semen donor from this evidence was submitted for search against

---

[1] Sexual assault evidence generally contains cells of two types of cells; non-sperm cells and spermatozoa cells. A convenient method has been devised that attempts to separate the DNA from the two types of cells. This results in a non-sperm fraction and a sperm fraction.

Figure 11.3 Example of a good report from a laboratory analyst. The headings for a report vary according to jurisdiction, and will not be included here.

25,000 felons and 200 cases. A hit was obtained at 4 independent RFLP loci.with a felon identified as Doit Agen, at 4 independent RFLP loci.

This sample, along with samples flanking it at the time of submission and the time of analysis, were re-examined by an RFLP technique. Results verify that the sample submitted with the name Doit Agen to our laboratory was the one analyzed and hit against the evidence profile.

Typically, a new sample will be obtained and analyzed by the casework laboratory.

TABLE 1

	3A Sperm	3B Sperm	Suspect	3A Non-sperm	3B Non-sperm	Victim
D1S7	2952	2938	7384	4741	4742	4733
	2202	2192	3488	4473	4473	4487
D2S44	1772	1772	1858	2139	2036	2038
	1129	1128	766	1931	1938	1932
D4S139	9375	9335	6169	2961	2962	2968
	4083	4064	5359	2673	2673	2577
D5S110	7176	7146	5148	4084	4101	4098
	4313	4294	4439	3024	3024	3016
D10S28	2225	2213	7856	2164	2164	2157
	1915	1915	1817	1017	1008	1008

DISPOSITION

All submitted items were returned to the submitting agency.

Date of report: _____   Examinations by: _____

Figure 11.3 (continued)

no way to reach the layperson who must ultimately understand the import of our results.

The whole issue is complicated by the fact that many of the terms we use are "terms of art." Criminalists don't agree among themselves about the intended meaning of several commonly used phrases, not to mention the lack of consensus between scientists and attorneys. Additionally, many analysts take advantage of "weasel words" that relieve them of the responsibility of crafting a statement that conveys their conclusions as accurately as possible. Finally, the terms we use to describe our laboratory results are also used in everyday language. They have acquired connotations that may or may not be appropriate to their use as descriptors of a scientific conclusion.

DNA ADVISORY BOARD
Standards for reports and review

11. REPORTS

STANDARD 11.1

The laboratory shall have and follow written procedures for taking and maintaining case notes to support the conclusions drawn in laboratory reports.

  11.1.1 The laboratory shall maintain, in a case record, all documentation generated by examiners related to case analyses.

  11.1.2 Reports according to written guidelines shall include:

  (a) Case identifier

  (b) Description of evidence examined

  (c) A description of the methodology

  (d) Locus

  (e) Results and/or conclusions

  (f) An interpretative statement (either quantitative or qualitative)

  (g) Date issued

  (h) Disposition of evidence

  (i) A signature and title, or equivalent identification, of the person(s) accepting responsibility for the content of the report.

  11.1.3 The laboratory shall have written procedures for the release of case report information.

12. REVIEW

STANDARD 12.1

The laboratory shall conduct administrative and technical reviews of all case files and reports to ensure conclusions and supporting data are reasonable and within the constraints of scientific knowledge.

  12.1.1 The laboratory shall have a mechanism in place to address unresolved discrepant conclusions between analysts and reviewer(s)

REFERENCES

Scientific Working Group for DNA Analysis Methods (SWGDAM). http://www.for-swg.org/swgdamin.htm

Figure 11.4 DNA Advisory Board standards for reports and review. (From *Scientific Working Group for DNA Analysis Methods (SWGDAM)*, available at *http://www.forswg.org/swgdamin.htm.*)

Probably the most contentious term is the word *match*. Interestingly, *Webster's* (1996) lists no fewer that 24 definitions for "match." Two (the first and third) are of particular interest to forensic science.

  1. A person or thing that equals or resembles another in some respect.
  2. A person or thing that is an exact counterpart of another.

It is the difference between these two statements that forms the basis of the confusion. It is technically correct, in our opinion, to say that the results of all tests done on two items match, or that two patterns match. This relies on the first definition listed above. The point, of course, is that we obviously cannot know if the two items match for some attribute that was not tested. It is therefore incorrect and potentially misleading to say that, based solely on the tests that were run, that the two *items* match. This statement is the second one listed above. One might make this inference, incorporating some assumptions in the process, or become convinced of it and form an opinion. However, because we, as scientists, have not explicitly stated which definition we mean to imply, and the word, as commonly used, has multiple definitions, the situation simply begs for misunderstanding and misuse. In particular, many laypersons easily equate "match" with "unique common origin." This may or may not be what the forensic scientist means to convey.

Another widely used term, and one that is equally successful at fomenting debate, is the phrase *consistent with. Webster's* (1996) gives the following as one definition of "consistent":

1.   Agreeing or accordant; compatible; not self-contradictory

This phrase is highly ambiguous because it encompasses such extremes of meaning that the reader could easily be misled regarding the strength of an inference. This is reflected in the weak and nonspecific common understanding of the term, as described above. For example, an evidence sample of type O blood is "consistent with" coming from an individual with type O blood. It is also "consistent with" coming from any other person in the 40% of the population that has type O blood. In contrast, an evidence sample typed at 15 RFLP loci and 13 STR loci is also "consistent with" coming from an individual who shows the same type at all 28 loci. The calculated frequency of this type is so rare, however, that it is unreasonable to believe that it describes more than one person on earth. Using "consistent with" to describe both of these situations potentially overstates the blood-typing results and also understates the DNA result. As a consequence, the layperson reading the report or hearing the testimony may give much more weight to the blood typing result than would be appropriate, and conversely, underestimate the strength of the DNA result. This is particularly true if no additional information is presented in the report to describe the strength of the inference. We do not find this phrase to be useful in communicating the results of a forensic analysis.

A term that we do find useful is *indistinguishable.* In part, because it is a six-syllable word and not common in everyday speech, it forces the reader to actually think about its meaning. Combined with the appropriate limitations, such as "indistinguishable by the tests performed" or "at this particular level of analysis," and a brief description of the tests and their limitations, this term can provide the reader or listener with a good feeling for the strength of the result.

We are not under the illusion that terms such as "match" and "consistent with" will disappear from forensic usage, nor do we believe that "indistinguishable" is the sole best solution to the dilemma of accurately describing our results. We do invite practitioners to think about the language that they use to describe their conclusions about a forensic analysis and suggest that the various professional groups might begin discussions about adopting a standard terminology. This would also assist attorneys to better understand the strengths and weaknesses of the physical evidence in the context of the case, and the trier of fact to decide how much weight to give to a particular piece of evidence.

d. Significant Figures

This is a relatively harmless complaint, but does go to the thoughtfulness of the analyst. We are all taught in Chemistry 101, if not long before, that no numerical weight or measure should be written with more significant digits than is reflective of our actual confidence in the accuracy of the measurement. For some reason, when calculators, and now computers, are used to make a calculation, people tend to record the number that flashes on the screen with absolutely no regard for whether the last 10 digits provide any meaningful information. Is the weight of the cocaine sample really accurate to five digits (1.3572 g) or is the scale only accurate to two digits (1.4 g). Can we really estimate a population frequency to four significant digits (0.1383) or is a more reasonable representation two digits (0.14). An example of an institutionalized misappropriation of significant figures by a company who should know better is shown in Figure 11.5. We make a plea here to apply some intelligent thought to the number of significant digits you record both in your notes and in your report. You will lose at least one opportunity to look silly on the stand when opposing counsel asks you if you can really measure the concentration of DNA in your tube to five significant figures.

2. The Big Picture

At one time, the same person who performed the blood typing would simply move over to another bench to examine fibers under a microscope or to compare two dermal ridge prints. At most, another analyst in the same laboratory might participate in analyzing the evidence in a single case. This is no longer the situation. It is not uncommon these days for various pieces of evidence in a case to be examined by multiple analysts in the same laboratory,

Table 1: DNA Standards and Concentrations		
DNA Standard	Concentration (ng/ µL)	Quantity DNA per 5 µL (ng)
A	2	10
B	1	5
C	0.5	2.5
D	0.25	1.25
E	0.125	0.625
F	0.0625	0.3125
G	0.03125	0.15625

Figure 11.5 Dilutions. In chemistry 101 we are taught the fundamentals of significant figures. This is an example of thoughtfulness put on hold.

multiple laboratories, multiple jurisdictions, or even public and private laboratories. The detective and ultimately the attorney is then left with numerous reports from different people in various disciplines, and no way to integrate the results into a meaningful whole. Many of the analysts who did the work may not have any expertise beyond their individual specialty. We, as workers in the field, need to think about how best to integrate this profusion of information and help those in the legal system who ultimately use our work product to understand how all the evidence fits together.

Things have gotten so specialized that disciplines that were once considered one have become distinct entities. This can cause problems when the analysts no longer speak the same language and in effect have stopped communicating with each other. We even know of one case in which analysts from the same DNA laboratory, analyzing literally the same piece of evidence, failed to communicate with each other, with potentially disastrous results.

Different cuttings from the same panty crotch were analyzed within a single DNA laboratory by individual analysts using different genetic marker systems. None of the analysts was aware of the results of any of the others, or of the initial serology results from the submitting laboratory. Each analyst was about to submit an isolated report, when an alert reviewer realized they were all from the same case, and that the typing results appeared to be internally inconsistent. Fortunately, after reviewing the history of the evidence and the case circumstances, the reviewer was able to reconcile the apparently discrepant results before the situation created any more confusion.

However, the preceding is not always the outcome. The following is an example involving serological typing and DNA.

> A private consultant was asked to review a DNA report from a private laboratory regarding an attempted rape. The initial serological screening was performed by a city laboratory, and a number of different evidence items were selected to forward for DNA analysis. One of the items, an apparent bloodstain taken from the defendant's car, was determined by DNA to show the same markers as the victim, and the laboratory submitted a report to this effect. However, nobody, either at the DNA laboratory or from the originating laboratory, bothered to compare the two reports. If they had, they would have noticed that the victim was *excluded* from contributing to this stain by ABO typing. Like most instances of this type, more work could have probably resolved that apparent discrepancy. As it was, the defendant obtained a plea-bargain for a substantially reduced sentence.

A major case file with lots of evidence will frequently contain reports from several different individuals covering a number of disciplines. These analyses may have been performed in a complete vacuum relative to each other, potentially compounding the problems described above.

Surprisingly few laboratories seem to have a formalized system for integrating interdisciplinary analyses from a single case (Zeppa, 1999). No one person reviews the entire case file and looks to see if the evidence appears to tell a coherent story. If contradictory results exist, the attorney and the investigator are left to sort things out. We would like to suggest that the final element of good laboratory practice is to generate a comprehensive report summarizing the results of all the different examinations and analyses. Such a report would provide a complete picture of the physical evidence in the case and lay the foundation for a reconstruction — the ordering of events (as defined by physical associations) in time and space.

3.   Testimony

A criminalist's work culminates in a court of law. Obviously, not all cases proceed to court, but the anticipation of court testimony is what sets forensic science apart from any other applied science. It is also probably the greatest deterrent to joining the profession and the downfall of many an examiner. Although no amount of external wisdom can fully prepare one for the rigors of the stand, it's helpful to define the general process, the expectations of the various players, and, in particular, to review the role of the scientist in the proceedings.

In the previous section, we covered the preparation that must take place before you set foot in a courtroom. The most successful and efficient testimony results from a solid foundation laid by both you and your attorney client, so that as little as possible is seat-of-the-pants guesswork once you are on the stand. This is not to say you shouldn't anticipate the possibility of having to think on the fly. You are rarely in control in the courtroom. You are an invited guest and you must abide by the rules and conventions of your host, the court. However, this is balanced by the desire of the scientist to ensure that his opinion is communicated as clearly and completely as possible.

As invited guests of the court, forensic scientists must understand how their role is viewed by the legal profession. Although each country, state, and local jurisdiction has its own set of rules governing the acceptance and conduct of expert witnesses, generally, they are quite similar. In the United States, many are predicated to at least some extent on the *Federal Rules of Evidence*,* Article VII of which is reproduced in Figure 11.6. Although the specifics vary, a main point is always that the expert witness, as opposed to the lay witness, is allowed to give opinion testimony. Further, expert witnesses are allowed to explain their answers.

a.   *Personal Preparation*

The criminalist must specifically prepare for testimony in a variety of ways. It is not advisable to assume that your natural intelligence combined with your familiarity with the evidence will be enough to get you through. The thought process that began when the evidence entered the laboratory must continue through testimony. You should review your notes, including the data and the interpretation that led to your conclusion. Having kept detailed written records helps immensely with this process. You think you will never forget how you came up with that complex interpretation of the data, but by the time the next case is on your desk, the previous one is probably gone from your conscious mind. You should never have to resort to literally reading from your notes on the stand. You should, however, refer to them to refresh your recollection about specific items of information, and when requested to do so. You should have clearly in mind your full set of conclusions, in particular the competing hypotheses, and how your data either support or disprove a particular hypothesis. This includes an intimate knowledge of the capabilities and limitations of both the evidence and the tests.

One of the most difficult preparatory activities is to keep up with the literature in your field. As a historical literature base develops, and the number of published papers continues to increase, this frequently seems like a losing battle. In addition, some relevant papers may be published in relatively obscure journals that may be difficult to both monitor and obtain. A general familiarity with who is doing what will help you concentrate on the most

---

* The *Uniform Rules of Evidence* are very similar to the *Federal Rules of Evidence*. They have begun to be adopted by states to accomplish a goal of standardization.

United States Federal Rules of Evidence
ARTICLE VII
OPINIONS AND EXPERT TESTIMONY

RULE 701. Opinion Testimony by Lay Witnesses. If the witness is not testifying as an expert, his testimony in the form of opinions or inferences is limited to those opinions or inferences which are (1) rationally based on the perception of the witness and (2) helpful to a clear understanding of his testimony or the determination of a fact in issue.

RULE 702. Testimony by Experts. If scientific, technical, or other specialized knowledge will assist the trier of fact to understand the evidence or to determine a fact in issue, a witness qualified as an expert by knowledge, skill, experience, training, or education, may testify thereto in the form of an opinion or otherwise.

RULE 703. Basis of Opinion Testimony by Experts. The facts or data in the particular case upon which an expert bases an opinion or inference may be those perceived by or made known to him at or before the hearing. If of a type reasonably relied upon by experts in the particular field in forming opinions or inferences upon the subject, the facts or data need not be admissible in evidence.

RULE 704. Opinion on Ultimate Issue. Testimony in the form of an opinion or inference otherwise admissible is not objectionable because it embraces an ultimate issue to be decided by the trier of fact.

RULE 705. Disclosure of facts or data underlying expert opinon. The expert may testify in terms of opinion or inference and give his reasons therefor without prior disclosure of the underlying facts or data, unless the court requires otherwise. The expert may in any event be required to disclose the underlying facts or data on cross-examination.

RULE 706. Court appointed experts.

(a) *Appointment.* The court, on motion of any party or its own motion, may enter an order to show cause why expert witnesses should not be appointed, and may request the parties to submit nominations. The court may appoint any expert witnesses agreed upon by the parties, and may appoint expert witnesses of its own selection. An expert witness shall not be appointed by the court unless he consents to act. A witness so appointed shall be informed of his duties by the court in writing, a copy of which shall be filed with the clerk, or at a conference in which the parties shall have opportunity to participate. A witness so appointed shall advise the parties of his findings, if any; his deposition may be taken by any party; and he may be called to testify by the court or any party. He shall be subject to cross-examination by each party, including a party calling him as a witness.

(b) *Compensation.* Expert witnesses so appointed are entitled to reasonable compensation in whatever sum the court may allow. The compensation thus fixed is payable from funds which may be provided by law in criminal cases and civil actions and proceedings involving just compensation for the taking of property. In other civil actions and proceedings the compensation shall be paid by the parties in such proportion and at such time as the court directs, and thereafter charged in like manner as other costs.

(c) *Disclosure of appointment.* In the exercise of its discretion, the court may authorize disclosure to the jury of the fact that the court appointed the expert witness.

(d) *Parties' experts of own selection.* Nothing in this rule limits the parties in calling expert witnesses of their own selection.

Figure 11.6 *U.S. Federal Rules of Evidence,* Article VII, Opinions and Expert Testimony.

useful and relevant papers. Also, attendance at meetings, or at least a review of the abstract book, will help keep you plugged in to the most recent developments. There is little worse than being challenged on the stand with an article that you had no idea existed refuting your opinion.

You should prepare both mentally and physically for what can be very grueling days. Even if you are a veteran, it's useful to discuss with both your colleagues and your attorney client the best way to present your conclusions, and what challenges might be posed (both reasonable and unreasonable). Moot court sessions can be useful for both an inexperienced analyst as well as a veteran with a tough case. Classes in testimony may also be helpful for the beginner to get tips and gain practice. Again, you are not taking a closed-book exam. You have the resources of the whole community at your disposal. It is prudent to take advantage of this body of knowledge and experience.

Know and understand your own personal limitations. Do you have annoying verbal or physical habits that you must work to control? Is your handwriting completely illegible, making it prudent to prepare exhibits ahead of time? Do you need to establish a personal routine to control nerves? What is your personal comfort level and what do you need to do to maximize it? Make sure that you are well rested (easier said than done) and that you eat properly before testimony. Someone in the courtroom will usually make sure you have water while you are testifying, but don't be shy about asking. There is nothing worse than trying to be clear when your tongue is sticking to the roof of your mouth. Last, appearance does count. Especially in front of a jury, you should make every effort to look professional. This may mean different things in different venues, so it pays to check out expected dress codes with your attorney client in advance.

b.   Preparing with Your Attorney Client

One of the most important and least-recognized roles the analyst must play is that of educator. To take our continuing paradigm one step farther, you can perform the most brilliant analysis, and write the most articulate report, but if the attorney who is examining you hasn't a clue what to ask, the whole exercise may turn out to be futile. Unfortunately, quality time with the attorney is the first thing to go in the crunch of preparing for trial. We cannot emphasize enough how critical it is that the attorney understand the full import of your results and how they fit into the case, and that you understand how the attorney plans to use your testimony. This is the time to clarify to the attorney the limitations that must be placed on your conclusions, and to discuss the scope of your testimony. Having this discussion prior to your examination on the witness stand can prevent an enormous amount of frustration for everyone, and advance the testimony in a much more effective and efficient manner.

Attorneys on both sides of the bar, with a few exceptions, usually have to be dragged kicking and screaming into a discussion of the nitty-gritty of scientific evidence. After all, as they so often remind us, many of them became attorneys in direct response to the realization that they were about to flunk chemistry. Nevertheless, it is up to you to make sure your client, be that a prosecutor or defense attorney, understands both the general ideas behind the test procedure and the details of the evidence in the case.

> In one DNA admissibility hearing, the scientist's failure to educate the prosecution team was in large part responsible for a rejection of the motion. The analyst simply couldn't be bothered to sit down with the prosecution team and instruct them in the particular procedures he had used and explain potential vulnerabilities they might face in their bid to introduce the testing at trial. The attorneys, working under the mistaken impression that DNA was a shoo-in, were not ready for an exceptionally aggressive and well-prepared defense team. In the wake of the court decision, they were still left wondering what went wrong. Although a number of factors contributed to this particular fiasco, the analyst's dereliction of his obligation to educate and prepare his clients for trial was a major determinant.

One of the common misconceptions that you will constantly battle is the idea that science can provide irrefutable facts. While the law makes clear distinctions between guilt and innocence, attorneys are often frustrated with our inability or unwillingness to commit to an unqualified conclusion. To their mind, testimony from experts includes too many instances of "could," "might," and "possibly." Sometimes attorneys think that if we can give opinion testimony, we always should; after all, we are the expert. However, because science is a process of constantly updating knowledge, the most we can do is offer our best explanation of the moment that remains unrefuted and to articulate our assumptions.

It is frequently useful to prepare a list of questions that the attorney can use as a road map to elicit the information from you that you together have decided convey the essence of your conclusion. You must be clear about what you are willing to say and especially what you are *not* willing to say. There should be no surprises during direct examination; there is enough opportunity for that during cross-examination. The use of exhibits should not be overlooked. Oversized charts and illustrations can be enormously helpful in assisting you to summarize the results. They provide a visual focus, especially for a jury, and seeing and hearing the same information simultaneously increases the chances that the jury will understand and retain your testimony. Finally, we have found it helpful to provide the court reporter with a glossary of technical terms. Interruptions to the testimony to ask for spelling clarifications are fewer and the final transcript is more accurate. Remember, the more you can simplify your testimony, while still retaining a reasonable degree of accuracy, the better chance you have to communicate the import of your conclusions.

i.   The danger of "expert attorneys."   Remember that *you* are the scientific expert, not the attorneys, the judge, or anyone else in the courtroom (save perhaps another expert). You should give your attorney enough background information for her to understand the meaning of the tests, but this does not and should not make the attorney a scientific expert. You should never be a shill for the attorney's opinion.

Just as dangerous as the ignorant attorney are "expert attorneys" who consider that they are indeed expert in the science, and could testify but for a technicality. There seems to be a trend for attorneys specializing in physical evidence to advertise themselves as "physical evidence experts," "scientific evidence experts," or, most often, "DNA experts." Attorneys can and should be an expert in the legal issues relating to scientific evidence; they cannot and should not represent themselves as scientific experts.

4.   Be Familiar with Legal Rules and Procedures

Just as attorneys should refrain from representing themselves as scientific experts, the scientist should not try to be a legal expert. Objections to "compound question" and "argumentative" coming from the stand will only annoy everyone and get you in trouble. However, you should be familiar with general courtroom procedure and the portions of the law that directly affect scientific and expert testimony. You should also make a point to review any statutory or case law that applies to the material you intend to present in a hearing or trial, and to discuss specific implications with your attorney client.

Your attorney should also be alert and attentive, not only during direct examination of you, but especially during cross-examination, so that she can pull you out of any legal quagmires using the appropriate objections. Because the attorney may be concentrating on preparing the next set of questions and not paying full attention, it is beneficial to the expert to familiarize himself with the expectations of, and limits on, expert testimony. For example, we know of an instance where opposing counsel wrote points on an easel pad, none of which was actually said by the witness. Opposing counsel attempted to move this page into evidence while the witness's attorney was not paying attention. Fortunately, the witness was familiar with the fact that attorneys cannot give evidence, and was able to get his attorney's attention to object before the deed was completed.

5. Admissibility Hearings

Depending on the discipline in which you work, and whether you have used any methodologies that might be considered "novel scientific evidence," you may have to testify in an admissibility hearing before you can present your results before a jury. In the United States, some states follow the federal *Frye* (*Frye v. United States*) standard for admissibility, which can be summarized as "generally accepted by the relevant scientific community." Others follow the statutory *Federal Rules of Evidence*, reincarnated as the *Daubert v. Merrill Dow Pharmaceuticals*, a standard for admissibility that can be summarized as "more probative than prejudicial." Most recently, the U.S. Supreme Court ruled that the *Daubert* standard may be applied to any sort of expert testimony, not just strictly "scientific" testimony (*Kumho Tire Co. v. Carmichael*). Whether or not you are personally involved in an admissibility hearing, you should be familiar with any case and statutory law pertaining to the admissibility of scientific evidence.

6. Educating the Judge and the Jury

One of the most important functions of the scientist in the courtroom is to educate the judge and jury so that they can appreciate the import of the examiner's conclusions. The witness should neither condescend to the lay audience, nor obfuscate the information in a flurry of technical terms. Clear, simple explanations, with the intention of communicating the sense rather than the explicit details, usually work best. Visual aids and well-crafted analogies can be enormously helpful in conveying technical information in a comprehensible way to nonscientists. If you lose the trier of fact, it does not matter how brilliant your work was, or how convincing your conclusion. If you cannot communicate it, you might as well not have done it.

The very process of simplifying technical information results in a loss of accuracy. This is the compromise we make in transporting our conclusions out of the scientific realm and into the legal arena. The expert witness must constantly balance the need to convey the information in a technically correct manner with the necessity to impart the take-home message clearly to a lay audience. This is precisely where a summary in lay terms is useful. This allows the expert the latitude to communicate the substance of his conclusion in easily understandable terms.

7. The Ethics of Communicating Your Conclusions

You alone have the power to communicate the full import of your conclusions to the trier of fact. Throughout a career, you will no doubt encounter opposition to achieving this goal from opposing counsel, from the court, and even from your own attorney. Attorneys often lose sight of the fact that, although their role is intended to be one of advocacy, the expert witness cannot be a party to the advocacy. You may get tremendous pressure to testify to only the part of your results that supports the attorney's position, or to change your wording subtly to something the attorney likes better because she can more easily argue it to support the cause. As much as you feel obligated to please the attorney for whom you are working, especially if she is paying you a hefty fee, your primary obligation is to communicate the scientific truth. Partial results aren't truth if the missing piece would substantively temper the conclusion. An example might be including a suspect as the source of some bloodstains on a garment without mentioning that he is excluded from other stains on the same garment. Intentionally providing results without mentioning the relevant limitations is misleading at best, unethical at worst. This is exemplified by the stereotypical example of stating that two hairs "match" without mentioning that the discrimination power of this test is low and the proportion of errors relatively high. This must be tempered with the understanding that the expert can only answer questions that are put to her. As frustrating as it is, all experts have had the experience of being stymied either by opposing counsel, or even by their own attorney, from providing the best answer to the question.

You take an oath to "tell the truth, the whole truth, and nothing but the truth." It is useful to remember that this really means the truth, which may or may not be the same as any one person's view of justice. You only have control over what you say; you have no control over how either attorney uses those words, or how the judge or jury interprets them. And sometimes, you don't even have complete control over what you are allowed to say.

8.   Navigating the Testimonial Wilderness — Pitfalls, Traps, and Ambushes

Although we cannot make a complete study of all the possible uncomfortable situations in which you might find yourself as an expert witness, we highlight a few common situations that arise with some regularity.

a.   Reasonable Certainty

Because the law works in absolutes, while science provides anything but, the never-ending struggle is for scientists to render their opinion in a way that is useful to the layperson in making a decision about guilt or innocence. In medical testimony, the phrase *to a reasonable medical certainty* is often used to convey the idea that, although we can never positively prove that the victim was killed by the third bullet, the pathologist's expert opinion carries enough weight that the trier of fact may accept it as true. From the medical model has come the phrase *to a reasonable scientific certainty.* Both the judicial system and some experts have latched onto this phrase as a convenient way to render an opinion as fact. As convenient as it might be, it is a *nonsequitor.* As we have repeatedly discussed throughout this book, the notion of scientific certainty does not exist. In our opinion, scientific experts should refrain from resorting to that phraseology in expressing their opinions.

b. Know What You Did

You must be intimately familiar with your contributions to the case. Never testify to what you think you would normally do in general practice if you aren't explicitly sure you did it in this case. In *Simpson,* an expert testified that he always wore gloves when handling evidence samples at a crime scene. The defense followed that testimony with a videotape of the witness grasping a piece of evidence with his bare hands (*People v. Simpson,* April 11). The credibility of the witness was effectively destroyed by that simple demonstration of his apparent lack of appreciation for specifics.

c. Knowing When to Say "I Don't Know"

It is not an uncommon cross-examination strategy for an attorney to play on every human being's natural tendency to want to provide an answer to every question. The best strategy to avoid being caught in this particular net is to have firmly in mind the limits of both the evidence in the case and the tests employed, as well as the limits of your own personal knowledge. Knowing when to say "I don't know" is just as important as knowing the correct answers to those questions for which they exist. Clever attorneys will evoke a string of "I don't knows" from a witness in an effort to convince those listening that he isn't the expert he claims to be. Regardless of how stupid you are starting to feel, the correct answer is still "I don't know" when you don't know.

d. Yes or No

Most experts have, at one time or another, been confronted with opposing counsel insisting that they limit their answer to "yes" or "no." As we mentioned previously, the *U.S. Federal* (and *Uniform*) *Rules of Evidence* explicitly permit expert witnesses to explain their answers. Although many states follow those guidelines, some jurisdictions may not. Either way, you may still find an judge who will rule that you cannot explain your answer. A sometimes effective rejoinder is to state that you cannot answer the question as asked without misleading the jury. Other times it is best simply to pick the lesser of the two evils and make sure that your attorney allows you to explain on re-direct.

e. Agreement by Default

One tactic of creative attorneys is to repeat your last statement with their own spin on it as a prelude to asking another question. If you allow the statement to stand, it appears as though you agree with it. If you try to correct the misstatement, you may seem argumentative. Without the help of an alert attorney and a sympathetic judge, there is, unfortunately, little you can do about this type of tactic.

f. Demeanor of the Expert

The demeanor of the expert plays a large role in the perception of his testimony by the judge and jury. In addition to maintaining professional (read that conservative with no apology) attire, the expert should be polite and accord the proper respect to the judge, attorneys on both sides of the bench, and also to the jury. Remember that, although experts are being paid for their services (either by a salary or fee), jury members are more or less volunteering their time to provide a civil service. Because they will make the final decision in most cases that go to trial, you want them at least receptive enough to consider your testimony seriously.

Sarcasm and intentional obfuscation may be the fastest way to get your testimony either dismissed or ignored. In a DNA admissibility hearing, the expert, in a reaction to having been hammered for many days on the stand, testified that "PCR can be done in a barn." Out of several weeks of testimony, this was the phrase that the judge remembered when it came time to write his opinion. The credibility of the expert was seriously undermined and his thoughtless remarks were a large (if unfounded) contributing factor to the judge's final decision not to admit evidence analyzed by the new methodology.

In another example of condescending testimony during an admissibility hearing the witness was asked:

Q: In your laboratory did you do any studies to compare PGM and DNA sensitivities in terms of —

A. Again, that's a different — you compare different thing. You say I compare your intelligence with my intelligence. That's not a legitimate comparison [sic].

g. Review Your Testimony

As painful as it is, regular review of your testimony can be very helpful in improving it. Most laboratories have a testimony monitoring program where a supervisor or one of your peers provides a critique after listening to live testimony. When transcripts are available, reading over your own testimony can enlighten you in terms of what you said as opposed to what you thought you said. In a situation, such as a deposition, where you are required actually to sign the transcript, it would be remiss not to review the document thoroughly before signing it to make sure your words were transcribed correctly.

B. Expressing Opinions — How Far Should the Analyst Go?

Throughout this book, we've related a number of concepts that justify the expression of an opinion by a qualified expert.

1. A scientific hypothesis can never be proved; we can only fail to disprove it (Popper, 1962).
2. In a Bayesian framework, we can compare the relative likelihood of competing hypotheses.
3. A conclusion of individuality can never be proved; we can only become convinced of it (Stoney, 1991).
4. A forensic scientist with appropriate education, training, and experience is the person best qualified to interpret scientific evidence, form a conclusion about it, and provide an opinion about its significance in the context of the case.
5. The law provides for the introduction of opinion evidence based on inferences by qualified experts (*Federal Rules of Evidence*).

The criminalist is not only justified in rendering an opinion, he is obligated to do so. This will commonly be an opinion concerning source determination, but, when appropriate, the qualified examiner may also speak to an inference of contact (association) or reconstruction. Because we provide a service to a group of people who are unable to understand our results for themselves, we must interpret the results for them and form a conclusion, often expressed in the form of an opinion. In simplifying the examination or analysis such that its import can be easily understood by the laypersons who fulfill the roles of counsel, judge, and jury, some technical accuracy is necessarily lost. Throughout this book, we have discussed how the forensic scientist must translate the legal question into a scientific question that can be answered by examining or analyzing physical evidence. Finally, the process must be reversed. The expert proffering the opinion is responsible for translating the scientific answers back into a form that is useful and understandable by the trier of fact.

C. Summary

We've spent this chapter exploring the different ways that forensic casework results are disseminated and communicated. The written report represents the final work product of the criminalist and, as such, must be complete and accurate. A scientific conclusion must be present, and any applicable limitations explicitly stated. This conclusion must also be summarized in a form that the layperson can understand. The culmination of our work on a case may be testimony in a court of law. Here, scientists must straddle the boundary between science and the law, a sometimes uncomfortable and precarious position. Realizing that he does not always have complete control, the criminalist's goal is to communicate his conclusions about the physical evidence as completely and accurately as possible.

References

Daubert v. Merrell Dow Pharmaceuticals, 509 U.S. 579, 1993.

Federal Rules of Evidence, Legal Information Institute, Cornell Law School, available at *http://www.law.cornell.edu/rules/fre/overview.html.*

Frye v. United States, 54 App. D.C. 46, 47, 293 F. 1013, 1014, 1923.

Heinlein, R. A., *Stranger in a Strange Land*, Ace Books, New York, 1961.

Kumho Tire Co. v. Carmichael, 526 U.S. 137, 1999.

People v. Simpson, CNN trial transcripts, available at *http://www.cnn.com/US/OJ/trial/.*

Popper, K. R., *Conjectures and Refutations: The Growth of Scientific Knowledge*, Basic Books, New York, 1962.

Stoney, D. A., What made us ever think we could individualize using statistics? *J. Forensic Sci. Soc.*, 3(2), 197–199, 1991.

Uniform Rules of Evidence, University of Pennsylvania Law School, available at *http://www.law.upenn.edu/bll/ulc/fnact99/ure88.html.*

Webster's Encyclopedic Unabridged Dictionary of the English Language, Gramercy Books, New York, 1996.

Zeppa, J. E., The primary examiner, paper presented at the Spring meeting of the California Association of Criminalists, Oakland, CA, 1999.

Ethics and Accountability — The Profession of Forensic Science

12

Figure 12.1 The profession of forensic science. A sampling of organizations committed to the ethical practice of criminalistics. (The CAC logo is a registered service mark of the California Association of Criminalists and is used with permission; use of the CAC logo does not imply endorsement of products or services, or opinions expressed herein. The ABC, IAI, AFTE, ABFDE, and NWAFS logos are used with permission; their use does not imply endorsement of products or services, or opinions expressed herein. The AAFS was unable to consider our request to use their logo because of a written policy that expressly precludes outside use of any kind.)

If the law has made you a witness, remain a man of science, you have no victim to avenge, no guilty or innocent person to convict or save — you must bear testimony within the limits of science.

Dr. P. C. Brouardel
—19th-century French medicolegalist

Almost 40 years ago, Dr. Paul Kirk asked, "Is criminalistics a profession?" (Kirk, 1963).

This is a difficult question to answer because the nature of a profession itself is not well characterized. Medicine and the law represent the traditional norms of the professions, but in popular usage, the word is loosely applied to almost any habitual occupation. We speak of the "oldest profession", and of the "professional housepainter" as distinguished from the amateur. Similarly, in golf and other sports the "pro" is sharply distinguished from the amateur. It seems clear that most informed persons recognize the difference between a true profession and what is only a vocation. The burgeoning of professional colleges in our universities has given respectability to the inclusion of numerous activities in the ranks of the professions, this move having followed careful scrutiny of the activity in question by learned men. The criteria generally applied by the universities would appear sufficient for a determination of status. Three basic criteria seem to apply:

1. A profession is based on an extensive period of training at a high educational level. In general, university or college work of considerable duration is necessary to qualify in the recognized professions. Far too slowly, but at a finite rate, the universities and colleges are beginning to offer training that may be considered at a professional level in criminalistics. Much progress in this direction is needed.
2. A profession is characterized by some generally recognized and accepted code of behavior or ethics. In the words of Vannever Bush, the professional must "minister to the people." The professional is in some degree set apart from the layman, and he must accept his responsibilities as he

exercises his prerogatives. The California Association of Criminalists has adopted a code of ethics as complete as could ever be required of any profession. Thus, a start has been made in meeting this essential requirement of professional activity. As a rule, even those practitioners not bound by any official code of ethics tend to be objective, fair and just in their relations to the people and the law. The exceptions are not more glaring than those in many of the established professions. It seems fair to state that criminalistics is inherently in accord with the principles of the recognized professions in this regard and may properly be considered to meet this requirement.

3. A profession requires established competence. This requirement may seem to be subsidiary to (1) Above. Actually this is not necessarily true. Graduates of medical schools may not immediately practice without being examined by a licensing board. Schools which claim to train in criminalistics may fall far short of their stated objectives, since there is no way of checking on the quality of their offerings. Even when satisfactory courses are available, there is no guarantee that a student who has passed these courses is ready to assume professional practice. Whether licensing, certification, or some other indication attesting a person's competence is adopted ultimately, there is a present no method of assuring the quality of practice by any individual except as the courts qualify him as an expert witness. As every witness knows, this process is not immune to error, nor is it uniform from jurisdiction to jurisdiction, or even from one court to another. There is great need for serious consideration of this problem, and for application of more uniform criteria of qualification. Despite the limitations still apparent in this relatively new field, the practice of criminalistics is clearly meeting the requirements of a professional discipline.

Although the above excerpt from Kirk's 1963 monograph, *The Ontogeny of Criminalistics*, perhaps reflected his hopes for the profession rather than the current reality, the three main criteria that he sets forth for an academically based profession, *formal education*, a *code of ethics*, and *demonstration of competency*, remain even today as defining factors. In this chapter, we consider each in turn.

A.   Educational Perspectives

In the second edition of *Forensic Science* (Davies, 1986), in a chapter on forensic education, Ralph Turner* asks, "Is forensic science education developing in an orderly and well-planned fashion?" In answer to this query, he

* School of Criminal Justice, Michigan State University.

notes that "the profession has advanced rapidly in the past decade, and education must have played an important role. The advancement, however, has probably not occurred in an orderly fashion." He mentions that criminalistics programs reached their peak in the 1970s and were, even then, declining. He laments the lack of a new generation of educators to fill the positions vacated by those who have retired, and in many cases are no longer with us. In the 15 years since Mr. Turner reviewed the state of forensic education, it has continued to decline. This has been to the detriment of the profession.

1. Programs in Forensic Science vs. Criminalistics

Education is one area where we cannot afford to tread lightly for fear of political incorrectness or offense. The requirements of those who examine or analyze physical evidence in a crime laboratory differ substantially from those who concentrate on crime investigation. They also differ from those who remain in the academic realm, and even from those who choose to work in the industrial or clinical arena. Now, more than ever, the onslaught of technology obligates the criminalist to draw on a strong background in the physical sciences, including an understanding of statistics and logic. The scientific background cannot be only theoretical, it must include copious laboratory experience. For laboratory exercises to be most useful, the problems that students are asked to solve must move past the standard chemistry and biology laboratory exercises into the more thought-provoking, and often unanswerable, questions likely to be encountered in forensic casework.

Although a number of programs can be found that list themselves as forensic science programs, a closer look shows that majority of these programs, be they at the undergraduate or graduate level, provide only a general curriculum most appropriate for an overview or introduction to forensic science in the broadest sense. Rarely are they combined with a rigorous physical science curriculum, including laboratory work. For this reason, many laboratory directors prefer to hire someone with a strong science and laboratory background over an individual with, in particular, a terminal undergraduate forensic science degree (Siegal, 1988). A 1986 survey showed that the educational background most preferred for a career in forensic science would consist of a B.S. degree with a major chemistry component, and an M.S. in forensic science (Siegal, 1988). A similar survey conducted more than a decade later indicated similar preferences. A survey taken in 1996 also concluded that those responsible for hiring are more interested in specific coursework than a named degree, perhaps in direct response to the lack of uniformity in forensic science program requirements (Furton et al., 1999).

This situation is truly unfortunate. As we have emphasized throughout this book, we believe strongly that criminalistics rests on a unique philosophy and framework of fundamental principles. A strong educational network would do much to strengthen, promulgate, disseminate, and continue to challenge the academic underpinnings of our profession.

a. Generalist Background

Although there is no turning back from the fact that specialization is here to stay, that does not relieve any one of us from the responsibility of understanding how our particular discipline fits with the other evidence into the case as a whole. A DNA analyst may not be able to place two bullets into the holders on a comparison microscope and proffer an expert opinion whether or not they were fired from the same gun, but she should understand the theoretical basis of the tests and the limitations on the conclusions from the examination. As a practical matter, she should be able to read a firearms examination report and have a pretty good idea of what it means. Unless one comes up through the ranks in a full-service laboratory, it's not a simple matter to acquire this generalist background once one starts working. It is not impossible, but it does require a measure of dedication and discipline. A more realistic approach is to include this information as part of a complete criminalistics program, along with the necessary physical science courses and associated laboratory work. As a minimum or interim solution, a criminalistics specialization could be offered as a fifth year after a more standard university curriculum. A certification program in criminalistics might culminate in the opportunity to take the General Knowledge Exam (GKE) offered by the American Board of Criminalistics (ABC). We will discuss the idea of analyst certification itself later in this chapter.

b. Graduate Education in Criminalistics

At present not one graduate program exists in the United States that specifically culminates in a named doctorate in criminalistics or forensic science. In fact, we are aware of only two institutions worldwide* that offer such a degree. To be sure, a number of universities provide for the possibility of completing a doctoral thesis on a forensically related topic, but this lacks the formal structure and community of a named degree program. Only a few master's programs exist that truly provide the opportunity to perform advanced research relating to a problem in criminalistics. Because it is possible to earn a degree called "Masters in Forensic Science" without ever

---

* University of Strathclyde, Glasgow, Scotland, United Kingdom and Institut de Police Scientifique et de Criminologie de l'Université de Lausanne, Switzerland.

having set foot in a laboratory or even having taken a core curriculum of hard science classes, the degree has been diluted to the extent that no one is sure what it means any more. This is unfortunate because those few programs that do offer a true criminalistics degree find it hard to distinguish themselves.

In the 1986 edition of *Forensic Science* (Davies), Kathleen Higgins, then of the College of (also now defunct) Criminal Justice at Northeastern University wrote a chapter entitled "Graduate Education, Forensic Science's Answer to the Future." She says:

> Training in criminalistics in the early 1950s seemed to be headed toward a unified scientific and professional program with a tremendous potential for further development. However, it has literally died in its own tracks (the number of graduate programs decreased from 12 in 1976 to 10 in 1984 and 9 in 1985), and because of a failure of implementation in facilities and faculty, a "turnoff" of research and development has occurred.
>
> In 1976, Joseph Peterson and Peter DeForest reported:
>
> Forensic science faces no problem more pressing than the education and training of the scientists who staff the nation's forensic laboratories. If one examines the critical research needs of the profession, the shortage of truly qualified laboratory scientists and supervisors, or the crisis of overwhelming caseloads and backlogs, one finds that the most essential element in satisfying these needs is a core of scientifically qualified personnel. Again, when the need for maintaining high quality control (assurance) standards or for developing high ethical awareness among the professionals is under discussion, we inevitably find that laboratory personnel and the quality of their educational backgrounds are the main focus.
>
> And now, 9 years later, everything Peterson and DeForest said is still fully applicable and embodies the basic needs of the profession.

As Higgins refers to Peterson and DeForest, we continue the lament. The future she predicts is now here, and we are in worse shape than ever with regard to graduate education in forensic science.

Although sophisticated instrumentation is now routinely employed in forensic analyses, and the technical complexity of the examinations performed continues to increase, this is not our main concern. A reasonably bright technician can reliably perform a competent instrumental analysis; advanced degrees are not needed for this aspect of the work. It is the interpretation of the data from those complex examinations that increasingly requires a complete and subtle understanding of the principles underlying the instrumentation, and the impact of many layers of electronics, hardware, and software on the final data. And, precisely because the laboratory work has become so refined, the questions regarding forensic evidence must shift to the areas of logical inference, statistical probabilities, and subtle interpretive issues. In our opinion, these areas of inquiry lie at the heart of criminalistics regardless of how the data are obtained. Graduate education provides the opportunity to learn how to formulate questions and solve problems in addition to acquiring specific laboratory skills. The diverse and distinctive nature of the problems presented by forensic casework requires an educational specialization, and at a high level.

A well-known medical talk show host answered a caller's question about a physician assistant performing some minor surgery. He said that the critical decision that the doctor needed to make was what procedure needed to be performed, and if surgery was the most appropriate option. The actual procedure, he maintained, was quite routine and could well be competently performed by a technical-level person. We can draw an exact parallel from this medical example to forensic science. The criminalist's most important job is to decide what evidence should be examined, using which analyses and, in fact, whether any analysis would be useful in answering the legal questions posed in the case. The knowledge to make the critical preliminary decisions regarding the evidence, and to interpret the final results thoughtfully, is what forensic science is all about; this is what forensic education should emphasize.

c.   *Academic Resources*

The last point in the realm of forensic education is that of research and development. One of the reasons for the longer than necessary lag time between a new scientific development and its adaptation for forensic use is simply a lack of time and resources. In the most efficient working crime laboratory, the case backlog may occasionally ebb, but it never recedes completely. A delicate balancing act always exists between clearing current cases and developing the technology to process future cases more efficiently and with better reliability and enhanced discrimination. Most professions rely on graduate research programs to provide a wellspring for new ideas, and to develop novel scientific breakthroughs to the point where they have practical application. Both undergraduate and graduate students provide the perfect vehicle for large comprehensive studies, screens, and validation. This lack of academic support continues to hamper the progress of criminalistics severely.

The emergence, or perhaps reemergence, and maintenance of forensic science as an autonomous branch of academic knowledge, and its recognition as a true and respected profession, depend on a strong educational and academic component. In spite of the valiant efforts of a few individuals who continue to maintain quality criminalistics programs, an adequate and comprehensive academic framework does not exist. The forensic community would do well to make this a priority (Stoney, 2000).

d. Apprenticeship

In addition to formal education and laboratory experience, some kind of apprenticeship is appropriate before a practitioner takes on independent casework. No amount of simulated casework truly prepares one for the real thing; working cases under the direct mentorship of an experienced colleague remains the best induction into the field.

B.   Demonstration of Competency

We began this book with a description of the "state of the practice" and a historical perspective on how that state came to be. Because the early forensic scientists were more or less lone practitioners of a yet-to-be-recognized discipline, each felt a pioneer of sorts. While this was certainly true a century or even half a century ago, this trail-blazing mentality is no longer appropriate. The profession has survived a rather tumultuous adolescence and has achieved young adulthood, if not quite maturity. Government laboratories abound, private laboratories are increasing, and both the courts and the public now expect the presentation of scientific evidence in every trial.

With this increased exposure comes increased scrutiny. Although the movement toward acquiring the accoutrements of professionalization began around the middle of the century (Appendix A), it was not until the 1990s that it really gained momentum. This was, at least in part, a reaction to suggestions of government regulation of forensic activities, instigated by the advent of DNA technology along with its potential power for both use and abuse. While the acceptance of the need for accountability has been slow, the community has finally come to grips with the reality of that necessity. We will describe several programs that have been developed from within the forensic community to provide a means for both laboratories and individuals to demonstrate competency and adherence to minimum standards.

1.   Certification

A certification program for general criminalistics has been a long time in coming. It was not until 1993 that a certification examination in criminalistics was nationally available. Interestingly, only a certification program for questioned documents examiners was, in the 1970s, implemented prior to the general examination.*

---

* Document examination is not always considered part of criminalistics. The AAFS, for instance, maintains a separate section for this specialty.

a.   Philosophy of Certification

The American Board of Criminalistics (ABC), under whose auspices the criminalistics certification program resides, supports the philosophy that forensic scientists must have a broad understanding of many aspects of forensic science. To this end the General Knowledge Exam (GKE) was developed. According to the ABC (see ABC in reference list):

> The ABC Board's goal for the GKE was to develop a process that answers the question, "Does this person have sufficient knowledge to be able to competently perform the work typically encountered by forensic scientists?" With the assistance of professional testing agencies, an examination was developed to answer that question.
>
> Criminalists must examine evidence within the context of an entire case. They are often the only scientist associated with an investigation, and must have sufficient knowledge and experience to make appropriate recommendations to investigators and attorneys.
>
> The purpose of the specialized examinations conducted is to piece together the crime, and a path to the perpetrator(s). Examiners do not work in isolation. What they do can, and will, impact what "pieces of the puzzle" other examiners can add, or light they can shine on the "path."
>
> The GKE sets a standard for professional knowledge needed to examine evidence within the context of an entire case. Forensic science does not have a standardized academic curriculum that the profession can rely on to teach the basic criminalistics that every examiner needs. This makes the need for obtaining and measuring that knowledge even more critical for our profession.
>
> This broad knowledge is a solid foundation for examiners to develop specialized understanding and skills. This is analogous to the approach taken with all science (i.e., B.S. before Ph.D. or physician before surgeon). This knowledge foundation facilitates thorough evidence analysis because the examiner is aware of what other tests might be done, their limitations or requirements, and how his/her action or inaction can affect the total forensic investigation. Using this broader knowledge, forensic scientists are better able to maximize evidentiary value and to avoid compromising/contaminating samples.

The written GKE examination is the first segment of a comprehensive certification program. Those who achieve a passing score on the GKE receive *Diplomate* status (D-ABC). To achieve *Fellow* status (F-ABC), the analyst must additionally pass another written specialty examination and also take and pass laboratory proficiency tests at prescribed intervals. As of this writing, specialty examinations are available in drug identification, forensic biology (including DNA), fire debris analysis, and trace evidence. We expect that specialty examinations in other areas will continue to be developed.

b. History of Certification

The ABC program is based in large part on the work done by the Criminalistics Certification Study Committee (CCSC). From 1975 to 1979, more than 25 individuals from all regions of the United States and Canada, representing many disciplines, all regional associations, and a diverse array of laboratories participated in the CCSC. Under the auspices of a National Institute of Justice (NIJ) grant, they studied and deliberated over the problems associated with testing and certification, and surveyed the profession on its views. Failing a majority vote by the members of professional associations polled, no certification program was implemented by the CCSC.

Building on the CCSC work and philosophy, the California Association of Criminalists (CAC) developed a certification program in the late 1980s. The initial stage of the CAC program was the development of an examination designed to assess the overall competence of certification candidates. Those candidates who passed the examination, and who met other professional requirements, were issued a Certificate of Professional Competency in Criminalistics. The CAC program recognized the inevitable trend toward specialization, but maintained a strong commitment to a solid foundation in the full range of criminalistics.

In 1989, the need for certification again encroached on the national consciousness, and the ABC was incorporated for the purpose of developing a national certification program. In 1991, a liaison with the American Society of Crime Laboratory Directors (ASCLD) was established, and, in 1992, the American Association of Forensic Science (AAFS) Criminalistics Section voted to join ABC. In 1993, the first GKE, based on the examination originally developed by the CAC, was offered at the Boston AAFS meeting and the first diplomate certificates were awarded later that year. In 1994, the first specialty examinations were offered at the San Antonio AAFS meeting, resulting in the first fellow certificates issued. In that same year, a proficiency testing program was also implemented and the ABC newsletter initiated. At this writing, over 450 people have been awarded ABC diplomate status. The number grows every year with approximately 50 people per year sitting for the GKE. Over 130 people have passed ABC Specialty Examinations and have been awarded fellow status.

As this book goes to press, the ABC has just announced the availability of a "Technical Specialist" examination. The examination was developed in response to a perceived need for those who perform only DNA or drug analyses. The argument was put forth that these workers neither have nor need a complete generalist background to perform their jobs adequately in the context of a case investigation. The examination will comprise a "Specialty Examination Component" and a "Forensic Science Core" set of questions reflecting essential knowledge, skills, and abilities of forensic scientists practicing in that specialized discipline. The technical specialist must already be performing the analyses and show a record of passing proficiency tests (Selavka, 1999). It remains to be seen how many people will take advantage of this examination, just how a Technical Specialist certification will be perceived in relation to diplomate or fellow status, and whether technical specialist examinations for other disciplines will follow.

c.   Proficiency Testing

The laboratory component of certification has been incorporated as proficiency testing. Current standards require that a working analyst complete a blind external proficiency test once a year. Proficiency testing complements the written certification examination in that it demonstrates a minimum level of competence. This is a concrete way that a laboratory and an analyst may demonstrate to the lay world that they can perform the work with skill and accuracy. It should be noted, however, that the very nature of proficiency testing (the need for the provider to produce many identical samples) precludes it from testing any but the most minimal analytical and interpretation skills. Also at issue is the question of how to establish reliability and consistency among the test samples themselves. Regardless of the difficulty of producing and disseminating such a test, the benefits to the profession and to the criminal justice system are worthy of the effort.

2.   Accreditation

While certification addresses the competency of individual examiners, accreditation is concerned with the larger scope of the laboratory in which the criminalist works. Accreditation relates to laboratory-wide issues such as evidence handling, validation, and institution of proper scientific protocols, education and training, proficiency testing programs, and case review procedures. Laboratory accreditation is provided under the auspices of the ASCLD. The program is managed and the standards established by the ASCLD Laboratory Accreditation Board (ASCLD/LAB), which is responsible to a delegate assembly composed of the directors of all accredited laboratories.

a.   Philosophy of Accreditation

ASCLD/LAB has adopted four official accreditation objectives to define the purpose and nature of the program:

1. To improve the quality of laboratory services provided to the criminal justice system.
2. To develop and maintain criteria which can be used by a laboratory to assess its level of performance and to strengthen its operation.

3. To provide an independent, impartial, and objective system by which laboratories can benefit from a total operational review.
4. To offer to the general public and to users of laboratory services a means of identifying those laboratories which have demonstrated that they meet established standards.

Like individual certification, an outside review for accreditation serves to identify criteria that can be used by a laboratory to assess its level of performance and improve its operations. It is also an impartial means by which those that depend on the laboratory's services, as well as the general public, can ascertain that a particular laboratory meets established standards. To qualify for accreditation, the laboratory must demonstrate that it meets the standards for management, operations, personnel, procedures, equipment, physical plant, security, and health and safety procedures. The laboratory analysts must also participate in a regular proficiency testing program. Accreditation is granted for 5 years, provided that a laboratory continues to meet the standard during this period. Both the initial accreditation, and reaccreditation on a 5-year cycle, require a full review of the laboratory including an on-site inspection.

Most recently, other organizations, notably the National Forensic Science Technology Center (NFSTC), headquartered in Florida, have begun to offer accreditation services. A new challenge will be to normalize the standards proffered by the various organizations offering accreditation, and to institute a means of establishing credibility for the accrediting bodies.

b. History of Accreditation

Although the issue of laboratory accreditation has achieved public notoriety only in the last decade or so, the crime laboratories themselves began to address the issue more than a quarter of a century ago. In the fall of 1973, a small group of about 30 crime laboratory directors from around the country met in Quantico, Virginia. A steering committee was formed and a constitution was drafted. In the fall of 1974 the ASCLD was born. One of the early committees appointed by ASCLD was the committee on laboratory evaluation and standards. The committee considered both certification and accreditation programs as a means to evaluate and improve the quality of laboratory operations. In 1981, a program of laboratory accreditation was approved by ASCLD, and the committee eventually became the ASCLD/LAB. In 1982, the eight laboratories of the Illinois State Police became the first laboratories accredited by ASCLD/LAB. As of June 1999, 182 laboratories worldwide have become accredited.

3.   Regulation and Enforcement

At present, both analyst certification and laboratory accreditation are voluntary and self-regulated. Neither laboratory accreditation nor analyst certification is required, but community and peer pressure to provide documentation of individual competency and a laboratory-wide quality assurance program is increasing. We fully expect that within the next decade, if not sooner, both certification and accreditation will be made mandatory for those who analyze evidence and produce a work product. What has not begun to be addressed is whether scientists whose sole involvement is to interpret the work of others, notably many independent consultants, should be required to demonstrate the same level of competency as the analyst who performed the work. Interestingly, the forensic science profession has absolutely no control over this issue; it is a matter totally within the purview of the courts.

C.   Ethics

The third and final defining characteristic of a profession is a written *code of ethics*. It is incumbent upon the forensic science community as a whole to monitor its members. As a group, those involved in forensic science on a daily basis are the best qualified to set analytical and ethical standards, and to judge the veracity of an opinion; they also have the most to lose if an analyst commits abuses that reflect on the forensic community as a whole. Peer pressure is often the most effective method of ensuring ethical conduct; however, peers must be willing to challenge each other for this to work.

1.   Codes of Ethics

One definition of *ethics* is:

> The rules of conduct recognized in respect to a particular class of human actions or a particular group, culture, etc.: medical ethics; Christian ethics (*Webster's Unabridged*, 1996).

In other words, individuals that choose to associate themselves with a particular group make a personal decision to abide by the rules of conduct espoused by that community. These rules of conduct are, by definition, codified into a written code of ethics along with instructions for enforcement. Specifications for determining whether a member has committed an ethical violation, and specific direction regarding the consequences of that violation, must accompany the code. The community must have both the means and the courage to enforce its code of ethics.

a. Morals and Ethics

People frequently confuse morals and ethics. Both describe codes of behavior. However, they differ in their origin and application. Each of us defines our own moral code, the rules by which we choose to live. A personal moral code encompasses each individual's understanding of "right" and "wrong." Individuals may choose a set of morals that have been codified as part of organized religion, or they may create their own set of morals or lack thereof.

Webster's (1996) distinguishes morals from ethics in this way:

> Morals refers to generally accepted customs of conduct and right living in a society, and to the individual's practice in relation to these: the morals of our civilization. Ethics now implies high standards of honest and honorable dealing, and of methods used, especially in the professions or in business: ethics of the medical profession.

Ethics and morals do not necessarily intersect. An individual might be highly moral, according to her own personal code, and still violate some particular rule of ethics. Conversely, someone might act immorally, by his own standards or someone else's, and remain in compliance with a specific ethical code.

2.   Codes of Ethics for Forensic Science

Numerous professional forensic organizations have adopted codes of ethics (Appendices B, C, D). Although the creation of ethical codes for the profession of forensic science is a step in the right direction, several problems remain. First, the existence of multiple codes of ethics for a single profession creates discord and confusion. Which set of standards should a criminalist choose? To which code should she be held? Second, the working criminalist is not required to accept *any* ethical code. Should he be? Finally, one may engage in the practice of forensic science without a prerequisite membership in the profession. Should those who examine evidence be required to join the profession formally? What about those who opine on evidence and cases, particularly in a court of law, but do not otherwise practice the profession?

a.   Which Code?

The most basic ethical considerations in forensic science (and other applied sciences) are shared with the academic sciences. These include but are not limited to:

1. Accurate representation of qualifications
2. True and accurate representation of data

3. Clear and complete documentation*
4. Reporting of colleagues who violate the profession's ethical code

Others considerations are specific to forensic science because of the special nature of our interaction with the justice system. These include but are not limited to:

1. Maintaining the integrity of the evidence
2. Impartiality of the examiner
3. Limitations on conclusions
4. Limitations on the examiner's expertise
5. Confidentiality and disclosure
6. Exculpatory evidence
7. Testimony
8. Fees**

The two codes of ethics espoused by the national forensic organizations, the ABC and the AAFS, and the various regional codes, differ from each other considerably. At one extreme, the AAFS code of ethics contains only four points, two of which concern themselves with the interests of the organization. The two parts of the code that actually concern the everyday activities of the practitioner cover the fundamental areas of misrepresentation of credentials or misrepresentation of data (Appendix B):

1. Every member of the AAFS shall refrain from providing any material misrepresentation of education, training, experience, or area of expertise. Misrepresentation of one or more criteria for membership in the AAFS shall constitute a violation of this section of the code.
2. Every member of the AAFS shall refrain from providing any material misrepresentation of data upon which an expert opinion or conclusion is based.

At the other end of the spectrum lies the CAC code of ethics which contains very specific instructions in the areas of:

1. Ethics relating to scientific method
2. Ethics relating to opinions and conclusions
3. Ethical aspects of court presentation

---

* Although clear and complete documentation is a cornerstone of academic science, its implementation in forensic science varies widely. In our opinion, the same high standard should apply.
** The special consideration for forensic work refers to refraining from working on contingency rather than imposing any limit other than "reasonable" on the fees actually charged.

4. Ethics relating to the general practice of criminalistics
5. Ethical responsibilities to the profession.

The CAC code (Appendix D) is extremely specific, and has been updated twice from its original 1957 version, the last time in 1985. The ABC code was derived from the CAC version, and is intermediate in length and specificity. It contains 18 points, one of which concerns itself with the interests of the organization. Each regional code is also slightly different.

No question exists that the greatest number of forensic scientists are members of the AAFS and presumably subscribe to its code of ethics. Membership in the AAFS, which includes virtually all of the forensic disciplines, criminalistics being just one section, requires only a couple of recommendations from current members, payment of yearly dues, and the satisfaction of some fairly minimal professional requirements. Most regional organizations have similar requirements, although the demonstration of active participation in the profession may, in some cases, be a bit more stringent. The only organization that requires a demonstration of professional knowledge is the ABC. Even to qualify to take the GKE examination, one must demonstrate an active and continuing participation in the profession of criminalistics, be sponsored by two members in good standing, and agree to abide by the ABC code of ethics. Predictably, the ABC membership is much smaller than that of the AAFS.

b. Membership in the Profession

Many, perhaps most, professions require actively practicing members to join the profession formally. This usually involves a demonstration of competence such as the bar exam for attorneys and the medical boards for physicians. The forensic profession is uncontrolled in that admission to the profession is not dictated by any formal process. For us to move forward in our recognition as a legitimate profession, we will need to require practitioners to join the profession and participate as peers.

However, the matter is complicated by the fact that this is not something totally under our control. Historically, forensic experts have been qualified by the courts under very different criteria than a group of peers might use. The legal requirements that permit experts to comment are quite minimal, often rest on academic credentials, and don't require witnesses actually to demonstrate any specific expertise in the subject about which they have been legally qualified to testify. The qualifying process is also completely up to a judge's discretion. Even if the profession, such as it is, begins to oversee its members actively, there is nothing to stop an attorney from calling any witness that he can qualify in a court of law. This is not a trivial matter. Historically, attorneys have been able to call any witness that they believe might assist their case. Defense attorneys, in particular, like to use witnesses from outside of the profession because they will more readily criticize forensic work.

It is not our intention to suggest that a scientist with only academic credentials and no forensic experience might not have some valuable insight into a forensic problem. For example, a fiber chemist from a manufacturing company might provide useful information regarding the chemical characteristics of a particular fiber, the amount manufactured, and its geographical distrubution. A molecular biologist who has participated in the development of a genetic typing system for a forensic application clearly has useful insight into its capabilities and limitations, and can testify regarding its reliability. Note, however, that in these examples, the scientist is testifying about his own specific area of expertise, rather than commenting directly on some work performed by a criminalist.

The question becomes more difficult when scientific experts who have no experience working in the forensic field are invited to comment directly on the forensic implications or interpretation of techniques or evidence. Courts have historically been quite lenient in permitting such testimony, in part because they are reluctant to deny the defense access to an expert. The question that must be asked in such cases goes beyond scientific qualification and enters the arena of ethics. What is the motivation behind the testimony of such experts? Do their suggestions that are intended to discredit some forensic work contain scientific merit, or is the goal simply to confuse, divert, or mislead. Do data exist to substantiate the issues proffered, or are the stated concerns vague and of no relevance to the particular case? (see Figure 11.2).

While we may never have complete control over who is allowed to offer expert testimony in a court of law, we can at least espouse and enforce minimum standards for those who examine and analyze evidence. If the profession sets and enforces a universal standard, and requires practitioners to join the profession, the court might follow our lead and ask other potential witnesses to meet this standard.

c. A Single Code of Ethics

In addition to requiring membership in a profession to practice, individuals are typically required to agree to the organization's code of ethics at the time of their induction. Frequently, this is incorporated into the knowledge examination, such as is done in medicine and law, and also by the ABC. A single code of ethics would unify the forensic profession. Multiple ethical standards make it too easy "code shop," and a lack of cohesiveness within the community lessens the influence of any one code, making it more acceptable to subscribe to no code. Apparent dissension also provides an easy target for outside criticism. However, it is unclear whose code should prevail and how this should be determined.

3.   When Ethics Fail

In every group, regardless of viewpoint, one or more individuals will inevitably decide that the end supersedes the means. At this juncture, even a code of ethics is insufficient to prevent the actions that follow from this decision. Whatever the agenda may be — convicting those we "know" are guilty, discrediting DNA analysis wholesale, or simply monetary profit — these people play by their own rules. Sometimes they act from maliciousness, sometimes from their perception of a greater good, sometimes from coercion or confusion. Whatever the intent, whatever the motivation, we know that unethical behavior occurs and, like laboratory contamination, we must do what we can to prevent it and, failing that, to detect and correct it.

Throughout this book, we have made a point of referring to criminalists or forensic scientists, rather than "prosecution experts" or "defense experts." This was done quite deliberately to emphasize that the science is the same, regardless of client or destination. However, at this juncture, we can no longer avoid the issue. Unscrupulous behavior by scientists frequently stems from choosing a "side" or being a "team player." As it so happens, the consequences of corrupt behavior by scientists working for the prosecution can be much more serious than that of a defense expert whose role is merely to comment on the work.

a.   Unethical Prosecution Experts

Because of the nature of the justice system, at least in the United States, crimes are charged by the prosecution, encumbering them with the burden of proof. However, this also gives the prosecution team the first chance at analyzing any physical evidence — or at destroying any possibility of analyzing it. Even should the defense choose to reanalyze some of the evidence, they accept it with choices that have already been made. These include decisions about collection, preservation, sampling, analysis, and consumption. There may simply be no evidence left to analyze. The consequent custodial responsibility of the scientists charged with the initial evidence evaluation and analysis also provides opportunities to mishandle, conceal, misrepresent, or otherwise manipulate the evidence or the data. The limited and ephemeral nature of forensic evidence provides few second opportunities for a full analysis. Additionally, the defense is usually lucky to find funding for an expert to review the data, never mind reanalyze the evidence, even if they suspect unscrupulous behavior. Finally, malevolent actions by prosecution scientists are more likely to result in a wrongful conviction of an innocent suspect than acquittal of a guilty one. For all of these reasons, the actions of unscrupulous prosecution experts typically have greater ramifications for the case, and ultimately the community, than those of defense experts.

Several scandals have erupted in recent years, including those perpetrated by Fred Zain at the West Virginia and Bexar County Crime laboratories (Sidebar 13) and by Allison Lancaster at the San Francisco Crime Laboratory (Zamora, 1994; 2000). Serious questions have also been raised regarding the internal workings of the FBI. The USDOJ/OIG Special Report documents instances of significant testimonial errors, substandard analytical work, and lack of requisite scientific qualifications for some examiners, in particular in the explosives section of the laboratory (Bromwich, 1997). While Zain and Lancaster have been taken out of commission, as a national government institution, the FBI continues to practice forensic science with a great amount of authority. While certain changes were made in response to the report, including rearrangement of personnel, the hiring of a new director, and acquiescence of the laboratory to accreditation, it is not clear if a true cultural revolution has occurred. It remains to be seen whether the serious criticisms that have been weathered as the millennium draws to a close will instigate a continuing evolution at the FBI laboratory.

b.   Unethical Defense Experts

A whole industry has been created by experts who limit themselves to defense work. Almost by definition, those who dismiss any possible value to forensic work wholesale cannot engage in it themselves, as the very performance of the works confers a measure of credibility. Independent laboratories do not generally fall into this category, as those who take both prosecution and defense work must accept the technology to at least the degree that the work is worth doing. Those who restrict themselves to commenting on the work of others need not labor under these restraints. Although "defense-only" consultants who work within ethical boundaries certainly exist and provide a valuable service to the defense community, the defense-only position is also a hallmark of those who engage in profiteering at the expense of the judicial system, legitimate forensic science, and, worst of all, the case. Because these "experts" don't perform analyses, they cannot influence a case by mishandling or destroying evidence. They can, however, waste an enormous amount of time and money, not to mention the seemingly endless annoyance and frustration they cause to legitimate workers and commentators on both sides. Worst of all, they occasionally succeed in introducing enough confusion and misinformation that legitimate work is either discredited or disregarded.

D.   Summary

Forensic laboratories must not only produce accurate, reliable, and unbiased analyses and interpretations, they must also convince the judicial system and

Sidebar 13

The Fred Zain Story — Crossing the Line

The unfortunate poster child for unethical conduct in forensic science is Fred Zain. However, it is important to realize that Mr. Zain, and others like him, do not exist in a vacuum. It took a whole system, from laboratory co-workers through the supervisors, to attorneys and the courts, to support, or at least ignore, the blatant and continued abuse that was perpetrated by Fred Zain over his decade and a half tenure as a forensic serologist in two public laboratories.

The story begins in about 1979, just after Zain was first hired by the West Virginia State Police as a serologist. It is impossible to say how it might have started — Zain himself could probably not say — but at some point during the 10 years he was to work for that agency, the means became only a barrier to the end. In the end, hundreds of cases worked by Zain would show an undeniable trend toward interpreting marginal or even nonexistent results so as to implicate a suspect.

The clues were there for any who chose to look. In the mid-1980s, two of Zain's co-workers allegedly filed a formal letter of complaint stating that they had routinely observed him reporting results from apparently blank enzyme plates. Nothing was done. They claim to have shown the blank plates and completed worksheets to Zain's supervisors. They were ignored. One employee would later testify that the fabricated result recorded on the worksheets always seemed to include the victim or suspect, in the correct pattern to inculpate the suspect. This pattern in Zain's work would later be confirmed by an independent investigatory group.

In 1989, Zain left West Virginia to become chief of physical evidence for the medical examiner in Bexar County, Texas. Interestingly, he continued to receive cases to analyze from prosecuting agencies in West Virginia. In several cases, items from which serologists at the West Virginia laboratory were unable to obtain results were sent to Zain in Texas. The prosecutors apparently preferred the results and interpretations that Zain was able to given them.

Suspicions about Zain's work finally came to the fore in 1992, when the rape conviction of Glen Woodall was overturned by DNA testing. In the original 1987 trial, Zain had testified that "the assailant's blood types … were identical to Mr. Woodall's." An independent expert would later say that Zain misrepresented and overstated the true significance of the results, but ironically, the serology results themselves were apparently not fabricated in this particular instance. Woodall's conviction was affirmed on appeal, but DNA testing done in a subsequent *habeas corpus* proceeding excluded Woodall from having contributed the semen evidence, simply because of its inherently better discrimination.

The review of the non-DNA evidence was probably more instrumental in first focusing suspicion on Zain. According to reports, Zain testified "he had no reason to believe" that a hair found in one rape victim's borrowed car "could not have originated from Mr. Woodall." Apparently, Zain initially described the sample as a pubic hair and only later testified that it was a beard hair. In addition, he reportedly never bothered to compare it with a hair sample from the man who owned the car. An independent expert later excluded Woodall as a possible source of the hair.

Following his release, Woodall sued the State of West Virginia for false imprisonment, thus initiating a chain of events that would culminate in criminal indictments of Fred Zain for perjury in both West Virginia and Texas. It began with an internal audit in 1992 that identified certain improprieties with respect to Zain's work, but, interestingly, concluded that "no material inclusion or exclusion errors were made," and culminated in an extraordinary investigation of the entire body of Zain's work as ordered by the West Virginia Supreme Court. In 1993, as part of that investigation, Barry Fisher, chairman of ASCLAD/LAB, was asked to organize a review of Zain's work by an independent group of forensic scientists. The two forensic serologists assigned to this task, James McNamara,

Laboratory Director of the Florida Department of Law Enforcement, and Ronald Linhart, Supervisor of Serology in the Crime Laboratory for the Los Angeles County Sheriff's Department, would eventually review hundreds of analyses. They would eventually find material problems in all 36 cases that they reviewed.

Holliday's investigative report listed 11 findings specifically regarding Zain's work:

> The acts of misconduct on the part of Zain included (1) overstating the strength of results; (2) overstating the frequency of genetic matches on individual pieces of evidence; (3) misreporting the frequency of genetic matches on multiple pieces of evidence; (4) reporting that multiple items had been tested, when only a single item had been tested; (5) reporting inconclusive results as conclusive; (6) repeatedly altering laboratory records; (7) grouping results to create the erroneous impression that genetic markers had been obtained from all samples tested; (8) failing to report conflicting results; (9) failing to conduct or to report conducting additional testing to resolve conflicting results; (10) implying a match with a suspect when testing supported only a match with the victim; and (11) reporting scientifically impossible or improbable results.

The reviewers also noted systematic deficiencies of a more general nature that allowed Zain to practice in the way that he did with no apparent checks or balances:

> (1) No written documentation of testing methodology; (2) no written quality assurance program; (3) no written internal or external auditing procedures; (4) no routine proficiency testing of laboratory technicians; (5) no technical review of work product; (6) no written documentation of instrument maintenance and calibration; (7) no written testing procedures manual; (8) failure to follow generally-accepted scientific testing standards with respect to certain tests; (9) inadequate record-keeping; and (10) failure to conduct collateral testing.

They concluded that:

> Irregularities were found in most of the cases reviewed in this investigation....

The 1993 West Virginia Investigative report concluded that:

> The overwhelming evidence of a pattern and practice of misconduct by Zain completely undermines the validity and reliability of any forensic work he performed or reported during his tenure in the serology department of the state police crime laboratory. If the information which is now available concerning the pattern and practice of misconduct by Zain had been available during the prosecution of cases in which he was involved, the evidence regarding the results of serological testing would have been deemed inadmissible.

So far, neither state has been successful in obtaining a conviction against Zain, due in part to statutes of limitations. West Virginia tried again in 1998 with charges that Zain had defrauded the state by accepting his salary and benefits while falsifying evidence and committing perjury. The charges were dismissed in January 1999, only to be resurrected by the State Supreme Court in November of the same year. The outcome is still pending. West Virginia has also launched a renewed investigation into the work of other serologists working contemporaneously with Zain who are also alleged to have fabricated test results.

At least nine men have been freed based on a postconviction review of evidence provided by Fred Zain, and many more are working their way through the system. Between West Virginia and Texas, over $5 million has already been paid to individuals suing the states for wrongful imprisonment.

While it is easy to criticize Fred Zain, an individual who was clearly led astray by motives at which we can only guess, we must also question the system that allowed Zain to exist for so long, in not only one, but two public laboratories, before he was finally exposed. Was it fear, ignorance, or apathy that prevented those in authority from taking action sooner? How can we foster a climate in which a Fred Zain would stick out like a sore thumb rather than blend seamlessly into the background? Identifying errant individuals can be accomplished with a reasonable amount of due diligence and vigilance. Changing the climate that produces and nurtures such individuals is the greater challenge.

Oversight comes in three different guises, and each functions at a different level in the process. Laboratory accreditation formalizes outside review of both procedures and case files; it can address the issue of institutional blindness. Analyst certification demonstrates minimal competence. More to the point, however, the organization in charge of administering certification examinations and proficiency testing, currently maintains the most specific and comprehensive ethical code of any national forensic organization, along with enforcement guidelines; individuals are required to agree to the code before they are allowed to take a certification examination. The most effective method of discouraging overinterpretation of borderline data, or even blatant falsification, however, remains review. A rigorous and objective internal review, with appropriate consideration of alternative hypothesis, and further review by an independent expert as the case demands, remains the best way of discouraging "interpretational drift" and identifying patent unethical conduct.

Zain, who was eventually fired from the Texas laboratory, now lives in Florida, and is no longer involved in crime laboratory work. He maintains his innocence.

References

Starrs, J. E., The seamy side of forensic science: the mephitic stain of Fred Salem Zain, *Sci. Sleuthing Rev.*, 17(4), 1993.

West Virginia Supreme Court Investigative Report on Fred Zain, available at *http://www.truthinjustice.org/zainreport.htm*.

Police Chemist Falsifies Huge Numbers of Rape Cases, AP wire, 1993, available at *http://www.vix.com/men/falsereport/cases/chemist.html*.

When experts lie, *Truth in Justice*, available at *http://truthinjustice.org/expertslie.htm*.

the general public that they hold to the highest possible standard. DNA testing, with its potential not only to exclude, but to individualize, has focused an enormous amount of scrutiny on forensic science in general. Recent events, including the homicide trial of O. J. Simpson, allegations of misconduct at the FBI laboratory, and the ever-increasing media and public attention to forensic science, bring into sharp relief issues of quality assurance, laboratory and analyst qualifications, ethical standards, and the continuing evolution of the state of the practice.

Forensic scientists are human beings; the question is not "Will an error occur?" but "When an error occurs, how can it be detected and corrected?" A series of checks and balances must be in place to ensure a reliable work product. Valid, proven, analytical techniques and thoughtful interpretation are obviously essential to a competent examination; the proper education, training, and certification of forensic analysts and independent reviewers, accreditation of laboratories, implementation of proper quality control and quality assurance protocols, and internal and external review procedures are no less critical to the output of a high-quality forensic work product. Although certification and accreditation programs exist to assess the general quality of a forensic work product, case review or evidence reanalysis by a qualified scientist remain the best methods of catching and correcting honest mistakes, as well as intentional falsification of results, before permanent damage is wrought. Additionally, but of no lesser importance, these measures provide a means by which the judicial system and lay public may judge a forensic work product.

References

American Board of Criminalistics (ABC), GKE Examination Philosophy, available at *http://www.criminalistics.com/ABC/abc002.htm*.

American Society of Crime Laboratory Directors — Laboratory Accreditation Board, available at *http://www.ascld-laboratory.org/*.

Bromwich, M, R. et al., USDOJ/OIG Special Report, The FBI Laboratory: An Investigation into Laboratory Practices and Alleged Misconduct in Explosives-Related and Other Cases, 1997, available at *http://www.usdoj.gov/oig/fbilab1/fbil1toc.htm*.

Davies, G., *Forensic Science*, American Chemical Society, 1986.

Furton, K. G., Hsu, Y. L., and Cole, M. D., What educational background do crime laboratory directors require from applicants? *J. Forensic Sci.*, 44(1), 128–132, 1999.

Kirk, P. L., The ontogeny of criminalistics, *J. Criminal Law Criminol. Police Sci.*, 54, 235–238, 1963.

National Forensic Science Technology Center (NFSTC), available at *http://www.nfstc.org/*.

Selavka, C., ABC update — a time of extension, *ABC Certification News*, 6(1), 1999.

Siegel, J. A., The appropriate educational background for entry level forensic scientists: a survey of practitioners, *J. Forensic Sci.*, 33, 1065–1068, 1988.

Stoney, D. A., A medical model for criminalistics education, *J. Forensic Sci.*, 33(4), 1086–1094, 1988.

Stoney, D. A., Criminalistics in the new millennium, *The CACNews*, 1st Quarter, 2000.

Webster's Encyclopedic Unabridged Dictionary of the English Language, Gramercy Books, New York, 1996.

Zamora, J. H., Lab scandal jeopardizes integrity of S.F. justice: sting uncovered bogus certification, *San Francisco Examiner*, 1994, unavailable at *http://www.catalog.com/hopkins/hemp/laboratory-scandal.html*.

Zamora, J. H., Procedure glitch undoes drug cases, *San Francisco Examiner*, 2000, available at *http://www.examiner.com/000209/0209chemists.html*.

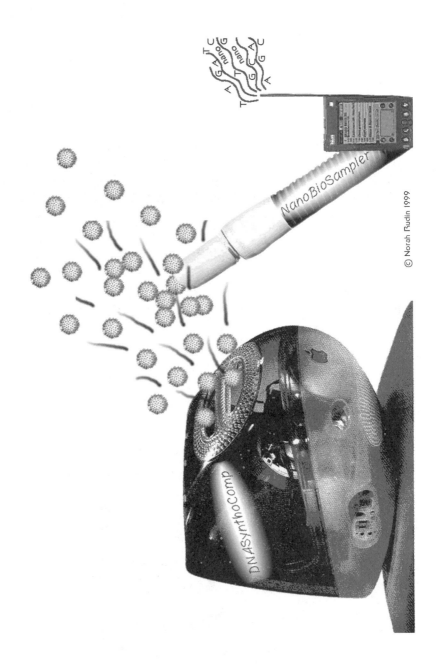

© Norah Rudin 1999

The Future of Forensic Science

13

To characterize the past accurately is difficult enough, but to attempt to predict the future is to tempt error... Whether DNA analysis and related methods of genetic engineering will be of value is more problematic; as sensitive as these methods are, the amount of DNA present in most biological evidence may be below practical detection limits. It would be good to be proven wrong on this matter because the DNA technology would open a new dimension in genetic-marker analysis.

—**George Sensabaugh**
"Forensic Science Research: Who Does It and Where Is It Going?" in Forensic Science, Geoffrey Davies, Ed.

This quote effectively demonstrates just how tenuous and unreliable any predictions about the future may be. Especially in the current climate, where technology is advancing at warp speed, it is sometimes all one can to do to hang on to the trailing edge, never mind forecast future directions. It is an interesting accident that this book is being written at the dawn of a new millennium. Pundits in all disciplines have spent the last year attempting to summarize what has been and prophesy what will be. Forensic science is no exception. For example, *The CACnews* devoted an entire issue to essays about the future of forensic science by prominent experts from around the world. Most of those writers wisely avoided the obvious — everything will get smaller, faster, better, and cheaper (or at least you will continue to pay the same price for more). Although funding and technology transfer received due acknowledgment, the topics of greatest concern were criminalistics education, the loss of generalist knowledge, and the professionalization of forensic science, all subjects that we discuss at length in this book. If criminalistics is to evolve into a truly autonomous, respected profession, these aspects must

Figure 13.1 The DNA SynthoComp. The future holds a synthesis of ideas and technologies that we cannot comprehend. The one link to the past and present is that *Thinking Is Required!*

actively be addressed. We hope that this book has made a contribution to that effort, and we invite the forensic community, and the larger field of forensic science to continue in that endeavor.

Our contribution to The CACNews Millennium issue is reproduced here.

The Purloined NanoBioSampler
by
Norah Rudin, Keith Inman and Peter Barnett
(first published in *The CACNews*, 1st quarter, 2000)

The year is 2050. Forensic science has finally been professionalized and unified. After completing their decade of criminalistics post-doc training, all criminalists are now required to take and pass the comprehensive IKR (Internationale Kriminalistiks Registry) examinations which traces its origins back to the old American GKE. Not everyone is happy with this situation.

2:00 AM, Sunday morning
A crime is reported in the Berzerkely computer laboratory in a remote region of the an alternate reality called California. The two scientists responsible for continuing development of the DNASynthoComp computer have been found dead in the laboratory. It is a bloody scene, relatively uncommon in the 21st century, so all three on-call criminalists are called to the scene. The coordinates of the scene are transmitted directly to the integrated GPS units in each criminalist's personal hover car, so they get an extra 10 minutes of sleep on the way to the scene.

2:30 AM
They take a few moments to chat before entering the scene:

DNAtyper794: I had the oddest conversation with my old friend who is now on Mars Colony. He received most of his training back in the late 20th century when everyone was DNA-happy and the emphasis was on specialization. He's tried several times to become IKR-qualified and failed. It is really hard to get training out on Mars. If he does not pass this time, he will be out of a job. He sounded really desperate. I hope he does not try anything stupid.

Criminalist976: (*a neophyte criminalist*) Wow, what a concept! You mean there was a time when limited criminalists were allowed to practice with only their specialist knowledge?

GunIDer 135: Yes, believe it or not, many in the profession felt that was the way to go. Good thing they all came to their senses. If all you could do would be to watch after the analytical computers, and occasionally replace a mutating Biopack processor, what kind of a job would this be? The only part of this job that is interesting is going to the crime scene to decide what evidence is important and what tests should be run, and later integrating all of the data. Where would all those limited criminalists be these days?

DNAtyper794:   Well, it's too bad about my friend, but it shows what happens when you cannot get your pension until you are 130 — a lot of folks trained in the last century need to be upgraded. Let's concentrate on the scene at hand. Been a long time since I've been at a scene with real blood and I'm looking forward to getting my hands on it.

Criminalist976:   Shouldn't we talk to the investigator first so we have some clue what we are looking for? He's already been through the HoloProjection of the scene and interviewed some of the witnesses over the CyberVideo link.

GunIDer135:   Good point.

A group CyberVideo link is established

Cop8957:   As you know, what we have here is a double homicide. These two scientists, the DNA specialist and the computer specialist, had apparently worked together harmoniously for years. Recently, however, they had been observed in arguments in which it was apparent that the biologist's only concern was with the nucleotide sequences and the computer guy's only concern was with bits and bytes. Their colleagues reported that these arguments had grown more and more animated recently. Now, all of a sudden, they're both dead. I've never seen anything quite like it.

DNAtyper794:   OK, thanks, we'll see what we can get. Meet you for breakfast when we are done?

Cop8957:   Fine, I'll keep my CyberCafe link on and order us all breakfast. The usual?

3:00 AM

The three criminalists enter the scene and begin to process it. The DNAtyper is observed cutting samples from the clothing of the two victims, taking swabs of bloodstains underneath them on the floor, scanning these samples with his Nano-BioSampler and finding out the obvious. The GunIDer spends his entire time at the scene making barrel and breach face casts of the gun collection of one of the deceased scientists who was a firearms collector and kept his collection in the laboratory for security reasons. The Criminalist neophyte is the only one of the three that seems to note that the two scientists stabbed each other to death.

6:00 AM

The criminalists pack up their stuff and disperse back to their respective offices where each sets up a CyberCafe link by putting on his CyberView goggles and accessing the secure band frequency reserved by law enforcement for such conferences.

6:30 AM

GunIDer135:   Well, the coffee is cold and the doughnuts are stale. I guess some things never change.

Cop8957:   The food servos never seem to work very well at this hour in the morning. Don't know whether it is overload on the power grid or the programmers do this on purpose.

DNAtyper794:   Back to our little crime, I've established with certainty that all the blood at the scene is from the two victims.

Criminalist976: What about the pattern of the blood spatter — anything unusual or unexpected?

DNAtyper794:   Well, I checked the World Database twice, and I'm sure the types are correct. No one else's blood was at the scene.

GunIDer135:   I compared all the guns in the collection with the World Database of guns. I found that these guns were manufactured before all guns were test-fired prior to being sold, and records kept of the bullet striae patterns. None of them match any of the guns in the database, even with extended computer simulations for predicted wear of barrel markings.

Cop8957:   Uhm — did anyone happen to collect the antique knives that the victims used to stab each other to death?

7:00 AM

As the conversation continues, the Criminalist neophyte realizes something is amiss. She has an idea, but she needs a NanoBioSampler. She is frustrated that she has not yet completed the one-week advanced training course after which she would be given her own NBS, but she has an idea. Setting the background of her CyberCafe projector to run a loop of her office background, she continues to engage her colleagues in aimless conversation while she sneaks off to the Forensic Mobile Unit and surreptitiously purloins her colleague's NBS and returns to the crime scene. She sets the unit to "robotic autosample" and sends it into the crime scene. When the SceneScan is completed, she changes the setting of the NanoBioSampler to "Determine Bioactivity," and hits the "execute" activator. The Biopack processor struggles with the analysis for an unusual number of gigglecycles, but finally issues a report. When she reads the report she realizes her suspicions are correct. The results from the samples recovered from the DNASynthoComp's internal environment monitoring port suggest an intriguing idea. She taps for a few moments on her personal computer, which is permanently connected to the worldwide directory of reference databases and confirms her suspicions. A few moments later her suspicions are confirmed, but she realizes she cannot report her findings to her colleagues. She leaves the investigator to keep them busy and contacts his partner.

8:00 AM

Criminalist976: I think I've solved your partner's case, but my colleagues have been affected and they are now useless. You have to help me.

Cop9007: OK, but make it fast and this better be good.

Criminalist976: Well, here's what I think. We know that the DNASynthoComp is powered by a DNA BioPack. In this particular model, it directs the synthesis of bioactive materials in the search for a drug to reverse the short-term memory loss in Alzheimer's patients. The NanoBio-Sampler reported that the sample from the vent area contains a "possible long term memory antagonist." When I queried it further, I found an unusual pattern of repeating amino acids specified by the DNA sequence coding for this long-term memory antagonist. There are long stretches of DNA triplets coding for Isoleucine–Lysine–Arginine. I thought to ask for the one letter codes for these amino acids. Turns out these long stretches are composed of *IKR IKR IKR*. This was the clue I needed.

I remembered a brief conversation we had just before we started this scene. A colleague of ours is apparently getting a bit irrational about his inability to pass the IKR and is concerned for his job. I checked the DNASynthoComp user log and found a hacked access linked to a computer which is registered to him. I then accessed the video records from the G.O-Cam in his study and watched as he managed to hack into the DNASynthoComp. He introduced a computer virus that changed the programming to direct the DNA fragments normally used to synthesize the memory agonist such that they now direct the synthesis of a compound long-term memory antagonist.

From what I have heard about the victims and saw with my colleagues, this virus has the effect of destroying a person's general knowledge, leaving only that more recently learned, highly specific knowledge. I have apparently remained unaffected because I have only recently acquired general knowledge, so it is still in my short-term memory. The viruses are programmed to be self-replicating, removing a safety feature of the bioactive material normally synthesized by the computer. They apparently begin to multiply and couldn't be contained in the computer. They exit via the fan vent. I put it all together when I realized that the Forensic Training and Development Laboratory is just across the hall. Apparently his idea was that everyone would forget their generalist training so his lack of the same would not be noticed, and he would still have a job. What I don't know is if the effect is reversible.

Cop9007:	Well, you've convinced me, but now we have another problem. Do we report this to the Violent Crimes Unit or the CyberCrime Unit? You know how territorial they are.
Criminalist976:	How about we leave it to them to resolve it and tell them they shouldn't open their e-mail if they cannot or we'll infect them with the virus.
Cop9007:	What do you think happens to an attorney who forgets all generalist knowledge?
Criminalist976:	I think I don't want to go there.

5:00 PM, Monday afternoon

Cop8957:	You'll be pleased to know that we apprehended, tried, and convicted your suspect. His sentence is a lifetime ban on practicing the profession of criminalistics.
Criminalist976:	Legitimately, at least.
Cop8957:	Now what do we do with your colleagues. I'm getting really tired of listening to them babble about DNA and Firearms.
Criminalist976:	I guess that will just have to wait until … the next episode of *FuturCrim*.

References

Davies, G., *Forensic Science*, American Chemical Society, 1986.

Stoney, D. A., Criminalistics in the new millennium, *The CACNews*, 1st quarter, 2000.

Forensic Science Timeline

B.C.E.   Evidence of fingerprints in early paintings and rock carvings of prehistoric humans.

A.D. 700s   Chinese used fingerprints to establish identity of documents and clay sculpture, but without any formal classification system.

ca. 1000   Quintilian, an attorney in the Roman courts, showed that bloody palm prints were meant to frame a blind man of his mother's murder.

1248   A Chinese book, *Hsi Duan Yu* (the washing away of wrongs), contains a description of how to distinguish drowning from strangulation. This was the first recorded application of medical knowledge to the solution of crime.

1609   The first treatise on systematic document examination was published by François Demelle of France.

1686   **Marcello Malpighi**, a professor of anatomy at the University of Bologna, noted fingerprint characteristics. However, he made no mention of their value as a tool for individual identification.

1784   In Lancaster, England, **John Toms** was convicted of murder on the basis of the torn edge of a wad of newspaper in a pistol matching a remaining piece in his pocket. This was one of the first documented uses of physical matching.

ca. 1800s   **Thomas Bewick**, an English naturalist, used engravings of his own fingerprints to identify books he published.

1810   **Eugène François Vidocq**, in return for a suspension of arrest and a jail sentence, made a deal with the police to establish the first detective force, the Sûreté of Paris.

1810   The first recorded use of questioned document analysis occurred in Germany. A chemical test for a particular ink dye was applied to a document known as the *Konigin Hanschritt*.

1813   **Mathiew Orfila**, a Spaniard who became professor of medicinal/forensic chemistry at University of Paris, published *Traite des Poisons Tires des Regnes Mineral, Vegetal et Animal, ou Toxicologie General l*. Orfila is considered the father of modern toxicology. He also made significant contributions to the development of tests for the presence of blood in a forensic context and is credited as the first to attempt the use of a microscope in the assessment of blood and semen stains.

1823   **John Evangelist Purkinji,** a professor of anatomy at the University of Breslau, Czecheslovakia, published the first paper on the nature of fingerprints and suggested a classification system based on nine major types. However, he failed to recognize their individualizing potential.

1828   **William Nichol** invented the polarizing light microscope.

ca. 1830s **Adolphe Quetelet**, a Belgian statistician, provided the foundation for Bertillon's work by stating his belief that no two human bodies were exactly alike.

1831   **Leuchs** first noted amylase activity in human saliva.

1835   **Henry Goddard**, one of Scotland Yard's original Bow Street Runners, first used bullet comparison to catch a murderer. His comparison was based on a visible flaw in the bullet which was traced back to a mold.

1836   **James Marsh**, a Scottish chemist, was the first to use toxicology (arsenic detection) in a jury trial.

1839   **H. Bayard** published the first reliable procedures for the microscopic detection of sperm. He also noted the different microscopic characteristics of various different substrate fabrics.

1851   **Jean Servais Stas**, a chemistry professor from Brussels, Belgium, was the first successfully to identify vegetable poisons in body tissue.

1853   **Ludwig Teichmann**, in Kracow, Poland, developed the first microscopic crystal test for hemoglobin using hemin crystals.

1854   An English physician, **Maddox**, developed dry plate photography, eclipsing **M. Daguerre**'s wet plate on tin method. This made practical the photographing of inmates for prison records.

1856   **Sir William Herschel**, a British officer working for the Indian Civil Service, began to use thumbprints on documents both as a substitute for written signatures for illiterates and to verify document signatures.

1862   The Dutch scientist **J. (Izaak) Van Deen** developed a presumptive test for blood using guaiac, a West Indian shrub.

1863   The German scientist **Schönbein** first discovered the ability of hemoglobin to oxidize hydrogen peroxide making it foam. This resulted in first presumptive test for blood.

1864   **Odelbrecht** first advocated the use of photography for the identification of criminals and the documentation of evidence and crime scenes.

1877   **Thomas Taylor,** microscopist to the U.S. Department of Agriculture suggested that "markings of the palms of the hands and the tips of the fingers could be used for identification in criminal cases. Although reported in the *American Journal of Microscopy and Popular Science* and *Scientific American,* the idea was apparently never pursued from this source.

1879   **Rudolph Virchow,** a German pathologist, was one of the first to both study hair and recognize its limitations.

1880   **Henry Faulds,** a Scottish physician working in Tokyo, published a paper in the journal *Nature* suggesting that fingerprints at the scene of a crime could identify the offender. In one of the first recorded uses of fingerprints to solve a crime, Faulds used fingerprints to eliminate an innocent suspect and indicate a perpetrator in a Tokyo burglary.

1882   **Gilbert Thompson,** a railroad builder with the U.S Geological Survey in New Mexico, put his own thumbprint on wage chits to safeguard himself from forgeries.

1883   **Alphonse Bertillon,** a French police employee, identified the first recidivist based on his invention of anthropometry.

1887   **Arthur Conan Doyle** published the first Sherlock Holmes story in Beeton's Christmas Annual of London.

1889   **Alexandre Lacassagne,** professor of forensic medicine at the University of Lyons, France, was the first to try to individualize bullets to a gun barrel. His comparisons at the time were based simply on the number of lands and grooves.

1891   **Hans Gross,** examining magistrate and professor of criminal law at the University of Graz, Austria, published *Criminal Investigation*, the first comprehensive description of uses of physical evidence in solving crime. Gross is also sometimes credited with coining the word *criminalistics.*

1892	**(Sir) Francis Galton** published *Fingerprints*, the first comprehensive book on the nature of fingerprints and their use in solving crime.
	Juan Vucetich, an Argentinean police researcher, developed the fingerprint classification system that would come to be used in Latin America. After Vucetich implicated a mother in the murder of her own children using her bloody fingerprints, Argentina was the first country to replace anthropometry with fingerprints.
1894	**Alfred Dreyfus** of France was convicted of treason based on a mistaken handwriting identification by Bertillon.
1896	**Sir Edward Richard Henry** developed the print classification system that would come to be used in Europe and North America. He published *Classification and Uses of Finger Prints*.
1898	**Paul Jesrich**, a forensic chemist working in Berlin, Germany, took photomicrographs of two bullets to compare, and subsequently individualize, the minutiae.
1900	**Karl Landsteiner** first discovered human blood groups and was awarded the Nobel prize for his work in 1930. **Max Richter** adapted the technique to type stains. This is one of the first instances of performing validation experiments specifically to adapt a method for forensic science. **Landsteiner**'s continued work on the detection of blood, its species, and its type formed the basis of practically all subsequent work.
1901	**Paul Uhlenhuth**, a German immunologist, developed the precipiten test for species. He was also one of the first to institute standards, controls, and QA/QC procedures. **Wassermann** (famous for developing a test for syphilis) and **Schütze** independently discovered and published the precipiten test, but never received due credit.
	Sir Edward Richard Henry was appointed head of Scotland Yard and forced the adoption of fingerprint identification to replace anthropometry.
	Henry P. DeForrest pioneered the first systematic use of fingerprints in the Umoted States by the New York Civil Service Commission.
1902	**R. A. Reiss**, professor at the University of Lausanne, Switzerland, and a pupil of Bertillon, set up one of the first academic curricula in forensic science. His forensic photography department grew into Lausanne Institute of Police Science.

1903   The New York State prison system began the first systematic use of fingerprints in United States for criminal identification.

            At Leavenworth State Prison, Kansas, Will West, a new inmate, was differentiated from resident convict Will West by fingerprints, not anthropometry. They were later found to be identical twins.

1904   **Oskar** and **Rudolf Adler** developed a presumptive test for blood based on benzidine, a new chemical developed by Merk.

1905   American President Theodore Roosevelt established **Federal Bureau of Investigation** (FBI).

1910   **Victor Balthazard**, professor of forensic medicine at the Sorbonne, with Marcelle Lambert, published the first comprehensive hair study, *Le poil de l'homme et des animaux*. In one of the first cases involving hairs, Rosella Rousseau was convinced to confess to murder of Germaine Bichon. Balthazard also used photographic enlargements of bullets and cartridge cases to determining weapon type and was among the first to attempt to individualize a bullet to a weapon.

            Edmund Locard, successor to Lacassagne as professor of forensic medicine at the University of Lyons, France, established the first police crime laboratory.

            Albert S. Osborne, an American and arguably the most influential document examiner, published *Questioned Documents*.

1912   **Masaeo Takayama** developed another microscopic crystal test for hemoglobin using hemochromogen crystals.

1913   **Victor Balthazard**, professor of forensic medicine at the Sorbonne, published the first article on individualizing bullet markings.

1915   **Leone Lattes**, professor at the Institute of Forensic Medicine in Turin, Italy, developed the first antibody test for ABO blood groups. He first used the test in casework to resolve a marital dispute. He published *L'individualità del sangue nella biologia, nella clinica, nella medicina, legale,* the first book dealing not only with clinical issues, but heritability, paternity, and typing of dried stains.

            International Association for Criminal Identification, to become The **International Association of Identification** (**IAI**), was organized in Oakland, California.

1916   **Albert Schneider** of Berkeley, California first used a vacuum apparatus to collect trace evidence.

1918   **Edmond Locard** first suggested 12 matching points as a positive fingerprint identification.

1920   **Locard** published *L'enquete criminelle et les methodes scientifique,* in which appears a passage that may have given rise to the forensic precept that "every contact leaves a trace."

1920   **Charles E. Waite** was the first to catalog manufacturing data about weapons.

ca. 1920s   **Georg Popp** pioneered the use of botanical identification in forensic work.

          Luke May, one of the first American criminalists, pioneered striation analysis in toolmark comparison, including an attempt at statistical validation. In 1930, he published "The identification of knives, tools and instruments, a positive science," in *The American Journal of Police Science.*

          Calvin Goddard, with Charles Waite, Phillip O. Gravelle, and John H Fisher, perfected the comparison microscope for use in bullet comparison.

1921   **John Larson** and **Leonard Keeler** designed the portable polygraph.

1923   **Vittorio Siracusa,** working at the Institute of Legal Medicine of the R. University of Messina, Italy, developed the absorbtion–elution test for ABO blood typing of stains. Along with his mentor, **Lattes** also performed significant work on the absorbtion–inhibition technique.

          In *Frye v. United States,* polygraph test results were ruled inadmissible. The federal ruling introduced the concept of *general acceptance* and stated that polygraph testing did not meet that criterion.

1924   **August Vollmer,** as chief of police in Los Angeles, California, implemented the first U.S. police crime laboratory.

1925   **Saburo Sirai,** a Japanese scientist, is credited with the first recognition of secretion of group-specific antigens into body fluids other than blood.

1926   The case of **Sacco and Vanzetti,** which took place in Bridgewater, Massachusetts, was responsible for popularizing the use of the comparison microscope for bullet comparison. **Calvin Goddard**'s conclusions were upheld when the evidence was reexamined in 1961.

1927   **Landsteiner** and **Levine** first detected the M, N, and P blood factors leading to development of the MNSs and P typing systems.

1928   **Meüller** was the first medicolegal investigator to suggest the identification of salivary amlyase as a presumptive test for salivary stains.

1929   **K. I. Yosida**, a Japanese scientist, conducted the first comprehensive investigation establishing the existence of serological isoantibodies in body fluids other than blood.

    Calvin Goddard's work on the St. Valentine's day massacre led to the founding of the Scientific Crime Detection Laboratory on the campus of Northwestern University, Evanston, Illinois.

1930   *American Journal of Police Science* was founded and published by staff of Goddard's Scientific Crime Detection Laboratory in Chicago. In 1932, it was absorbed by *Journal of Criminal Law and Criminology*, becoming the *Journal of Criminal Law, Criminology and Police Science*.

1931   **Franz Josef Holzer**, an Austrian scientist, working at the Institute for Forensic Medicine of the University of Innsbruck, developed the absorbtion–inhibition ABO typing technique that became the basis of that commonly used in forensic laboratories. It was based on the prior work of Siracusa and Lattes.

1932   **The Federal Bureau of Investigation** (FBI) crime laboratory was created.

1935   **Frits Zernike**, a Dutch physicist, invented the first interference contrast microscope, a phase contrast microscope, an achievement for which he won the Nobel prize in 1953.

1937   **Holzer** published the first paper addressing the usefulness of secretor status for forensic applications.

    Walter Specht, at the University Institute for Legal Medicine and Scientific Criminalistics in Jena, Germany, developed the chemiluminescent reagent luminol as a presumptive test for blood.

    Paul Kirk assumed leadership of the criminology program at the University of California at Berkeley. In 1945, he formalized a major in Technical Criminology.

1938   **M. Polonovski** and **M. Jayle** first identified haptoglobin.

1940   **Landsteiner** and **A. S. Wiener** first described Rh blood groups.

Vincent Hnizda, a chemist with the Ethyl Corporation, was probably the first to analyze ignitable fluid. He used a vacuum distillation apparatus.

1941   **Murray Hill** of Bell Labs initiated the study of voiceprint identification. The technique was refined by **L. G. Kersta**.

1945   **Frank Lundquist**, working at the Legal Medicine Unit at the University of Copenhagen, developed the acid phosphatase test for semen.

1946   **Mourant** first described the Lewis blood group system.

         R. R. Race first described the Kell blood group system

1950   **M. Cutbush**, and colleagues first described the Duffy blood group system.

         August Vollmer, chief of police of Berkeley, California, established the school of criminology at the University of California at Berkeley. **Paul Kirk** presided over the major of criminalistics within the school.

         Max Frei-Sulzer, founder of the first Swiss criminalistics laboratory, developed the tape-lift method of collecting trace evidence.

         The **American Academy of Forensic Science** (AAFS) was formed in Chicago, Illinois. The group also began publication of the *Journal of Forensic Science* (JFS).

1951   **F. H. Allen** and colleagues first described the Kidd blood grouping system.

1953   **Kirk** published *Crime Investigation*, one of the first comprehensive criminalistics and crime investigation texts that encompassed theory in addition to practice.

1954   **R. F. Borkenstein**, captain of the Indiana State Police, invented the Breathalyzer for field sobriety testing.

1958   **A. S. Weiner** and colleagues introduced the use of H-lectin to determine positively O blood type.

1959   Hirshfeld first identified the polymorphic nature of group-specific component (Gc).

1960   **Lucas**, in Canada, described the application of gas chromatography (GC) to the identification of petroleum products in the forensic laboratory and discussed potential limitations in the brand identity of gasoline.

1960s   **Maurice Muller**, a Swiss scientist, adapted the Ouchterlony anti-body–antigen diffusion test for precipiten testing to determine species.

1963   **D. A. Hopkinson** and colleagues first identified the polymorphic nature of erythrocyte acid phosphatase (EAP).

1964   **N. Spencer** and colleagues first identified the polymorphic nature of red cell phosphoglucomutase (PGM).

1966   **R. A. Fildes** and **H. Harris** first identified the polymorphic nature of red cell adenylate cyclase (AK).

          Brian J. Culliford and **Brian Wraxall** developed the immuno-electrophoretic technique for haptoglobin typing in bloodstains.

1967   **Culliford**, of the British Metropolitan Police Laboratory, initiated the development of gel-based methods to test for isoenzymes in dried bloodstains. He was also instrumental in the development and dissemination of methods for testing proteins and isoenzymes in both blood and other body fluids and secretions.

1968   **Spencer** and colleagues first identified the polymorphic nature of red cell adenosine deaminase (ADA).

1971   **Culliford** published *The Examination and Typing of Bloodstains in the Crime Laboratory*, generally accepted as responsible for disseminating reliable protocols for the typing of polymorphic protein and enzyme markers to the United States and worldwide.

1973   **Hopkinson** and colleagues first identified the polymorphic nature of esterase D (ESD).

1974   The detection of gunshot residue (GSR) using scanning electron microscopy with electron dispersive X-rays (SEM–EDX) technology was developed by **J. E. Wessel, P. F. Jones, Q. Y. Kwan, R. S. Nesbitt**, and **E. J. Rattin** at Aerospace Corporation.

1975   **J. Kompf** and colleagues, working in Germany, first identified the polymorphic nature of red cell glyoxylase (GLO).

          The *Federal Rules of Evidence*, originally promulgated by the U.S. Supreme Court, were enacted as a congressional statute. They are based on the *relevancy standard* in which scientific evidence that is deemed more prejudicial than probative may not be admitted.

1976   **Zoro** and **Hadley** in the United Kingdom first evaluated GC–MS for forensic purposes.

1977   **Fuseo Matsumur,** a trace evidence examiner at the Saga Prefectural Crime Laboratory of the National Police Agency of Japan, notices his own fingerprints developing on microscope slides while mounting hairs from a taxi driver murder case. He relates the information to co-worker Masato Soba, a latent print examiner. Soba would later that year be the first to develop latent prints intentionally by "Superglue®" fuming.

ca. 1977   The *Fourier transform infrared spectrophotometer* (FTIR) is adapted for use in the forensic laboratory.

             The FBI introduced the beginnings of its Automated Fingerprint Identification System (AFIS) with the first computerized scans of fingerprints.

1978   **Brian Wraxall** and **Mark Stolorow** developed the "multisystem" method for testing the PGM, ESD, and GLO isoenzyme systems simultaneously. They also developed methods for typing blood serum proteins such as haptoglobin and Gc.

1983   The polymerase chain reaction (PCR) was first conceived by **Kerry Mullis,** while he was working at **Cetus** Corporation. The first paper on the technique was not published until 1985.

1984   **(Sir) Alec Jeffreys** developed the first DNA profiling test. It involved detection of a multilocus RFLP pattern. He published his findings in *Nature* in 1985.

1986   In the first use of DNA to solve a crime, **Jeffreys** used DNA profiling to identify Colin Pitchfork as the murderer of two young girls in the English Midlands. Significantly, in the course of the investigation, DNA was first used to exonerate an innocent suspect.

             The human genetics group at **Cetus** Corporation, led by **Henry Erlich,** developed the PCR technique for a number of clinical and forensic applications. This resulted in development of the first commercial PCR typing kit specifically for forensic use, HLA DQ-α (DQA1), about 2 years later.

             In *People v. Pestinikas,* **Edward Blake** first used PCR-based DNA testing (HLA DQ-α), to confirm different autopsy samples to be from the same person. The evidence was accepted by a civil court. This was also the first use of any kind of DNA testing in the United States.

1987   DNA profiling was introduced for the first time in a U.S. criminal court. Based on RFLP analysis performed by **Lifecodes**, Tommy Lee Andrews was convicted of a series of sexual assaults in Orlando, Florida.

New York v. Castro was the first case in which the admissibility of DNA was seriously challenged. It set in motion a string of events that culminated in a call for certification, accreditation, standardization, and quality control guidelines for both DNA laboratories and the general forensic community.

1988   **Lewellen, McCurdy,** and **Horton** and **Asselin, Leslie,** and **McKinley** both publish milestone papers introducing a novel procedure for the analysis of drugs in whole blood by homogeneous enzyme immunoassay (EMIT).

1990   **K. Kasai** and colleagues published the first paper suggesting the D1S80 locus (pMCT118) for forensic DNA analysis. D1S80 was subsequently developed by **Cetus** (subsequently Roche Molecular Systems) corporation as a commercially available forensic DNA typing system.

1991   **Walsh Automation Inc.**, in Montreal, launched development of an automated imaging system called the Integrated Ballistics Identification System, or IBIS, for comparison of the marks left on fired bullets, cartridge cases, and shell casings. This system was subsequently developed for the U.S. market in collaboration with the **Bureau of Alcohol, Tobacco, and Firearms** (**ATF**).

1992   In response to concerns about the practice of forensic DNA analysis and interpretation of the results, the National Research Council Committee on Forensic DNA (**NRC I**) published *DNA Technology in Forensic Science.*

Thomas Caskey, professor at Baylor University in Texas, and colleagues published the first paper suggesting the use of short tandem repeats (STR) for forensic DNA analysis. **Promega** corporation and **Perkin-Elmer** corporation in collaboration with Roche **Molecular Systems** independently developed commercial kits for forensic DNA STR typing.

The **FBI** contracted with **Mnemonic System**s to developed Drugfire, an automated imaging system to compare marks left on cartridge cases and shell casings. The ability to compare fired bullets was subsequently added.

1993   In *Daubert et al. v. Merrell Dow*, a U.S. federal court relaxed the Frye standard for admission of scientific evidence and conferred on the judge a "gatekeeping" role. The ruling cited **Karl Popper's** views that scientific theories are falsifiable as a criterion for whether something is "scientific knowledge" and should be admissible.

ca. 1994   **Roche Molecular Systems** (formerly Cetus) released a set of five additional DNA markers ("polymarker") to add to the HLA-DQA1 forensic DNA typing system.

1996   In response to continued concerns about the statistical interpretation of forensic DNA evidence, a second National Research Council Committee on Forensic DNA (**NRC II**) was convened and published *The Evaluation of Forensic DNA Evidence.*

            The **FBI** introduced computerized searches of the AFIS fingerprint database. Live scan and card scan devices allowed interdepartmental submissions.

            In *Tennessee v. Ware*, mitochondrial DNA typing was admitted for the first time in a U.S. court.

1998   An FBI DNA database, **NIDIS**, enabling interstate cooperation in linking crimes, was put into practice.

1999   The FBI upgraded its computerized fingerprint database and implemented the Integrated Automated Fingerprint Identification System (IAFIS), allowing paperless submission, storage, and search capabilities directly to the national database maintained at the FBI.

            A Memorandum of Understanding is signed between the FBI and ATF, allowing the use of the National Integrated Ballistics Network (**NIBIN**), to facilitate exchange of firearms data between Drugfire and IBIS.

References

Block, E. B., *Science vs. Crime: The Evolution of the Police Lab*, Cragmont Publications, 1979.

Dillon, D., A History of Criminalistics in the United States 1850–1950, Doctoral thesis, University of California, Berkeley, 1977.

Else, W. M. and Garrow, J. M., *The Detection of Crime*, The Police Journal, London, 1934.

Gaensslen, R. E., Ed., *Sourcebook in Forensic Serology, Unit IX: Translations of Selected Contributions to the Original Literature of Medicolegal Examination of Blood and Body Fluids*, National Institute of Justice, 1983a.

Gaensslen, R. E., *Sourcebook in Forensic Serology*, U.S. Government Printing Office, Washington, D.C., 1983b.

Gerber, S. M., Saferstein, R., *More Chemistry and Crime*, American Chemical Society, 1997.

German, E., *Cyanoacrylate (Superglue) Discovery Timeline 1999*, available at *http://onin.com/fp/cyanoho.html*.

German, E., *The History of Fingerprints*, 1999, available at *http://onin.com/fp/fphistory.html*.

Kind, S. and Overman, M., *Science against Crime*, Aldus Book Limited, Doubleday, New York, 1972.

Morland, N., *An Outline of Scientific Criminology*, Philosophical Library, New York, 1950.

Thorwald, J., *The Century of the Detective*, Harcourt, Brace & World, New York, 1964; translation, Richard and Clara Winston, 1965.

Thorwald, J., *Crime and Science, Harcourt*, Brace & World, New York, 1966; translation, Richard and Clara Winston.

American Association of Forensic Science
Article II. Code of Ethics and Conduct

SECTION 1 — THE CODE: As a means to promote the highest quality or professional and personal conduct of its members, the following constitutes the Code of Ethics and Conduct which is endorsed and adhered to by all members of the American Academy of Forensic Sciences:

A. Every member of the American Academy of Forensic Sciences shall refrain from exercising professional or personal conduct adverse to the best interests and purposes of the Academy.

B. Every member of the AAFS shall refrain from providing any material misrepresentation of education, training, experience or area of expertise. Misrepresentation of one or more criteria for membership in the AAFS shall constitute a violation of this section of the code.

C. Every member of the AAFS shall refrain from providing any material misrepresentation of data upon which an expert opinion or conclusion is based.

D. Every member of the AAFS shall refrain from issuing public statements which appear to represent the position of the Academy without specific authority first obtained from the Board of Directors.

Appendix C

American Board of Criminalistics
Rules of Professional Conduct

These rules describe conduct in the profession of forensic science (criminalistics) and are meant to encompass not only work done by Applicants, Affiliates and Diplomates, but to the extent possible, work supervised by them as well. They meet general acceptance by peers in that profession. They specify conduct that must be followed in order to apply for, receive, and maintain the certification status provided for by the American Board of Criminalistics.

Applicants, Affiliates and Diplomates of the ABC shall:

1. Comply with the by-laws and regulations of the ABC.
2. Treat all information from an agency or client with the confidentiality required.
3. Treat any object or item of potential evidential value with the care and control necessary to ensure its integrity.
4. Ensure that all exhibits in a case receive appropriate technical analysis.
5. Ensure that appropriate standards and controls to conduct examinations and analyses are utilized.
6. Ensure that techniques and methods which are known to be inaccurate and/or unreliable are not utilized.
7. Ensure that a full and complete disclosure of the findings is made to the submitting agency.
8. Ensure that work notes on all items, examinations, results and findings are made at the time that they are done, and appropriately preserved.
9. Render opinions and conclusions strictly in accordance with the evidence in the case (hypothetical or real) and only to the extent justified by that evidence.
10. Testify in a clear, straightforward manner and refuse to extend themselves beyond their field of competence, phrasing their testimony in such a manner so that the results are not misinterpreted.
11. Not exaggerate, embellish or otherwise misrepresent qualifications, when testifying.

12. Consent to, if it is requested and allowed, interviews with counsel for both sides prior to trial.
13. Make efforts to inform the court of the nature and implications of pertinent evidence if reasonably assured that this information will not be disclosed to the court.
14. Maintain an attitude of independence and impartiality in order to ensure an unbiased analysis of the evidence.
15. Carry out the duties of the profession in such a manner so as to inspire the confidence of the public.
16. Regard and respect their peers with the same standards that they hold for themselves.
17. Set a reasonable fee for services if it is appropriate do so however, no services shall ever be rendered on a contingency fee basis.
18. Find it appropriate to report to the Board, any violation of these Rules of Professional Conduct by another applicant or Diplomate.

The Code of Ethics of the California Association of Criminalists

Adopted May 17, 1957
Revised April 11, 1958 and May 17, 1985 (Section V.F)

Preamble

This Code is intended as a guide to the ethical conduct of individual workers in the field of criminalistics. It is not to be construed that these principles are immutable laws nor that they are all-inclusive. Instead, they represent general standards which each worker should strive to meet. It is to be realized that each individual case may vary, just as does the evidence which the criminalist is concerned, and no set of guides or rules will precisely fit every occasion. At the same time the fundamentals set forth in this Code are to be regarded as indicating, to a considerable extent, the conduct requirements expected of members of the profession and of this Association. The failure to meet or maintain certain of these standards will justifiably cast doubt upon an individual's fitness for this type of work. Serious or repeated infractions of these principles may be regarded as inconsistent with membership in the Association.

Criminalistics is that professional occupation concerned with the scientific analysis and examination of physical evidence, its interpretation, and its presentation in court. It involves the application of principles, techniques and methods of the physical sciences, and has as its primary objective a determination of physical facts which may be significant in legal cases.

It is the duty of any person practicing the profession of criminalistics to serve the interests of justice to the best of his ability at all times. In fulfilling this duty, he will use all of the scientific means at his command to ascertain all of the significant physical facts relative to the matters under investigation. Having made factual determinations, the criminalist must then interpret and evaluate his findings. In this he will be guided by experience and knowledge which, coupled with a serious consideration of his analytical findings and the application of sound judgment, may enable him to arrive at opinions and conclusions pertaining to the matters under study. These findings of fact and his conclusions and opinions should then be reported, with all the accuracy and skill of which the criminalist is capable, to the end that all may fully understand and be able to place the findings in their proper relationship to the problem at issue.

In carrying out these functions, the criminalist will be guided by those practices and procedures which are generally recognized within the profession to be consistent with a high level of professional ethics. The motives, methods, and actions of the criminalist shall at all times be above reproach, in good taste and consistent with proper moral conduct.

I.   Ethics Relating to Scientific Method:

A. The criminalist has a truly scientific spirit and should be inquiring, progressive, logical and unbiased.

B. The true scientist will make adequate examination of his materials, applying those tests essential to proof. He will not, merely for the sake of bolstering his conclusions, utilize unwarranted and superfluous tests an attempt to give apparent greater weight to his results.

C. The modern scientific mind is an open one incompatible with secrecy of method. Scientific analyses will not be conducted by "secret processes", nor will conclusions in case work be based upon such tests and experiments as will not be revealed to the profession.

D. A proper scientific method demands reliability of validity in the materials analyzed. Conclusions will not be drawn from materials which themselves appear unrepresentative, atypical, or unreliable.

E. A truly scientific method requires that no generally discredited or unreliable procedure be utilized in the analysis.

F. The progressive worker will keep abreast of new developments in scientific methods and in all cases view them with an open mind. This is not to say that he need not be critical of untried or unproved methods, but he will recognize superior methods, if and when, they are introduced.

II.   Ethics Relating to Opinions and Conclusions:

A. Valid conclusions call for the application of proven methods. Where it is practical to do so, the competent criminalist will apply such methods throughout. This does not demand the application of "standard test procedures", but, where practical, use should be made of those methods developed and recognized by this or other professional societies.

B. Tests are designed to disclose true facts and all interpretations shall be consistent with that purpose and will not be knowingly distorted.

C. Where appropriate to the correct interpretation of a test, experimental controls shall be made for verification.

D. Where possible, the conclusions reached as a result of analytical tests are properly verified by re-testing or the application of additional techniques.

E. Where test results are inconclusive or indefinite, any conclusions drawn shall be fully explained.

F. The scientific mind is unbiased and refuses to be swayed by evidence or matters outside the specific materials under consideration. It is immune to suggestion, pressures and coercions inconsistent with the evidence hand, being interested only in ascertaining facts.

G. The criminalist will be alert to recognize the significance of a test result as it may relate to the investigative aspects of a case. In this respect he will, however, scrupulously avoid confusing scientific fact with investigative theory in his interpretations.

H. Scientific method demands that the individual be aware of his own limitations and refuse to extend himself beyond them. It is both proper and advisable that the scientific worker seek knowledge in new fields; he will not, however, be hasty to apply such knowledge before he has had adequate training and experience.

I. Where test results are capable of being interpreted to the advantage either side of a case, the criminalist will not choose that interpretation favoring the side by which he is employed merely as a means of justify his employment.

J. It is both wise and proper that the criminalist be aware of the various possible implications of his opinions and conclusions and be prepared to weigh them, if called upon to do so. In any such case, however, he will clearly distinguish between that which may be regarded as scientifically demonstrated fact and that which is speculative.

III. Ethical Aspects of Court Presentation:

A. The expert witness is one who has substantially greater knowledge of a given subject or science than has the average person. An expert opinion is properly defined as "the formal opinion of an expert." Ordinary opinion consists of one's thoughts or beliefs on matters, generally unsupported by detailed analysis of the subject under consideration. Expert opinion is also defined as the considered opinion of an expert, or a formal Judgment. It is to be understood that an "expert opinion" is an opinion derived only from a formal consideration of a subject within the expert's knowledge and experience.

B. The ethical expert does not take advantage of his privilege to express opinions by offering opinions on matters within his field of qualification which he has not given formal consideration.

C. Regardless of legal definitions, the criminalist will realize that there are degrees of certainty represented under the single term of "expert opinion." He will not take advantage of the general privilege to assign greater significance to an interpretation than is justified by the available data.

D. Where circumstances indicate it to be proper, the expert will not hesitate to indicate that while he has an opinion, derived of study, and judgment within his field, the opinion may lack the certainty of other opinions he might offer. By this or other means, he takes care to leave no false impressions in the minds of the jurors or the court (sic)

E. In all respects, the criminalist will avoid the use of terms, and opinions which will be assigned greater weight than are due them. Where an opinion requires qualification or explanation, it is not only proper but incumbent upon the witness to offer such qualification.

F. The expert witness should keep in mind that the lay juror is apt to assign greater or less significance to ordinary words of a scientist than to the same words when used by a lay witness. The criminalist, therefore, will avoid such terms as may be misconstrued or misunderstood.

G. It is not the object of the criminalist's appearance in court to present only that evidence which supports the view of the side which employs him. He has a moral obligation to see to it that the court understands the evidence as it exists and to present it in an impartial manner.

H. The criminalist will not by implication, knowingly or intentionally, assist the contestants in a case through such tactics as will implant a false impression in the minds of the jury.

I. The criminalist, testifying as an expert witness, will make every effort to use understandable language in his explanations and demonstrations in order that the jury will obtain a true and valid concept of the testimony. The use of unclear, misleading, circuitous, or ambiguous language with a view of confusing an issue in the minds of the court or jury is unethical.

J. The criminalist will answer all questions put to him in a clear, straightforward manner and refuse to extend himself beyond his field of competence.

K. Where the expert must prepare photographs or offer oral "background information" to the jury in respect to a specific type of analytic method, this information shall be reliable and valid, typifying the usual or normal basis for the method. The instructional material shall be of that level which will provide the jury with a proper basis for evaluating the subsequent evidence presentations, and not such as would provide them with a lower standard than the science demands.

L. Any and all photographic displays shall be made according to acceptable practice, and shall not be intentionally altered or distorted with a view to misleading court or jury.

M. By way of conveying information to the court, it is appropriate that any of a variety of demonstrative materials and methods be utilized by the expert witness. Such methods and materials shall not, however, be unduly sensational.

IV. Ethics Relating to the General Practice of Criminalistics:

A. Where the criminalist engages in private practice, it is appropriate that he set a reasonable fee for his services.

B. No services shall ever be rendered on a contingency fee basis.

C. It shall be regarded as ethical for one criminalist to re-examine evidence materials previously submitted to or examined by another. Where a difference of opinion arises, however, as to the significance of the evidence or to test results, it is in the interest of the profession that every effort be made by both analysts to resolve their conflict before the case goes to trial.

D. Generally, the principle of "attorney-client" relationship is considered to apply to the work of a physical evidence consultant, except in a situation where a miscarriage of justice might occur. Justice should be the guiding principle.

E. It shall be ethical for one of this profession to serve an attorney in a advisory capacity regarding the interrogation of another expert who may be presenting testimony. This service must be performed in good faith and not maliciously. Its purpose is to prevent incompetent testimony but not to thwart justice.

V. Ethical Responsibilities to the Profession:

In order to advance the profession of criminalistics, to promote the purposes for which the Association was formed, and encourage harmonious relationships between all criminalists of the State, each criminalist has an obligation to conduct himself according to certain principles. These principles are no less matters of ethics than those outlined above. They differ primarily in being for the benefit of the profession rather than specific obligations to society. They, therefore, concern individuals and departments in their relationship with one another, business policies, and similar matters.

A. It is in the interest of the profession that information concerning any new discoveries, developments or techniques applicable to the field of criminalistics be made available to criminalists generally. A reasonable attempt should be made by any criminalist having knowledge of such developments to publicize or otherwise inform the profession of them.

B. Consistent with this and like objectives, it is expected that the attention of the profession will be directed toward any tests or methods in use which appear invalid or unreliable in order that they may be properly investigated.

C. In the interest of the profession, the individual criminalist should refrain from seeking publicity for himself or his accomplishments on specific cases. The preparation of papers for publication in appropriate media, however, is considered proper.

D. The criminalist shall discourage the association of his name with developments, publications, or organizations in which he has played no significant part, merely as a means of gaining personal publicity or prestige.

E. The C.A.C. has been organized primarily to encourage a free exchange of ideas and information between members. It is, therefore, incumbent upon each member to treat with due respect those statements and offerings made by his associates. It is appropriate that no member shall unnecessarily repeat statements or beliefs of another as expressed at C.A.C. seminars.

F. It shall be ethical and proper for one criminalist to bring to the attention of the Association a violation of any of these ethical principles. Indeed, it shall be mandatory where it appears that a serious infraction or repeated violations have been committed and where other appropriate corrective measures (if pursued) have failed.

G. This Code may be used by any criminalist in justification of his conduct in a given case with the understanding that he will have the full support of this Association.

Sample Likelihood and RMNE Calculations

1. **Assuming the presence of the boyfriend**

The probability of the profile is this many times more likely if the boyfriend and suspect are the donors than if the boyfriend and a random man of the indicated race are the donors

$$\frac{P\left(E\,|\,\text{Boyfriend} + \text{Suspect}\right)}{P\left(E\,|\,\text{Boyfriend} + \text{random man}\right)} = \frac{1}{\text{5.7E-10}} = 1,700,000,000$$

AfAm	5.7E-10	1,700,000,000
Cauc	6.6E-10	1,500,000,000
Hisp	7.7E-11	13,000,000,000

2. **Assuming neither donor is identified**

The probability of the profile is this many times more likely if the suspect and a random man are the donors than if two random men of the indicated race are the donors

$$\frac{P\left(E\,|\,\text{Suspect} + \text{random man}\right)}{P\left(E\,|\,2\ \text{random men}\right)} =$$

AfAm	$\dfrac{4.0\text{E}-09}{1.2\text{E}-16}$	=	33,000,000
Cauc	$\dfrac{4.1\text{E}-08}{9.1\text{E}-16}$	=	45,000,000
Hisp	$\dfrac{2.7\text{E}-07}{1.3\text{E}-15}$	=	200,000,000

3. **Assuming neither race, number, nor identity of donors**

RMNE   Freq = 5.4E-07   = 1 in 1,800,000

Fundamental Principles and Concepts of Criminalistics

> ## Thinking Is Allowed

The Origin of Evidence

The Principles of Criminalistics

- **Divisible matter**
  Matter divides into smaller component parts when sufficient force is applied. The component parts will acquire characteristics created by the process of division itself and retain physicochemical properties of the larger piece.

  Three corollaries:
  Corollary 1: Some characteristics retained by the smaller pieces are unique to the original item or to the division process. These traits are useful for individualizing all pieces to the original item.
  Corollary 2: Some characteristics retained by the smaller pieces are common to the original item as well as to other items of similar manufacture. We rely on these traits to classify the item.
  Corollary 3: Some characteristics of the original item will be lost or changed during or after the moment of division and subsequent dispersal; this confounds the attempt to infer a common source.

- **Transfer** (*Locard exchange principle*)
  Conventionally: every contact leaves a trace.
  As defined here: when two objects come in contact, material may be exchanged.

The Crime

The Crime

The Practice of Criminalistics

> **If you don't ask the right question,
> you won't get the right answer,
> no matter how brilliant your analysis.**

At the crime scene

What? | When? | Where? | Who? | How? | Why?

We see what we want to see

Recognition and **detection** of evidence

Goals of Evidence Collection

- Maintain physical integrity
- Limit degradation
- Prevent contamination

Contamination: Any substance inadvertently introduced into or onto an item of evidence after its recognition by a responsible party.

The Processes of Criminalistics

Identification
Defining the physicochemical nature of an evidence item.

Classification
Inferring multiple potential common sources for an evidence item.

Class Characteristics
Traits that are produced by a controlled process. They are used to group like objects into sets.

Individualization
Concluding a singular common source for two items

Individualizing Characteristics
Traits that are produced by a random, uncontrolled process. They are used to individualize items to a common source.

Association
An inference of contact between two objects, the source of the evidence, and the target on which it was found.

Reconstruction
The ordering of events in relative space and time based on the physical evidence.

The results
   The true result
   A false negative result
   A false positive result
   An inconclusive result
   No result

What does it mean?

$$(A)ssumptions + (F)acts = (I)nference$$

Inference: to conclude from something known or assumed.

Opinion: a judgment not based on absolute certainty or positive knowledge, but on what seems true, valid, or probable to one's own mind.

Conclusion: the last division of a discourse, usually containing a summing up of the points and a statement of opinion or decisions reached.

Communication

  The report

- Summary
- Purpose
- List of evidence received and examined
- Examination and results
- Interpretation and conclusion

Criminalistics and the Law

- Identification evidence is direct evidence. It does not require an inference to be relevant evidence.
- Potentially individualizing evidence is circumstantial evidence. It requires an inference to be relevant evidence.
- Evidence must be relevant (answer a question about a fact in question) to be admitted into a court of law.

Appendix G

Physical Evidence by Origin

Nonbiological

Physical Match
- -
  Anything that can divide and retain its shape[1]

Prints and Impressions
- -
Prints
  Shoeprints
  Tire tracks

Impressions
  Shoe impressions
  Tire impressions
  Toolmarks
- -
    Firearms

"Trace"
- -
  Fibers, Particles, Soil, Paint, etc.

Drugs
- -
  Solid dose drug analysis
  Toxicology

Questioned Documents
- -
  Handwriting/typesetting
  Paper and ink

Biological

Physiological
- -
  Biochemical/antigenic (serology, blood groups)
  DNA

Somatic
- -
Prints
  Friction ridge
  Other body parts (ears, lips, etc.)

Retinal patterns

---

[1] Shape shifters do not meet these requirements.

This organization of physical evidence emphasizes the difference between biological and nonbiological physician evidence. Biological evidence, or what we refer to as personal identification evidence, can be linked directly to an individual. Nonbiological physical evidence can be linked to a person only through inferring multiple intervening associations.

Index

A

AA analysis, see Atomic absorption analysis
AAFS, see American Academy of Forensic Sciences
ABC, see American Board of Criminalistics
Abiotic material, 124
ABO
  in ants, 215
  testing, 32
Absence of evidence, 173
Academic resources, 305
Accreditation, philosophy of, 309
Accuracy, 225
Acid phosphatase test, 32
Admissibility hearing, 292, 295
Adventitious traits, 92
Advocacy, system of, 15
AFTE, see Association of Firearms and Toolmark Examiners
Agreement by default, 295
Alternative hypothesis, 6, 168, 175, 248
Ambiguity, in absence of physical matching, 90
Ambiguous traits, 92
American Academy of Forensic Sciences (AAFS), 11, 65, 308, 313
American Association of Forensic Science Article II, 343
American Board of Criminalistics (ABC), 65, 303, 307, 313
American Board of Criminalistics Rules of Professional Conduct, 345–346
American Society of Crime Laboratory Directors (ASCLD), 308
American Society for Testing and Materials (ASTM), 231
Analyst, 10
  bias, 250
  education, training, and experience of, 252
  job of, 15
  judgment, 262
Analytical evidence, 255
Anthropometry, 29, 30, 44
Antibodies, immunological tests using, 40

Applied science, 7, 8, 286
Apprenticeship, 306
ASCLD, see American Society of Crime Laboratory Directors
Association, 18, 56, 77, 151, 167, 188
  evidence, 56, 165
  inference of, 170
  levels of, 57
  significance of, 79
  strength of, 95
Association of Firearms and Toolmark Examiners (AFTE), 178
Association and reconstruction, 157–190
  association, 158–177
    associating two objects through inference of contact, 170–176
    definition of association, 169–170
    evidence and law, 158–160
    inferential reasoning in forensic science, 165–169
    inferential reasoning in science, 160–165
    making of inference, 176–177
  reconstruction, 177–188
    capabilities of reconstruction, 178–181
    limitations of reconstruction, 181–188
    state of practice, 177–178
ASTM, see America Society for Testing and Materials
ASTM Committee E-30, 231
Atomic absorption (AA) analysis, 38
Authenticity of similarities, 133

B

Bacon, Francis, 8
Ballistics, 86
Bar exam, 314
Bayes' theorem, 144, 147
  framework, 6, 170
  statistics, 172
  thinking, 108
Bertillon, Alphonse, 27, 29, 31, 48
Bias(es)

T